CRAFT IN THE MACHINE AGE
1920–1945

CRAFT IN THE MACHINE AGE
1920-1945

THE HISTORY

OF

TWENTIETH-CENTURY

AMERICAN CRAFT

Janet Kardon, Editor

with essays by

Rosemarie Haag Bletter

Kate Carmel

Harvey Green

Janet Kardon

April Kingsley

Karen Lucic

Marcia Yockey Manhart

Barbara Perry

Mary Schoeser

Jewel Stern

Resource List by Tara Leigh Tappert

Harry N. Abrams, Inc., Publishers, in association with the American Craft Museum

This book is published on the occasion of the exhibition
"Craft in the Machine Age: 1920–1945"
American Craft Museum, New York
October 18, 1995–February 25, 1996

The History of Twentieth-Century American Craft: A Centenary Project
Janet Kardon, Project Founder and Director
Betsy Jablow, Project Coordinator
April Kingsley, Publications Coordinator, Assistant Editor

For Harry N. Abrams, Inc.:
Editor: Ruth A. Peltason
Designer: Judith Hudson

For American Craft Museum:
Editor: Barbara Ross Geiger

Front cover: Winold Reiss. *Harlequin Panel, Hotel Alamac, New York.* 1923
Background: Clayton Knight. *Manhattan. 1925–26*
Back cover: Frederick Carder. *Six Prong Green Jade Vase.* c. 1930

Captions for pages 1–6:

Page 1: Frederick Carder. *Dancing Faun Panel.* 1930s. *Pâte de verre,* 9 x 9¼"
Collection The Corning Museum of Glass, Corning, New York. Bequest of Gladys C. Wells

Page 2: Clayton Knight. *Manhattan.* 1925–26. Designed for Stehli Silk Corporation. Silk crepe, 6'1" x 37¼"
Collection The Newark Museum. Gift of L. Bamberger & Co., 1926

Page 5: Paul V. Gardner. *Empire State Building Architectural Panel.* 1931. Crystal; intaglio, 10¼ x 13¼"
Collection The Corning Museum of Glass, Corning, New York. Gift of Corning Glass Works

Page 6: Anonymous. *Tires and Tire Treads (Speed Age Silk Print).* 1929
Designed for Marshall Field and Company. Silk, 5⅛ x 4⅞"
Collection The Museum at the Fashion Institute of Technology, New York

The History of Twentieth-Century American Craft: A Centenary Project is a decadelong program of symposia, exhibitions, and catalogues organized by the American Craft Museum to write the history of twentieth-century American craft by the year 2000. "The Ideal Home: 1900–1920" was the first in the series of planned exhibitions; "Revivals! Diverse Traditions 1920–1945" was the second; "Craft in the Machine Age: 1920–1945" is the third. We greatly appreciate the generous support the Centenary Project has received from the Lila Wallace–Reader's Digest Fund; the National Endowment for the Arts, a federal agency; The Rockefeller Foundation; The Norman and Rosita Winston Foundation, Inc.; and The Cowles Charitable Trust.

Library of Congress Cataloging-in-Publication Data

Craft in the Machine Age, 1920–1945: the history of twentieth-century
American Craft/Janet Kardon, editor; with essays by Rosemarie
Haag Bletter . . . [et al.].
p. cm.
Includes bibliographical references and index.
ISBN 0–8109–1968–0 (Abrams: cloth)/ISBN 0–8109–2639–3 (Mus: pbk.)
1. Decorative arts—United States—History—20th century.
2. Decorative arts—United States—Foreign influences.
3. Decorative arts—United States—Technological innovations.
I. Kardon, Janet. II. Bletter, Rosemarie Haag.
NK808.C69 1995
745′.0973′09041—dc20   95–7849
                                                                                CIP

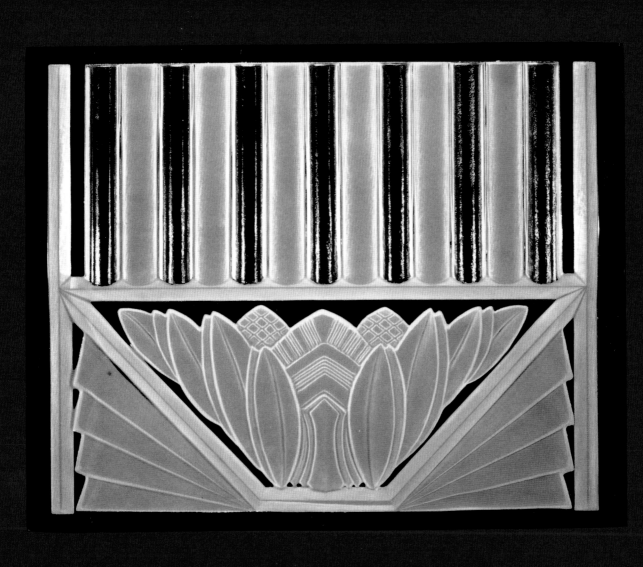

CONTENTS

Contributors

Rosemarie Haag Bletter is professor of art history at the City University of New York. She was a guest curator for the Whitney Museum of American Art exhibition "High Styles—Twentieth Century American Design" in 1985. Among her many publications are *Skyscraper Style—Art Deco New York* and *Venturi, Rauch, and Scott Brown: A Generation of Architecture.*

Kate Carmel is senior curator at the American Craft Museum. She was formerly curator for David A. Hanks & Associates, Inc., where she organized "Frank Gehry: New Bentwood Furniture Designs" and was coauthor of *Design 1935–65: What Modern Was.*

Harvey Green is professor of history at Northeastern University. He has published many articles and reviews on American history and material culture and written three books—*Light on the Home: Women in Victorian America, Fit for America: Health, Fitness, and American Society, 1830–1940,* and *The Uncertainty of Everyday Life, 1915–1945.*

Janet Kardon, director of the American Craft Museum and founder and director of the Centenary Project, is the chief curator of "Craft in the Machine Age: 1920–1945" and editor of the catalogue. Formerly director of the Institute of Contemporary Art at the University of Pennsylvania, in Philadelphia, she has curated and written the catalogues for more than fifty exhibitions of contemporary art and craft.

April Kingsley is curator and Centenary Project publications coordinator at the American Craft Museum. Formerly an independent art critic, curator, and historian, she has organized over twenty exhibitions and written dozens of catalogues. She is also the author of *The Turning Point: The Abstract Expressionists and the Transformation of American Art.*

Karen Lucic is assistant professor of art history at Vassar College. She is the author of *Charles Sheeler and the Cult of the Machine* and, under the name Karen Davies, has curated and written the catalogue for "At Home in Manhattan: Modern Decorative Arts, 1925 to the Depression."

Marcia Yockey Manhart is a clay artist, curator, educator, and administrator. She is the executive director of the Philbrook Museum of Art in Tulsa, Oklahoma, where she co-curated "Nature's Forms/Nature's Forces: The Art of Alexandre Hogue"; she was the curator of "The Eloquent Object" exhibition, which toured nationally for two years after opening at Philbrook in 1987.

Barbara Perry is director of the Tyler Art Gallery, State University of New York at Oswego. Formerly curator at the Everson Museum of Art, she organized the 27th and 28th Ceramic National Exhibitions. She is the author of *Fragile Blossoms, Enduring Earth: The Japanese Influence on American Ceramics* and *American Ceramics: The Collection of the Everson Museum of Art.*

Mary Schoeser was born in California and educated in England, where she still lives. She is a curator, writer, editor, lecturer, and consultant to many public and private textile collections. She is the author of *French Textiles 1760–1960* and coauthor with Celia Rufy of *English and American Textiles from 1790 to the Present.*

Jewel Stern is an artist, art and architectural historian, guest curator, and consultant in twentieth-century American silver and metalwork. Her conceptual and photographic projects have been exhibited at the Washington Square East Galleries, New York; the Akron Art Institute; Lowe Art Museum, Miami; and the Museum of Modern Art, Oxford, England. She is currently working on a monograph of the Art Deco architect Ely Jacques Kahn.

Tara Leigh Tappert (Resource List) is an independent arts consultant and archivist. She has written a biography of Cecilia Beaux, and has organized the 1995 exhibition "Cecilia Beaux and the Art of Portraiture" for the National Portrait Gallery, Smithsonian Institution, Washington, D.C. Tappert has worked in various museums, art galleries, archives, and libraries for more than twenty years.

Lenders to the Exhibition

Albright-Knox Art Gallery, Buffalo

American Craft Museum, New York

Dr. Thomas F. Armour, Hermitage, Pennsylvania

John P. Axelrod, Boston

Tony Berlant, Santa Monica

The Brooklyn Museum

Constance R. Caplan, Baltimore

The Cleveland Museum of Art

Cooper-Hewitt Museum, National Museum of Design, Smithsonian Institution, New York

The Corning Museum of Glass, Corning, New York

Cowan Pottery Museum at Rocky River Public Library, Rocky River, Ohio

Cranbrook Academy of Art Museum, Bloomfield Hills, Michigan

Cranbrook Educational Community, Bloomfield Hills, Michigan

Lucia Eames Demetrios, Eames Office, Los Angeles

Detroit Institute of Arts

William Waldo Dodge, III, Blowing Rock, North Carolina

Dr. Martin Eidelberg, New York

Helene Barbara Fisher Eldred, East Boothbay, Maine

Mr. and Mrs. Peter Esherick, Orefield, Pennsylvania

Everson Museum of Art, Syracuse, New York

Dr. Tom Folk, Bernardsville, New Jersey

Denis Gallion and Daniel Morris, Historical Design Collection, Inc., New York

David Gebhard, Santa Barbara

The Globus Collection, New York

Bertrand Goldberg, Chicago

Goldstein Gallery, University of Minnesota, St. Paul

Carol and Robert Goodman, Gladwynne, Pennsylvania

Wayland Gregory Collection, Warren, New Jersey

Frances and Michael Higgins, Riverside, Illinois

High Museum of Art, Atlanta

Mrs. William W. Hughes, Newport Beach, California

Indianapolis Museum of Art

Christopher Kende, New York

Myron and Lois Kozman, New York

Harvey K. Littleton, Spruce Pine, North Carolina

Mrs. Mildred Loew, New York

Los Angeles County Museum of Art

Sharron Martin, Cupertino, California

Mark A. McDonald, New York

The Metropolitan Museum of Art, New York

The Milwaukee Public Museum

James L. Murphy, Columbus, Ohio

The Museum at the Fashion Institute of Technology, New York

Museum of Fine Arts, Boston

The Museum of Modern Art, New York

National Museum of American Art, Smithsonian Institution, Washington, D.C.

The Newark Museum

New Jersey State Museum, Trenton

North Carolina Museum of Art, Raleigh

The Oakland Museum

Ruth Penington, Seattle

John C. Petterson, Park Ridge, Illinois

Philadelphia Museum of Art

Radio City Music Hall Productions, Rockefeller Center, New York

Mr. and Mrs. W. Tjark Reiss, Claverack, New York

Rhode Island School of Design, Museum of Art, Providence

Rockwell Museum, Corning, New York

Rose Family, Cleveland

San Francisco Museum of Modern Art

Seattle Art Museum

Stanley H. Shapiro, Bala Cynwyd, Pennsylvania

Patricia Shaw, West Bloomfield, Michigan

Fred Silberman, New York

Fern Simon, Winnetka, Illinois

Alexander B. Slater, Locust Valley, New York

Steuben Glass, New York

William Straus, New York

The Toledo Museum of Art, Ohio

Jorie Marshall Waterman, New York

Mary Lou Wickham, Glen Arm, Maryland

The Wolfsonian Foundation, Miami Beach and Genoa, Italy

Yale University Art Gallery, New Haven

GILBERT ROHDE
Dressing Vanity. 1939
Rosewood, burl redwood veneers, brass, brassplated
steel, Plexiglas, vinyl-coated fabric, glass, ebonized
plywood, 48 x 47 x 15"
Collection High Museum of Art, Atlanta. Purchase
in honor of Hilda Cyphers, Associate Manager of
the Members' Guild, 1979–94, with funds from the
Decorative Arts Acquisition Trust

PORTER GEORGE BLANCHARD

Coffee Set. c. 1938–40

Silver, ebony; coffee pot: 6½ x 8¼ x 3¾";

creamer: 4 x 4¼ x 2"; sugar bowl: 4¼ x 5⅛ x 2⅝"

Collection Mrs. William W. Hughes

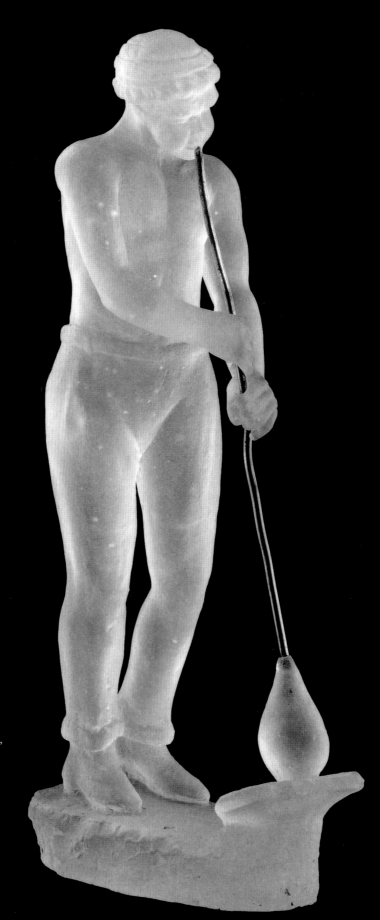

FREDERICK CARDER
Standing Glassblower. 1937
Cast crystal, 12¹¹⁄₁₆ x 3³⁄₁₆ x 6"
Collection The Corning Museum of Glass,
Corning, New York. Gift of Grace Fraas

FREDERICK CARDER
Elephant Bowl. c. 1940
Crystal; *cire perdue,* 7⅛ x 5¼ x 5¼"
Collection The Corning Museum of Glass,
Corning, New York. Gift of Corning
Glass Works

WAYLANDE DESANTIS GREGORY
Nautch Dancer. 1930
Earthenware, 17⅛ x 8⅛ x 4¼"
Collection The Cleveland Museum of Art.
Dudley P. Allen Fund

R. GUY COWAN
Scarf Dancer with Bowl. 1925
Designed for Cowan Pottery Studio

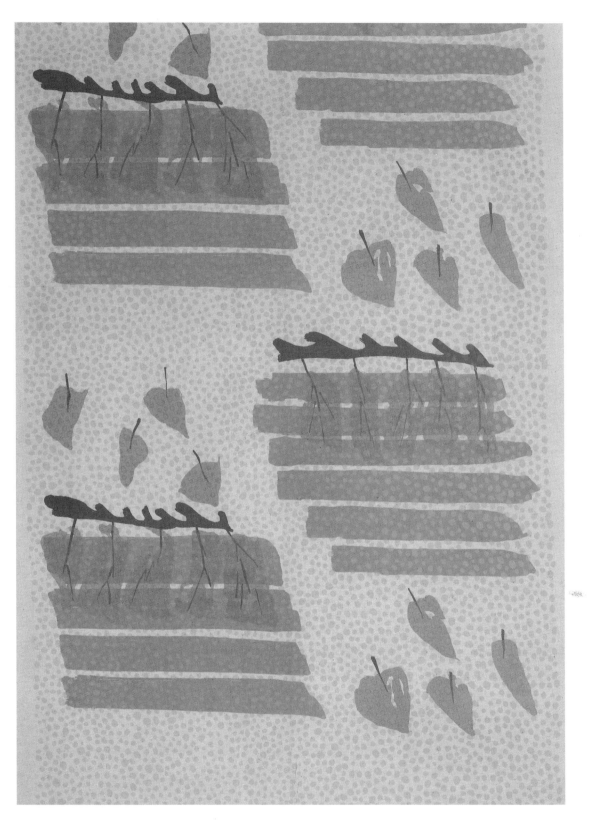

ANTONIN RAYMOND
Strips, Trunks, Trees, Dots Fabric Panel. c. 1941
Cotton; handscreened, 7'4" x 50"
Collection The Museum of Modern Art, New York.
Gift of the designer

ACKNOWLEDGMENTS

The History of Twentieth-Century American Craft: A Centenary Project is the American Craft Museum's decadelong pioneering effort to produce the first historical overview of the American craft movement. "Craft in the Machine Age: 1920–1945," documents the third exhibition in this ambitious series.

The Centenary Project has been made possible by a major grant from the Lila Wallace–Reader's Digest Fund; the National Endowment for the Arts, a Federal agency; the Peter T. Joseph Foundation; The Rockefeller Foundation; the Cowles Charitable Trust; and The Norman and Rosita Winston Foundation, Inc. On behalf of the museum, I express my heartfelt gratitude.

Planning for the exhibition began four years ago. It was agreed that the period 1920 to 1945 was too complex and varied to be encompassed within a single framework. In fact, it split naturally along two parallel temporal lines. Indigenous developments within our shores—the Colonial, Hispanic, Native American, Southern Appalachian, and African-American craft revivals and survivals were treated in "Revivals! Diverse Traditions: 1920–1945." During the same time period, there was the influence from outside our shores of European modernism, brought by artists who, fleeing Nazism, immigrated to this country. These developments, and the effect that our own industrial and architectural images, such as the skyscraper, had on craft and design are traced in this third volume and exhibition in the Centenary Project series.

The structure for the exhibition was outlined in the symposium "Craft in the Machine Age—European and American Modernism" in the spring of 1991, and was further redefined in a roundtable conference and many informal discussions with the participants: Rosemarie Haag Bletter, professor of art history, City University of New York Graduate Center; Karen Lucic, assistant professor of art and program in American culture, Vassar College; Jeffrey L. Meikle, associate professor of art history and American studies, University of Texas; Otto Natzler, ceramist; Lotus Stack, curator of textiles, The Minneapolis Institute of Arts; Jewel Stern, consultant, The Wolfsonian Foundation; and Tran G. Turner, curator of decorative arts, The Minneapolis Institute of Arts.

The Centenary Project has been strengthened by the expertise of many outside scholars; this book and exhibition reflect their conscientious efforts. It has been a rewarding experience for all of us to work with them. I am particularly grateful to the writers of the essays in *Craft in the Machine Age*: Rosemarie Haag Bletter; Kate Carmel, senior curator, American Craft Museum; Harvey Green, professor of history, Northeastern University; April Kingsley, curator and Centenary Publications coordinator, American Craft Museum; Karen Lucic; Marcia Yockey Manhart, executive director, Philbrook Museum of Art; Barbara Perry, director, Tyler Art Gallery, State University of New York at Oswego; Mary Schoeser, curator and writer; and Jewel Stern. Their considerable expertise has enabled us to present this complex chapter in American art history.

The extensive resource section was entrusted to Tara Leigh Tappert, who performed a challenging task with admirable precision. Natalie Goldstein, our picture researcher, was exceptionally resourceful at fulfilling difficult assignments. It has also been a great pleasure to collaborate again with the publishing house of Harry N. Abrams, Inc., and its representatives, in particular, Paul Gottlieb, president, publisher, and editor-in-chief; Ruth Peltason, senior editor; and Judith Hudson.

The entire staff of the American Craft Museum has been exemplary. Betsy Jablow, Centenary Project coordinator, has overseen all aspects of this complex project with uncommon organizational skill and diligence. The support of Project Registrar Marsha Beitchman, who executed the myriad details of this project, was of great importance. April Kingsley's research on this time period and her commitment have made her an indispensable coordinator of the Centenary publications. She has also been a splendid assistant editor.

Many other members of the American Craft Museum staff have made vital contributions to the project, but I want to mention particularly Kate Carmel, senior curator; Lillian Piro, assistant director; Elizabeth Reiss, curator of education; Joan McDonald, communications manager; and Scott VanderHamm, collections manager. We have had the inestimable benefit of the assistance of interns: Urszula Lazowski, Clarissa Hutton, Meredith Harper, and Danielle Malavade.

Special thanks go to our curatorial colleagues from across the country: Jane Adlin, Bruce Altshuler, Kathy Bogus, Mark Coir, Gail Davison, Martin Eidelberg, G. Eason Eige, Jonathan Fairbanks, Jeannine Falino, Suzanne K. Frantz, David Gebhard, Adrian Grad, Pat Kane, Robert Leonard, Mark McDonald, Cara McCarty, David McFadden, Anita McNeece, R. Craig Miller, Milo Naeve, Sara Nichols, Robyn G. Peterson, David Rago, Kevin Stayton, Davira Taragin, and Gay Taylor.

For their assistance with research, thanks are extended to Mary Dellin, Robert Di Corcia, Ulysses Dietz, Anita Duquette, Dr. Tom Folk, Thomas Grischkowsky, Lisa Hartjens, Mary Husjak, Victoria Peltz, Anne Poor, David Rau, Renate and W. Tjark Reiss, Noelle Soper, William Straus, Eileen Sullivan, William Warmus, Bobbie Xuereb, and Alice Maria Zrebiec.

The Board of Governors of the American Craft Museum, led with admirable vision by Jerome Chazen, former chairman, and now Barbara Tober, chairman, have steadfastly and enthusiastically supported this project. Museums across the country have been remarkably generous in extending loans from their collections, and private lenders have kindly parted with beloved objects to make this exhibition possible. We are immensely grateful to them all.

Ultimately, our appreciation must go to the artists themselves, many of them new citizens, who generated and transformed craft teaching institutions in this country. They also created splendid objects.

JANET KARDON
DIRECTOR
AMERICAN CRAFT MUSEUM

CRAFT IN THE MACHINE AGE

by Janet Kardon

The History of Twentieth-Century American Craft: A Centenary Project is the American Craft Museum's pioneering, decadelong effort to write the first comprehensive historical overview of American craft since 1900. "Craft in the Machine Age: 1920–1945," the third exhibition in the Centenary Project series, is documented by this volume.

The Centenary Project, initiated in 1990, is divided into eight chapters. For each one, planning meetings are conducted with our curatorial staff and other professionals in the field. Eventually, some one hundred scholars and artists from across the country representing the disciplines of craft, the decorative arts, art history, material culture, and political and social history will be involved. Appropriate curators and authors are then selected by the museum for each project. Through this rigorous process, plans have emerged for major exhibitions relating to each period, each to be documented by a comprehensive publication such as this one. The first two were "The Ideal Home: 1900–1920," which examined the ideals of the American craft movement as exemplified by domestic objects; and "Revivals! Diverse Traditions: 1920–1945," which brought together revival styles of African-American, Hispanic, Native American, and Southern Appalachian crafts, as well as the Colonial revival. The widespread and positive response to earlier segments of this project has affirmed the critical need for a text, a history of twentieth-century American craft. The Centenary Project will engage outside scholars and the resources of the American Craft Museum for at least a decade.

In the years between the wars, isolationists and supporters of the League of Nations opposed one another in the political arena. These political poles had an aesthetic counterpart. There were radical differences between objects made by artists reviving traditional American craft forms, and those made by artists affected by modernist ideas. These disparate expressions seemed better served if separated into two exhibitions and publications. Political isolationism was reflected in such diverse artistic traditions as the popular Colonial revival style, the indigenous "folk" handcrafts of Southern Appalachia, and the expressions of African-American, Hispanic, and Native American communities. The revivals and survivals of these historic styles were the subject of the exhibition "Revivals! Diverse Traditions: 1920–1945," presented in 1994, dealing with objects made in craft media that emerged from regional and cultural activity contained within our shores. Against the pervasive backdrop of the Colonial revival, pluralist, multicultural, and regional expressions were examined in the light of new scholarship.

Internationalist in spirit, "Craft in the Machine Age: 1920–1945" reports on transcontinental interaction, focusing on artistic developments resulting from the influx of European émigrés and ideas, and the direct experience of American artists who traveled to Europe. Wherever or however informed, the artists represented in this exhibition were strongly influenced by European modernism. They broke with tradition, rebelling against the past to form a new artistic and expressive vocabulary that can best be described as modernist, since it embraced the present.

EUROPE AND AMERICA BETWEEN THE WARS

The American social, economic, and political climate between 1920 and 1945 was affected at beginning and end by world wars and riven by the Great Depression. In an era of challenge and change, the farmer suffered from droughts of epic proportions and the city dweller was placed in straitened circumstances by the stock market crash of 1929. In the following decade, the promise of the New Deal and the rise of unions gave hope to the out-of-work factory worker. Abject poverty contrasted with conspicuous affluence, exemplified by the austere life of the mountaineers and the self-indulgent society that frequented the speakeasy. The Eighteenth Amendment to the Constitution brought Prohibition in 1919; the next amendment, ratified in 1920, gave women the right to vote.

These were decades when the machine upstaged the hand, decades when American products, particularly artworks, were undervalued, decades when industrial production and craft constantly shifted relationships, ultimately leading to an unfriendly "divorce." Two books bracketed the period: *The Age of Innocence* (1920), by Edith Wharton, and *Animal Farm* (1945), by George Orwell. Wharton contrasted European and American societies by underscoring American materialism and the rigidity of the European establishment, while Orwell predicted a rise in material incentives and increased competition for power. *Animal Farm* was prescient of the power struggles that would take place between East and West after World War II, the outcome of which empowered the United States to assume a position of world leadership. Power was the consuming agenda of this era, during which the focus changes from societal to political hierarchies.

Century of Progress Exposition, Chicago, 1933–34

The United States was the site of a virtual technological revolution. Speed—in mass production or in travel on or above the ground—had become a compelling social force. Transportation and communication networks exploded—it was the era of the ocean liner, air travel, the family car, railroad vacations to the Southwest, the radio, and the telephone. Mass production of the automobile had an enormous influence on road systems, homes, and other design spheres. The theme of the 1933–34 Century of Progress Exposition in Chicago was the application of science to industry. As new appliances enhanced domestic life, new designs were created to house them, and were made with new materials—Formica, Bakelite, Micarta. But the response to the new, to technology, was often ambivalent. A radio, for example, might be encased, for nostalgia, in a Colonial clock or in a futuristic streamlined box made of wood, metal, and mirrored glass. The ambivalence about technology reached an apogee when the atomic bomb was dropped on Hiroshima in 1945, ending a war, but disastrously, and with ominous portents.

In Europe, the period began with the formation of the League of Nations in Paris and concluded at the end of World War II. The years between the wars were strained and sinister. Adolf Hitler announced his twenty-five-point program in 1920 at the Hofbrauhaus in Munich, introducing a period when free expression in Europe was crushed by Soviet repression and the Nazi siege. In 1921, the Communist Party took official control of artistic expression in Russia. In 1933, Hitler ordered "degenerate" abstract art removed from the walls of museums throughout Germany, and the Bauhaus was disbanded. By this time, hundreds of artists had immigrated to this country from Europe—authors, architects, designers, painters, sculptors, musicians, and artists working in clay, fiber, glass, metal, and wood.

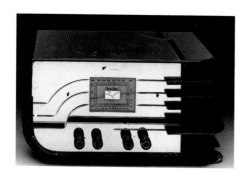

Walter Dorwin Teague, Sr. *Sparton Radio.* c. 1936. Manufactured by Sparks Withington Company. Glass, metal, wood, plastic, 17¾ x 9". Mitchell Wolfson, Jr. Collection The Wolfsonian Foundation, Miami Beach and Genoa, Italy

"Craft in the Machine Age: 1920–1945" provides the first retrospective look at the evolution of craft during this period, and the movement away from highly elaborate, finely wrought, and prohibitively expensive objects—identified with wealth and the past—toward unique and manufactured works that embodied a modernist aesthetic: simplicity, informality, and practicality. The rectilinear, obviously handcrafted objects of the Arts and Crafts movement, tied to nature and the ideal of an integrated living and working environment, were supplanted by elemental geometric forms reflecting a modernist impulse, and devoid of the mark of the hand.

In this transition, European influence upon American craft was enormous. With the influx of European artists early in the century and in the prelude to World War II, new technical skills, an innovative vocabulary of forms and motifs, and philosophical agendas arrived in the United States. As artists working in craft media, they showed their work in the major exhibitions of the time, enabling craft to be perceived side by side with other art forms. These years of intense technological, industrial, political, and social change saw American craft transform under the influence of European modernism. Emigrating mostly from Germany, Scandinavia, Austria, and France, many artists became teachers. Tremendous changes occurred in the various craft media, first through the private studio instruction they provided, and later at the schools they spawned, such as Black Mountain College, the Cranbrook Academy of Art, and the New Bauhaus in Chicago.

A partial list of these influential artists, architects, and designers is imposing. Jules Buoy arrived from Belgium before World War I, as did Elie Nadelman, from Poland, and William Zorach, from Lithuania. Paul T. Frankl and Joseph Urban emigrated from Austria before 1920. In the late 1920s and 1930s, Wolfgang and

Pola Hofmann, Gertrud and Otto Natzler, and Vally Wieselthier arrived from Austria; Erik Magnussen from Denmark; Maija Grotell and Loja and Eliel Saarinen from Finland; Robert Laurent from France; Josef and Anni Albers, Walter Gropius, Ludwig Mies van der Rohe, László Moholy-Nagy, Walter von Nessen, Bruno Paul, Kem Weber, and Marguerite Wildenhain from Germany; Mariska and Ilonka Karasz from Hungary; Alexander Archipenko from Ukraine; and Carl Milles from Sweden.

In addition, many American artists visited Europe and were directly informed by European aesthetics. To cite a few examples, the textile designer Ruth Reeves studied in Paris with Fernand Léger in the 1920s, while ceramists Henry Varnum Poor and Viktor Schreckengost attended the Slade School of Art in London and the Vienna Kunstgewerbeschüle, respectively. Donald Deskey studied painting in Paris and visited the Bauhaus in Germany. Janet Payne Bowles was among the many Americans who visited the seminal 1925 Exposition Internationale des Arts Décoratifs et Industriels Modernes in Paris.

The Paris "Art Deco" exposition, as it came to be called by the 1960s, contained neither German nor American entries—Germany due to a purposely late invitation. The United States, however, declined because Herbert Hoover, then Secretary of Commerce, felt that objects of American design could not meet the guidelines of "new inspiration and real originality."[1] Instead, he sent a committee of over one hundred members of trade organizations and art guilds to review the exposition. Its report was enthusiastic about modern design. Charles R. Richards, director of the American Association of Museums, was charged with selecting approximately four hundred objects from the Paris Exposition for an eight-city traveling exhibition that arrived at The Metropolitan Museum of Art in New York in 1926. Department stores across the country reacted, presenting thirty-six exhibitions within the next few years. Thus, French modernism was disseminated in this country through the dual efforts of museums and retailers, as stores competed with museums to define good taste. The department store was often the pioneer in displaying domestic objects influenced by a modernist sensibility. Two landmark exhibitions were mounted in 1928 by New York retailers: Lord & Taylor's "Exposition of Modern French Decorative Art" and R. H. Macy's "International Exposition of Art in Industry."[2]

New objects were often installed in modernist "period rooms." Design historian Jeffrey L. Meikle notes that "the rise of the *ensemblier* proved influential in America. Most French designers created complete rooms by carefully designing

Robert Bonfils. *Exposition Internationale des Arts Décoratifs et Industriels Modernes*. 1925. Color lithographic poster, 36¾ x 23⅛". Museum of Fine Arts, Boston. Gift of John P. Axelrod

American Designers' Gallery, New York, 1928. From *The American Architect* (December 5, 1928)

Raymond Hood in collaboration with Henry V. K. Henderson. "Business Executive's Office," room setting designed for "The Architect and the Industrial Arts: An Exhibition of Contemporary American Design," Eleventh American Industrial Art Exhibition, The Metropolitan Museum of Art, New York, February 11–September 6, 1929

Raymond Hood. "Apartment House Loggia," room setting designed for "The Architect and the Industrial Arts," The Metropolitan Museum of Art, 1929

and orchestrating furniture, rugs, tapestries, wallpaper, and minor accessories for a unity of effect."[3] In the United States, the architect was the key creative figure, and co-opted the interior designer's territory in designing coordinated domestic or commercial environments for their buildings. At New York's American Designers' Gallery, important exhibitions were presented in this manner. The architect's viewpoint was also crucial to the rooms assembled for The Metropolitan Museum of Art exhibition "The Architect and the Industrial Arts" of 1929.

By the 1930s, Europe's influence was no longer confined to French *art moderne*. Although the reduced geometric forms of the Wiener Werkstätte had been known here previously, the primary artistic import in this period was the ideology of the German Bauhaus. When Walter Gropius founded the Bauhaus, a school to unite all the arts, in Weimar in 1919, there was a heavy bias toward craft. Bauhaus founders attempted to provide a teaching environment in which craft, design, architecture, sculpture, and painting each had a voice; only later would the importance of the hand succumb to architectural and industrial imperatives. When Bauhaus ideas influenced American expression and teaching practices, it was as part of an altruistic effort to unite the artist and industry in order to produce affordable, well-designed objects for everyone. Bauhaus principles were readily absorbed in this country, partly due to our fascination with the machine. A geometric form was far easier to replicate in a factory than any expressionist endeavor and, ideally, artists could work creatively with the manufacturer. Bauhaus theory as well as other concepts entered this country without the benefit of annual exhibitions such as the Paris salons, or those of the Deutscher Werkbund and the Austrian Hagenbund.

THE EDUCATION OF THE ARTIST

Artists from Europe had a profound impact on the education of the American artist. Before their arrival, there was a scarcity of innovative teachers and little information about new materials or techniques. Our art schools were conservative, expecting students to model their works on historic styles, such as Art Nouveau or Gothic Revival.[4] Certain individuals and their allied institutions played major roles in transmitting new ideas to a new generation. Charles Fergus Binns brought the aesthetics of Asian pottery to Alfred University. Josef Albers arrived with his wife, Anni, to teach at Black Mountain College in North Carolina in 1933. Anni Albers's weaving program at Black Mountain was an alternative to craft classes, where a little ceramics, metalwork, and some enameling would result in what Albers herself described as "ashtray art." For Albers, weaving was a serious and complex process of responding to materials, the structure of textiles, and to function. Black Mountain, and the New Bauhaus in Chicago, founded by László Moholy-Nagy in 1937, were centers for the Central European ideas that were disseminated in only a few other United States art schools, such as Syracuse University and the Cleveland School of Art.

Under the leadership of architect-designer Eliel Saarinen, the Cranbrook Academy of Art became a nurturing ground for Scandinavian ideology. Saarinen wished to have visiting artists from various parts of the country as well as from foreign countries in residence at Cranbrook. Under their tutelage, aspiring designers and artists learned a respect for natural materials and a sense of the interrelatedness of the applied arts.

The School for American Craftsmen was founded at Dartmouth College at the end of this period to train artists to become self-sufficient through production work. The school, as well as America House, an important showplace for American craftsmen and a predecessor of the American Craft Museum, was founded by Aileen Osborn Webb in 1940. The American Craft Council was founded in 1943, and in 1956, the American Craft Museum opened its doors.

THE MODERN SPIRIT

During the period 1920–45, modern industry, the machine, and its products infiltrated every aspect of American culture. Henry Ford's mass-produced automobile symbolized the overturning of the unique and the individual, informing films such as Fritz Lang's *Metropolis* (Germany, 1926) and Charlie Chaplin's *Modern Times* (United States, 1936). There was a universal drive to invent a new lifestyle, to pass new social reforms, and to create new music, literature, and art. Expressions were sought that overturned the past rather than imitated it.

In the 1920s, the urge to infuse painting and sculpture with modern spirit and form was paralleled in craft objects. Exhibitions of modern art included works that today might be marginalized as craft. Craftspeople focused on new uses for old materials and devised objects that could be made with the newly invented synthetics and metal alloys. These exploratory designs were often one of a kind and made by hand, but terminology and the prominence of the industrial designer cloud our perception of those years. Much of what was then called design

Art Deco set, inspired by the New York skyline, designed for Fritz Lang's *Metropolis* (1926)

America House, New York, 1943

or industrial art would be called craft today, since the objects were unique, displayed a reverence for natural or exotic materials, and evidenced technical prowess. Even "modern-looking" metal objects with reduced industrial forms that appear to have been manufactured were actually handmade, and unique. Too, works intended for factory production were produced in such small quantities that they could be defined more appropriately as limited studio production.

During the Depression, however, economic necessity forced a shift from the handmade toward industrial design and mass production. Exotic natural materials such as ivory, ebony, and onyx were replaced by synthetics. As Alastair Duncan observes: "The impact of the crash cannot be overstated. Among its influences on the decorative arts was the creation of the profession of industrial designer, which, in turn, led to a vast project of product redesign, carefully staged to re-stimulate consumer buying in the 1930s."[5] Artists were enlisted as designers for industry—to create furniture, functional glass, and ceramics—and designers were elevated to the status of artists.

Streamlined forms replaced the ornamented surfaces of the 1920s. Streamlining, an aesthetic best represented by the airplane and the zeppelin, could be noted in objects in all craft media. Smooth, machine-made materials, such as plastics, composite metals, and wood laminates reflected the national obsession with speed at a time when efficiency and productivity were passwords to a fast-paced future.

Craft and design in the Machine Age looked ahead with hope. Futuristic fairs, such as the Century of Progress Exposition and the "World of Tomorrow Exhibition" at the 1939–40 New York World's Fair, attempted to satisfy the need for optimism in a time of universal depression, as did Hollywood musicals, sky-scraping architecture, and planned urban complexes like New York's Rockefeller Center. Hollywood films embraced modernism, popularizing the movement. New, sleek, machined designs could be seen in recreational objects, such as the cocktail glasses and ashtrays adopted by the "speakeasy" culture; in recreational atmospheres, such as jazz clubs; and in the workplace. Technological advances expressed a concern with practicality but also with style. The adherence to a particular style—smooth and streamlined, simple and precise—demanded the evolution of certain materials. The essayists in this volume discuss the relationship between the emergence of new materials and the development of craft techniques that followed.

Dirigibles salute the New York World's Fair, 1939

Installation view of "Machine Art,"
The Museum of Modern Art, New York,
March 5–April 29, 1934

Manhattan was the center of industrial design, and the mutation into the streamlined was primarily processed within the domain of certain East Coast museums: The Brooklyn Museum, The Metropolitan Museum of Art, The Newark Museum, and from 1929 onward, the newly founded Museum of Modern Art in New York. The Pennsylvania Museum of Art (now the Philadelphia Museum of Art) presented "Design for the Machine" in 1932, giving design prominence in the museum's hierarchy, as did The Museum of Modern Art's "Machine Art" show of 1934. By the 1940s, much well-designed furniture and other domestic objects were being manufactured. New industrial materials, such as a more flexible plywood, enabled artists to create organic forms, abandoning the right angle and simple geometric shapes.

The skyscraper is this country's signature image, and perhaps its most significant contribution to the modern era. Ornamented with Art Deco motifs in the 1920s and 1930s, its imagery influenced several generations of objects in this country and abroad. The architectural setback, created in response to a 1916 New York zoning law to insure that sun would permeate the city's expanding grid of high-rises, became the unifying theme of American Art Deco design, appearing in textile patterns, furniture, and accessories.[6] Manhattan was rapidly altered by modernist structures—Rockefeller Center and the Empire State, Chrysler, and Chanin buildings were completed by the early 1930s—establishing the modern urban norm. However, the skyscraper, a unique American phenomenon, was not universally embraced; Lewis Mumford and Frank Lloyd Wright were outspoken critics.

Last stone being placed on the world's largest office building to date, Rockefeller Center, New York, 1932

From the Depression emerged a capitalist vision of the skyscraper as a redeemer. The machine was also a compelling social force, transforming the appearance of all kinds of objects and inspiring a contagious acquisitive attitude as streamlining infiltrated design and permeated homes. A profusion of new domestic appliances was invented. Kitchens and bathrooms were the beacons of modernism, replacing the drawing room as the aesthetic showcase in the home. It was also the era of the movie house, gas station, diner, and night club, and mechanistic designs were created for these new needs. It was thought that lifestyles, altered by Prohibition and the Depression, could be enhanced by modernist signals and new domestic objects. As many slid from positions of great wealth, new appliances for a servantless life were appealing, and domestic furnishings were

Gottlieb Eliel Saarinen. "Room for a Lady," room setting designed for "Contemporary American Industrial Art," Thirteenth American Industrial Art Exhibition, The Metropolitan Museum of Art, New York, 1935

Gottlieb Eliel Saarinen. Master bathroom, Saarinen House, Cranbrook Educational Community, Bloomfield Hills, Michigan, c. 1930

scaled down for more modest quarters. The modern New York apartment would contain modular furniture, and spaces might serve more than one function, as in a living-dining room. The need to escape made movies and travel vacations popular pastimes. Travel, particularly to the Southwest, brought Native American motifs into the design vocabulary. Prohibition led to the advent of the discreet, at-home cocktail party; many accessories were invented to enhance this new social occasion. Cocktail bars, tables, shakers, and glasses appeared, often incorporating the new plastics. Smoking, considered a sophisticated companion activity to drinking, had its own paraphernalia—cigarette cases, lighters, and holders, small cigarette tables, and ashtrays. The Hollywood set became the model of an urbane life, and movie stars wore clinging evening gowns that attenuated and streamlined their bodies.

CRAFT IN THE MACHINE AGE

The overriding issue in this period differs from that of the two earlier chapters in the history of twentieth-century American craft. The machine and the hand were the protagonists of the exhibition "The Ideal Home: 1900–1920." In "Revivals! Diverse Traditions: 1920–1945" the differences between folk art and craft were examined. In this era, craft confronts design, particularly as practiced by the industrial designer. As unique objects became too costly to produce, the craftsperson looked for ways to work more economically, often as part of a designer/maker team. Thus, the splendid objects of the period range from a unique and completely handmade desk by Wharton Esherick—the embodiment of the craft ideal—to a Gilbert Rohde radio that incorporates traditional craft materials in a slick, modern design produced in quantity.

The ever-reaching threat of industry and the machine-made, and the separation of the designer from the maker, impinged upon the purity of the unique, handmade object. At the same time, the contribution of industry to the period was a critical one. Industry's mandate was to modernize products and their means of manufacture. Streamlining swept through the design universe, rounding corners, smoothing surfaces, attenuating forms, proselytizing speed. Modernism was like a cult, practiced with fervor and compliance to the doctrine. Everything in American life was affected; craft would be irrevocably altered. The artist could work within a factory system or create objects that looked streamlined or machine-made, but both choices blotted out the evidence of the hand.

CRAFT IN THE MACHINE AGE: THE EXHIBITION

The works in the exhibition were selected by five curators, one for each of the traditional craft disciplines. Barbara Perry, director of the Tyler Art Gallery, State University of New York at Oswego, curated the ceramics section, while Mary Schoeser, an independent curator, writer, and lecturer, selected the textiles. Jewel Stern, a consultant at The Wolfsonian Foundation, chose the works in metal, and April Kingsley, American Craft Museum curator, the works in glass. I acted as curator of the section on wood.

There are about one hundred and fifty objects in the exhibition, representing a spectrum of developments within each of the craft disciplines. The emphasis has been placed on the unique object rather than the manufactured product, although mass-produced objects inspired by the unique example and engendered with a similar sensibility do appear. Much glass, for example, was factory-made, and some furniture was destined to be manufactured as well. All of the objects meet the rigorous expectation that they be innovative within craft tradition, and evidence technical prowess and a reverence for materials and process. In addition, since this is only one chapter in an extensive history of American craft in this century, an effort was made to identify those objects of historical importance that influenced future developments in craft; others were selected because they were signposts of the period.

Murals were among the most visible artistic manifestations of the 1930s, involving European and Latin American artists as significant as Pablo Picasso, Henri Matisse, Diego Rivera, and José Clemente Orozco as well as numerous Americans. But generally, the interval between the wars is an undervalued and relatively unrecorded period across the arts, a twenty-five-year hiatus—or at best, a period of hibernation before postwar activity. Therefore, documenting artistic expression in this period is a challenge, design history is underrecognized, and Art Deco has been considered a playful interlude rather than a serious style. In addition, we have examined the period to trace the development of craft, an area that is particularly obscured in conventional art histories.

Karen Davies, in *At Home in Manhattan: Modern Decorative Arts, 1925 to the Depression* (1983), first drew concerted attention to the period's decorative arts; subsequently, there have been several other important publications as well as exhibitions. This is the first time, however, that the influence of European modernism on American artists working in craft media has been surveyed. It is little recognized that the machine was such a powerful aesthetic force at the time that unique and handmade objects may not *look* handmade. A program of modernity erased these signs. They are objects born of economic depression, an impending holocaust, and war, and they promised an escape. Part of this transaction was a break with tradition in all ways possible. This mission—to escape to a new world—bestowed a seamless consistency, a modern look that declared the primacy of speed and the luxury of convenience.

Though modernism and the machine formed the rubric, diverse aesthetic forces, originating from different European countries as well as elsewhere, coexisted within it. These sources have been noted, as has the European influence upon American art education. But how did the presence of European ideas affect the appearance, the form and shapes, the materials, and the function of objects? Early twentieth-century Cubist painting and sculpture was reincarnated in glass and metal objects with multifaceted surfaces. French *art moderne* brought an ideal of luxury and simplified Art Nouveau forms. Another vocabulary, based upon pure geometry, can be traced to the Bauhaus. Although the Bauhaus litany—form follows function—was acknowledged, geometry often obscured an object's use, subsuming function in an abstract shape—a cube, a square, or a cylinder. Forms were reduced to such a degree that common objects like a teapot or a chair might seem to have emerged as brand new and without historical precedent.

Coexisting with functional objects were nonfunctional figurative ceramics, derived from Viennese Expressionism and characterized by a fanciful presence and exuberant polychromy. Scandinavian-influenced forms, primarily in wood, silver, or fiber, enlisted a purist, almost classical approach while respecting the nature of the material itself. The elegant curvilinear aspect of many of these works positions them on the borderline between historicism and modernism. By the 1930s, abstract patterns were inspired by other historic sources, such as Native American Pueblo patterns. Derivations of African portrait busts and classical Greek furniture also appeared. The American skyscraper hovered as backdrop, influencing the forms of many domestic and commercial objects. Considering these diverse sources, it is astounding that the objects have such a cohesive look.

This cohesiveness emerged from a universal formal vocabulary—the zeitgeist of the moment—that may be exemplified by the treatment of surfaces. Inspired by the machine aesthetic and new materials, surface and form achieved a synergy. The slick, smooth surfaces of the new synthetics, as well as those of glass and metal, initiated a blatant and important change in the surface treatment of traditional materials. The rising popularity of lacquer and metal may even have been due to their affinities to Bakelite's shiny "new" surface. Surfaces were also enhanced by combining materials, mixing metal and glass or wood and chrome, or by incorporating synthetic fibers with wool, silk, or cotton. The increasing importance of luxurious materials in the 1920s was probably inspired by French *art moderne,* but it was acceptable in this country to state luxury through a surface. It could be truly "skin deep," as evidenced in the prevalent use of exotic veneers instead of solid wood, lacquer to disguise wood graining, and silverplate instead of sterling.

Surface treatment is one unifying theme; a romantic geometry is another. *Art moderne* also inspired the stylized organic and geometric relief patterning that clad the surfaces of many New York skyscrapers; these patterns are ubiquitous in textiles and glass and metal objects of the period. Assertive circles, rectangles, or

Paul Theodore Frankl. Room with a skyscraper bookcase, c. 1929. As published in Paul T. Frankl, *Decorative Art* (New York: Albert and Charles Boni, 1929)

squares interact or are elegantly distorted in every kind of object, from a martini shaker to a case piece. Patterns of stylized geometric or natural forms appear in every material. Streamlining is a constant presence, and stepped motifs, zigzags, telescope forms, and concentric shapes proliferate.

CRAFT IN THE MACHINE AGE: THE PUBLICATION

In these pages I have reported crosscurrents between Europe and America that nurtured the growth of art schools and changed the nature of craft during the period. The prominence of the American skyscraper and the attendant focus on the machine and streamlining have veiled the importance of craft during the period between the wars. I have directed attention to the important presence of craft artists, even within the factory system, in order to increase awareness of the actual preponderance of significant craft objects. This book contains several essays that provide a backdrop for these major developments.

Harvey Green traces the political and economic causes and effects of modernism. He discusses the roles of the industrial and graphic designer, the relationship of abstract painting to craft, as well as the part played by unions in the "industrialization" of craft. He describes the "marriage of engineering and art" that underlies modernist theory, and notes the importance of the Chicago Century of Progress Exposition and the New York World's Fair, with its "World of Tomorrow" theme.

Karen Lucic dismisses the notion that American craft is inferior to that of Europe. It is undervalued, she feels, because it must be understood within its own context, rather than compared with the European. Material culture, she points out, is a discipline that can enable us to understand these works better. While she notes that the "rhetoric of mass production," rather than traditional craft practice, has dominated the discourse, most modern works were actually unique and handmade. Manufacturers, concerned with sales potential, were slow to produce modern works.

Rosemarie Haag Bletter proposes a revisionist view of the period that questions the dominance of Le Corbusier. She calls attention to the more conservative strains of German modernism as well as the influence of Ludwig Mies van der Rohe and Alvar Aalto. She reassesses the influence of the Bauhaus and German Expressionism on American architecture.

Marcia Yockey Manhart examines developments in the teaching of craft and design. She contends that the acceptance of craft as a legitimate course of study in colleges and universities is due to the influx of artists and architects between 1930 and 1944. European émigrés founded the Cranbrook Academy of Art, the New Bauhaus, Black Mountain College, and other schools. She notes that The School for American Craftsmen at Dartmouth College was the first such institution to offer a degree in woodworking. Ceramics, however, was—and remains—the most common course offering.

Individual artists have been treated in the five essays, focusing upon each of these craft disciplines. Barbara Perry writes on ceramics, identifying specific Asian and European sources—German, French, Scandinavian, and Viennese—and describes their impact on artists and schools in this country. Attention is drawn to the Cowan Pottery Studio and its interaction with the Cleveland School of Art. She characterizes the period as one of vigorous experimentation. The strong belief in remaining true to the nature of the material is evident in both "purist" mass-produced pottery and expressive clay sculpture.

Jewel Stern discusses the metalwork of the period, noting the influence of the Paris Exposition of 1925 and that of émigré silversmiths, while commenting on the works of American artists who abandoned Arts and Crafts forms in order to produce modernist works. She also cites important schools where metalwork was featured, such as the Cranbrook Academy of Art. Elegant accouterments for the consumption of alcohol and cigarettes were commonly made of metal. Some craftspeople not only created luxurious accessories but also designed mass-produced tableware.

April Kingsley's essay traces the origins of the Studio Glass movement back to the post-retirement activities of Frederick Carder of Steuben Glass, and to the work of independents like Waylande DeSantis Gregory, Maurice Heaton, and Frances Higgins. Carder, working in a studio outfitted with small glass-melting kilns, experimented with cast crystal, *pâte de verre,* and complex double-wall castings. Simultaneously, design for glass was being revolutionized in the factories. Steuben's revamped design and promotion strategies for the perfectly clear crystal it developed in 1933 were an early model for future conjoinings of craft and industry. Special projects for Steuben, such as the "Twenty-seven Artists in Crystal" series and spectacular glassworks created for the New York World's Fair, also demonstrate the influence of modern European stylization on American glassmaking of the period.

Mary Schoeser explores the ties between the handmade and the machined in the handscreening and block printing of textiles in the 1920s. The impact of modernist abstraction on textiles saw a shift from tapestries imitating paintings to textiles in which fibers and construction were emphasized. Loja Saarinen, Anni Albers, and Marli Ehrman established weaving departments in three schools—Cranbrook, Black Mountain, and the Chicago School of Design, respectively—from which the first generation of American studio weavers emerged in the 1940s. Like hand screenprinting and weaving, rugmaking adapted well to modernism. Contemporary artists like Marguerite Zorach designed traditional hooked rugs, and the craft collectives that produced them were an important vehicle for carrying modernism to a broad public. Thus craft—in the development of prototypes by hand—and craftsmanship—in creating new standards for the exploration of new fibers and weave structures, and in the modification of printing techniques—set the parameters for a modern idiom in textiles.

Kate Carmel's essay focuses on wood objects. Unique, original works were either made in the studio by an artist-craftsperson or crafted by others to the artist-designer's specification out of carefully selected, often rare woods. Wharton Esherick's early furniture and turned wood pieces by James Prestini were completely handmade. Donald Deskey's designs for Radio City, as well as other furniture of this period, were exquisitely handcrafted outside the design studio. Many architects designed the furnishings for the interiors of their buildings, in the tradition of Frank Lloyd Wright.

CRAFT BETWEEN THE WARS

In the period 1920–1945, a foundation was laid for future growth and increased strength in the crafts. Schools were established, and the teaching of craft was elevated to a profession, led by educated and inspired individuals from abroad as well as artists born in this country. Museums organized exhibitions on craft and design and began to collect objects in both fields.

The prelude to a second world war lessened the power of an ocean to divide artistic communication by bringing leading artists to our shores. This, combined with our own innovative spirit and innate attraction to the new, enabled this country to join, and eventually lead, the modernist movement. The interwar period was permeated by a drive toward modernism that homogenized the appearance of domestic and industrial artifacts, imparting a machine-made look. Yet artists working in craft media played critical roles in this achievement. Craftspeople worked with designers in order to reach mass markets, and industrial designers in turn sought craftspeople whose special knowledge and skills would increase the aesthetic appeal of their products and the efficiency of their production. Craftspeople knew materials and how to use them. They understood function at a moment when it was a primary concern. And, perhaps most importantly, they had the rare talent for refining and inventing forms.

Whether working within industry, for industrial designers, or alone in their studios, craft artists played a significant role during the Machine Age. They enabled the machine to produce extraordinary functional objects, and if the machine was ignored, provided steady support for the continued appreciation of the handmade object. American craft of the period is inventive, beautifully made, and magnificent in form. There is a unity of intent reflecting a universal commitment to modernism. New materials were exploited, and traditional ones transformed. Scale was transcended, as the smallest object took on the monumentality of the skyscraper and expressed the force of the machine.

One cannot imagine the Paris Exposition Internationale des Arts Décoratifs et Industriels Modernes occurring today without the participation of Americans. Yet the period 1920–45 in this country remains in need of further attention. It is hoped that this exhibition and publication will be perceived in two ways: as a foundation for the further examination of an underdeveloped chapter in twentieth-century American craft, and as an attempt to acknowledge an American spirit that can absorb many sounds and still resonate as a singular voice.

JANET KARDON
DIRECTOR
AMERICAN CRAFT MUSEUM

THE PROMISE AND PERIL OF HIGH TECHNOLOGY

by Harvey Green

Our capacity to go beyond the machine rests upon our power to assimilate the machine. Until we have absorbed the lessons of objectivity, impersonality, neutrality, the lessons of the mechanical realm, we cannot go further in our development toward the more richly organic, the more profoundly human.[1]
—Lewis Mumford, *Technics and Civilization* (1934)

In *Technics and Civilization* Lewis Mumford offered an alternative set of ideas for comprehending what many Americans viewed as inevitable: the loss of a benign, agrarian society to the impersonal and superior power of mechanized industry. Unlike Stuart Chase, Joseph Wood Krutch, Robert Penn Warren, and other cultural critics, Mumford claimed that high technology and mechanization were not the necessary enemies of an organic human culture.[2]

After a decade of work in which he consistently pilloried the effects on society of mechanization and industrial capitalism,[3] Mumford developed a new synthesis in *Technics and Civilization* to explain how the West in general, and the United States in particular, had gone awry, and to chart a course toward a more humane and socially responsible civilization. According to his sweeping historical analysis, the chief culprit of the social and economic catastrophes bedeviling Europe and America was liberal capitalism's unbridled pursuit of profits, combined with the reckless assertion of individual liberties. By centering his critique on political economy rather than the means of production or the nature of the goods produced, he established a middle ground between the nationalistic and antimodern sentiments of social reformers such as William Morris, who proposed a retreat into the medieval guild concept of handwork, and the aggressive advocacy of efficiency and industrial production by Progressive politicians, political economists, and celebrants of the "machine arts" that had characterized the first three decades of the twentieth century.[4]

It is tempting to conclude that modernism and folk/historic revivalism are two poles in the development of craft in the United States between 1920 and 1945. (Revivalism was treated in Volume II of the Centenary Project.) Certainly the products of craftspeople influenced by one or the other tendency look dissimilar and seem to have radically different design sources. But both strains of craftwork emerged from a critique of liberal capitalism, which for decades had revolved around a virtually unquestioned belief in individualism, democratic principles, and laissez-faire economics.[5] Both also sought to rescue the worker from the alienation that urban industrialization had brought.

The "revival" of traditional crafts, however—whether in the form of Appalachian textiles and furniture or the Native American, African-American, and Anglo-American material culture of the seventeenth and eighteen centuries—was in direct opposition to the modernist ethos. Revivalists combined a conservative, even reactionary, nationalism with an emphasis on the proto-capitalist methods and design forms of an earlier, allegedly more organic culture. The revival of the Colonial and indigenous folk handcrafts, whether for personal profit or as therapy, were isolated and essentially rearguard actions against the overwhelming transformation that had taken place in the factory, the marketplace, and the home.

This tangible change was an outgrowth of the industrial revolution of the nineteenth century. But faster means of production and the resulting panoply of goods had not come about without dislocation, criticism, and protest. Domestic and foreign observers of the United States marveled at the availability of material goods, the fluidity of American social relations, and the rapidity with which we built, tore down, and rebuilt machines and communities. Yet many saw in these conditions a tendency toward instability and disruption—"the restlessness and din of the railroad principle,"[6] as it was described in 1840. Artists and patrons worried about the authenticity of the arts in an age in which mechanical reproduction—chromolithography, photography, and sound recordings—brought art to the masses. By the time Henry Ford introduced the assembly-line mode of production to the automobile industry in 1914, it seemed that the majority of workers employed by the industrial sector would be overwhelmed by the potent combination of mechanization and wealth—reduced to seeming automata, albeit with more goods available to them.

Cultural and political retrenchment followed World War I. President Woodrow Wilson's plan for a League of Nations was rejected by the United States Senate. Prohibition became law by Constitutional amendment. Laws enacted in 1921 and 1924 severely restricted immigration. The war had shown that science and mechanization—poison gas, the biplane, the tank—could be used to kill in ways only imagined before. Overexpansion in agricultural and industrial productivity, combined with war reparations and trade restrictions, culminated in the economic collapse of the late 1920s, transporting the American worker from the assembly line to the bread line. By 1930, the machine had become an emblem of fascism, a tool to control the masses, as evidenced by the mechanized precision of the marching columns of the Third Reich.

A NEW DEAL

Under the New Deal, the federal government became an agent rather than an arbiter of economic and social reform. Increased government sponsorship of the crafts after Franklin D. Roosevelt took office in 1933 indicated that policymakers did not view the industrial economy as a wholesale cure for the country's monumental socioeconomic problems. Traditional handcrafts were often viewed as a means of social and economic amelioration for disadvantaged rural folk, or as a form of nation-building therapy for Americans who had lost both jobs and hope. Indeed, most of the buyers of these handmade goods were the middle class and the wealthy, whose purchasing power was largely a result of the very industrial system to which the producers of crafts were a counterpoint.

Modernists acknowledged the potential evils of mechanized mass production, but they came to more optimistic conclusions about the patterns of social and economic change established in the nineteenth and twentieth centuries. Their ideology was an outgrowth of the Progressive doctrine of economic nationalism, social improvement by government action, and a reliance on engineering, technology, and planning of all sorts. Long-range economic planning—in the form of public-works projects, urban and regional development schemes, and the programs of the Works Progress Administration and the Farm Security Administration—was certainly at the heart of many of the New Dealers' (if not President Roosevelt's) proposals for economic recovery and social reform. The Left also clearly favored government planning, if businessmen and industrialists, wary of federal controls on a free-market economy, did not. Industry's encroachment on the self-sufficient community led to attempts to construct more humane living and working environments, from the Rockefeller Center complex, New York (1929–39), and planned towns such as Greenbelt, Maryland (1935–41), to more ambitious projects like the *Regional Plan for New York City and Environs* (1929).

Advocates of the synthesis of science, engineering, and planning could point to numerous large-scale public-works projects of the late 1920s and 1930s to prove the efficacy of their positions. Hoover Dam (1931–36); the various projects of the Tennessee Valley Authority, incorporated in 1933 to improve navigation and provide cheap hydroelectric power; the George Washington Bridge, New York (1927–31), and Oakland Bay Bridge (1933–37); and California's Arroyo Seco Parkway (1937–40) were evidence that modern engineering could transform and control nature for the benefit of the human race in previously unimagined ways. For many, these projects were not merely feats of engineering skill but also works of art, a resculpting of the American landscape.

After 1920, Progressives had attempted to define a new order, one promising the goods and services an eager consumer society craved, the regulation of big business, and the safeguarding of private property and the rights of the individual. Modernism as a central organizing concept in the crafts was built upon this Progressive synthesis, combining technological innovation in design and materials with a marked emphasis on individual hand production—with or without the use of machines.

Modernism was profoundly urban in character, and as firmly rooted in the present as the craft revivals were rooted in the past. Art Deco, perhaps the preeminent visual style of the era, appropriated so-called "primitive" design sources, such as Middle Eastern and African textiles.[7] Its geometry—ordered, controlled, if exuberantly polychromatic—often imitated the setback of the urban skyscraper.

Model kitchen for a one-room apartment in the planned community of Greenbelt, Maryland, 1938. Photograph by Russell Lee

Thomas Hart Benton. *City Activities with Dance Hall* from America Today. 1930. Distemper and egg tempera with oil glaze on gessoed linen, 7'8" x 11'12". Collection The Equitable Life Assurance Society of the United States

The McGraw-Hill Building (1930), Empire State Building (1931), and Rockefeller Center, in New York, are aggressively modern in scale, construction, and decoration—or lack of it. Despite superficial vagaries in style, these buildings are unified by a machine-as-parts aesthetic and the use of modern industrial materials such as steel and aluminum.

The new, liberated musical form of jazz, a progressive synthesis of earlier forms, exemplified contemporary urban life. Jazz was a distinctly American idiom, and its rhythms captured the restlessness and anxiety of this transitional period. By the 1920s, Louis Armstrong had become an anchor in Chicago, and Jelly Roll Morton, Kid Ory, and Mutt Carey were captivating audiences in Oakland. By mid-decade, the faster-paced American cakewalk, Charleston, turkey trot, and monkey glide competed with the more sedate waltz and sensual maxix—Europeanized dance forms—in the increasing number of huge ballrooms in many major American cities.[8]

Speed had become an important social value. Automobile races, faster trains, "aeroplanes," and their pilots were trumpeted in the print media and, increasingly, over the airwaves. Feats of individual daring and the mastery of complex machines, exemplified by Charles Lindbergh's solo nonstop transatlantic flight in 1927, were celebrated by Americans of all classes, and are an example of the reconciliation of individual discipline and the complexities of mechanization. Science-fiction heroes such as Buck Rogers, popularized through serialized films and in print, combined the ethos of individual liberty with the beneficence (or at least usefulness) of high technology.[9] Buck and Lucky Lindy could handle "modern times."

Americans wanting to adopt an attitude of urban sophistication embraced functionalist design and the new materials modernists hawked. In the immediate postwar era, Art Deco–influenced crafts and manufactured goods often were made of natural, if luxurious, materials such as ivory, onyx, ebony, and silver. In the mid-1920s, however, new industrial materials such as plastics, industrial enamels, chromium, and aluminum for the most part superseded the use of natural materials. Economic necessity and the opportunity to tap a potentially huge market occasioned a shift from the luxury handmade object to the mass production of useful objects made to serve a specific purpose.

Russel Wright was one of the more visible purveyors of commercial modernism in the United States from the late 1920s through the 1950s.[10] An appren-

The Twentieth Century Limited

"ACF" Console radio, model 333, 1929

39

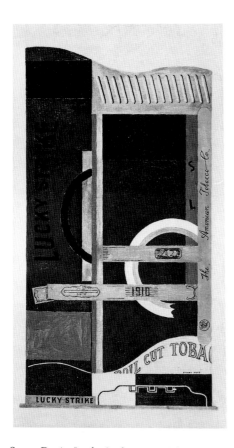

Stuart Davis. *Lucky Strike*. 1921. Oil on canvas, 33¼ x 18". The Museum of Modern Art, New York. Gift of The American Tobacco Company, Inc.

tice to theater designer Norman Bel Geddes in 1923–24, Wright launched his career as a designer of functional objects for the home in the 1930s. His first products were Bauhaus-inspired rounded forms in spun pewter—an alliance of machined forms and a material associated with the Colonial era. Wright soon adopted aluminum; it was easier to machine-tool and therefore less expensive to produce than pewter. Still enamored of the Colonial, however, he finished the aluminum goods with abrasives to emulate the matte look of pewter. Wright's greater commercial, and cultural, success lay in his later designs for mass-produced dinnerwares and furniture, especially his Modern Living (1935) and American Modern (1939) designs. Characterized by smooth lines and, in the case of his ceramic dinnerwares, pastel colors, the goods were marketed as appropriate to the less formal and faster-paced lifestyle that Wright accurately had sensed to be central to middle-class American life.

Wright's designs were consistent with the broad diffusion of European modernism that occurred between the wars. Abstraction was a signal characteristic of European modernist architecture, art, design, and craft. In American painting and sculpture, synthetic, or decorative, Cubism—as exemplified by the works of Pablo Picasso and Fernand Léger—and to a lesser degree, German Expressionism, were the most influential.

Partial to jazz and other popular art forms, the American painter Stuart Davis sought to inject new, urban rhythms into Cubist conventions.[11] In *Lucky Strike* (1921) he dissected the package of the popular cigarette, transforming it into a collagelike composition of line and form akin to the International Style architects' explorations of space and volume. Charles Sheeler's Cubist-realist *Rolling Power* (1939) is perhaps the most dynamic American exponent of the power of the machine.

Popular foreign films such as Fritz Lang's *Metropolis* (1927) and Robert Wiene's *Cabinet of Doctor Caligari (Das Cabinet des Dr. Caligari)* (1920) employed abstract design in their scenery. (Many of the muralists and sculptors employed by the New Deal federal arts programs would use similar—though somewhat more restrained—abstraction in their work.) The stylized abstraction of these films in turn influenced the Hollywood films of the period.[12]

The Bauhaus was the most important single design influence of the 1930s. Founded by Walter Gropius in Weimar, Germany, in 1919, the Bauhaus formulated a pragmatic approach to the problems of industrial design and a new method of teaching designers. Its premise was simple: The form of an object, or a building, derives from its function. Bauhaus designers rigorously avoided the use of applied ornament and attempted to give their objects a machine-made look, yet their creations were "in reality craft products which through the use of geometrically clear basic shapes gave the appearance of industrial production."[13] Mies van der Rohe's furniture designs often required impeccable handcraftsmanship in order to produce, paradoxically, a machine-made appearance. The tubular-steel chair, introduced by Bauhaus architect-designer Marcel Breuer in 1925, is a hallmark of modern functionalist design. Like much of the furniture produced at the Bauhaus, however, it was actually custom-made by the individual artisan.

The precise geometric shapes of seemingly undesigned machines and hand tools had become a matter of conscious aesthetic preference. Painters, sculptors, architects, and even craftspeople were influenced by these pure, "rational" forms. This new aesthetic was advanced by such seminal exhibitions as "Design for the Machine," at the Pennsylvania Museum (now the Philadelphia Museum of Art) in 1932; and The Museum of Modern Art's "Machine Art" show of 1934, which later traveled throughout the United States.

Variations on the new styles were disseminated chiefly through mass-circulation periodicals and films. The public's apparent fascination with speed and technology was reflected in the graphic arts. Streamlined, sans-serif typefaces, often with variations of thickness within a single letter, gave the appearance of movement and speed, conveying at least a proto-minimalist approach to typography consistent with the unadorned lines of Bauhaus design.[14] Advertisers also used the clean, sharply delineated style of "modern" illustration to signify the up-to-the-minute sophistication of the new products.

American industrial designers—Norman Bel Geddes, Donald Deskey, Raymond Loewy, and Walter Dorwin Teague, Sr., among others—redefined the look of manufactured goods, from automobiles and locomotives to pencil sharpeners and radios. Loewy's redesign of the Coldspot refrigerator for Sears, Roebuck, and Company in 1935 transformed a boxy apparatus with a visible motor into a smoothly curved rectangular solid sheathed in hospital-white enamel.[15] There seemed to be no place for dirt to hide in or on the new machine—an important selling point for a sanitation-conscious public—and it looked like the epitome of science brought into the home. By the late 1930s, variations on the tubular-steel chair—functional, durable, yet stylish—were mass-produced, extensively advertised, and widely purchased by middle- and upper-class Americans. The working class, which was still struggling to survive the ravages of the Depression, could afford few of these "luxury" conveniences. But many could acquire cheap, mass-produced kitchen cabinets, encased in white enamel and fitted with glass doors and shelves. Machines could oppress workers and, less directly, all of society, but they also promised better health, less work, and, for some, an optimistic post-Depression future.

Advertisement for Arrow shirts, *Saturday Evening Post,* November 14, 1931. As published in Roland Marchand, *Advertising the American Dream: Making Way for Modernity, 1920–1940* (Berkeley: University of California Press, 1985)

THE POPULAR FRONT

Locating the sources of the American character and strength in ordinary people and the prosaic objects of their lives connected many artists and craftspeople to the programs of the New Deal and the leftist politics of the Popular Front.[16] The Popular Front, which emerged after 1935, marked a change in strategy for the Communists, the socialists, and to some extent the "progressive" elements of the American political spectrum. For some on the Communist left, it represented no more than a change in tactics—a necessary delay—in the process of world revolution, prompted by the need to combat the rapid rise of fascism (as evidenced by Mussolini's invasion of Ethiopia, Hitler's expansionist designs in Central Europe, and the Japanese invasion of China). Others, ranging in political orientation from social democrats to middle-class moderates, shared the Popular Front's commitment to democratic government and the maintenance of peace. By 1938, the Popular Front had embraced the New Deal, and while it acknowledged that Roosevelt had acted primarily to save capitalism, it defended its new position as the most expedient means of advancing the rights of the American worker.

Workers in the industrial sector had experienced gradual improvements in wages, job security, and working conditions during the 1920s, but their gains had been sporadic and often undermined by inflation. When laborers did try to bargain or strike for a better deal, they often failed. In 1922 striking African-American farm workers gained minimally for their actions, and only after being tried for, and acquitted of, conspiracy. California oil workers, sardine fishermen, miners, and many other unionized workers lost protracted and bitter strikes. They eventually returned to their jobs (if they hadn't been fired and replaced) for little or no increase in salary, and sometimes for lower wages than they had earned when they went out. Union membership declined, from five million in 1921 to two and a half million in 1933.

But the Depression stiffened the resolve of the unions, and a new tactic—the

Ben Shahn. *Scotts Run, West Virginia*. 1937.
Tempera on cardboard, 22¼ x 27⅞".
Collection Whitney Museum of American
Art, New York

sit-down strike—enabled workers in the giant steel and automobile industries to
win broad concessions from management in the mid-1930s.[17] Union membership
surged to above four million by 1937, and many of the new members were part of
the recently formed Congress of Industrial Organizations, an industry-based (as
opposed to craft-based) union under the leadership of the charismatic and hard-
nosed John L. Lewis. Lewis and other labor leaders stressed bread-and-butter
issues such as hours, working conditions, job security, and wages. They were
less interested in issues of worker alienation or the dehumanizing effects of
assembly-line production. In this sense, they were far removed from the concerns
of social reformers such as Eleanor Roosevelt and the heirs of the Arts and Crafts
movement. Organized labor operated for the most part on the assumption that
industrial capitalism was a viable and desirable system of organization and production, and that labor's place within that system was that of a powerful interest
group in competition with management for available capital. This interpretation
received considerable support in 1935, when the Wagner Act, which guaranteed
labor's right to organize and restricted some antiunion management practices,
became law.

Although advocates of traditional craftwork often advanced their system as
an antidote to the baleful effects of industrial mass production, their arguments
failed to convince either the working class or management. The power of industry to efficiently produce affordable goods, and, at least in theory, to generate profits in a potentially vast global market, outweighed the benefits of reform. Like the
ultimately unsuccessful socioeconomic programs of William Morris and other
turn-of-the-century reformers, grass-roots craft remained grounded in the preser-
vation of pre-industrial skills, the celebration of individual workmanship, and the
lingering public enthusiasm for the Colonial revival and co-opted Arts and Crafts
styles in the furniture and decorative arts of the era.

CRANBROOK

Modernism as a visual style and urban attitude exerted a powerful influence upon
the formally trained arts and crafts communities in the form of design. Central to
the "formal" stream of craft activity after 1920 was the establishment of the Cran-

brook Academy of Art in Bloomfield Hills, Michigan.[18] Cranbrook was the result of the vision and finances of George G. Booth and the design sense of the Finnish architect Eliel Saarinen. Though it emerged from the Euro-American tradition of the small utopian community and the Arts and Crafts ideology of Morris, Elbert Hubbard, and Gustav Stickley,[19] the work produced there was wholly modernist in approach. Finnish design, characterized by a linear abstract geometry and natural materials, was at home in the expansive midwestern landscape and amidst the buildings of Prairie School architects Frank Lloyd Wright and William Purcell. It was equally at home among the Scandinavian immigrants who had settled in the Upper Midwest.

What seemed so novel to the American eye was the amalgam of hard-edged geometric form and the studied concentration on hand production that Cranbrook offered. Eliel Saarinen's ocher-painted birch side chairs of 1929, for example, are stylishly curved (as opposed to the right-angularity of most Arts and Crafts furniture), yet without the devalued historicism of, for example, the rococo furnishings popularized through mass-marketing venues such as the Sears, Roebuck and Company mail-order catalogue. Moreover, furniture and accessories such as Saarinen's were obviously different from the Colonial revival goods then popular. Though the seats of these particular chairs are covered in horsehair—an old American standard for upholstery—they do not refer to any previous American styles. No one could confuse them with the ever-popular Windsor chair or the rediscovered "settin" chairs of Appalachia.

The determining factor in these goods—what makes them "modern"—is the level of abstraction in both form and design. Whether their designers and fabricators consciously or unconsciously derived forms and decorative patterns from the native peoples of Latin and North America, the abstract geometric designs harmonized with the architecture and industrial and graphic design that was everywhere in the United States between 1920 and 1945. The spine of Jean Eschmann's 1931 binding for *The Odyssey of Homer* looks like any other fine leather binding of the previous two hundred years, but the front cover, with its small central rectangular space filled with interlocking multicolored diamonds makes it new. Arieto (Harry) Bertoia's silver-and-cherrywood coffee and tea service of 1940 appears to be without precedent in either form or decoration. The

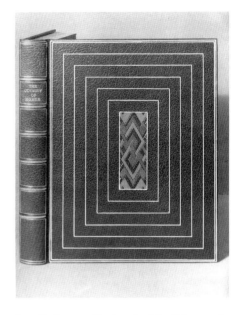

Jean Eschmann. Binding for *The Odyssey of Homer*. 1931. Tooled leather

Arieto (Harry) Bertoia. *Coffee and Tea Service.* 1940. Silver with cherrywood handles; tray: diameter 15½"; coffee pot: height 8"; water pitcher: height 9¾". Collection Cranbrook Academy of Art Museum, Bloomfield Hills, Michigan. Gift of Mrs. Joan R. Graham

seeming geometric perfection of the gracefully arched handles and curvilinear bodies suggests the marriage of art and engineering that formed at least the theoretical underpinnings of the modernist aesthetic.

The impact of modernism on amateur craftspeople is less evident, although membership in the art and craft societies that had been founded at the turn of the century continued to flourish. Many young people had been introduced to the crafts through school, in part as an introduction to skilled trades, and in part as a result of the growing influence of John Dewey's theories of education, which stressed the importance of learning by doing and the integration of the arts and sciences in school curricula.

There was also a burgeoning home hobbyist/do-it-yourself magazine culture in this period. Monthlies such as *Popular Mechanics* and *Modern Mechanix* or *Ladies Home Journal* were packed with how-to articles, primarily about woodworking, auto mechanics, the use and repair of small engines, or textile and culinary arts. By the early 1930s, when the Depression had cast millions out of work, these magazines provided not only a work-as-therapy opportunity for those with altogether too much spare time but also a chance to make or save now-precious cash.

Cover of *Modern Mechanix* (November 1935)

The form and design of furniture and other potentially homemade goods portrayed in periodicals were usually those of the Colonial revival or lingering "mission" style. Where modernism did find a home was in the use—and the celebration—of machines. There was little dignity in handwork when one could get a machine to do it faster, and perhaps better. The machine-as-hope ideology embraced by Mumford and the technocrats of the New Deal was pervasive in these magazines. The cover of the November 1935 issue of *Modern Mechanix* shows a streamlined locomotive barreling into the foreground—into the future. By contrast, inside are conservative "revival" style furnishings to be built by the do-it-yourself handyperson (the reassurance of the familiar in a rapidly changing world), as well as an array of self-improvement schemes, correspondence-school opportunities, and tips on how to succeed in Depression-era America.

THE CHICAGO AND NEW YORK EXPOSITIONS

Two of American modernism's defining moments between the wars were the Chicago Century of Progress Exposition of 1933–34 and the New York World's Fair of 1939–40, both of which were promoted as harbingers of the new age of high technology. The Chicago exposition took as its symbols a log cabin and a skyscraper, but visitors were probably most struck by the rhythmic geometric forms of the buildings grouped on the shores of Lake Michigan. The General Exhibits Group was a staccato succession of angular, machined solids with bright zones of color, set in a row along a broad *allée,* an enormous "Firestone" sign at its endpoint. The Goodyear blimp was ever-present, and the streamlined Burlington *Zephyr* locomotive, toured by nearly three-quarters of a million visitors, was indicative of the impact and popularity of high technology at the Fair.[20]

The historical vision presented by the Chicago exposition—the thematic center of which was, after all, the idea of change over time—was virtually nonexistent at the New York World's Fair. Originally planned to coincide with the sesquicentennial of George Washington's inauguration as president of the United States, the Fair quickly became, in planning, execution, and marketing, a celebration of science and technology—"The World of Tomorrow." The Trylon and Perisphere, not the statue or stature of Washington, became the symbols of the Fair.[21]

Modernism's faith in technology, science, planning, and capitalism was the informing ethos of the Fair, and it was synthesized in its architecture and design exhibits. Nearly every famous name in industrial design—Norman Bel Geddes, Donald Deskey, Raymond Loewy—had a major commission for the Fair's exhibits. Sweeping walkways carried visitors into svelte buildings; compact electric cars and futuristic "rocketports" showed modes of transportation to come. Ornament in the traditional sense was banished; streamlining was everywhere.

In its tidal wave of color and neon light, the Fair marked a significant departure from one of the central organizing principles of previous international exhibitions. Rather than displaying the wonders of magnificent, even magical machines, the "World of Tomorrow" exhibitors concentrated on processes, and in so doing recognized both the public's ambivalence about mechanization and their Depression-inspired need for confidence in an economy and a national ideology that seemed off-track, even out of control.

In the end, modernism, and the New York World's Fair, aimed to restore society's faith in science and technology, but more importantly, in the human spirit and the ability to overcome cataclysmic change. It was in this sense as much as in any other way that modernism and the crafts intersected and interacted in the years between the wars.

Opening night of the second season of the New York's World's Fair, May 11, 1940

THE MYTHS OF MODERNISM

by Rosemarie Haag Bletter

Marcel Breuer. *African Chair*. 1921
(now lost). Upholstery by Gunta Stölzl

With the rise of postmodernist architecture in the 1970s and the attendant back-lash against modernist principles,[1] early twentieth-century modernism came to be defined as a unilateral movement of the avant-garde in Europe. This simplistic definition of modernism had its origins in Henry-Russell Hitchcock and Philip Johnson's presentation of 1920s architecture as a visually coherent style in the Museum of Modern Art exhibition "Modern Architecture: International Exhibition," which opened in New York in 1932 and was later shown in Milwaukee, Los Angeles, and numerous other American venues.[2] The accompanying book, *The International Style: Architecture Since 1922*,[3] with its highly selective images (most are examples of German architecture) and clear principles of design, became the primer for American students of avant-garde style.

Modernism, however, should be seen as a more inclusive development, one in which many disparate factions played pivotal roles. To understand what modernism meant before its reduction to a uniform and all-powerful orthodoxy, it is instructive to look at several German publications of the 1920s, most of them written by architects: Walter Gropius's *Internationale Architektur* (1925); Adolf Behne's *Der moderne Zweckbau* (Modern Functional Building; 1926); and Ludwig Hilberseimer's *Internationale neue Baukunst* (International New Architecture; 1927).[4] While Hitchcock and Johnson focused on the external appearance of architecture and stylistic continuity, these authors identified the new architecture through an underlying conceptual understanding. Contemporary expression was therefore seen as a reflection of the architects' philosophical attitude toward modernity—a view allowing for greater visual diversity, since a balanced correlation between idea and form was difficult, if not impossible, to define. Reinforcing this characteristic attitudinal difference, these texts referred to contemporary architecture not as a style but as *neues Bauen*—"new building." In the Netherlands, modernist architecture was also referred to as "new building" (*nieuwe bouwen*), probably because in both countries social housing, not just high-style architecture, played a significant role in the way modernism was conceived.

Clichés like "Bauhaus architecture" and "Bauhaus functionalism," commonly used as shorthand for a European modernism, have helped to perpetuate another aspect of this misreading. The Bauhaus was not, in fact, a school of architecture, but a school of painting, sculpture, craft, and design; architecture was taught only to fourth-year students, and functionalist design, as it is understood today, was not included in its pedagogical program for much of its existence.[5]

From its inception in Weimar, Germany, in 1919 until about 1923, the Bauhaus was under the influence of the color theorist and mystic Johannes Itten, Expressionism, and folkloristic-primitivizing tendencies, evident in Marcel Breuer's *African Chair* (1921) and Gerhard Marcks and Theo Bogler's Inca-inspired *Dual Pot* (1921). From 1923 until Gropius's departure as the school's director in 1928, Bauhaus designs were informed by the rigorous Constructivist practice of László Moholy-Nagy and by the neoplasticist theories of Theo van Doesburg and the Dutch de Stijl group. This middle period of the Bauhaus, when it incorporated in eclectic fashion the various avant-garde styles of the 1920s, is its most well known. Its products were sleek and elegant-looking, such as the coffeepot and water jug designed by Wilhelm Wagenfeld, W. Roessger, and Friedrich Marby in 1924, and Marianne Brandt's nickel-silver and ebony teapot of 1924. Yet these objects, which are modern in their elementary geometrical forms, are more concerned with aesthetics than utility; ostensibly designed for use, these containers have handles that are difficult to grasp.

It was only from 1928 to 1930 that the Bauhaus, under the directorship of Hannes Meyer, followed an overt program of utilitarian functionalism that excluded any consideration of aesthetics, fracturing the unity of art and technology that had been the central tenet of Gropius's pedagogy after 1923 (a radical change in direction that led many students and teachers to leave the Bauhaus after Meyer's appointment). Meyer stated in 1928: "All things on this earth are a product of the formula: (function times economy). . . . Building is not an aesthetic process . . . building is only organization."[6] Under the direction of Josef Albers, in 1929, the cabinet workshop produced folding chairs that may have been practical and economical but that have none of the modern elegance of the designs of the middle period.

Bauhaus teaching, therefore, was hardly uniform, but consisted of a series of rather different approaches. Gropius was responsible in part for the widely accepted reductive view of the school, for in his later institutional career, as the head of Harvard University's Graduate School of Design, he tended to stress only its middle period, and did not consider in his reassessment its early Expressionist phase or the utilitarian functionalism of the Meyer era.

Although functionalism was a minor aspect of Bauhaus pedagogy, the notion of *Sachlichkeit* (objectivity) did in fact play a central role in the way early modernist architecture was defined. In general, however, *Sachlichkeit* did not describe a utilitarian functionalism. For instance, Gropius freely admitted the existence of individual and national characteristics in current architecture, but despite this he discerned unifying tendencies—in effect an "international" architecture—which he described as a shared *Gestaltungswille* (creative will); *Sachlichkeit* was subsumed under this idealistic concept.[7] Hilberseimer, a teacher at the Bauhaus in its later phase, also found unity in contemporary architectural practice: "The creative will of the architect dominates everything. . . . The new architecture is the expression of spiritual permeation. . . . It is not based on a stylistic conception."[8] Both Gropius and Hilberseimer seem indebted to Alois Riegl's idealist notion of *Kunstwollen,* or artistic intention.[9]

Behne, whose *Der moderne Zweckbau* was conceived in 1923, was the most prescient in unmasking many of the ideologies and assumptions of functionalism, rationalism, and European modernism. He wrote that "man is not strictly utilitarian. From the beginning of human culture, the urge to be playful is coupled with the practical."[10] What does change continually, in Behne's view, is the balance between function and form. Design should always aim for an equilibrium between these factors. Though he did not insist on the primacy of functionalism

Gerhard Marcks and Theo Bogler. *Dual Pot*. 1921. Glazed stoneware, height 13½". Staatliche Kunstsammlungen zu Weimar

Josef Albers cabinetmaking shop. *Folding Deck Chair*. 1929. Wood, fabric

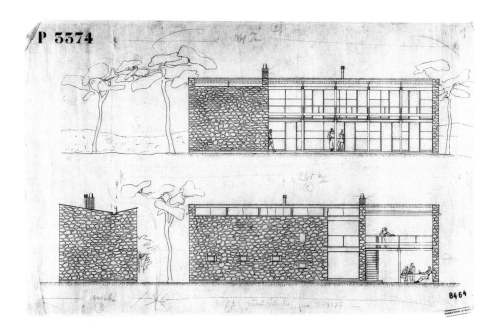

Le Corbusier (Charles-Édouard Jeanneret). *Drawing of Villa "Les Mathes."* 1935. Fondation Le Corbusier, Paris

as such, a perceived overemphasis on formalism in the nineteenth century led Behne to suggest that the current stress should be on functionalism. Shifts from one to the other implied neither cultural regression nor progress; Behne merely demanded that they be seen as related, interdependent concepts. His belief that function and form should be balanced also allowed him to be critical of a pure, or absolute, functionalism. *Der moderne Zweckbau* constitutes early modernist theory that contained within it the possibility of a *post*-modernism.

Regarding functionalism, Behne proposed an expanded notion of this term that clarifies the difference between utilitarianism and functionalism as conceived by most of his contemporaries: "Functionalists are concerned with solving a problem of general significance to our culture. Utilitarians only ask: 'What is the most practical way for me to act in this case?' Their attitude inclines towards philosophy and has a metaphysical basis. . . ."[11] Because of the tremendous influence of English utilitarianism in America, later discussions of functionalist architecture, despite Louis Sullivan's deep concern that building serve the good of the society, are usually mistakenly interpreted as exclusively utilitarian in nature.

Similar misunderstandings have clouded the interpretations of the work of Le Corbusier, the most influential European architect of the twentieth century. His rational approach, combined with his interest in machine metaphors, often have led to an exclusively technocentric assessment of his work. His Villa Savoye, Poissy (1928–31), a seminal design of the period, has a prominent sunscreen on the rooftop terrace. The form of the screen appears cylindrical from the entry façade, and can be read as an allusion to the smokestack of a steamship. As one moves around the building, however, it unfolds to reveal extraordinary sculptural forms and a poetic sensibility.

Le Corbusier had been deeply interested in vernacular architecture from the beginning of his career, as is evident in the houses he designed in 1905–08 at La Chaux-de-Fonds, his hometown in Switzerland. In 1911 he made a wide-ranging study trip—to Berlin, Prague, Belgrade, Istanbul, Athens, and Rome, among other sites—during which he recorded both well-known works and folkloristic architecture. And while he was certainly concerned with the technocentric imagery of cars, airplanes, and steamships in his *Vers une Architecture* (1923),[12] this must be seen against his equally strong convictions about the lyrical powers of the designer as form-giver. From the 1930s onward, Le Corbusier revealed an increasing disillusionment with rationalism—particularly in his designs for country houses—and began to develop a new, more tactile architectural language. His unexecuted project for the Errazuris House (1930), the de Mandrot Villa (1931), the Pavillon Suisse (1932), the Villa le Sextant (1935), and his Maison de Week-end (1935) all feature prominent fieldstone walls. These projects form a transition to the better-known works of the postwar period, such as Notre Dame du Haut, Ronchamp (1950–55), and Maisons Jaoul, Neuilly (1954–56), in which bold, rough textures, a self-conscious primitivism, and a reassertion of the handcrafted are brought together to express a quasi-preindustrial approach to building. The Neo-Expressionist, non-Euclidean, "organic" forms that dominate Ronchamp represent the culmination of Le Corbusier's shift toward a more anthropocentric architecture, a shift that may have been influenced by Surrealism in the 1930s.

A similar argument can be made for the work of the Finnish architect Alvar Aalto. His buildings of the 1920s seem to belong to the high-modernist International Style, yet, as one analyzes them more closely, a distinct interest in vernacular traditions, tactile surfaces, and the handcrafted detail can be discerned. As in Le Corbusier's oeuvre, this change is clearly evident in Aalto's work of the 1930s: in the undulating interior wall of his Viipuri Library (1927–35); in the emphasis on handcraft in the subtly varying textures—for instance, the raffia-wrapped columns—of the Villa Mairea (1937–39); and in the textured wood slats and massive undulating walls of his Finnish Pavilion, designed for the New York World's Fair of 1939–40. These "soft" forms are echoed by his furniture designs, most notably, the Paimio armchair (1940), and the Savoy glass vases of the same period.

While it is useful not to think of the avant-garde as a hegemonic group, one needs also to reposition the avant-gardists vis-à-vis the traditionalists. The classic

Alvar Aalto. Interior view of the Finnish Pavilion, New York World's Fair, 1939

Frank Lloyd Wright. Storer House,
Hollywood, 1923–24. Photograph by
Anthony Peres

modernist texts tended to address only the avant-garde; it is important, however,
to recognize that the avant-garde exists in opposition to more conservative
approaches—the normative base—which may vary from one country or region to
another. In the United States, for example, conservative architects of the early
twentieth century primarily followed the Beaux-Arts approach.

Henry-Russell Hitchcock, in *Modern Architecture: Romanticism and Reintegration* (1929),[13] a less polemical work than his *International Style* of 1932, established the terms "New Pioneers," or the avant-garde, and "New Traditionalists,"
encompassing modernists with a sense of tradition, such as H. P. Berlage and Josef
Hoffmann. With these terms Hitchcock provided a richer view of history than the
more influential books on modernism by Siegfried Giedion and Nikolaus Pevsner, both of which concentrate solely on progressive architecture.[14] If full-fledged
traditionalists such as Edwin Lutyens and John Russell Pope are added to Hitchcock's historical schema, one begins to see the interlayering of the various architectural conventions. In this scheme, Art Deco architecture, for example, should
be positioned between the avant-garde International Style and traditional Beaux-Arts architecture.

If one begins to look for a more differentiated type of modernism, one that
does more than single out sleek forms or new technology, one can also find within the context of American modernist architecture numerous references to "handicrafts" coexisting with an interest in "traditional" modernism, with its trust in a
progressivist, technological future. Frank Lloyd Wright's California houses of the
early 1920s, particularly the Millard, Freeman, and Ennis Houses of 1923–24,
employ so-called textile-block construction, and are an intriguing case in point.
For these designs Wright adopted the use of precast concrete blocks, a "found"
building material that he injected with extraordinary dignity by using different
geometric patterns for the blocks in each house. The blocks and the interweaving
of the reinforcement rods that hold them in place create the effect of a geometrically patterned fabric. It seems to derive from a strong crafts tradition as well as
from the theories of Gottfried Semper concerning textiles as fillers between
structural supports, in his definition of the elements of building that were being
adopted for contemporary architecture in Chicago in the late nineteenth century.[15]

During the same period, Wright retained a singular interest in the automobile, as his project for the Gordon Strong Automobile Objective and Observatory (1925) demonstrates. Its double spiral prefigures Wright's 1943–59 design for
the Solomon R. Guggenheim Museum in New York; here, however, the spiraling
ramps are intended expressly for the movement of cars up and down the observatory tower. At the same time, the spirals are reminiscent of natural forms. As in
many of Wright's buildings, there is no clear-cut division between organic and
technological references; the two coexist in an ambiguous relationship.

Like Wright's work, Art Deco skyscrapers—usually designed by architects
who had been trained in the Beaux-Arts tradition, but who wanted to be seen as
modernists—are modern, yet they acknowledge an older, more decorative architectural tradition. The New York architect Ely Jacques Kahn had a special historical awareness of the confluence of the Wiener Werkstätte and Austrian design
in general in the 1925 Exposition Internationale des Arts Décoratifs et Industriels
Modernes in Paris. Despite the public-relations effort to present Art Deco as the
new "French style," Kahn observed in a review of the exhibition, "It is Vienna
warmed over."[16] In the vivid polychrome terracotta panels and intricate brickwork
of his office buildings at 2 Park Avenue (1927) and 261 Fifth Avenue (1929) in
New York, Kahn incorporated a full awareness of European design traditions
together with his familiarity with Wright's work. The tactile density and woven,
fabriclike quality he created with these materials do not jibe with our normal

understanding of the skyscraper as a structure that addresses primarily futuristic expectations.

After the stock market crash of 1929, architects and their patrons turned to a somewhat more pared-down look. The polychrome richness of the preceding decade was replaced by a grayer, more workaday mode. Increasingly, streamlining was used in architectural as well as industrial design to allude to the everyday modern world of speed and locomotion. As design historian Jeffrey L. Meikle has pointed out, such industrial-looking designs were commonly used as modern styling, as a public-relations gesture to compete for the limited buying power of the public during these years.[17]

In design during the 1930s, as in the architecture of Le Corbusier and Aalto, one can also detect resistance to the "machined" look preferred by industrial designers like Raymond Loewy and Walter Dorwin Teague, Sr. Russel Wright's armchair of 1934; Frederick J. Kiesler's aluminum nesting tables of 1938, and the sculpture pedestal and rocker he designed for Peggy Guggenheim's New York gallery, Art of This Century, in 1942; Isamu Noguchi's articulated table, designed for collector A. Conger Goodyear in 1939; and the experimental plywood chairs of Charles and Ray Eames from the early 1940s—all attest to the influence of Surrealism in their anthropomorphic and biomorphic forms, and can be seen as a reaction against the more technocentric forms of streamlining.[18]

In The Brooklyn Museum's exhibition of 1986, "Machine Age in America, 1918–1941," the 1920s and 1930s were presented as a monolithic period dominated by the machine. (While the machine and a technocentric future were no doubt powerful and appealing concepts, undercurrents that actually ran counter to this tendency were nevertheless subsumed under the exhibition's notion of a machine aesthetic.) Thus, the setback design of skyscraper pinnacles is described as a "machine-as-parts aesthetic,"[19] although there is no evidence that the detailing of these terminations intentionally referred to machine parts. On the contrary, the pinnacles of the Empire State Building, the Chrysler Building, and the General Electric Building in New York all vie with each other for attention through their stagy, idiosyncratic stylistic interplay, which appears intensely artful rather than machined. Similarly, biomorphic design of the 1930s is presented as simply a further development of streamlining,[20] when, in fact, architecture and design in the United States was rather distinct during these decades. During the 1920s there was a joyful engagement with ornament and the tactile surface, while during the Depression this exhibitionism was toned down to more somber colors and textures. Nor are the biomorphic designs of Kiesler or Russel Wright an extension of streamlining, with its suggestions of fast-moving machines and, on a metaphoric level, the speed of the modern age. Kiesler, Noguchi, and the Eameses were more directly involved with developments in painting and sculpture than with streamlined design. Surrealism had reintegrated the body, the personal, and the psychological. Architects and designers gradually responded to this shift in emphasis, rejecting technological imagery and progressivist futurism. What makes the period of high modernism of interest today is that it was neither uniform nor orthodox; that modernists such as Le Corbusier and Aalto proposed a new architectural language long before the postmodernists began to deconstruct modernism; and that streamlined commercial products reached a popular audience at the same time that artist-designers like Kiesler were questioning common assumptions about the meaning of modernism.

Ely Jacques Kahn. 2 Park Avenue, New York, 1927. Photograph by Cervin Robinson

Frederick J. Kiesler. *Two-part Nesting Table*. 1935–38. Cast aluminum, 9¾ x 34½ x 22¼". Estate of Frederick Kiesler. Courtesy Jason McCoy, Inc., New York

SEEING THROUGH SURFACES:
AMERICAN CRAFT AS MATERIAL CULTURE

by Karen Lucic

For many years an assumption prevailed about useful, artistically designed objects—whether craft, decorative arts, or industrial design—made in the United States during the 1920s and 1930s. Judged inferior to its European counterparts, this American material was largely ignored and deemed unworthy of study, especially in the museum setting. It was not until the 1980s that exhibitions surveyed pioneering developments in modern American design,[1] and though a scholarly reassessment was begun in the last decade, contemporary treatments still occasionally include invidious comparisons with European examples. As a result, American objects of the period are too often derided and dismissed.

Granted, when examined using conventional canons, these objects are not easily categorized. Their idiosyncrasies derive from the fact that the environment for design and production in the United States during the 1920s and 1930s was replete with contradictory impulses and blurred conceptual boundaries. With the exception of work by Frank Lloyd Wright, such as the tubular metal lamp designed for the Storer House in Hollywood, California, in 1923, artists working in the United States produced few modern designs for useful objects in the immediate postwar period. Instead, an array of period revival styles dominated. Not until 1925, when the Exposition Internationale des Arts Décoratifs et Industriels Modernes in Paris generated interest in modern alternatives, did opportunities evolve for European-trained immigrants and native-born craftspeople and designers interested in new, if not yet fully synthesized, ideas. Even so, these individuals encountered a more rigid status quo and limited patronage than abroad. The United States also lacked the government-sponsored schools and workshops that encouraged innovation and experimentation in, for example, Germany and Austria.[2]

In this problematic context, stylistic mergers were commonplace: influences from French *art moderne,* the Wiener Werkstätte, and German functionalism would converge in a single object; combinations of material, form, and manufacture could connote both luxury *and* utility, elitism *and* populism. Such is the case with Kem Weber's eccentric and evocative side table of 1929. An innovator in the design of multifunctional furniture, Weber was born and trained in Germany before immigrating to the United States during World War I; by the late 1920s, he was among the most successful designers for modern urban living in the country.[3] This side table, part of a coordinated bedroom ensemble, is dramatically thin and vertical, and the ingeniously designed drawers swivel sideways to open;

commentators of the time considered such features a boon to apartment dwellers living in close quarters. In addition, the elongated proportions mimic period skyscrapers, while the electric lights crowned by stacked metallic disks are especially evocative of modern technology. (This detail in fact anticipates the distinctive spire that crowns the Empire State Building, which was originally designed to be used as a dirigible mooring mast.) Weber effectively cloaked this economical form in somewhat incongruous luxury materials—sage-green painted wood with silvered details, and richly figured walnut-burl veneer.

In the headlong rush to embrace the modernist aesthetic after the Paris exposition, designers often transformed their handmade objects into forms suggesting mass production. A typical example is Walter von Nessen's Bakelite, aluminum, and brushed aluminum table of 1930, a spare and unornamented object composed of shiny, planar forms that intersect with geometric precision. Von Nessen, like Weber, emigrated from Germany, arriving in 1923. This table, which is symbolic of the Machine Age in both materials and form, indicates the broad influence of the design theories of the Bauhaus. Its individual elements look industrially manufactured, and von Nessen undoubtedly intended it as a prototype for mass production; yet the table was actually made in a small artisan's shop using rather traditional methods of handcraft. This object attests to the fact that work in the crafts survived during this era, but often in disguised forms. Social and aesthetic values discouraged the celebration of craft—sometimes even its acknowledgment. As Jeffrey L. Meikle has pointed out, rhetoric and the reality of production often diverged in this transitional period, before the canons and conceptual boundaries so familiar to us now had solidified.[4]

The terminology of the era embodies this fluidity. Well into the 1930s, the term "industrial art" denoted not only mass-produced objects but also unique creations made by hand. It was a synonym for what we now might call the "applied" or "decorative" arts. The defining feature of industrial art (as opposed to the so-called fine arts) was its *usefulness,* not its method of manufacture. Similarly, artists and critics identified many different decorative styles as "modern" or "modernistic." The term "*moderne*" usually indicated pieces showing French influence, but beyond that, there was little differentiation in reference to a wide variety of novel stylistic modes—at least in the American context.[5]

Another example that embodies the fusion of styles and associational significance characteristic of American work is a silver tea service made in 1930 by the Danish émigré Erik Magnussen. This exotic ensemble of teapot, creamer, and sugar bowl rests on a long, rectangular tray. The teapot and bowl are low, capacious forms, while the creamer is more vertically oriented. All of the pieces have elongated handles accented by carved jade. Like contemporary French examples,

Walter von Nessen. *Table*. 1930. Aluminum, Bakelite, brushed aluminum, 18½ x 15¼ x 15¼". The Metropolitan Museum of Art, New York. Purchase. Gifts in memory of Emil Blasberg, 1978 (1978.492.2)

Erik Magnussen. *Tea Service*. 1930. Sterling silver, New Zealand jade; teapot: height 6³⁄₁₆"; creamer: height 5⅜"; sugar bowl: height 4¹⁵⁄₁₆". Private collection

Jean E. Puiforcat. *Kettle, Stand, and Lamp.* c. 1923. Silver, lapis lazuli, 9½ x 11⅛". The Metropolitan Museum of Art, New York. Purchase, Edward C. Moore, Jr. Gift, 1925 (25.230.2 ab)

Marianne Brandt. *Teapot.* 1924. Brass, silver, ebony; height 3". Bauhaus archiv, Museum für gestaltung, Berlin

such as Jean Puiforcat's silver, ivory, and lapis lazuli teapot of about 1923, the precious materials give the Magnussen service a fashionable modernity. Yet Magnussen's forms are more geometrically simplified than those in Puiforcat's teapot, with its elegantly ascending profile and decorative flourishes. The American piece in fact suggests an awareness of contemporary Bauhaus metalwork, exemplified by Marianne Brandt's extraordinarily spare teapot of 1924, with its squat arrangement of seemingly machine-tooled planes and spheres. As an exercise in the rigorous reduction of forms to essential geometric elements, the design of Brandt's object asserts both vanguard aesthetic principles and mass production as an ideal.

The Magnussen service gestures toward such avant-garde models in its reduced decorative embellishment and eccentric angular forms, yet it remains a one-of-a-kind, elitist object—an elegant response to diverse modern trends in metalwork and quite representative of luxury silver production in America at the time.

However, when compared with European examples using solely formalist criteria, the Magnussen piece is at a disadvantage. Puiforcat's service displays more lavish materials and more elaborate craft techniques. To those beguiled by the extravagance of the French style, the American piece might appear to be a shy, less prosperous provincial cousin. Alternately, to those partial to the spartan functionalism and formal simplification embodied in the Bauhaus teapot, the American ensemble might look positively decadent, with its high-style materials and more traditional forms.[6] Such American work has been criticized both for being derivative and for not matching the elegance—or, alternatively, the rigor—of its foreign sources of inspiration. Caught between the two extreme polarities of European design during the interwar years—French *art moderne* and German functionalism—the American object is vulnerable to attack from both directions, at least from those who insist on evaluating it solely within the context of contemporary European production.

Traditional standards of connoisseurship and absolutist definitions of quality have obscured our understanding of the emergence of modernist trends in American craft. An alternative methodology is to view such objects through the lens of material culture study rather than to judge them by conventional aesthetic standards alone. As outlined by Jules David Prown, the premise of material culture study is that objects "reflect, consciously or unconsciously, directly or indirectly, the beliefs of individuals who made, commissioned, purchased or used them, and by extension the beliefs of the larger society to which they belonged."[7] This approach allows not only for the appreciation of an object's inherent qualities but also for unexpected insights into its context.

Interestingly, some strategies employed in the study of material culture overlap with those of traditional connoisseurship. Both begin with a meticulous examination of the artifact itself; both use painstaking visual analysis and informed intuition to uncover meaningful patterns in groups of related objects. The differences arise in the processes of interpretation and evaluation. The connoisseur seeks superior aesthetic quality and generally dismisses that considered second-rate. The student of material culture looks for the interrelatedness of object and context—the values, social conditions, aesthetic norms, or other features relating to the culture from which the object emerged. Visual delight and evidence of technical skill can still be considered important, but only within a complex matrix of meaningful factors. Seen in this light, the material environment of any social group is worthy of serious analysis.[8]

This last point is an important one, because our project to reconstruct the history of twentieth-century craft in America will not benefit from a narrow, unreflective perspective. Claims that American material is superior to other national traditions or untouched by European influences need not arise from an expanded interest in its significance. In fact, it would be counterproductive to advocate scholarly isolationism. What seems unnecessary is an automatic dismissal of American works when compared to European analogues.

When we see beyond the surfaces, the idiosyncratic features of American objects—those features that look peculiar when compared with European examples—can be important clues in the process of interpretation. They reveal the specific concerns of individual makers and, by extension, the social groups to which their makers belonged.

A ceramic punch bowl by Viktor Schreckengost will serve as an appropriate example. At first glance, the piece appears whimsical and perhaps somewhat frivolous; with patient study, however, it acquires complex meaning. This glazed porcelain bowl with *sgraffito* decoration is one of several versions made by the Cowan Pottery Studio in 1931. Its shape is simple and classical, with a subtly curving profile culminating in a footed base—an appropriate foil for the intricate iconography on the ceramic surface. Its colors are deep blue and black, giving a nocturnal cast to Schreckengost's ebullient collage of New York imagery. The colors suggest that Manhattan is most glamorous and exciting after dark.

Imagery interlocks and undulates around the bowl. Dramatically ascending skyscrapers, surrealistically overscaled playing cards, and blaring saxophones dwarf the human revelers. Mammoth champagne glasses emit effervescent bubbles, while corked liquor bottles indicate a risqué, even dangerous, substance within. The label of one displays repeated *X*'s, as if to warn of lethal contents, while the other includes the artist's signature, establishing his identification with, and presence in, the scene. The assertive forms of alcoholic beverages signify not only a festive occasion (undoubtedly a New Year's Eve celebration) but also a defiance of Prohibition, which was still in effect in 1931. Furthermore, the saxophones and the fanlike arrangement of clarinets complement the words "jazz," "follies," and "dance" emblazoned on the side of the bowl. Suggesting illuminated signs, these words establish a nightclublike atmosphere, with pulsating rhythms by jazz musicians. Jazz, like the skyscraper, was a phenomenon hailed as uniquely American during this period, and through its imagery the bowl establishes a sense of nationalistic self-definition.

There is a playful, celebratory spirit embodied in this work, but the mad, convulsive gaiety depicted on Schreckengost's bowl does not simply reflect contem-

Viktor Schreckengost. *Jazz Bowl*. 1931. Designed for Cowan Pottery Studio. Earthenware, 11⅛ x 16⅜ x 16⅜". Collection Cowan Pottery Museum at Rocky River Public Library, Ohio

porary New York nightlife. Seen in context, the imagery is multivalent, even contradictory. In thumbing its nose at laws outlawing alcohol consumption, it allies itself with the transgressive behavior of the social elite during America's dry years.[9] In terms of craft traditions, Schreckengost's work rebels against the norms of American art pottery of the period; its humor and satire undercut the traditional earnestness of Arts and Crafts and Art Nouveau ceramics,[10] while its invocation of the Machine Age shuns the conventional preference for natural motifs. Perhaps most strikingly, the buoyant iconography defies the conditions of the Depression then gripping the nation. The mood of devil-may-care urbanity is actually more characteristic of the 1920s than 1931, which was the worst year of the Depression. Ironically, this work was one of the last productions of the Cowan Pottery, which closed because of the economic crisis. Against this backdrop, Schreckengost's creation becomes a poignant swan song to America's Jazz Age—or perhaps an attempt to evade the grimness of the present moment through a wishful regression to past times of greater prosperity.[11]

Curiosity about the object *and* its context opens up a wide variety of interpretive avenues. As the analysis of the Schreckengost bowl suggests, one context for such objects produced in the United States during this period is the search for a national identity, a postwar project embraced by crafts artists as well as writers, painters, and intellectuals. Georgia O'Keeffe's 1927 painting *Radiator Building, Night, New York* represents one artist's attempt at nationalistic self-definition. Its subject, a skyscraper designed by Raymond Hood, became upon its completion in 1925 a glamorous icon on the Manhattan skyline. Like Schreckengost's bowl, O'Keeffe's painting depicts a nighttime view, and it embodies features of the cityscape in a dynamically rhetorical form: The soaring, illuminated skyscraper surrounded by klieg lights and neon signs suggests that technological transformation is the essence of urban life.

Analogous attempts to define national character by creative individuals in all fields was not a unified, programmatic movement. People argued constantly about what characteristics constituted "Americanness." Nor was this project new: It had been a recurring issue in the nation's cultural life since the first Europeans began colonizing the North American continent. But for each generation, this search for a national identity took on variable attributes. In the interwar period, attempts to define America in terms of the machine characterized the effort.

Americans were not the only machine-intoxicated people in the 1920s; the fascination was international. But artists in different countries gave different inflections to the machine aesthetic. In the United States, the mode was overtly representational and dramatically emblematic, employing motifs allied with the country's prestige in the urban and industrial arenas: skyscrapers, factories, advertising, and mass-produced consumer products. These elements formed an internationally recognized iconography that signified America's quintessential modernity. The emphasis was on the impersonal, on methods of mass production, and on advanced engineering. Bookcases took on the characteristics of the New York skyline; serving vessels resembled industrial machine parts.

This cultural strategy of self-definition was particularly challenging and paradoxical for those who labored by traditional methods to make one-of-a-kind, handcrafted objects. A futuristic cocktail shaker by Russel Wright, made in his small New York City workshop in about 1931, clearly demonstrates this paradox. Originally involved in theater design, Wright began to produce informal accessories in 1930.[12] Since alcohol consumption evoked a forbidden glamour during Prohibition, serving vessels such as Wright's were often made in modern styles. However, this vessel's severe cylindrical form with a bulging spherical center is so unlike traditional beverage containers that the viewer could easily mistake its

Georgia O'Keeffe. *Radiator Building—Night, New York.* 1927. Oil on canvas, 48 x 30". Carl van Vechten Museum and Gallery of Fine Arts, Fisk University, Nashville

function. With its gleaming polished pewter surface, it seems more like a mass-produced component destined for a shiny new automobile rather than for the living room of a Manhattan apartment. This object reveals Wright's fascination with sleek industrial forms, which had potent symbolic appeal in the 1930s. As one reviewer noted, "Cylindrical and spherical forms are indicative of the speed of our age."[13] This commentator overlooked the fact that Wright made the shaker by hand. Its simplified, impersonal appearance suggests the swiftness of the assembly line, as well as the streamlined vehicles of the time, sufficiently establishing its Machine Age credentials. Again, the contradiction of symbolic associations and means of manufacture underlies its production.

Despite its Machine Age profile, Paul T. Frankl's bookcase of 1928 is also a handmade object. The irregular silhouette of the piece reproduces the setback forms of skyscrapers in the 1920s, and the asymmetrical arrangement of drawers, cubbyholes, and cabinets creates disjunctive patterns emblematic of both modern art and contemporary urban life. In fact, Frankl studied architecture and engineering in his native Vienna, as well as in Berlin, Munich, and Paris, before emigrating in 1914. For his books *New Dimensions* (1928) and *Form and Re-form* (1930),[14] Frankl included photographs that emphasized the dramatic angles and verticality of his skyscraper bookcases and desks. For these and other designs he used the image of New York's modernistic urban environment to challenge the dominance of period-revival décor in the domestic sphere.

Russel Wright. *Cocktail Set.* c. 1930. Pewter; shaker: 9 x 4⅞ x 4⅞". Denis Gallion and Daniel Morris, Historical Design Collection, Inc., New York

Paul Theodore Frankl. *Skyscraper Furniture.* c. 1928. As published in Paul T. Frankl, *New Dimensions: The Decorative Arts of Today in Words and Pictures* (New York: Payson & Clarke Ltd., 1928)

Although such novel contributions to the home evoked associations with engineering rather than with craft, in reality virtually all work in the modern style was handmade until the early 1930s. Makers rarely emphasized this fact, however, because their search for a national identity was allied with a rhetoric of mass production based on a machine aesthetic, and not on traditional craft practice. Ironically, only objects in period-revival styles—objects that often suggested elaborate hand manufacture—were predominantly machine-made during this time. Therefore, both period-revivalist and nascent modernist designs put forward an artifactual symbolism at odds with an object's actual method of manufacture, but in inverted ways.

In the modern movement, such incongruities inevitably arose because manufacturers were at first extremely reticent to adapt innovative designs for large-scale production. Many designers wanted their handmade prototypes mass-produced, but often remained studio craftspeople because of circumstances rather than by choice. However, they geared their rhetoric to an imagined future that included widespread acceptance of modernism in the United States, and therefore a mass market for their products. Significantly, they conceived of this effort in overtly nationalistic terms. Frankl wrote in 1928: "The modern skyscraper is a distinctive and noble creation. It is a monument of towering engineering and business enterprise. . . . Decorative arts and furniture design are already under the powerful modern architectural influence. This can only resolve into one thing: a decorative art that is in keeping with the country and the people who live in it. It will resolve into an American decorative art, original and at the same time satisfying."[15]

Regarding this statement, one might ask why Frankl was so insistent on the *American* character of the evolving modernist mode. Why was his rhetoric so urgent and nationalistic? After all, the United States had emerged victorious from World War I, and basked unrivaled in terms of industrial prestige. But in the cultural arena, an embattled and self-critical mentality prevailed. For American painters and sculptors, European modernism was a source of inspiration and of anxiety. For those like Frankl who produced artful objects intended for use, the authority of Europe engendered a similar ambivalence. Although well-trained at continental institutions and conversant with modern Austrian design, Frankl identified most strongly with his newly adopted country. He, like his native-born contemporaries, wanted not only to create an original American mode but also to receive recognition for his efforts.

During the 1930s, modernism finally found a place in large-scale manufacturing, and figures like Russel Wright, whose American Modern dinnerware, designed in 1937, became enormously popular, eventually saw their work reproduced for a mass market. Yet Wright still felt one-down compared to his European counterparts. In 1938 he wrote: "Why can't someone, a Museum of Modern Art or a New York World's Fair, put on an exhibit in which they would dramatize all design that is American? First, let them parade those unconscious developments, free from any aesthetic inferiority complexes. Our bridges. Our roads. Our factory machinery. Our skyscrapers. . . . Roll out our trick gadgets— our streamlined iceboxes—our streamlined pencil sharpeners. . . . Let them put a magnifying glass (if they feel they need it) over these things to find the American character. . . . Let them do this without recourse to European standards in their selection. It has never been done. But I know that they will find that there is a distinct American character of design in all that is American and that our home furnishings tie in to this character. Not until then will we know of what elements this American character consists."[16]

As Wright's impassioned statement indicates, a sense of defensiveness about

American accomplishments in the aesthetic sphere persisted late into the 1930s. But if America was so closely identified with a triumphant Machine Age, why did critics, designers, and craftspeople have to lobby so hard for recognition of their country's aesthetic achievements? The answer lies in the waves of criticism following the disruption of trade between Europe and America during World War I. This event revealed a slavish dependence on foreign ideas in the industrial arts. When European imports ceased, foreign patterns were no longer available to copy. Manufacturers and tastemakers in this country suddenly felt an acute vulnerability in their relationship to the continent. As one observer noted, "A world cataclysm was necessary to make Americans aware of their shortcomings in industrial art; nothing less than a total deprivation of [European] designers was required to make clear to manufacturers and other producers the dearth of well-trained artists here. . . ."[17] For those who cared about such things—and a surprisingly large number of people did—it was a mortal blow to the national honor that American arts (both fine and applied) were not considered equal to foreign competition. This did not match the nation's self-conception as the world's trendsetter. In response to criticism, a good deal of defensiveness surfaced even in those, like Frankl, who had solid European training before immigrating to America. As a compensatory strategy, the rhetoric of the times—verbal as well as visual—made explicit references to national accomplishments, or at least to national potential.

The postwar criticism of the industrial arts in the United States was not unprecedented, of course. Arts and Crafts reformers had previously lodged similar complaints against manufacturers of American products. But by the late 1920s, the Arts and Crafts movement was out of fashion because it idealized nature and the medieval past, not the icons of Machine Age modernity that were allied with the current quest for national identity. And the remedy of individual craft production as an alternative to shoddy, mass-produced wares now seemed quixotic, especially during the Depression, when many judged luxurious, one-of-a-kind objects as socially irresponsible. Therefore, reform efforts in the 1920s and 1930s called for modern designs inexpensively fabricated by machine.[18]

Yet this fervent interest in the iconography and productive capabilities of the machine did not entirely eclipse the appreciation and support for craft in America. George Booth's Cranbrook Academy of Art in Bloomfield Hills, Michigan, provided one of the most conducive environments for emergent modernism in the crafts. Although Cranbrook's president, Eliel Saarinen, denied the charges that the institution unrealistically perpetuated the Arts and Crafts ideal, he clearly valued hand production as well as machine fabrication. In 1931, he stated that "if the form is there, it is of minor importance if we use the hand of man or the machine. . . . Both are necessary."[19] In Cranbrook's textile and ceramic workshops, artists such as Lillian Holm and Majlis (Maija) Grotell made unique objects never intended as prototypes for mass production.[20] Although the Depression limited Cranbrook's support for the crafts, artists such as Grotell and Holm remained as teachers at the Academy and the adjacent Kingwood School, and thereby were able to continue producing their unique creations throughout the 1930s.[21]

Even here, however, craft and the machine symbolically merge. The decoration on Grotell's vessel of circa 1938 is explicitly urban and industrial, with setback buildings ascending to the sky and factory smokestacks bellowing stylized plumes. In Holm's *First Sight of New York,* the skyscrapers of Lower Manhattan transfix the awestruck immigrants as they approach the wondrous city. The disjunctive, aspiring forms of the buildings recall not only Frankl's bookcase and Schreckengost's bowl but also O'Keeffe's *Radiator Building.* The identification with the Machine Age results in a specific iconography that underscores its national origins to a much greater extent than most analogous examples made in Europe.

HALL IN HOUSE OF ROBERT LAW, PORT CHESTER, N. Y.
DWIGHT JAMES BAUM, ARCHITECT
A characteristic Elizabethan staircase, true in every line, detail and proportion to the old style

From *The American Architect Journal* (February 1925)

A later vase by Grotell, completed in 1951, indicates that work done at Cranbrook subsequent to World War II had moved in another direction. Here the thick, pocked glaze drips heavily down the side of the vessel in discernible but highly irregular organic patterns. Although the red-and-black V-shapes near the rim suggest growing flowers, the piece invites us to appreciate its textured surface primarily in terms of abstract form and innovative technique. Typical of studio ceramists of the time, Grotell no longer employed overt symbols of the Machine Age. Like the so-called fine arts of the postwar era, her work followed the modernist preference for self-referentiality, highlighting materials and processes, not nationalistic symbolism.

Concurrently, the industrial design profession had established its own separate sphere, and designers (some of the most prominent trained at Cranbrook) were no longer limited to handmade prototypes, but realized their goal to have their work mass-produced. Charles and Ray Eames, both associated with Cranbrook, enjoyed a productive relationship with the Herman Miller Furniture Company. Their 1949 design for an armchair made innovative use of fiberglass; it was a practical, modern concept that found ready acceptance by a manufacturer who put the design into widespread production.[22] Projects such as Grotell's vase and the Eames fiberglass chair mark the dramatic separation of studio crafts from industrial design after World War II, widening the split between craft and the machine. Craft did not die in the age of mechanical reproduction, as many had

Lillian Holm. *First Sight of New York*. 1930s. Linen, wool, cotton, 6'10" x 64⅛". Flint Institute of Arts, Flint, Michigan. Gift of Lillian Holm in memory of Ralph T. Sayles

Majlis (Maija) Grotell. *Vase*. 1951. Stoneware, 13 x 11¼ x 11¼". Collection Cranbrook Academy of Art Museum, Bloomfield Hills, Michigan

predicted it would during the interwar years. But craft was reconceived and reconstituted, and moved closer to the realm of fine arts in terms of practices, training, and exhibition venues. Industrial designers and studio craft artists therefore pursued very different avenues after the war; as a consequence, some of the incongruities of rhetoric and practice that characterized the interwar years diminished. Simultaneously, aesthetic judgments and canons became standardized, inevitably influencing how American objects of earlier periods were viewed.

But in the period 1920–45, the creation of separate realms for craft and industrial design was only a dimly perceived possibility. The worlds of hand and machine production continually overlapped. The rhetoric of the era favored the machine because it seemed the most promising vehicle for self-definition at a time when confusion and self-criticism reigned. Drawing on areas of previously established national prestige, individuals such as Paul Frankl and Russel Wright evolved an eclectic repertoire of handcrafted objects that embodied a deep psychological investment in America's Machine Age. In this essay, I have contextualized the objects discussed in terms of this quest for communal identity, but material culture study of American craft opens up countless other avenues of interpretation. However, we miss opportunities for future discoveries if American material is snobbishly dismissed at the outset on the grounds of inferior quality.

CHARTING A NEW EDUCATIONAL VISION

by Marcia Yockey Manhart

The acceptance of craft as a legitimate course of study in American higher education is in large part the result of the more than one thousand European artists and architects who emigrated to the United States between 1930 and 1944. Prior to this influx of foreign philosophies and ideas, the teaching of art and what was considered craft were institutionally segregated. Colleges and universities taught art history, drawing, painting, and sculpture, while trade schools taught the traditional crafts of pottery, woodworking, metalworking, and weaving.[1] This bifurcation prevented fluidity and harmony, and stifled intellectual cross-fertilization.

Many of the European émigrés came from countries strongly influenced by William Morris's Arts and Crafts movement in England and the design theories of the Weimar Bauhaus, founded by Walter Gropius in 1919. Though they differed radically in approach, both Morris and Gropius believed that art should be an integral and vital part of life, and that its creation should be "a unity of discipline, a stimulating moral force towards a common goal."[2] Through the establishment of studio programs at the Cranbrook Academy of Art, Black Mountain College, the Carnegie Institute of Technology, the Chicago School of Design, Alfred University, and Ohio State University, their methods and ideals were synthesized and the process of teaching art and craft became a congruous whole.

The Cranbrook Academy of Art, founded in Bloomfield Hills, Michigan, in 1932, was first inspired by the Arts and Crafts ideals of Morris. George G. Booth, a Detroit newspaper publisher and arts patron, created a resident-artists community that included an art academy, housing, and a place of worship. In conceiving Cranbrook, Booth followed Morris's ideas. Like Morris, he believed that art should be produced "by the people and for the people," and by hand, and that the "ugliness of towns and buildings [should be] abolished and replaced with tasteful designs"; he also sought "an integration of daily life, social values, and the act of production."[3]

In 1925, Booth commissioned Finnish architect Eliel Saarinen to design an art academy, to be built on his farm estate outside Detroit. Both men were fascinated by the idea of interconnecting a school of design, a community of resident artist-teachers, and a museum providing invaluable resources in original art for both students and faculty. They chose as their model the Victoria and Albert Museum, London, and its associated School of Design (later the Royal College of Art). The project, which eventually encompassed several related buildings, required the skills of many gifted artists and craftspeople, a number of whom accepted Booth's invitation to remain and become a part of the Cranbrook community. Under Saarinen's leadership and Booth's patronage, the first traditional atelier system was established in the United States.

Cranbrook was experimental in both physical plant and educational theory. Saarinen not only incorporated the crafts into his architectural plans, he also chose a faculty of renowned artists who soon developed departments that went beyond designing for architecture: sculptor Carl Milles; weaver Marianne Strengell; ceramist Maija Grotell; metalworker Harry Bertoia; and, of course, Saarinen himself.[4] With the exception of Bertoia, an Italian émigré, all were influenced by Scandinavian thought and methods, and believed that the arts—especially the applied arts—were instruments to protect an authentic cultural inheritance.[5]

Initially, craft studios were formed to execute and embellish Saarinen's architectural scheme. Beginning in 1928, Loja Saarinen, Eliel's wife, produced hangings and carpets for the Cranbrook campus, among other commissions, in her own studio at the Academy; the following year, she established the Cranbrook weaving department. Since she was not a teacher, it was necessary to find a resident artist-instructor in the design and weaving of modern textiles. Marianne Strengell became that artist in 1937. Strengell saw weaving "in direct relationship to architecture. . . . [T]his concept included the idea of the interconnection between a specific environment and everything that was to finish it. Design became the means by which this theory could be achieved."[6] Strengell's style of teaching was informal, and she emphasized working within a limited framework, whether executing a design for the hand- or powerloom, handspinning, blockprinting, or silkscreening: "Aside from experimentation with design, fibers and colors, she required her students to consider seven criteria while planning projects: materials, price, climate, labor equipment, architectural placement and personalities. Her teaching was forward-looking."[7]

During her twenty-four-year teaching career, Strengell influenced many notable weavers, including Jack Lenor Larsen and Ed Rossbach. In 1944, Robert D. Sailors, a student of Strengell's, became the first graduate of the Cranbrook weaving department to teach in the capacity of assistant director and instructor in that department. Like Strengell, Sailors "dealt strictly with nonpictorial creations,"[8] experimenting with weaving materials that ranged from floor mops to unraveled copper wire from a Chore-boy pot-scrubber.[9]

The expectation to fabricate Eliel Saarinen's designs extended to other Cranbrook workshops. English silversmith Arthur Nevill Kirk, a member of the Royal Society of Miniature Painters in London, was invited by Booth to teach at the Art School of the Detroit Society of Arts and Crafts, and to execute several commissions for Christ Church, Cranbrook. An adherent of Arts and Crafts ideals, Kirk taught jewelry and enameling at Cranbrook beginning in 1927 and metalworking beginning in 1929, remaining until the metals workshop was closed for financial reasons in 1933. It would be reopened upon the arrival of the skilled sculptor and metalworker Harry Bertoia in 1937.

Bertoia not only revived metalworking at Cranbrook during his five-year tenure, he also pushed its practice and design firmly into the modern age.[10] He eagerly experimented with technological advances in metalworking, combining various materials to enhance his highly polished, formal style. His Kamperman silver tea service with Lucite handles (c. 1938–39) epitomizes this approach. Although Bertoia stopped producing holloware after leaving Cranbrook, he continued to make jewelry throughout his career, freely exploring space, texture, and movement. The jewelry is improvisational by nature and incorporates an organic liveliness that characterizes Bertoia's larger sculptures. His training at Cranbrook under sculptor Carl Milles allowed him to move easily among various media, bor-

Arieto (Harry) Bertoia. *Ornamental Centipede.* c. 1942. Brass, 19¾ x 8". Collection Cranbrook Academy of Art Museum, Bloomfield Hills, Michigan

Maija Grotell at Cranbrook, c. 1941

Majlis (Maija) Grotell. *Vase.* 1945. Stoneware, 17 x 9⅞ x 9⅞". Everson Museum of Art, Syracuse, New York. Purchase Prize, given by Encyclopaedia Britannica, 11th Ceramic National Exhibition, 1946

rowing and adapting the techniques of one to suit the other.[11] He would later join Charles and Ray Eames on the West Coast as a furniture designer.

The ceramics department at Cranbrook was less formally conceived. Initiated in 1933 under the direction of Waylande DeSantis Gregory, a graduate of the Cleveland School of Art (now the Cleveland Institute of Art) and a former designer for the Cowan Pottery Studio, the experiment lasted only one year. From 1934 to 1938, Cranbrook was without a formal ceramics program. The department as we know it today began in 1938 with the arrival of Finnish ceramist Maija Grotell, who brought from her native country a lively interest in all the arts and looked to nontraditional sources for inspiration.[12] Grotell had studied with Charles Fergus Binns at Alfred University; a strong and independent nature allowed her to break away from his rigorous methods to greater freedom of expression.

Grotell's thrust was directed toward preparing teachers for the college level. Students were not given the latitude to explore a more individual form of expression until they were accomplished in the basics of throwing, glazing, and firing.[13] "As a former student recalled, 'Maija's (as most called her) influence on my life and work came through her ability to create an atmosphere for productive thought—rather than specific instruction. . . . I gained the freedom of spirit to see such answers for myself.'"[14] Grotell "tried not to squash" her students with her thinking, stating, "I am against influence."[15] Indeed, she was extremely liberal, encouraging almost any conceivable style, as evidenced by the mature work of her former students Richard DeVore, John Parker Glick, Howard Kottler, Harvey K. Littleton, John and Suzanne Stephenson, Toshiko Takeazu, and Marie Woo. In her own work, Grotell focused on vessels embellished with architectonic Art Deco motifs. They are precise and impose a larger-than-life scale. Grotell's sensibility gradually changed the Cranbrook ceramics program into one committed to a "vessel aesthetic."[16]

Through their various departments and workshops, Strengell, Bertoia, and Grotell contributed significantly to the studio craft movement in America. But it was the vision of Eliel Saarinen that chartered some of the most significant changes in twentieth-century American design. Saarinen's aesthetic had been informed by the 1925 Exposition Internationale des Arts Décoratifs et Industriels Modernes in Paris, where he saw the work of the French *ébénistes*. The classical elegance associated with *art moderne* was exquisitely applied in the dining room furniture, armchairs, and table he designed for Saarinen House in the late 1920s. Executed by the gifted Swedish cabinetmaker and Cranbrook artist-in-residence Tor Berglund, these are among the finest examples of Art Deco furniture produced in the United States.[17]

From the beginning, Cranbrook's approach was holistic, emphasizing cultural context rather than curriculum and methods; it was the first educational institution in the United States to develop a comprehensive craft and design program, thus perpetuating the Arts and Crafts ideals of Morris. The faculty was accessible. The open channels of communication between instructors and students were an integral part of the Cranbrook experience. The collaborations of a younger generation of students and faculty—Benjamin Baldwin, Charles Eames, Florence Knoll, and Eero Saarinen—would have a profound influence on American design after World War II. "Cranbrook's history is symptomatic of the decisive developments occurring in American design during this century. It not only chronicles the struggle for a reconciliation between the ideals of the Arts and Crafts movement and the demands of industrial design . . . , it affirms the paramount role played by architects in the battle for modern design."[18]

In the 1930s, another community of resident artists was evolving at a liberal-arts college in the Southeast. In 1933, Josef and Anni Albers emigrated from Germany to teach at Black Mountain College in Asheville, North Carolina, at the invitation of founder John Andrew Rice. Rice wanted to create an educational environment that would integrate the artistic process with intellectual pursuits and social behavior. At Black Mountain, the arts were central, rather than peripheral, to a liberal-arts education.[19] Classes were based upon a system whereby Albers tried to involve both intuition and the intellect in the search for form and its fundamental laws.[20] Like Gropius, he stressed the concept of the nonstatic, ever-changing world in which problems are solved through information-gathering. Albers did not make a distinction between "fine" and "applied" art. For him, art included all fields of artistic purpose—music, dramatics, dancing, theater, photography, literature, religion, and so on.[21] His method was one of discovery and invention, "a 'pedagogy of learning' rather than a 'pedagogy of teaching.'"[22]

At Black Mountain, the crafts were viewed as a means of helping students "to learn to see and develop discipline, taste, and judgment."[23] The basic curriculum was supplemented by workshops that, like Cranbrook's holistic approach to design, evolved from the college's need for furniture, fabrics, printed materials, and bound books. Both Cranbrook and Black Mountain reflected the aesthetic values of their directors; both were responsive to the resources at hand—generous, in Cranbrook's case, modest in the other—in creating their communities of learning.

The weaving workshop was the most successful, surviving until 1946. Led by Anni Albers, weaving and textile design were taught as a "preparatory step" to machine production,[24] while workshop programs at the Institute of Design (until 1944 the Chicago School of Design), The Art Institute of Chicago, and Cranbrook stressed designing for industry. Albers emphasized the structure of the weave rather than color or texture, though she did draw upon unconventional materials. The textiles at Black Mountain are distinguished by their limitation of color,

Anni Albers. *Monte Alban*. c. 1936. Silk tapestry, 57½ x 44½". The Harvard University Art Museums, Cambridge, Massachusetts. Gift of Mr. and Mrs. Richard Leahy

being principally black, white, and natural hues. Reflecting Albers's aesthetic, they are modest and do not compete, but serve as a foil for other objects.[25] (Her own elegant geometric designs paralleled the development of her husband's paintings.) Albers's program produced the first generation of studio artists working with fiber: Ruth Asawa, Trude Guermonprez, Sheila Hicks, and Dorothy Ruddick.

One of the most important additions to the visual arts curriculum at Black Mountain was architecture. Again, there are obvious affinities to the Cranbrook curriculum. Josef Albers, assisted by A. Lawrence Kocher, taught basic courses in modern architectural design, furniture design, and practical construction methods that were combined with hands-on experience in the craft workshops. Within this structure, a program in woodworking was formalized under the direction of Molly Gregory in 1941. Her teaching emphasis was on good craftsmanship, traditional joinery techniques, and inventive solutions to problems. Gregory was both a pragmatist and an idealist—a rare combination for faculty outside of Black Mountain.[26] Aware of the demands of industry, Albers believed that photography as well as graphic and industrial design should be taught along with painting and sculpture. In 1944, James Prestini, a colleague of László Moholy-Nagy at Chicago's Institute of Design and a research assistant at the Illinois Institute of Technology, was added to the faculty to teach hand- and machine-made sculpture. Prestini is known for his large, thin, and gracefully balanced wood vessels and plates.

The extraordinary Black Mountain College experiment is continuously studied and rethought relative to present-day education and the search for a more integrated approach to art education. Faculty and students alike joined in the quest to bring art into everyday life and to integrate intellectual pursuits with the solutions to the community's needs. "Since art remains the basis and measure of culture, any education separated from art is no general education. Also, any art training unrelated to general human development is no education. But the integration of both general education and art education constitutes comprehensive education."[27] Young people who sought an education at Black Mountain College were taught to think in new ways and, through exploration and experimentation, to integrate their ideas into a total way of life.

The impact of the Paris Exposition of 1925, reflected in advertising, department store displays, and numerous museum exhibitions, awakened the American public to modern design. The economic austerity caused by the Depression provided the catalyst for Americans to experiment with and to accept new materials, manufacturing techniques, and stylized design in the production of basic household items: appliances, furniture, tableware, and kitchenware. When manufacturers' profits declined, they sought competent designers to design affordable mass-produced goods for all consumers.[28] Widespread interest impelled mainstream schools and colleges to consider industrial design as a new program.[29]

In 1935 the U.S. Government, through the Works Progress Administration (WPA), took an interest in funding the nation's first school of industrial design. The Design Laboratory, in New York, provided an educational opportunity for students who could not afford private training. Project codirectors Gilbert Rohde and Josiah P. Marvel adopted a modified Bauhaus curriculum, one that included not only aesthetics and product design but also practical studies in machine fabrication and merchandising; its faculty included, among other designers, Henry Dreyfuss, Ruth Reeves, and Walter Dorwin Teague, Sr. Unfortunately, as federal appropriations collapsed, so did the school; it closed in 1937.[30]

In the 1930s, Ohio, particularly Cleveland, became another important center for the Federal Art Project (FAP) of the WPA. A highly successful program was established at The Cleveland School of Art by Edris Eckhardt, director of the school's ceramic sculpture department. Eckhardt "concentrated on adapting ceramic techniques to the large-scale architectural embellishment of public buildings, thereby extending the medium of ceramic art into new areas of monumentality and social impact."[31] Made of readily available and relatively inexpensive clay, these decorative architectural panels—for example, Eckhardt's *Johnny Appleseed* and *Woman with Apple* (for Woodhill Homes)—began to replace those carved of stone and bronze.

The Cleveland School of Art initiated a unique cooperative program with the Cowan Pottery Studio and The Cleveland Museum of Art. Public awareness and acceptance of nonutilitarian ceramic sculpture was enhanced by R. Guy Cowan's production pottery and through the Museum's annual juried exhibition, the May Show. Eckhardt not only directed the program but participated as an artist in the May Show, gaining recognition for her narrative work, most notably, a five-figure series based on *Alice in Wonderland* that was reproduced and displayed in public libraries throughout the country.

Working with Eckhardt and Cowan at the Cleveland School of Art was Viktor Schreckengost, who would become one of the most important ceramic sculptors and industrial designers in Ohio. In 1929–30, following his studies at the Cleveland School, Schreckengost went to Vienna for postgraduate work with Michael Powolny, then one of Europe's leading ceramicists, at the Kunstgewerbeschüle. Although France was the center for European modernism, it was the Viennese style that most influenced American ceramics in the 1930s and 1940s.

As a WPA artist, Schreckengost was commissioned by the Brownell-Lambertson Gallery, New York, on behalf of Eleanor Roosevelt, to produce twenty punch bowls for the Governor's mansion in Albany, New York, that were evocative of "modern taste."[32] These beautifully designed bowls reflect Schreckengost's experience abroad. Words and images drawn on both inner and outer surfaces are poignant reminders of the short-lived Jazz Age of the 1920s, and suggest parallels with both Cubist and Futurist painting.[33] Always timely, many Schreckengost pieces served as comic relief during the Depression; one of his greatest works, *The Apocalypse '42*—created in 1941 but not exhibited until the spring of 1942, just a few months after the bombing of Pearl Harbor—caricatures Hitler, Hirohito, and Mussolini. His cerebral approach brought a new dimension to American ceramic sculpture. As an industrial designer for several firms, he redefined the look of dinnerware, appliances, toys, and theater sets, all of which were marked by a sleek simplicity.

By 1940, John Paul Miller, another graduate of the Cleveland School of Art, had joined the faculty of his alma mater. Inspired by teachers Kenneth Bates (an enamelist) and Schreckengost, Miller taught general techniques in color, design, drawing, watercolor, painting, jewelry, and metalwork. A naturally gifted teacher, he showed his students how to be responsible to themselves and to their work—in short, how to establish self-respect.[34] Today, Miller's name is synonymous with gold granulation, the ancient process he rediscovered after many years of research and experimentation.

In New York, Augusta Savage, a leading African-American ceramic sculptor, was developing another WPA/FAP program. The Savage Studio of Arts and Crafts, established in 1932 in a basement apartment on West 143rd Street in Harlem, would become the largest community arts program of its kind in the United States.[35] Some fifteen hundred people of all ages participated in the Savage Studio's weaving, potterymaking, and quilting workshops, which also included discussion groups.[36] Savage, who was born in the brickmaking town of Green Cove Springs, Florida, came naturally to clay modeling. She studied sculpture at

Edris Eckhardt. Alice in Wonderland series. 1935–36. Ceramic, 6⅜ x 4¼". Cleveland Public Library

Augusta Christine Savage. *Lift Every Voice and Sing*. 1939. Plaster with black paint, height 16'. Beinecke Rare Book and Manuscript Library, Yale University, New Haven, Connecticut. One of four statues commissioned for the 1939–40 New York World's Fair, this plaster was highly popular and the subject of numerous postcards and metal souvenirs.

Cooper Union and with Félix Bueneteaux at the Académie de la Grande Chaumière in Paris, and in 1936 held an assistant supervisory position with the FAP. By 1938, she had become a consultant and project supervisor for the World's Fair Commission, and the following year she created the powerful and moving work *Lift Every Voice and Sing (The Harp),* a celebration of African-American music. (The piece was destroyed because there were no funds available to cast it in a permanent material.)

WPA/FAP programs were also being developed on the West Coast. Here, the aesthetic experience differed from the mainstream in that Asian and Native American cultures, as well as those of Latin America, were freely explored and adapted. Sargent Johnson, who had studied with the well-known sculptors Ralph Stackpole and Beniamino Bufano at the California College of Arts and Crafts, became a senior sculptor and project supervisor for the WPA in 1936; of Swedish, African-American, and Cherokee descent, he was one of the first minority artists hired. Like Savage, Johnson was also interested in studying the African-American slave and his roots. A daring innovator, he worked in many different media— wood, terracotta, marble, copper, plastic, and terrazzo. The WPA provided Johnson the opportunity to create large-scale ceramic sculptures. His 1940 commission for the monumental athletic frieze at George Washington High School in San Francisco, which was influenced by Mayan and Aztec designs seen on his travels in Latin America, exemplifies the cultural diversity of the West Coast scene.[37]

Gradually, after several attempts, institutions of higher learning began to introduce industrial design programs into their curricula, among them, Pratt Institute, in Brooklyn (under Donald Dohner with Gordon Lippincott); New York University (under Donald Deskey); and Columbia University, New York (under Frederick J. Kiesler).[38] In 1935, the Carnegie Institute of Technology in Pittsburgh established the first degree program in industrial design, under the direction of Peter Mueller-Munk.[39] Trained as a silversmith, Mueller-Munk had immigrated from Berlin in 1926 and briefly designed for Tiffany and Company.[40] With the Depression and the decline in demand for fine handwrought silver objects, he turned to industry. Mueller-Munk employed new metals such as spun aluminum, chromium-plated metals, and Monel (a copper-nickel alloy that was a precursor to stainless steel) to create sleek and simple forms with highly polished surfaces. These refined objects, energized with new materials, soon found their way into many American homes and businesses.

In 1937, Hungarian émigré László Moholy-Nagy was invited by the Association of Arts and Industries (AAIC) in Chicago to direct its newly formed school of design, which was intended to provide instruction for industry employees in changing product image, designing new products, and creating commercially viable designs for those products. The school would become known as the New Bauhaus because Moholy-Nagy endeavored to embody in it the ideals of the Weimar Bauhaus, where he had headed the metalwork shop under Gropius. (It was Gropius, newly appointed to the faculty of the Graduate School of Design at Harvard University, who recommended Moholy-Nagy to the AAIC.)

Moholy-Nagy's educational theories were both all-encompassing and integrated, and were aimed at the education of the individual within the context of a democratic social structure. The Bauhaus had been dedicated to the idea that art is practical enrichment and an integral part of life in a machine age; the machine was seen as a tool to produce art. Gropius and his followers—Moholy-Nagy among them—believed that art was not a luxury but an essential, and that the study of art was a spiritual as well as an intellectual pursuit. Manual dexterity and a thorough knowledge of materials, tools, and processes were accepted as basic to art education, but it was also considered vital that the student keep in touch with life and society during the learning process.

The New Bauhaus may have derived from the Weimar Bauhaus, but "the pragmatic life-oriented approach espoused by John Dewey,"[41] and the stringent demands of everyday life in Depression-era America, exerted their influences on the school, its concepts and realizations. The New Bauhaus increasingly strove to come to terms with its own Americanization,[42] but the experiment lasted for only one year: Moholy-Nagy's ideas for "total education" were too innovative.

In 1939, philanthropists Walter and Elizabeth Paepche helped Moholy-Nagy reopen the school under a new name: the Chicago School of Design.[43] Prior to the school's accreditation in 1944, students were taught in a workshop context that integrated weaving, painting, photography, filmmaking, and sculpture with the formal departments of architecture, industrial design, and commercial art. Students experimented with both natural and the new man-made materials, spatial and volumetric relationships, and texture. Art studies were directed toward analysis and exploration; practical studies included the use of hand and power tools. The emphasis was not on materials, however, but on process and the realization of ideas. Also included was Moholy-Nagy's program of "intellectual integration," which expanded on the Bauhaus theme of unifying culture and technology:[44] "An education in the crafts develops responsibility toward the product as a whole and through this it teaches the student discipline. But the crafts are not emphasized in opposition to machine work. The Machine is understood as a very efficient 'tool' which—if properly used—will serve the creative intention as well as the traditional handtool."[45] Like Albers, Moholy-Nagy saw art as interaction and sought to change society through education.

In 1941, Margaret De Patta, a distinguished jeweler, studied with Moholy-Nagy in Chicago. It was from him that she learned the optical and spatial possi-

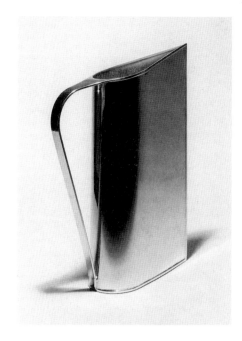

Peter Mueller-Munk. *Normandie Water Pitcher*. c. 1935–41. Chromeplated brass, 11¹⁵/₁₆ x 9⅝ x 3¹/₁₆". Manufactured by Revere Copper and Brass, Inc., Rome, New York. Musée des Arts Décoratifs de Montréal. Gift of Mr. Geoffrey N. Bradfield

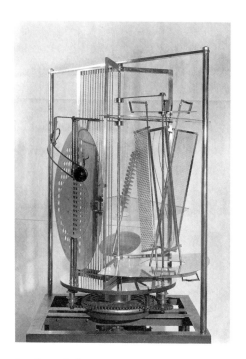

László Moholy-Nagy. *Light Space Modulator.* 1923–30. Kinetic sculpture: steel, plastic, wood, other materials, with electric motor, 59½ x 27½ x 27½". The Harvard University Art Museums, Cambridge, Massachusetts. Gift of Sibyl Moholy-Nagy

bilities—the multidimensionality—of her art form, thus becoming a master controller of space and light. "De Patta's work shows the indelible mark of her mentor: the use of semi-transparent stones, such as quartz, cut to manipulate light; industrial screens; and moving elements. [Moholy-Nagy's] three-dimensional constructions became 'light modulators,' and 'space modulators.' These were derived from his experimentations with light and its transmission through plastic sheets and kineticism."[46] In the Chicago School of Design's educational "laboratory," De Patta and students like her developed their own creative potential while receiving professional training in the crafts as well as the fields of architecture, industrial design, photography, and graphic design.

As the public demand for mass-produced ceramics increased, so did the requirements for qualified technicians, designers, and decorators. Some universities and art schools reacted by adding ceramic engineering, design, and, later, what was to become known as studio pottery to their curricula. Universities located near production potteries were especially responsive to the industry's design concerns. Both Alfred University, in Alfred, New York, and Ohio State University, in Columbus, developed curricula emphasizing ceramics. They also expanded their ceramic engineering programs, creating a resource for research in glazing and clay as well as new firing techniques.

The New York School of Clayworking and Ceramics at Alfred University was the first institution of higher learning to focus on all aspects of pottery, including its application to industrial design, and the first to offer a degree program in ceramics. The "father" of contemporary American ceramics and the creator of the program was Charles Fergus Binns, who served as department head from 1900 to 1931. His approach, like that of Saarinen at Cranbrook, was initially grounded in the Arts and Crafts movement. Binns believed that "intelligent design depends largely upon a knowledge of materials."[47] He wrote voluminously about ceramics materials and techniques in glazing and firing; *The Potter's Craft,* originally published in 1910, remained the studio potter's "bible" until the publication of Bernard Leach's *A Potter's Book* in 1940.[48]

Binns's curriculum at Alfred was designed to provide an education in ceramics as well as the liberal and the applied arts.[49] He stressed technical competence in both glaze chemistry and clay bodies, and believed that the objects produced should reflect the intrinsic characteristics of the clay; if they did not, students were encouraged to destroy their work. "Binns' special contribution was in setting the standard for a new concept, the artist-potter. What had been a divided labor in industry—the designer and the mechanic—he pulled together as one, making the craftsman responsible for the complete process. That responsibility created the artist."[50] A purist, Binns followed the Bauhaus dictum "form follows function" to the end. His forms were small, pristine, their flawless surfaces exquisitely, richly glazed. His students would carry forward the "Alfred aesthetic" to other institutions and to various commerical potteries: Arthur Baggs, R. Guy Cowan, Myrtle French, Marion Heard, Harold Nash, Adelaide Alsop Robineau, and Binns's successor at Alfred, Charles Mabry Harder.

In 1932, the school legally changed its name to the New York State College of Ceramics at Alfred University. The college was organized into three departments: applied art, general technology, and glass technology.[51] Within the applied arts, the focus was ceramics. (Although jewelry and metalwork, under Erma Hewitt, and decorative textiles were reintroduced into the curriculum, these were seen as superficial attempts to acknowledge the widening interest in the crafts.[52]) In 1935–36, Harder studied industrial design theory and production methods at the New Bauhaus in Chicago, an experience that was to have a profound influence on the program at Alfred.[53] The ideas to which he was exposed, including

Charles Fergus Binns. *Bowl*. 1929.
Stoneware, diameter 7½". The Metropolitan
Museum of Art, New York. Gift of Miss
Henrietta M. Crawford, 1934 (35.91)

the writings of Moholy-Nagy, Herbert Read, and Lewis Mumford, equipped Harder with a new theoretical language, practical applications, and a commitment to functional design.

Upon his return to Alfred in 1936, Harder continued the traditions of Binns. (A story told by many of his students was that "he could throw a pot dressed in a tuxedo and not splash."[54]) He was admired by his students, who would take his principles, ideas, practices, and aesthetic values with them when they left Alfred to establish their own studios: Sheldon Carey, Roger Corsaw, Dorothy Perkins, and Hal Riegger. "To French and to Binns, [Harder] was their protégé who deeply understood the educative force of clay as sure knowledge, and a pot as a making of a shaped thing of pleasantness, of character, and integrity. To his colleagues he was a restless shaker and doer. To his students he was a shaper of clay, of ideas, and of people."[55]

The School for the American Craftsman, conceived by the American Craftsmen's Educational Council, opened at Dartmouth College in Hanover, New Hampshire, in October 1945. That same year, the school's Board of Managers, chaired by Aileen Vanderbilt Webb, made an offer to affiliate with Alfred University. Founded on the belief that "craftsmen, their skills and products must be entirely representative of the cultural, social and economic patterns of their times," the Craftsman school was structured around "a combination of the old apprenticeship system and present day production methods. . . ."[56] Harder, who was chair of Alfred's industrial design program at the time, had difficulty in accepting a degree program in the new Fine and Hand Arts Division of the Liberal Arts College. In 1950, after four tenuous years, the School for American Craftsmen left Alfred and joined the Rochester Institute of Technology, where it still thrives.

Arthur Eugene Baggs continued the "Alfred aesthetic" at Ohio State University from 1927 to 1947, following a three-year tenure at the Cleveland School of Art. At Ohio State, his main objective was to train designers for industry. Prior to his arrival, the only degree offered was in ceramic engineering. Baggs implemented a program that balanced technical and artistic skills. As in the Cranbrook workshops, he and fellow faculty members Carlton Atherton, Paul Bogaty, and Edgar Littlefield were accessible to students; there were "no secrets," "no private glazes."[57]

Baggs's utilitarian designs were classically simple and almost void of decoration, except for the glaze. He spent much of his career pursuing viable formulas for a self-glazing clay body, which led him to salt-glazed ware and the rediscovery of a formula for Egyptian paste.[58] Baggs believed that complete technical control was necessary in order to have complete artistic freedom.[59] His salt-glazed stoneware cookie jar of 1938 exemplifies his technical mastery, the seamless integration of form and decoration: how the glaze fits the form and the form, the glaze.

Former students Herbert Sanders and Viktor Schreckengost remember Baggs as a purist, a sound craftsman, and a master of skills and techniques; most of all, he proffered that a completed work should be a unified whole.[60] He expected his students to adhere to the same standards. His "high regard for craftsmanship, inherent in scientific pursuit of ceramic technology, and reconsiderations of design problems were two reasons that . . . [he] and the ceramic program at Ohio State gained recognition."[61]

Fertile California provided a new "field" for the nourishment of the ceramic arts in higher education. Those who taught did not come from the Alfred or Ohio State mold. In fact, very little information or materials were available to these pioneers of ceramic education on the West Coast; in time, it was the ground beneath them that provided the materials necessary for their art form.

In 1931, Glen Lukens established a program at the University of Southern California (USC), Los Angeles, under the auspices of their School of Architecture, wherein ceramics would be intimately coordinated with architectural design. Lukens, who had studied with Myrtle French at The Art Institute of Chicago, taught the simple methods of coil building indigenous to Southwest Native American pottery. His simple, straightforward forms are adorned with brightly colored crackle glazes, in sharp contrast to the somber surfaces found on the East Coast. Lukens and his students were meticulous researchers of their environment, studying its geology and collecting clay and glazing materials from nearby deposits. The search for native materials led him to an alkaline deposit in the dry lake bed of Death Valley, enabling Lukens, after years of research, to develop a formula for Egyptian paste.[62] It was Lukens's rugged, individualistic approach that provided the foundation for the Otis Art Institute, in Los Angeles, and the revolutionary concepts of students like Peter Voulkos.

One other ceramics program was developed in California during the 1930s. Laura Andreson pioneered that effort at the University of California, Los Angeles, taking ceramics from the area of art education and into the forefront of the fine arts program; between 1936 and her retirement in 1970 she would share her knowledge with over five thousand students. Andreson received her graduate degree from Columbia University and was trained as a painter. She claims to be a "self-taught" potter. An inspired teacher, Andreson did not separate her creative endeavors from her teaching. She worked actively alongside her students, imparting a sense of design as well as her knowledge of simple handbuilding techniques, low-firing clays, and glazes. She taught her students to "see" nature as an inspiration for forms and glazes. In 1944, she learned wheel throwing from four students she had sent to study with F. Carlton Ball at Mills College, Oakland; the Austrian ceramist Gertrud Natzler was also a teacher. Like Lukens, Andreson did extensive glaze research; her clean, simple forms were often created especially for the glaze. Leach's *A Potter's Book* provided invaluable information to her.[63]

Farther north, in the San Francisco Bay Area, the California College of Arts and Crafts (CCAC) pottery curriculum was also contributing significantly to the popularity of the ceramic arts. Ball, who had learned his craft under Glen Lukens at USC, joined the faculty of CCAC in 1935. Ball was known for his monumental wheel-thrown forms, which were produced at a time when colleagues throughout the country were shifting to ceramic sculpture. Kathryn Uhl Ball collaborated with her husband, producing the decorative elements for his glazed forms. Influential as a teacher, Ball authored many articles and books, most notably, *Making Pottery Without a Wheel: Texture and Form in Clay* (1965), which he coauthored with Janice Lovoos.[64]

Shortly after Ball's departure for Mills College, Marguerite Wildenhain arrived from the Netherlands to teach at CCAC. Rejecting mass-production meth-

Glen Lukens. *Death Valley Plate*. 1941.
Earthenware, 3¼ x 18¾ x 18¾". Everson
Museum of Art, Syracuse, New York. Gift of
IBM Corporation

ods, Wildenhain advocated a return to handcraftsmanship. In 1942, she opened
her own workshop-studio at Pond Farm, an artists' community in Guerneville,
California. Wildenhain stressed the unification of form and function and had a
significant role in bringing the Bauhaus aesthetic to West Coast ceramics and utilitarian pottery. Like Ball, her teaching and her writings, especially her book *Pottery: Form and Expression* (1962),[65] left indelible imprints on both students and
colleagues.

Two other institutions of higher learning have contributed significantly to the
study of art and craft: Howard University in Washington, D.C., and the Tuskegee
Institute (now Tuskegee University) in Alabama, two of the nation's foremost colleges for African-Americans. Joseph Gilliard, who followed Henry Letcher as
ceramics instructor at Howard (both had studied under Harder at Alfred), influenced ceramic artists for at least four decades. Tuskegee was actually built by its
students in the late nineteenth century, probably the most significant accom-
plishment African-American artisans in the post-Reconstruction era. Tuskegee's
mission was to teach trades and the crafts, including masonry, tinsmithing, blacksmithing, and mechanical drawing; it also provided the first school of architecture
for African-Americans. Isaac Hathaway established the ceramics department in
1937, later instituting a similar program at Alabama State Teachers College (now
Alabama State University) in Montgomery. Hathaway was recognized as the dean
of African-American ceramics. Like Savage, most of his commissions were official
portrait busts; the most famous are of Frederick Douglass, Paul Lawrence Dunbar, and Booker T. Washington.

An entire generation of American students and artists were propelled to new
aesthetic ideas, philosophies, and approaches by these schools and their leaders.
Their methods were new, and nonformulaic. They encouraged exploration,
experimentation, and most importantly, new ways of thinking. As a result, the
course of art education in the twentieth century was altered dramatically.

AGAINST THE GRAIN:
MODERN AMERICAN WOODWORK

by Kate Carmel

The period from 1920 to 1945 falls between the expiration of the American Arts and Crafts movement and the robust craft revival that occurred just after World War II—eras in which craftsmanship and the beauty of woods were held in high esteem. In those intervening years, Americans were introduced to various forms of modern design from Europe, a cavalcade of hybrids from *moderne* and "zigzag" styling to Scandinavian Modern, the International Style, and biomorphism.[1] As distinctive American styles began to evolve, the sleek machine aesthetic and the exigencies of industrial production were of much greater interest to designers than the charms of natural wood or the idiosyncrasies of handcrafted objects. Yet this period is important to the history of American woodworking, not only for the pioneering of interesting shapes, methods of construction, and materials made possible by the machine but also for the endurance of wood as a favored material for craftspeople and, ultimately, the renewal of public interest in organic beauty and in the unique handcrafted object as an antidote to the anonymity of mass production.

During this period, woodworking was marked by a wide fluctuation in levels of skill, often dictated by variations in modern styling. In the creation and production of wood furniture and objects (whether decorative or functional), some very distinct models emerged. In the 1920s, designers working in the decorative *moderne* or zigzag style provided drawings to established artisanal firms for refined execution using traditional skills. Beginning in the 1930s, craftspeople skilled in the fabrication of wood models and prototypes were employed in the emergent field of industrial design, which addressed the need for uniform construction techniques and the use of more economical materials. A striking aspect of modernism was the de-emphasis of expert carving and craftsmanship as standards of quality and their eventual replacement by simplified forms designed for large-scale production.

The potential of new wood products was frequently explored and expanded by architects and craftspeople working in studio settings. Craft training became the basis for industrial design education, setting standards of quality and providing modelmaking skills. Many modern architects, continuing an Arts and Crafts tradition, controlled all aspects of a project, favoring simple built-in and freestanding furniture of their own design, constructed by carpenters on the building site. Finally, and least common of all, there was the artist-craftsperson who conceived and made unique functional objects. The fusion of the many branches of modernism and the various modes of execution gave rise to a confusing plethora of hybrids that prevents a simple line of development in this narrative.

EARLY MODERNIST AMERICAN FURNITURE

Furniture of the early 1920s shows striking links with the Arts and Crafts movement as well as with the first wave of modern style. Three chairs demonstrate interesting parallels and distinctions, and reveal how American Arts and Crafts advocates and European modernists began to consider ways to adapt older ideals to the new vocabulary of modern art.

By 1920, Munich-trained Winold Reiss had established a considerable reputation in art circles as the designer of two of New York's earliest modern commercial interiors, the Busy Lady Bakery (1915) and the Crillon Restaurant (1919).[2] Yet the Voysey-esque aspects of the armchair he designed about 1920 for his own Christopher Street art school are late manifestations of Arts and Crafts form, complete with heart-shape cutout, plank-style construction, and exaggerated articulation of the joints. The totally unexpected, modern element is the brilliantly painted surface of ultramarine blue edged with vermillion.[3] Strong, contrasting colors were to become a fundamental characteristic of modern design.

Frank Lloyd Wright's plank-style chair of around 1921 was designed as part of his commission for the Imperial Hotel in Tokyo (1916–22). Wright's vocabulary of angular shapes, repeated as surface decoration, unified the exterior and interior of the building. Variations on the hexagon were used in the seatback and sides of this chair; even the legs cant inward to form a half-hexagon, thus uniting the decorative and the structural. (The composition of overlapping planes is consistent with the Cubist-inspired motifs with which Wright had been experimenting since 1912.[4]) Wright later described how he had brought examples of furniture from his home and taken them apart in order to teach the Japanese workmen how to build according to the structural considerations of his new designs.[5] The original chair had a cane back, which revealed the chair's structure. (The caning was later replaced by vinyl upholstery.)

Viennese architect and stage designer Joseph Urban became the designer of Florenz Ziegfeld's theatrical productions, creating the dazzling style of the Ziegfeld Follies. The harsh economic conditions in Central Europe after World War I prompted Urban to open the Wiener Werkstätte of America in New York

Winold Reiss. The Busy Lady Bakery, New York, 1915. From *M.A.C.* (*Modern Art Collector*), February 1916

in 1922.[6] In typical Urban manner, the shop installation at 501 Fifth Avenue was sophisticated and dramatic. The theatrical highback "tub" chairs he designed for the showroom suggest Werkstätte forms of the turn of the century, while the black painted finish and overall pattern of circles recall Viennese modernist design.

DELUXE ART DECO WOOD FURNITURE

American interest in modern European design was quickened by the Paris Exposition Internationale des Arts Décoratifs et Industriels Modernes in 1925. The furniture seen in those elaborate installations was bulky yet simple, and encased in smooth and sumptuous veneers or lacquered finishes. Surfaces were brilliantly ornamented in a variety of motifs adopted from modern, African, and classical art; while surface decoration reflected modernist trends, the same exacting techniques used by French artisans of the past two centuries for *objets de luxe* were used for construction and finishing.

Through touring exhibitions, department store displays, magazine promotions, and temporary presentations organized by associations of architects, artists, and designers—many of them European émigrés eager to present their own work—French *moderne* decoration infiltrated American architecture and design. By 1927, the vocabulary of pyramids, circles, zigzags, and stylized fountains—rendered in bright colors or glittering metallics—could be seen on the facades and interiors of skyscrapers and on the surfaces of furniture. For the most part, designers working in this idiom followed the French model of refined execution and superb hand craftsmanship. Although many saw the potential for the mass production of their designs, U.S. manufacturers were unwilling to experiment with new forms when the production of period-revival furniture was so profitable. Consequently, this Jazz Age style remained largely unaffordable to the general public.

By the time the architect-designer Eliel Saarinen arrived in Bloomfield Hills, Michigan, in 1925 to begin planning the various buildings envisioned for a new utopian art and craft community at Cranbrook, he had already established an impressive reputation as a modernist in his native Finland. Strongly attached to the aesthetic of quality craftsmanship and materials, Saarinen was not particularly interested in the issues of industrial production. Evidently stirred by the work of the French *ébénistes,* which he had seen at the 1925 Paris Exposition, Saarinen designed furniture for his own house (1929–30) that specified exotic wood veneers and geometrically patterned inlays. The cabinet and dining room chair demonstrate his interest in fine woodwork and in the classicizing mode of French *moderne* styling. The chair, for example, has a gently fluted, grooved back, crisply

Gottlieb Eliel Saarinen. "Dining Room" (detail), room setting designed for "The Architect and the Industrial Arts: An Exhibition of Contemporary American Design," Eleventh American Industrial Art Exhibition, The Metropolitan Museum of Art, New York, February 11–September 6, 1929

defined edges, and legs enhanced with black, suggesting Viennese Biedermeier and Werkstätte antecedents. Saarinen contracted with the Company of Master Craftsmen, the deluxe workshop division of the New York furniture retailer W. & J. Sloane, for the fabrication of the dining chairs and the accompanying table.[7] The cabinet was made by Tor Berglund, the master cabinetmaker whom Saarinen had invited to work on-site at Cranbrook to fabricate much of the project furniture.[8] Though similar in design to the case pieces Saarinen designed for the house, this cabinet was intended to be kept as a "museum piece," a glorious summation of Berglund's craft skills.[9]

The modernist architect and designer Eugene Schoen was known for designing luxurious furniture and quietly elegant interiors. American-born and -educated, Schoen kept up with progressive design practices in Europe.[10] Encouraged by the enthusiastic American response to the Paris Exposition, he started an interior design enterprise in New York in 1925, and was advantageously positioned for the rush of interest in modernist style that occurred in the late 1920s within cosmopolitan circles. Responding to the increased regard among fashion-minded Europeans for austere block forms, the broad, flat surfaces of the c. 1930–32 cabinet are surfaced in a two-tone pattern of veneer squares that serve to heighten the rigorous geometry of the case. In combining the simplicity of geometric form with the suavity of elegant wood veneers, Schoen managed to reconcile the modern and the traditional. Influenced by the exclusive French design houses, Schoen remained faithful to the concept of the unique object and was fastidious about craftsmanship.[12] In this case, the cabinet was made to his specifications by the New York cabinetmakers Schmieg, Hungate and Kotzian, known for traditional craft skills.[13]

Trained in Vienna and Berlin, Paul T. Frankl was an early champion of modernism in the United States. In 1922, he opened a gallery of modern decorative art in New York and launched a vigorous crusade to enlighten the largely conservative American public. He favored handcrafted quality, and most of his furniture was one-of-a-kind or limited-production work,[14] "carefully executed in a high-class cabinet-shop, created with excellent workmanship out of carefully selected woods. It was addressed to a small, exclusive, and somewhat sophisticated clientele."[15]

Paul Theodore Frankl. Silvered vanity with lacquered stool, c. 1925. Also pictured: lacquered screen and metal table designed by Donald Deskey. From *Good Furniture* (September 1927)

Frankl worked in several modernist idioms at the same time. The graceful curule bench of 1927, similar to a campstool with curved legs, was designed to accompany a mirrored vanity with Egyptian Anubis head terminals and silvered surfaces in the French style.[16] Frankl was one of the first designers to create furniture inspired by America's unique urban landscape. As early as 1925, he began designing furniture with setbacks like those of American Art Deco skyscrapers. He sold his "skyscraper" furniture in his own gallery, promoting it as a practical space-saving device for the cramped city apartment. It was produced in many sizes and shapes to fit any room; a full assemblage could suggest the Manhattan skyline.[17]

Donald Deskey won the 1932 competition to design the interiors of Radio City Music Hall in Rockefeller Center by convincing the project manager that the public's awe of modern technology offered psychological advantages over the extravagant historic styles then typical of large motion-picture theaters.[18] Deskey made inventive use of new, less costly industrial materials. In the simple rectilinear sideboard designed for the manager's office he combined exotic wood veneers with steel, a rich mix intended to satisfy the manager's taste for the opulent. Though streamlined and industrial-looking, this furniture was made to order.[19]

Classical revivalism translated smartly into the uncluttered modern manner while retaining enough comfortable familiarity to be acceptable to clients reluctant to abandon tradition; it was therefore extremely popular with the fashionable

Donald Deskey. J. B. Patterson apartment, River House, New York, 1928–32

decorators. Terrence Harold (T. H.) Robsjohn-Gibbings, best-known for his unique, neoclassical modern style, made a specialty of designing for the wealthy and socially prominent on both sides of the Atlantic. After receiving his architectural degree in England, Robsjohn-Gibbings took a job in the late 1920s with the antique and home furnishings dealer Charles Duveen (Charles of London). He continued to study design and began researching antique Greek furniture at the British Museum, developing a feeling for the classical forms that would dominate his designs. He established his own firm in New York in 1936.[20]

Robsjohn-Gibbings's glass-topped occasional table of limewood and syca-more with carved ram's head terminal and acanthus decoration is one of a pair made around 1936 for the home of Mrs. J. O. Weber in Bel Air, California. Known as Casa Encantada (1934–38), this modernized "Georgian" house with Grecian influences was designed by an architect and a fashionable decorating firm, which engaged Robsjohn-Gibbings to provide classically styled furniture. The furniture he created had a good deal of "authentic" classical detail, carved, applied, and assembled in rather playful and often unusual combinations.[21] This highly individual hand-carved furniture negated the anonymity of the machine aesthetic, which Gibbings claimed to despise.

After the economic collapse of 1929, building as well as furniture production declined dramatically. Deluxe cabinetry and the jazzy style associated with the 1920s were abandoned as sales diminished. Forms were simplified as efficient mass production became a major concern. In the early years of the Depression, a handful of U.S. furniture manufacturers looked to progressive design as a possible avenue of survival, developing effective relationships with a new breed of consultant: the industrial designer.

In 1927, the German émigré Kem Weber, an architect and designer, opened an independent design studio in Hollywood, California. Listing himself as an "industrial designer," Weber quickly garnered commissions for interiors and furnishings for hotels, department stores, restaurants, and residences. He was one of only three American designers included in R. H. Macy's well-received "International Exposition of Art in Industry" in 1928, for which he executed designs addressing the modern necessity of creating interior spaces that could serve a variety of purposes.[22] While Weber's early designs were influenced by *art moderne,* in the late 1920s he began to develop a more serene style that emphasized horizontality, softly rounded corners, and smooth surfaces in "California" colors such as sage greeen, yellow, orchid, and rose. This "streamlined" style soon displaced the jazzy 1920s manner, emerging in the 1930s as America's own modernist idiom.

A transitional sideboard of around 1930, designed by Weber and produced by the Grand Rapids Furniture Company, is interesting for its residual Parisian influence in the silver-leafed horizontal banding, the sharp contrast of "soft" body color and the richly grained walnut top, base, and drawer pulls, and the stepped motif carved on the fascia. Nonetheless, the lacquered sage-green surface and sophisticated formal treatment give the sideboard a fully realized streamlined look.

When the young American designer Gilbert Rohde approached D. J. De Pree of the Herman Miller Furniture Company, a Zeeland, Michigan, manufacturer of quality period furniture, he had already produced a successful and inexpensive line for the Heywood-Wakefield Company in Massachusetts. De Pree saw the potential of quality production in the relatively uncompetitive arena of modern design.[23] Rohde's designs were muted interpretations of austere German modernism, often softened with the rounded corners characteristic of streamlining. Although his designs often took advantage of the structural economies that materials such as molded plywood and tubular steel allowed, the assembly and finishing of the furniture was on a semi-custom basis and was dependent upon high-quality handwork.[24]

Rohde featured the Herman Miller furniture in room settings he designed for the "Design for Living House," one of thirteen model houses at the 1933–34 Chicago Century of Progress Exposition. These models received extensive national press exposure and were duplicated for department store installations around the country.[25] The unpretentious, comfortable traits of "modern" design found enthusiastic consumers in the middle class, which for the first time was presented with good modern design at affordable prices.

In the late 1930s, Rohde responded to the appetite for showier and more elaborate products that economic recovery had made possible. A dressing vanity of 1939 features a mix of traditional and new industrial materials. The drawers of the serpentine front are faced with rosewood-burl veneers, and synthetic leather is used on the inset, top, and sides. Brass inlays, drawer pulls, and nail heads, and brass-plated tubular-steel mountings for the mirrors, were specially fabricated, and a demi-lune Lucite working surface is set into the top—all carried on an ebonized bent-plywood base. The emphasis on plain surfaces, veneered edges, mitred joints, and similar details depended on meticulous workmanship in the factory.[26]

THE EXPLORATION OF INDUSTRIAL WOOD MATERIALS

Certainly the current concept of the history of design has reinforced the notion that the introduction of tubular steel marked a decisive turn in twentieth-century furniture design. In fact, though many leading European and American architects and designers responded favorably to industrially produced tubular metal, wood remained the dominant material for furniture fabrication. Not only was tubular steel expensive, but the American public was not receptive to the use of "cold" metal in domestic settings. With its warm tone and sensuous feel, wood overcame resistance to the perceived coldness of modern furniture.

The newly refined and inexpensive industrial plywoods—a major technical advance of the 1930s—helped focus attention on the innovative possibilities of wood. Tougher and springier than natural wood, plywood could be bent or molded. Its resistance to shrinkage and the large size of standard plywood sheets eliminated dependence on frame-and-panel construction. Simplified structural systems in turn made possible the development of economical assembly systems for the furnituremaking industry. Plywood became recognized for its great potential in creating new structural and decorative forms, especially by the European architect-designers Alvar Aalto and Marcel Breuer.

Following Hitler's rise to power, many of Europe's great functionalist designers immigrated to the United States, often to teach, bringing with them principles of architecture and design that were to have a profound effect on American design. When former Bauhaus director Walter Gropius was invited in 1937 to join the faculty of the Harvard Graduate School of Design, he asked fellow Bauhaus architect-designer Marcel Breuer to join him in teaching and in architectural practice. Their earliest American houses were far less austere than the functionalist buildings for which they were originally noted. The integration of indigenous natural materials such as rugged stone and wood siding with plywood paneling and broad expanses of plate-glass windows opening onto the landscape indicate a warmer, more tactile idiom that was characteristic of modernist architecture and design in the late 1930s.

The cutout plywood chair designed by Breuer for the Gropius-Breuer collaboration on the Frank House (1939) in the Pittsburgh suburbs is similar to the plywood furniture with which he had experimented during a stay in England in 1935–37.[27] For this furniture, two flat side pieces cut from a single sheet of plywood replaced the traditional assemblage of legs, arms, and back stiles; the sides were then joined by seat and back elements.

There were compelling reasons for Breuer to investigate cutout furniture. First, furniture made from flat pieces of plywood offered a simplified construction method since the pieces could be cut out with a jigsaw and assembled inexpensively in a small workshop; second, plywood could be cut and pierced with holes without splitting, which held the promise of new and engaging shapes.[28] The cutout biomorphic shapes that form the sides of the chair illustrate Breuer's continued interest in Hans Arp's stencil-cut wood sculptures, which he had first seen in the early 1930s.[29]

Frederick J. Kiesler also explored biomorphically-shaped furniture of cutout plywood construction. The novel multipurpose furniture he designed in 1942 for Peggy Guggenheim's Art of This Century gallery in New York was in keeping with a gallery devoted to Surrealist art. Kiesler, an Austrian émigré who fiercely

Walter Gropius and Marcel Breuer. Dining room, Frank House, Pittsburgh, 1939. Photograph by Ezra Stoller

resisted the rigidity of "Bauhaus" functionalism, had been experimenting with free-form and interrelated organic shapes since the mid-1930s, and was at the time director of the Laboratory for Design Correlation at Columbia University.[30]

Bertrand Goldberg, an American architect who studied at the Bauhaus in 1932, recalls that plywood was in use there at the time but was not often molded or bent.[31] While at Dessau, Goldberg received a commission for a bent-plywood chair from the inventor of a cold-process plywood-bending machine. The prototype he made for the machine was, however, never produced. Upon returning home to Chicago in 1933, Goldberg began his architectural apprenticeship and resumed experimenting with new materials. Dorothy Wright Liebes, organizing the presentation of modern American design for the 1939–40 Golden Gate International Exposition in San Francisco, invited Goldberg to participate. The molded plywood chair and a related settee in that display were designed in 1938; fabricated of five-ply mahogany board in Mexico City, they reiterated his Bauhaus designs. The structural concept of these self-bracing scrolled forms was learned through the paper-bending classroom exercises of Josef Albers, which illustrated how strength derived from structure.[32]

In the late 1930s, Frank Lloyd Wright began work on the Usonian houses, which were intended to make the contemporary Wrightian home available at a moderate price. To control costs, unconventional materials and techniques were developed, including the construction of furniture on-site. Each house was designed on a modular unit—often hexagonal—that was repeated as a decorative motif. Single-storied, with expanses of glass windows and doors connecting the interior to the landscape, and organized around a central area devised for informal family living, the Usonian house was in many ways the precursor to the ranch house—the archetypal postwar suburban dwelling.[33]

Wright applied many of his Usonian concepts to Auldbras Plantation—the Leigh Stephens house, in Yemassee, South Carolina—in 1939. The floorplan was based on hexagonal modules, a motif repeated in the freestanding furniture; hexagonal plywood chairs and tables and triangular ottomans were grouped in flexible clusters that could be rearranged as needed. Made of cypress, a native tree that is resistant to moisture, the furniture matches the cypress boards of the walls. The chair is formed of a planklike seat and back, with a flat triangular "leg" that slopes out beyond the back of the chair to correspond to the cant of the building's walls.[34] The surfaces were stained and waxed to accentuate the warm tones of the wood and reveal the natural grain. The chair's unpretentious character reflects Wright's roots in the Arts and Crafts movement, but its structure is predicated on the development of plywood panels that could be fabricated of woods indigenous to a particular region and suitable to its climate.

Rudolph M. Schindler moved with Wright to Los Angeles in 1920, opening a private practice there in 1921 to take advantage of the area's apparent receptivity to innovative modern architecture. Trained in Vienna, Schindler rejected the Arts and Crafts ideal of an overall interior design concept controlled by the architect, limiting his architectural contribution to a backdrop for a harmonious life.[35] Most of his houses were sparely furnished with built-in furniture and a few freestanding sculptural chairs constructed on-site by project carpenters. Carpenter-made furniture eventually came to characterize Schindler's nonelitist stance toward design. Spurning the cold practicality of functionalism, he designed furniture appropriate to the more relaxed social and cultural conventions of modern life. His furniture, such as the chair designed for the Van Paten House of 1934, and interiors focused on comfort and flexibility.[36] Though the Van Paten chair was assembled on the building site, the arc of the arm was formed at a specialized woodworking shop equipped with molds for bending the plywood.[37]

Frederick J. Kiesler. Furniture designs for Art of This Century, New York, 1942. Estate of Frederick Kiesler. Courtesy Jason McCoy, Inc., New York

Charles O. Eames and Ray Eames. Experimental plywood chairs with different leg, spine, and support configurations, 1945. Photograph courtesy Lucia Eames Demetrios, Eames Office, Los Angeles

The collaborative wood furniture designs produced by architects Eero Saarinen and Charles Eames in the years just before World War II presage the influential position that would be established by American furniture designers by midcentury, and indicate the laboratory research and art studio effort that characterized developments in technology and form in this period. Extensive experimentation resulted in the fabrication of the winning chair design submitted by Saarinen and Eames to The Museum of Modern Art's "Organic Design in Home Furnishings Competition" of 1940–41. Their innovation was to bend the plywood into compound curves, producing a single sculptural seat-back-arm unit separate from the legs.[38] The molded plywood shell, padded with foam rubber and upholstered with fabric, was then set on the slenderest possible legs—a minimal base intended to set off the sculptural beauty of the form. The objective of this design was to produce a functional factory-made object with the aesthetic appeal of a sculpture. Unfortunately, production technology of the time was not capable of manufacturing the chair at an affordable price.[39]

In 1941, when Charles Eames moved to Southern California with his wife, the painter and sculptor Ray Kaiser Eames, their goal was to develop a system to mass-produce high-quality low-cost organic furniture.[40] Experimenting in their apartment, they developed a device to mold plywood in compound curves that became the basis for all further developments in molded plywood.[41] Based on their knowledge of plywood molding, the Eameses developed a prototype for a compound-curved leg splint for the U.S. Navy and the equipment necessary for its manufacture. During the war years they produced over 150,000 leg splints as well as a great variety of specialty products in molded plywood commissioned by the various armed forces.[42]

When military orders declined at war's end, the Eameses began to apply their expertise to furniture production, developing prototypes adaptable to assembly-line production.[43] In 1945, the basic tooling necessary for mass-producing compound-curved furniture was begun. Chairs assembled of independent modules appeared to be the best prospect for manufacturing an inexpensive, high-quality product using the technologies developed during the war. The development of a narrow spine to which all of the components could be attached eliminated much superfluous material from the chair and emphasized the minimal aesthetic of its design.[44]

ARTIST-MADE FURNITURE

With the focus on developing wood furniture for industrial production, craft in wood tended to be ignored by the East Coast design press and relegated to the domain of the therapeutic. As industrial designers and architects eagerly turned toward standardization, artists began exploring the possibilities of creating functional objects as self-expressive sculptures: furniture as art.

Kansas-born painter Henry Varnum Poor played an important role in modern American art and design circles. One of the most respected artists of his day, Poor first achieved success in ceramics in the early 1920s, and a major part of his reputation rests on his accomplishments as a studio potter. Poor was uncompromising in developing his diverse interests, producing accomplished work in painting, graphics, small- and architectural-scale ceramics, handcrafted furniture, and in the design and building of a group of distinctive homes for friends. He was a vital part of the circle of artists and designers who organized and presented their work in exhibitions of modern design and craft in the late 1920s.

Upon his return from military service in Europe in 1919, Poor had settled in a community of artists in New City, New York, and launched a home-building

Henry Varnum Poor. Living room, Crow House, New City, New York, c. 1920

project. Boyhood training in carpentry and farm repairs provided basic skills, and the artist proceeded to design and construct the buildings, studios, and all the furnishings for his rustic domain, asserting his independence from the familiar and creating imaginative new forms that served as inspiration for many friends.[45]

The earliest of Poor's furniture suggests the solid rusticity of European peasant furnishings, with tenon construction and made of rough-hewn wood embellished with chip carvings. Although he never developed a sustainable, recognizable personal style in his furniture designs, Poor did experiment freely with many forms, always retaining that element of wood boldly treated in an almost primitive way and removed from the refined surface techniques of high-style furniture of the period. In a tiered table designed for the house in the mid-1930s, each of the tiers has a decorative and textural surface made of the generally oval but entirely natural cross-sections of a small tree limb set into a plumber's "goop."[46] The vertical structural elements of the table are formed of a split, forked limb that has been stripped of bark and sanded but otherwise left intact. Poor was never a skilled technician in wood, yet he seems to have been a generic force in American craft furniture whose influence has not yet been fully explored.

In 1916, the painter Wharton Esherick moved with his family from Philadelphia to rural Paoli, Pennsylvania, where he restored and converted the old house and barn on his property. In the 1920s, his interest in carving wood frames with designs reflecting the subject matter of his paintings and in carving woodcuts in the manner of the German Expressionists helped turn his attention to wood as his personal medium of expression.[47] In 1926, stimulated by the similiar venture of his friend Henry Varnum Poor, Esherick began to build a studio and all of its furnishings. Wood was used for every detail—stairs, ceilings, sinks, furnishings—resulting in a highly unified decorative scheme. Far outstripping Poor's undertaking, Esherick's studio was daring in concept, sculptural yet entirely functional, and exemplified the two-fold aspect of Esherick as artist and craftsman. The early furniture made for the studio in 1928 looks almost medieval. Designed for use around an eccentric five-sided plank table, four different but related rough-hewn wood chairs, their seatbacks rising in wildly erratic pointed arches, are closely connected to the aesthetic of the Expressionist woodcuts he was producing at that time.

Esherick's success in furniture design and his use of wood in interiors led to a succession of important commissions from progressive, art-minded Philadel-

Henry Varnum Poor. *Tiered Table*. c. 1935. Wood, wood burls, 34½ x 28 x 28". Collection Estate of Henry Varnum Poor

phians.[48] His sewing cabinet of 1933, a faceted Cubist-Expressionist form, demonstrates the artist's liberation from the constraints of traditional furniture design and a move into the realm of functional sculpture. The cabinet rises to a peak like a prism; the hinged doors open and fold back to reveal a serviceable interior.

By the mid-1930s, curving, flowing forms and surfaces began to appear in Esherick's work. Esherick accounted for this quite clearly: "Some of my sculpture went into the making of furniture. I was impatient with the contemporary furniture being made—straight lines, sharp edges and right angles—and I conceived free angles and free forms; making the edges of my tables flow so that they would be attractive to feel or caress."[49] The side chair designed for the board room of the Philadelphia Schutte-Koerting Company in 1942–44 is representative of Esherick's work in this style. The structural supports—sinewy and organic branch forms—were to influence the generation of artists who succeeded him, among them, Sam Maloof, George Nakashima, and Wendell Castle.

The sculptor Isamu Noguchi, discouraged by his inability to earn income consistently from anything but portrait busts, began entertaining ideas of making and selling "a really new creation [that] could rise above the demeaning categories of applied art and the like."[50] The idea of making furniture apparently had come from French designer Jean-Michel Frank (a refugee from the war then living in New York), who, while leading the Paris design world in the 1920s, had employed the sculptor Alberto Giacometti to make furniture. Noguchi received commissions for sculptural tables from A. Conger Goodyear, president of The Museum of Modern Art (1939), and designer T. H. Robsjohn-Gibbings (both 1939), and a commission for a carved and pierced pedestal (1941) from Philip L. Goodwin, codesigner, with Edward Durrell Stone, of the new Museum of Modern Art building. This history serves as an interesting barometer of where patronage was to be found, especially for such avant-garde design.[51]

Noguchi's furniture, as in the Goodyear table, was consonant with the organic and surging curvilinear forms of his sculpture of the 1940s. The artist's concern with sculpted furniture—whether unique examples or industrially produced designs—was limited to a single decade of his career, but his innovative forms helped change the direction of wood furniture design.

Craft flourished on the West Coast in the 1930s quite removed from the restraining domination of the Eastern schools of architecture, design, and art. The journal *Californian Arts and Architecture,* first published in 1929, frequently reported

Wharton Esherick. Five-sided table, chairs, and bench designed for Esherick's Paoli, Pennsylvania, studio, 1928

George Nakashima. *Slab Coffee Table.* c. 1945–46. American black walnut, 14¼ x 64 x 18". Private collection

on individual craftspeople disregarded in the East. The handcrafted modernist furniture designs of George Nakashima first appeared in those pages in 1941. Trained at the Massachusetts Institute of Technology, Nakashima had spent most of the 1930s in Asia, eventually working for the European modernist architect Antonin Raymond in Tokyo. The threat of war forced him to return home to Seattle in 1940, where he set up a small furniture craftshop. He completed several projects for custom-designed handmade furniture at that time, including the work illustrated in *California Arts and Architecture* in November 1941. This austere furniture was closely related to the rectilinear designs of his contemporaries, and certainly within the limited technical capabilities of Nakashima, who was new to the craft. The accompanying text by Nakashima indicates his dissatisfaction with the separation of design and craft: "Essentially, the best designer should be a mechanic, but unfortunately most mechanics cannot design. To carry the point further, the contractor is unable to design and the architect usually doesn't know much about building. The guilds and master builders have degenerated into mass-productionists and specialists. The so-called industrial designers smell too much of the studio, of watercolor renderings, and not enough of the workshop."[52]

Isamu Noguchi. Rosewood articulated table designed for A. Conger Goodyear, 1939

The element that most distinguished Nakashima's designs from those of his contemporaries was the tentative use of a raw, untrimmed tree edge on the top of a modular cabinet and bookcase from the early 1940s.[53] As seen in the low table designed for the Brogen House of 1945–46, by mid-decade he was making confident use of the unshaped natural edges and forms of tangentially cut wood sections with perforations purposefully left intact.[54] This emphasis on the forms inherent within organic materials comprised the basic aesthetic of Nakashima's subsequent work.

There are obvious similarities between Nakashima's later work and that of Raymond. Raymond, whose Tokyo firm catered to the most Europeanized of the Japanese community as well as to foreign companies, was greatly influenced by the work of Le Corbusier. By the mid-1930s, Le Corbusier and his design team of Pierre Jeanneret and Charlotte Perriand had shifted their interest away from the refined metal furnishings of their earlier interiors toward more robust, even rugged wood furniture that emphasized organic forms and often unprocessed natural materials.[55] Photographs of selected projects designed by Raymond and his assistants from 1933 onward reveal tables and chairs of peeled wood logs with knots and other imperfections left intact.[56]

Support for handcrafted wood furniture and objects came, surprisingly enough, from Russel Wright, the industrial designer who most successfully marketed mass-produced modernism in America. The "Russel Wright" label signified comfortable and useful contemporary design to a large U.S. market. Wright's first success came with the useful bar and serving pieces he had handspun of aluminum in Bauhaus-pure, undecorated shapes.[57] His own philosophy was suspended somewhere between Bauhaus social views and dedication to the craft element of the Arts and Crafts movement. Working for the most part alone, Wright was most successful functioning as an artist-craftsman sculpting directly in his materials. The handcrafted chair he designed in 1932 for his own office-apartment marks a move away from the machined forms of his previous work and demonstrates his inclination for natural materials, animated carved forms, and the individuality of hand production.[58]

Perhaps more interesting than the chair itself are Wright's views of craft. An interview published in the new magazine *Craft Horizons* in 1943 indicates his expectations for the emergence of a new kind of craftsperson: "The Craftsman today must find an entirely new role to play; and I don't believe he has yet found it. That is, the whole trend for Craftsmanship should be away from making use-

Members' Penthouse, The Museum of Modern Art, New York, c. 1939–44. The lounge included industrially produced furniture designed by Marcel Breuer, Bruno Mathsson, and Russel Wright, whose handmade armchair is visible at center (back view).

ful articles (he must forget his medieval past) and work toward the realm of the Fine Arts. He can make useful objects but they should always offer something the machine can't offer—like a more sensitive employment of materials, . . . form and decoration. . . . [B]ut with this background being created by Industrial Designers of impersonal and anonymous design of houses, rooms, furniture, and all articles of service—there will be a need for a different standard of Craftsmanship and of Fine Arts—a concentration of the personal and individualistic must be produced by the Artist and the Craftsman to relieve our new machine made surroundings."[59]

FUNCTIONAL ART OBJECTS IN WOOD

The Oceana line of wood table accessories reflects Wright's enthusiasm for adapting the sculptural possibilities of handcraft to industrial production techniques. In 1935 he began working with the Klise Woodworking Company of Grand Rapids to develop free-form organic objects based on marine motifs, sea shells, and sea plants. Many of the pieces, though sculptural in appearance, were designed within the capabilities of contemporary woodworking machinery, achieving a handmade look for objects that were not. Various colored and grained woods—cherry, gum, blonde maple, and hazelwood—reflect the taste for natural texture, materials, and colors prevalent in the late 1930s modernist house. Although the line was recognized by many for its elegant modernism, potential buyers apparently decided that the marine motifs were only appropriate for summer home use, and lack of their support forced the discontinuation of the line in 1940.[60]

Like Breuer and Goldberg, another Bauhaus alumnus to affect the course of wood in the United States was László Moholy-Nagy, a Hungarian artist who had been one of the most renowned teachers at Dessau. Wood was one of the materials explored as part of Moholy-Nagy's extension of the Bauhaus primary course at the New Bauhaus, the progressive design school he established in Chicago in 1937.[61] The "hand-sculptures" created by his students represent a classic classroom exercise that involved experimenting with sculptural form through modeling or carving basic organic shapes. A 1945 *Art News* article described the program: "As in the Dessau Bauhaus, materials are examined for their potential properties. Wood is perforated or ridged or slitted to give it elasticity or flexibility or torsion. Metals and plastics are bent or rolled or crumpled according to the student's individual line of experiment. Since this exercise is designed to develop his inventive faculties and ingenuity, there can be no standardized approach."[62]

James Prestini also recognized the significance of craft in the setting of standards for industry and as training for the role of industrial designer. A mechanical engineer by profession, Prestini began experimenting with lathe turning in 1932. After a year's apprenticeship with furniture designer and craftsman Carl Malmsten in Stockholm, he enrolled at the Chicago School of Design, working simultaneously as student and craft instructor. In true Bauhaus custom, he as craftsman and Moholy-Nagy as artist shared the teaching of the foundation course.[63]

In his early lathe-turned works Prestini confined himself to symmetrical, elemental wood bowls that implied a utility that their exquisite refinement denied. Flaring gracefully from base to rim in the manner of a fine porcelain cup, a Prestini object was largely confined to visual or tactile appreciation. This self-imposed limitation was consonant with the austerity of his modernist aesthetic.

One of the paradoxes of modernism in America was The Museum of Modern Art's institutional endorsement of industrially produced design objects and the consequent denial of the validity of the unique object conceived and made by the craft artist. This paradox, and the ensuing confusion regarding the unique craft object, is well expressed in the writings of the man who after the war would become the museum's curator of architecture and design, Edgar J. Kaufmann, Jr.: "But if this view of Prestini's turned wood forms as art is admissible, what about craftsmanship? Unlike crafts practiced by many enthusiasts, Prestini's revives no lingering local skills, it achieves no vibrant surfaces charged with personal touch and its contribution is minor to the convenience of household routine. Spare, smooth, and evenly accented, it has more often borrowed from mechanization than protested against it. In short, it is hard to make place for Prestini among conventional craftsmen, and his place among artists would be exceptional and marginal. Yet his place is secure as a maker of beautiful, pure shapes."[64]

The confusing implications of this new, unnameable art form were to have profound repercussions in the postwar years as we grappled once again with issues of industry and craft. At the close of World War II a generation of young American designers supplanted all preceding modern styles with industrial techniques capable of producing seductive sculptural wood furniture and objects. Their deliberate choice of wood was predicated on evoking reassuring connections with historic furniture traditions while simultaneously expressing the most advanced and inventive forms of modernism.

The links between the Arts and Crafts furniture in the period before World War I and the post–World War II craft revival furniture are clear. Each movement favored the special beauties of wood and sought individuality in hand production. The rekindling of interest in woodcraft, first apparent in the mid-1930s, continued to gather momentum after the war. Industrial design and production methods had fulfilled the democratic goal of providing good contemporary design at affordable prices for a mass market. But the loss of individuality implied by mass production, and the desire for relief from the mechanistic qualities of modern life, led to a replacement of the slick surface with bold natural materials and the sensory pleasure of the handcrafted object.

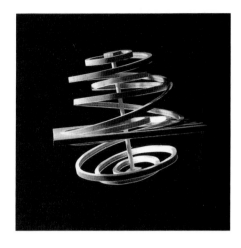

James L. Prestini. *Multiple Spiral* (extended). Photograph by Barbara Morgan

THE MAKING OF MODERN ART GLASS

by April Kingsley

Two divergent tendencies emerged in glassmaking in the years between the wars and both led to the future. One put a new spin on the guild tradition to give us modern industrial design; the other drew on the holistic tradition of the independent craftsperson to provide the basis for what would become known as the Studio Glass movement. European modernism provided the initial impetus for change in the field and shaped the developmental course of both industrial glass design and studio glassmaking. While not a cohesive concept or "look" in Europe, where it encompassed everything from the late Cubist excesses of Picasso to the rigorous linear discipline of Piet Mondrian, once it made America its home, modernism found its identity in craft as it did in all of the arts.

Louis Comfort Tiffany's studios epitomized the Arts and Crafts movement in America, while controverting its emphasis on the unique artist-crafted object. Indeed, the guild tradition of team-crafted production in a factorylike setting probably held on longest in glassmaking because the process necessitated handwork; and yet no single pair of hands could complete the entire process. The heavily embellished Art Nouveau look of the more luxurious Arts and Crafts objects, many of which were still produced by the Tiffany studios in the 1920s, was, however, on the wane. The curvilinear complexities of Art Nouveau simply did not speak to flappers in the fast lane, with their bobbed hair and streamlined sports coupes. Fine work was still being done in his factory, but Tiffany's trademark iridescent glass was being challenged by that produced in other, more commercially viable companies such as Steuben Glass Works. In 1920 the Tiffany Foundation established a school at Laurelton Hall, Tiffany's Long Island estate overlooking Oyster Bay.[1] The mandate of this "art institution," as it was called, was "art education directed toward both art appreciation and production, within the scope of industrial as well as the fine arts."[2] The school did not, however, make any significant inroads into educating craftspeople in innovative ways, or establish new criteria for the collaboration of art and industry.[3] Rather, Tiffany continued to cater to the elite, breaking no new ground in design for mass production and therefore failing to reach a larger market. The firm was sold in 1928.

Frederick Carder of Steuben had been Tiffany's strongest competitor since his arrival in the United States in 1903.[4] Carder had been lured to Corning, New York, from a successful career at the Stevens and Williams glassworks in Stourbridge, England, by Steuben glass engraver Thomas G. Hawkes. Hawkes wanted a glass manufacturer of his own to provide the necessary blanks for his engravers, and Carder managed this with ease.[5] He quickly set about experimenting with colored and iridescent glass, patenting one of them, Aurene, by mid-1904.[6] A scientist at heart, fondly mixing chemicals and powders in his lab, Carder drew inspiration from the entire history of glass, and the results were quite eclectic.[7] His wholly experimental approach to colored glass enabled him to keep it commercially viable until the 1930s. From the Tiffany-like Aurene wares he moved on in the 1920s to the Intarsia series—color abstractions cased between two layers of clear crystal.[8] Inspired by the Graal glassware developed at Orrefors in Sweden, the exquisite craftsmanship of one particular eighth-inch-thick Intarsia vase established it as a masterpiece in the history of glass.

Carder could design for, or work in, the entire panoply of glass techniques, from *pâte de verre* (glass paste fused and hardened by firing), *millefiore* (flower-like patterns formed by fused bundles of colored glass rods), and *cire perdue* (lost-wax casting), to the myriad possibilities of blown glass, including opalizing and marbelizing, acid etching, and the incorporation of mica and air bubbles within the glass.[9] A sparkling Cintra cologne bottle (1927–31), with a bubbled core cased in colored heavy crystal with threadings and massive cutting, is a sculptural tour-de-force with jewel-like faceting and strong allusions to Art Deco and contemporary French glass. Carder ostensibly disdained Deco, yet in pieces like the *Six Prong Green Jade Vase* of 1930 he handled the style as if it were his own. Carder was among the members of trade organizations and art guilds who viewed the Paris Exposition Internationale des Arts Décoratifs et Industriels Modernes in 1925 at the behest of the Hoover Commission of the United States Department of Commerce. In his report to the commission he commented specifically on Maurice Marinot's thick-walled, bubble-permeated bottles, which may well have been the design source for Carder's Cintra cologne bottle and other heavily etched glass works of the late 1920s.[10] In any event, he seems to have accepted the commercial viability of *art moderne*. In the late 1920s he also produced architectural glass panels with Art Deco designs.

Between 1903 and 1932, Carder introduced over 8,500 designs and 140 colors to glass. In the early 1930s, however, colored glass began to go out of favor. In 1932 Corning Glass Works, which had incorporated Steuben during World War I, brought in design consultant Walter Dorwin Teague, Sr., to test some new,

Frederick Carder designing engraved decoration for a goblet, c. 1930

more modern-looking designs. The following year, in a successful "palace coup" staged by Arthur Amory Houghton, Jr., the new young director of Corning, Carder was relieved of his design duties, and Houghton proceeded to revolutionize industrial glass design in ways to be discussed later in this essay.

In recognition of his three decades of service to the company, Carder was given space in a little-used Steuben factory building for his own experiments. Then age sixty-nine, but undaunted, he promptly installed a gas kiln and an electric oven for melting glass, establishing a one-person glassmaking studio. Here he would work happily for the next twenty-seven years, initially concentrating on a series of important cast-glass sculptures and reliefs. Among the first was a *Head of Christ* (1934), cast in uncolored glass from a plaster Carder created in 1933 upon hearing that Corning had purged its stockrooms of his now unfashionable colored glassware in a highly symbolic smashing session.[11] (While sculpting the head, Carder is said to have announced, with obvious double meaning, "This is a crucifixion."[12]) Carder also made portrait heads, bas-reliefs, and cast-glass sculptures such as the *Standing Glassblower* of 1937, with its echoes of Greek pipe-playing figures of Pan. Carder's works in *pâte de verre*—a technique that dates back to ancient Egyptian times—are likewise both modern in appearance and historically resonant. According to glass historian Paul Hollister, "Frederick Carder understood intuitively how *pâte de verre* could be applied to enhance *cire perdue* casting. His 1930s *Dancing Faun* panel shows the beautifully modelled figure, faun, and foreground in marble-white relief against a grainy green background like a hedge."[13] Starting in the 1930s, Carder took *cire perdue* glass casting to previously unheard of degrees of complexity with his Diatreta "cage" cups.[14] It wasn't until the 1950s, when he was in his nineties, that he perfected a method of casting double-walled glass cups like the Roman cut-glass beakers he was emulating.

Frederick Carder. *Head of Christ*. 1934. Lead crystal; *cire perdue,* height 15¼". The Rockwell Museum, Corning, New York

Though their scale of ambition was quite a lot smaller, the precursors and role models of the Studio Glass movement in the United States were independents like Carder (after 1933), Maurice Heaton, Waylande DeSantis Gregory, and Frances and Michael Higgins, all of whom came to glassmaking through ceramics, enameling, or some other artform, and who melted glass at home in their studios.[15]

Heaton was the third generation in a family of glassmakers. His grandfather had been a manufacturer of Gothic Revival stained glass in England, and his father was a cloisonné enameler who had been swept up in the Arts and Crafts movement. Upon moving to New York, his father established a stained-glass studio, in which Maurice worked after briefly studying engineering. Maurice found his niche in 1928, when, at the suggestion of his friend, textile designer Ruth Reeves, he began creating glass lamp shades as well as laminated glass walls and window decorations. He and Reeves, Donald Deskey, Raymond Hood, and Joseph Urban were among the artists involved with the American Designers' Gallery, a Manhattan cooperative formed to promote its members' work in a midtown showroom. As a result of that exposure, the Lightolier company commissioned Heaton to design a special line of handcrafted fixtures for them that did not appear in their catalogues. Heaton often created lighting fixtures for friends and acquaintances in the New City–area artists' colony such as Maxwell Anderson, Burgess Meredith, Henry Varnum Poor, and Rube Goldberg.[16] He later branched out into tableware with glazed and enameled undersurfaces, thereby bringing his grandfather's and his father's influences full circle.[17]

Heaton adapted his technique from stained glass and continued to use the flat sheets of bubbled glass called for in stained glass. For a work like the shallow bowl of 1930 in the collection of The Metropolitan Museum of Art, he would apply vitreous glazes, fusing them to the glass sheet through firing. Then a white glaze was applied, which silhouetted the colors when the sheet was slumped over an inverted, and customarily convex, mold; when turned upright after cooling, the plate or bowl would be concave and the white would appear to be beneath the color. Powdered enamels, which he would sift through templates placed on the flat glass using tiny sieves, replaced the glazes sometime in the 1940s. Working on a see-through turntable, Heaton cut the glass and ground its edges before the colors were applied. Whereas the glazes changed color and flowed together when fired, creating a freer, more painterly look like that of the "plaid" plate in the collection of the Metropolitan, the enamels fired hard and unchanged in color. The steel molds over which he slumped the finished glass sheet were made by hand, and at least two shapings of the glass sheet and readjustments of the mold were required before he achieved the result he wanted.[18] It was a complex process that yielded mysterious objects of deceptively simple appearance.

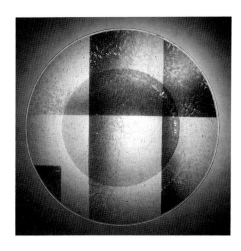

Maurice Heaton. *Plate.* c. 1930. Glass, diameter 9⅞". The Metropolitan Museum of Art, New York. Gift of Maurice Heaton, 1979 (1979.194)

The working structure Heaton evolved has the labor-intensive, long-term continuity that became the archetype for the American Studio Craft movement. The lifestyle surrounding it was archetypal as well; other craftspeople of Heaton's time, including Henry Varnum Poor, Wharton Esherick, and Waylande Gregory, to name only a few, led lives similarly picture-perfect in their fusion of home life and career. A visitor to Heaton's studio in Valley Cottage, New York, later wrote: "Maurice Heaton believes that it is better to be happy in one's work, as a craftsman can, than to be regimented. Something of the good life he and his family lead shines through in the soft whites and delicate enamel tones of his glass. His eleven-acre farm just west of the Hudson River has meadows where sheep graze, a pine grove . . . , a weathered barn converted into a great studio with a tremendous cathedral-like window at one end. He built his house himself, a house that has brownstone masonry and a beautiful brick terrace . . . , a patriarchal dining table well-laden with home grown food and surrounded by a large family."[19]

Heaton's definition of his calling has a similar purity: "Craftmanship to me is the making and designing of a useful and beautiful object in one creative operation. Whether, in the making, machines are used as tools, or the hand is used with tools, is of no importance. Whether, in the duplication of objects, part or even all of the work is done by apprentices is of no importance. As one craftsman said to me, you 'borrow hands' and train them to do what your own hands would do. The important thing is to create in the material."[20] Despite his obvious preference for "hands on" craftwork, Heaton did complete several commissions for murals and windows. The largest of his commissions was the seven-by-fourteen-foot fused, laminated glass mural honoring the achievements of Amelia Earhart that was a prime attraction in Radio City's Center Theatre, until it vanished during preparations for the building's demolition.[21]

Waylande Gregory, well known for ceramic sculptures such as *The Fountain of the Atom* created for the 1939–40 New York World's Fair, had his studio in a

Maurice Heaton. Amelia Earhart mural (now lost), Radio Center Theatre, New York, 1932

bucolic setting on the side of a New Jersey hill overlooking a beautiful, undeveloped valley. It was there in the early 1940s that he developed and patented a method of binding glass to clay. In these utilitarian bowls and ashtrays, thickly pooled glazes and sharp, light-refracting shards lie beneath a perfectly smooth glass surface, which Gregory termed "internally fractured glass."[22] Pieces of glass are actually embedded in the underlying clay of the *Mermaid Crystal Bowl* and *The Airman,* both made about 1942. The large *Mermaid Bowl* (c. 1940) in the collection of the New Jersey State Museum in Trenton, however, is all glass and was painted before firing. As these varied techniques indicate, Gregory took a highly experimental approach to glazing, even using uranium to achieve unusual color effects.[23]

After their marriage in 1948, Frances and Michael Higgins left the academic world to work independently "in a medium then barely touched anywhere."[24] Except for a later-regretted stint of adapting their designs to utilitarian tableware for Haeger Potteries, they have been creating glass art objects, jewelry, and architectural commissions ever since. It was "a precarious living, producing and selling fused, enameled glass in all forms from earrings to screens and church windows,"[25] but it provided one of the earliest models for the incipient Studio Craft movement in America. Georgia-born Frances taught craft and design at the University of Georgia in Athens, where she began heat-shaping glass in 1942. She has re-created the first piece she ever made in this medium for the current exhibition, using the original mold. Michael had emigrated from England in 1938 and was teaching visual design at the Institute of Design in Chicago in 1947 when Frances went there to study. After their marriage, their joint experiments with laminating metals and glass in intricate overlays introduced wholly new techniques and types of glass to the craft world.[26]

Makers of paperweights and other "lampworkers"—glasscrafters using gas burners or blowtorches to work glass—also had been busy in their studios for decades before Paul Perrot directed public attention to them in his 1960 *Craft Horizons* article "New Directions in Glassmaking." The situation he described then was actually that of Carder, Heaton, the Higginses, and other glassmakers in the 1930s and 1940s: "Contemporary technology, which has made easily available pure and consistent raw materials and dependable, inexpensive sources of fuel, has for the first time permitted the craftsman to go it alone, or almost so. Fuel is as far as the nearest gas jet, materials as close as the nearest wholesaler. Furnaces can be built with standard refractories; molds and pots can be thrown from readily available clays; and the total investment need be little more than for a good pottery kiln."[27]

Harvey K. Littleton was a member of the Corning "family."[28] His father, Jesse Littleton, was director of research and the developer of Pyrex, and young Harvey worked in different areas of the factory during his summer vacations. As an adult he remained attached to Carder in particular, visiting him whenever he returned to the area, though by the 1940s he was primarily a ceramist and remained one until the 1960s. Although Littleton used the facilities at Corning to cast his first multiform glass *Torso* in 1942, and again in 1946, when he cast a second torso, he became more and more anxious to prove that a glass artist could work independently of a factory. None of Frederick Carder's procedures involved working with hot glass, blowing it, adding to it, or shaping it outside the oven. This is probably the reason Littleton modeled his idea of a personal glass studio on the small workshops established in Paris by Jean Sala, and in Murano, Italy, by a number of Venetian glass artists, rather than on Carder's studio. Littleton did not melt glass in his own ceramics kiln until 1958 and did not blow "hot" glass until March 1962, during a week-long workshop sponsored by The Toledo Museum of Art that is

Harvey K. Littleton. *Torso.* 1942. Slip-cast Vycor multiform glass; fused, height 11¼". The Corning Museum of Glass, Corning, New York. Gift of Mr. and Mrs. Fred A. Bickford

now famous as the beginning of "solo" hot glass. Michael and Frances Higgins were the only other glassworkers at the seminar, the rest of the attendees being ceramists like Littleton. Dominick Labino, director of research at Johns Manville, set up Littleton's small pot furnace and provided special low-melting, long-working glass marbles he had developed. These two factors were essential to the project's success. Glassblowing instruction was provided by Harvey Leafgreen of the Libbey Glass Company.

Littleton shared with his colleagues the desire "to show that the individual craftsman working alone could melt decent glass and handle the technical aspects of blowing it and annealing it without being born in the industry and without going through an arduous apprenticeship"[29] Yet in a certain sense glass can only be a one-person product if it is relatively small and technically uncomplicated in the hot phase. Even the European models he used were two-man demonstration set-ups, and everyone needs assistance working hot glass of any considerable size or high level of ambition.

Simultaneous with these beginnings of the studio glass movement, a glorious, final efflorescence of factory art glass occurred in the 1930s. Following the successful "palace coup" of 1933 and the ouster of Frederick Carder, Steuben Glass entered a new phase of streamlined industrial design geared toward a broader, but discriminating, market. This "revolution of industrial design"[30]—its beginnings symbolized by the smashing of Carder's outmoded glassware—would ultimately result in the association of modernism with things American in the world's mind.

The hiring of Walter Dorwin Teague by Steuben's parent company, Corning Glass Works, in 1932, was among the opening salvos of the revolution. During his one-year consultancy Teague designed over thirty sleek, modern-looking glassware patterns, among them, the elegant, stepped *Lens Bowl* of clear crystal. He also offered solutions to the division's production and sales problems, outlining advertising and image strategies calculated, as he put it, "to establish Steuben as the finest glassware in America, worth all we ask for it. I believe we can make the ownership of Steuben glass one of those evidences of solvency—like the ownership of a Cadillac . . . or a house in the right neighborhood."[31] In a policy memo of 1932 Teague outlined what would become Steuben's motto, the "Steuben Trilogy": material, workmanship, and design.[32]

These three elements came together in 1933. First, Steuben's researchers developed a perfectly clear crystal, with no mineral tinting of any kind, so they had the finest glass material to work with. Second, Arthur Amory Houghton, Jr., at twenty-four one of the youngest Houghton family members to be named a director of Corning, proposed taking over the Steuben division and devoting its best glassblowers and engravers to working with the new crystal. Third, Houghton brought in a close friend, John Montieth Gates, a successful young architect, to restructure Steuben's approach to design. Gates in turn hired the New York sculptor Sidney Biehler Waugh to design for the new crystal. All three men were under thirty and full of ambition.[33]

One of Waugh's first designs was for a massive, double-walled (the fusion of two separately blown units), cut-crystal vase that was decidedly sculptural in feeling. Its somewhat stepped, rectilinear projections give it a *moderne,* architectural look as well. Waugh's *Gazelle Bowl* of 1935 is also a sculptural mass, but single-walled, and is supported on a chunky rectangular crossbrace, the simplicity of which probably was inherited from Swedish glass coming out of the factories of Orrefors, Kosta, and Boda. The gazelles leaping through the bowl's limpid space would have looked quite at home in any exhibition of contemporary sculpture, yet they, too, reflect the classicism of contemporaneous Swedish wheel engraving.

Sidney Biehler Waugh. *Vase.* 1935. Glass, 11¼ x 10½ x 10½". The Metropolitan Museum of Art, New York. Purchase, Edward C. Moore, Jr. Gift, 1935 (35.94.2)

Steuben staff designers at work in the Corning-Steuben Building, 718 Fifth Avenue, New York, c. 1937. Known as "The House of Glass," the building was the site of Steuben's New York shop from 1937 to 1959.

The Corning-Steuben Building, 718 Fifth Avenue, New York, late 1930s

Waugh exercised his innate tendency toward the three-dimensional when he created a glass gazelle for the top of an illuminated crystal fountain comprised of a column of concentric glass cylinders. This fountain was installed in the elegant Steuben shop, designed by Gates, that opened in 1934 at 748 Fifth Avenue near the Plaza Hotel. Instead of the network of small retail outlets favored during the Carder era, Houghton exhibited Steuben's new crystal only in New York, and only in the most dignified, gallerylike setting, with dramatically subdued lighting and gray and white surfaces.[34]

Houghton's next move was even more important than, though not nearly as dramatic as, the glass-smashing episode: He hired six graduates of architectural schools to design glass for Steuben. There were no trained glass designers then; traditionally, the blowers themselves (or their superior, as was the case during Carder's tenure at Steuben) were responsible for the final look of the piece, which often veered toward the overelaborate—a look out of favor in the 1930s. Houghton oriented his designers to the glassmaking process and insisted they spend several days each month at the factory to work out design problems with the glassblowers and engravers. But Houghton based his design team in New York rather than in Corning, so that they would be exposed to the latest cultural influences. The tendency toward artisanal niceties and the pull of the familiar were thus minimized for Steuben's designers, leaving them free to explore the new and untried.[35]

Houghton then fashioned a radical publicity campaign to establish Steuben glass as among the finest glass in the world. With a great deal of showmanship, he arranged for its exhibition, first in the elite Knoedler Gallery in Manhattan, then in London, where Waugh's *Zodiac Bowl* (1935) was presented to the Victoria and Albert Museum with much fanfare in the press.[36] Everything Houghton did created the impression that Steuben glass was a status symbol—exactly Teague's marketing concept. Houghton continued in this vein in the following years, arranging exhibitions at prestigious American museums and opening expensive retail shops in the best locations, culminating in 1937 in the opening of the Corning-Steuben Building at 718 Fifth Avenue. With its Pyrex-block walls, the building became known as "The House of Glass"; the designers worked on the upper floors, and the objects they created were sold amid bouquets of fresh flowers on the mezzanine and ground floors.[37]

A meeting between Gates and Henri Matisse in 1937 resulted in the collaboration of twenty-seven world-famous artists with Steuben's engravers on limited editions of their designs for glass. Isamu Noguchi's simple line drawing of a cat, Paul Manship's *Woman and Centaur* (1939), and Pavel Tchelitchew's *Acrobats Vase* (1939) were among the most successful translations of drawing into carved glass. All of the designs were displayed together in the Steuben gallery on Fifth Avenue in the 1940 exhibition "Twenty-seven Artists in Crystal."[38]

Steuben's representation at the New York World's Fair occupied much of Houghton's, Gates's, and Waugh's attention beginning in 1937. Gates designed a World's Fair Cup (1939), a large commemorative vessel crowned by a trylon and perisphere, while Waugh created a three-foot-high, three-hundred-pound mermaid in cast glass, titled *Atlantica* (1939), as a symbol of glassmaking—the first industry to cross the Atlantic to America in the seventeenth century. Monumental, muscularly articulated, with hair and lower limbs rolled up in huge waves, *Atlantica* took five men to pour and three to polish over the course of many months.[39]

Houghton readily admitted that the reason Steuben's new crystal generally took simple shapes was that they did not yet know how to make more complex forms in the new crystal,[40] but the influence of Scandinavian glass should not be discounted, nor the more modern glass being produced by Steuben's competitors in lines intended for a broader market. Among the latter were Libbey Glass's Modern American and Syncopation lines in particular, as well as the high-end production glassware of Phoenix and Consolidated, the Fostoria Glass Specialty Company, the Heisy Glass Company, and the Cambridge Glass Company.

Libbey (formerly the New England Glass Company), which is credited with introducing lead crystal to the United States, became internationally renowned after its spun and cut glass was shown at the 1893 World's Columbian Exposition in Chicago. Its deeply cut crystal of the Brilliant Period (1880–1915) lost its popular appeal during the 1920s; efforts to revive it in the following decade, with new designs by A. Douglas Nash, were not successful, largely because they were too elaborate to be cost-efficient.[41] The repeal of Prohibition in 1933 loosed a flood of cocktail glassware, none so unusual as Syncopation, the novelty cocktail glass Nash designed for Libbey—one must imagine with humorous intent. Bulky cubes surround its stem above a pyramidal base, combining references both to Cubist sculpture and ice cubes.

Nash's designs, extravagantly expensive to produce, came out at a time when American consumers were least able to afford them, and Libbey soon began to founder. In 1936 the company became a division of the Owens-Illinois Glass Company, which focused its energies on the mass production of its Safedge tumblers. A promotional tie-in with Walt Disney's animated *Snow White and the Seven Dwarfs* brought Owens-Illinois "carload customers," with sales in the millions. As a result, the company decided it could afford to try to regain a top position in the field of fine art glass, hiring Edwin W. Fuerst to design modern, if somewhat conservative, prestige glassware. Libbey's streamlined Modern American cut crystal of 1940, the last of its handcrafted glassware lines, was discontinued in 1942, when the exigencies of war compelled most of the industry to adopt more efficient modes of mass production.[42]

Two other colorful attempts to introduce Cubist modernism into the low-income American home were made by Fostoria Glass of Moundsville, West Virginia, and Consolidated Lamp & Glass Company of Coraopolis, Pennsylvania. Fostoria had patented its extremely popular clear-glass American pattern (no. 2056) in 1915. Its advertising stressed the line's appeal to "up-to-date" buyers in Europe and the United States, and noted how different its cubic faceting looked in reproduction, "where the 'cube' is brought out prominently," yet on close

John Monteith Gates. *The World's Fair Cup.* 1939 (now lost). Crystal, 28 x 10½ x 10½". Steuben Glass. This one-of-a-kind piece, inscribed "Building the World of Tomorrow," was created to commemorate the 1939–40 New York World's Fair. The figure of the goddess Mithrana adorned the fair's Administration Building.

Sidney Biehler Waugh. *Atlantica.* 1939. Crystal, height 36". The Corning Museum of Glass, Corning, New York. *Atlantica* was designed to symbolize the arrival of glassmaking in America in the early seventeenth century. Weighing 300 pounds, it was the largest casting of clear crystal to date.

examination "this cube effect is almost entirely obliterated by the prismatic brilliancy of the pattern."[43] Amber, blue, green, and canary were added to its color range in the mid-1920s. The line remained in production until the 1970s, and is the look one associates with the company.

Fostoria also brought in the well-known designer George Sakier to create fine, modern-looking dinnerware for large-scale production. Stemware with square bases, elegant, vertically ribbed vases, and the company's Mayfair line (no. 2419) resulted. The Mayfair dishes, made in rose, green, amber, and topaz, are characterized by stepped, seemingly Deco-inspired corners and handles. Introduced in 1930, it was discontinued in 1944.[44] Sakier's design for an amber vase has the elegant simplicity that characterizes Eliel Saarinen's Cranbrook furnishings.

Instead of regimenting Cubism, as Fostoria seemed to have done, designer Reuben Haley's Ruba Rombic line for Consolidated Lamp & Glass is more playful, its facets at odd angles, its edges jagged. The zigzagging motion of a decanter set seems to celebrate the effects of inebriation. When looking at the tall, stately French crystal vase in the collection of The Toledo Museum of Art, one is reminded of John Marin's fractured skyscrapers painted during the same period. Frosty white, the edges of its facets catch the light like quartz crystals. The sculptural feel of Ruba Rombic may derive from Haley's practice of modeling his designs in clay (he was also a sculptor and metalworker). Uncertain how to market its new giftware line, Consolidated hired Howard G. Selden as its factory sales representative for art merchandise.[45] Selden started off the Ruba Rombic advertising campaign with an unprecedented seven-page spread in a widely circulated gift-shop magazine. Original labels for the line called it "An Epic in Modern Art," and its perceived parallels to modern poetry were part of the sales pitch: "ruba," from "Rubaiy (meaning epic or poem) Rombic (meaning irregular in shape)."[46] There were thirty-seven items in this highly popular line, which was discontinued in 1932, when Consolidated merged with the Phoenix Glass Company.

Among the less expensive glassware produced in huge quantities in the 1930s, those that were modernistically stylized include the Manhattan series produced by Anchor Hocking, and Tea Room and Pyramid by the Indiana Glass Company. This was really modernism for the masses, but the rays, steppings, and concentricities that signified newness remain satisfying to the contemporary eye.

In 1939, Russel Wright designed a line of glassware (manufactured after the war by Century Metalcraft of New York and Morgantown, West Virginia) to accompany his American Modern tableware, but few of the other industrial

Advertisement for Ruba Rombic glassware. From *The Gift and Art Shop* (February 1928)

Indiana Glass Company. *Depression Glass.* 1930s. Glass; Tea Room pitcher: 10 x 9 x 6¼"; Pyramid candy and condiment dishes; Manhattan sugar and creamer. Collection William Straus

designers who had changed the look of the American home in the preceding decades made similar forays into glassware. Even more than his dinnerware, Wright's glassware expressed the gentle humanity of his Quaker background in its subdued grays and smoky earth tones. The satisfyingly simple, rounded shapes are so right for the hand that they, and variations on them, remain popular to the present day. Pipsan Saarinen Swanson, daughter of Finnish architect-designer Eliel Saarinen, was one of the few women who designed for glass, creating vases and ashtrays for U.S. Glass in Tiffin, Ohio, and lamps for the Mutual Sunset Lamp Company of New York and Trenton, New Jersey. In collaboration with her husband, J. Robert F. Swanson, and other Cranbrook craftspeople and designers, she introduced Flexible Home Arrangements (F.H.A.) through the Johnson Furniture Company of Grand Rapids, Michigan. By 1945, the Saarinen-Swanson Group, as it became known, included sixteen manufacturers of modern home furnishings.[47]

Many of the best American designers became involved in lighting design or experimented with the use of glass in furniture. Leading designers of modern lighting fixtures include Donald Deskey, Ilonka Karasz, Walter von Nessen, and Gilbert Rohde. Von Nessen used frosted-glass lampshades in fixtures noted for their "brazen modernity,"[48] and combined the newly invented material Bakelite with crystal in a curved chevron vase for Heisy Glass of Newark, Ohio. Rohde designed a number of lamps, probably including a plumbinglike chrome fixture with inset candle-shaped opaque glass cylinders. Deskey used glass sheeting in zigzag configurations reminiscent of French designer Jean Perzel's lamps.[49] Another lamp designed for and manufactured by Deskey-Vollmer, New York, resembles a miniature building in its four-square rectilinearity; diagonal lines divide the front glass panel into geometric planes in the manner of a Dutch de Stijl painting.

Clear glass characterized the modern look in lighting fixtures, as it had art glass in general. It might be etched or sandblasted when used for architectural purposes, as were Paul V. Gardner's glass panels for the Empire State Building, or otherwise textured to diffuse the light. The architectural element is prevalent in the furniture designed with glass during this period, such as Kem Weber's three-tiered circular table with square columnar supports fastened to the glass by stepped Deco clamps. A black-glass table by architect Raymond Hood, who designed some of the quintessential buildings of this period, including the American Radiator, Daily News, and McGraw-Hill buildings in New York, epitomizes machined modernity with its radio antenna–like legs, and it does so with an exquisite elegance. The most startling piece of glass furniture, however, is the chair believed to have been designed in 1939 by Louis Dierra for the Pittsburgh Plate Glass Company's display at the New York World's Fair. The soft seat floats in a semicircular column of clear, molded glass, its edges rounded like the upholstery. The tubular metal supports are minimally articulated, creating a sensation of the cushion floating, cloudlike, in the air.

It was the development of a perfectly clear, pure crystal in the first years of the 1930s at Steuben/Corning that sent Carder, the master of colored glass, into the studio to work independently and become a model for the nascent Studio Glass movement. And it was the team concept structured around that same transparent crystal at Steuben, where high-level material, craftsmanship, and promotion joined forces to establish a model for art in industry, which put American glass at the forefront of modernism in that medium. The effects of both are still being felt today.

Gilbert Rohde. *Lamp*. c. 1933. Designed for Mutual Sunset Lamp Company. Opaque glass, chrome, 14 x 6¾ x 2½". Collection William Straus

Donald Deskey. *Table Lamp*. c. 1926–27. Glass, wood, chromeplated brass, 11 x 8⅝ x 5⅜". The Metropolitan Museum of Art, New York. Purchase, Theodore R. Gamble, Jr. Gift, in honor of his mother, Mrs. Theodore R. Gamble, 1982 (1982.33)

MODERNISM AND AMERICAN CERAMICS

by Barbara Perry

Dina Kuhn. *Das Wasser.* c. 1927. Earthenware, 14½ x 7¼ x 7¾". The Cleveland Museum of Art. Dudley P. Allen Fund

American ceramics experienced a burst of creative energy in the period between the wars. Western civilization had been changed irrevocably by World War I, and the old formal vocabulary no longer seemed adequate, or even appropriate. Few of the art potteries, so productive at the turn of the century, were still active, and their wares held little relevance for younger ceramists, who tuned in to the latest jazz, went to the movies, and accepted the machine as a de facto part of modern life. Their search for new forms to reflect a new way of living would touch both the studio potters and the manufactories that centered on serial production.

Throughout the art pottery era, ceramics were produced by group effort in various commercial potteries. There was a clear division of labor, with potters, decorators, and glaze technicians working on their own particular aspect of production and no other. However, there were also a few artists who preferred to pursue their art more independently—studio potters who completed each step of production themselves, from mixing the clay bodies and throwing the forms to decorating and glazing. Adelaide Alsop Robineau, Susan Goodrich Frackleton, and George Ohr all worked alone, producing unique works of great individuality. As art pottery production fell off after the war, it was to this kind of production that younger American ceramists turned.

Most of the important ceramists to emerge during the 1920s did not experience the guildlike system of the art pottery. Rather than learning the craft in a production pottery, they studied in established art schools and universities, and were often directly influenced by developments in European art and design. Many began as painters or sculptors and moved into ceramics as yet another aspect of their work. The studio ceramist Carl Walters studied with Robert Henri and initially pursued a career in painting. His ceramic sculptures betray this early influence; their surfaces are decorative and colorful, and the figures are fully represented by sculptural mass. Henry Varnum Poor studied painting at Stanford University and in London and Paris, where he was introduced to Cubism and the modernist movement. Poor approached clay with the abandon of a painter, creating monumental, casually wrought forms decorated in an expressionistic manner. He was not exclusively a ceramist and effectively combined ceramics and architecture, demonstrating that clay objects, even utilitarian ones, need not have the sterility and monotony of production wares.

Alexander Archipenko arrived in the United States in 1923 with a modernist philosophy and the experience of Moscow and Paris behind him. Cubism in its most stringent form found few supporters in this country, but Archipenko's Cubist-inspired figures, with their classical symmetry and sinuous curves, were well received when they were shown in New York in 1924–25, and in the Sixth and Seventh Ceramic National Exhibitions (now the Ceramic Nationals) in Syracuse. His work in clay occurred mainly during the 1920s, but his abiding interest in combining painting and sculpture, as well as the "fleshlike" color of fired clay, prompted him to continue exploring the medium for figural works. In 1937, he accepted a teaching position at the New Bauhaus in Chicago, where he continued his investigations into the unification of painting and sculpture.

ART DECO CERAMICS

Art Deco, or *art moderne*—a neoclassical revival—enjoyed enormous popularity in the decade following World War I. It stressed solid mass and a clear delineation of parts. Surface was of primary importance, with shallow carving, bold colors, and often exotic motifs.

One of the major proponents of Art Deco ceramics in the United States was R. Guy Cowan and his Cowan Pottery Studio in Rocky River, Ohio, a suburb of Cleveland. Cowan specialized in limited-edition porcelain figurines, some of which he designed himself in the style of the bronze and ivory figures by the French sculptors Ferdinand Preiss, Pierre le Faguays, and others. He also employed the finest sculptors, including Waylande DeSantis Gregory, Paul Manship, and Alexander Blazys, a Russian émigré who taught at the Cleveland School of Art (now the Cleveland Institute of Art). Eventually, Viktor Schreckengost, Russell Barnett Aitken, and Thelma Frazier Winter were to produce ceramic sculptures and vessels at the Cowan pottery as well.

Cowan was one of the most important figures in American ceramics in the 1920s and 1930s. He considered clay a fitting medium for the sculptor, and encouraged, in fact demanded, innovation and originality. As a result of his interest, there would grow up in Cleveland a school of clay sculpture that was to be a dominant element in the development of ceramics in the United States.

Although the sculptural ceramics produced at the Cowan pottery varied in form and influence—for instance, the allusions to Cubism and Futurism in Blazys's work—much of it can be placed within the exuberant and playful Art Deco style, of which Gregory was the pottery's leading exponent. His work there ranged from a set of candelabra with angel motifs, to a rendition of Salome holding the head of John, her veils creating a dramatic sweep behind her, that was produced in a variety of glazes. Gregory would later work independently in his own studio, creating large ceramic sculptures as well as limited editions of plates, bowls, and vases, predominately in the Art Deco style. His plates and dinnerware are the most intriguing, with elegant abstract patterns or clever renditions of figures, such as polo players, in action.

The most important and best known of the Art Deco works produced at the Cowan pottery were the magnificent *Jazz* bowls (1931) by Viktor Schreckengost. The bowls were commissioned anonymously for the New York Governor's mansion in Albany, New York, by Eleanor Roosevelt, who explicitly asked for something modern in spirit. Schreckengost, an habitué of New York's jazz clubs, immediately chose a New York theme. The bowls were individually decorated in *sgrafitto,* with a turquoise glaze over black. Images of cocktail glasses, skyscrapers, and musical notes are interspersed with abstract Art Deco motifs—parallel wavy lines, zigzags, stars, and bubbles—and words such as "jazz," "follies," and "cafe," recalling the paintings of Schreckengost's contemporary, the American painter Stuart Davis.

Schreckengost made three *Jazz* bowls for Mrs. Roosevelt. Cowan was so pleased with them that a limited edition of fifty hand-decorated bowls was produced, some with straight sides and others with a flared rim.[1] Schreckengost made copies of his designs, which were then transferred to the bowls by other decorators. A second edition of 150–200 smaller bowls, the "poor man's bowl," was cast from molds that eliminated the need for hand incising of the exterior. The *Jazz* bowls, particularly the initial examples without the flared rim, are among the finest Art Deco objects ever produced in this country.

The Cowan pottery was not the only source of American Art Deco ceramics. The ubiquitous forms of the doe, the gazelle, and other animals were used repeatedly by Wilhelm Hunt Diederich, a Hungarian émigré who worked in metal as well as clay. Diederich's vessels are decorated with figures that express the sense of spontaneity and vitality seen in the best French *moderne* design. His influence was mainly in the area of decoration and extended to American design in general; it was not limited to ceramics.

The Roseville Pottery Company, in Zanesville, Ohio, was one of the few art potteries to produce objects of any quality in the Art Deco style. Its Futura line, introduced in 1924, was by far the most successful. Many of the forms are sleek and streamlined, while others are angular and geometric, with bright colors and no surface decoration. Their affinities to postmodern design lend these objects a contemporary appeal.

Art Deco ceramics were also produced at the Rookwood Pottery Company in Cincinnati, finely crafted by hand in the best Rookwood tradition. The decorations of Sara Saxe and Lorinda Epply, for example, were in an elegant and colorful Art Deco style. Kataro Shirayamadani, the Japanese artist whose work represents the best in Rookwood decoration, created a modernist vase form that lent itself perfectly to the Art Deco motifs of Epply.

THE CLEVELAND SCHOOL AND THE INFLUENCE OF VIENNA

The Cowan Pottery Studio closed in 1931, a casualty of the Depression. While the manufactory was in receivership, however, Cowan provided workspace and materials to a number of young ceramists, some of them students at the Cleveland School of Art, and allowed them free reign to experiment on their own work. This group formed the nucleus of what would come to be known as the "Cleveland school."[2] These ceramists worked in a similar style, often used the same subject matter, and found their stylistic roots in the witty and sophisticated clay sculpture being produced in the various workshops in Vienna.[3]

While still a student, Viktor Schreckengost saw the work of contemporary European ceramists in a traveling exhibition in Cleveland.[4] He was intrigued by the work of the Viennese in particular, especially the sculpture of Michael Powolny and Valerie (Vally) Wieselthier. What so impressed him about their work was the way the clay was handled.[5] Whereas American artists usually tried to hide the nature of the clay, striving to make it look like bronze, wood, or marble, the Austrian artists used its distinctive characteristics expressively, allowing them to play a vital role in the realization of the work.

Schreckengost's teacher at the Cleveland School of Art, Julius Mihalik, had taught at the Kunstgewerbeschüle, Vienna, and arranged for his young student to receive a scholarship to study there. When Schreckengost arrived in 1929, he discovered the works of a group of bright young ceramists who worked at the Wiener Werkstätte and other workshops in the city. Their work was not in the austere geometric style of Josef Hoffmann and the Secessionists, but in the more relaxed, playful style initiated by Dagobert Peche and expressed in the work of Wiesel-thier, Dina Kuhn, Reni Schaschl, Susi Singer, and others. Vessels and sculptures were loosely modeled, with bright, free-flowing glazes that complemented rather than concealed the nature of the clay. The Austrians were also committed to traditional methods of ceramic production, and created sculptures built of hollow forms created on the wheel. Wieselthier defined their approach: "Ceramics, more than any art, works by experiment. . . . Every touch of the finger on the clay as it is rolled out from the kick-wheel reveals new possibilities, so plastic is the material, so vast the range of colors in which the material may be diversified."[6] Wieselthier had studied at the Kunstgewerbeschüle with Hoffmann, Koloman Moser, and Michael Powolny before joining the Wiener Werkstätte. She was not only a ceramist but also designed furniture, fabrics, wallpaper, glass, and jewelry, and was one of the most important Viennese artists in the transmission of the Austrian style to the United States. When she arrived in New York in 1929, she brought with her a ceramic style that was unique at the time.

There is a spirit of abandon about Wieselthier's work that is typical of the Viennese school. Her *Europa and the Bull* (1938) is a playful interpretation of the ancient myth, with Europa clinging to the head of a rather silly-looking bull. The technique is totally Viennese: hollow forms, applied details, and the slim, elongated figure, with almond eyes, small mouth, and an opaque glaze. Wieselthier treats her *Taming of the Unicorn* (1946) with a bit more seriousness, but the applied curls and dripping glazes are again exemplary of the Viennese style.

Susi Singer also worked at the Wiener Werkstätte and brought the Austrian style with her when she emigrated to the United States in the late 1930s. Her slim

Reni Schaschl. *Ceramic Figures*. 1917. Earthenware. Courtesy Dr. Christian Brandstatter

Valerie (Vally) Wieselthier. *Vase*. c. 1923. Earthenware, 10 x 7". Everson Museum of Art, Syracuse, New York. Museum purchase with funds from the Dorothy and Robert Riester Ceramic Fund

figures, usually with opaque white glazes, are typically Viennese, but with more movement and a certain seething energy.

Schreckengost visited Vienna in 1929–30 and again in 1931–32. While in Vienna, he completed his *Chinese Head* (1929), with forms thrown on the wheel; the applied rectangular bars on the neck and hat are typical of contemporary Viennese work and illustrate a Cubist influence. Upon his return, he began to turn out witty, sophisticated, and often slightly irreverent vessels and sculpture in an original, modern style. His *Seasons* vase of 1931 is in the Art Deco style, but his ceramic sculptures are clearly Viennese in origin. *Water* (1939) and *Keramos* (1938) are monumental clay sculptures conceived as masks—hollow forms, with details in clay added to the basic structure.

The four elements—Earth, Fire, Air, and Water—were popular subjects during this period, and the Viennese ceramists as well as the Americans Waylande Gregory, Thelma Frazier Winter, and Carl Paul Jennewein, among others, used this theme. Both Schreckengost and Winter drew upon the motifs used by Dina Kuhn in the ceramic head *Das Wasser* (c. 1927), which they would have seen in Cleveland. All three used the theme of water, depicting a woman's head with fish and starfish intertwined in the watery waves of her hair. But each artist interpreted this theme in an entirely personal way, and each piece is unique stylistically.

Schreckengost had sensed the seriousness of the political situation on his last visit to Europe, and he produced two works with direct political references, unusual for ceramic artists of that period. The first was *The Dictator* (1939); the second, and more pointed, was *The Apocalypse '42,* completed in 1941 but not exhibited until the following year, several months after the bombing of Pearl Harbor. Here, the figure of Death, in the uniform of a German officer, sits astride a wildly galloping horse while holding a bomb. This frightening figure is accompanied by caricatures of Hitler, Hirohito, and Mussolini. Though Schreckengost was discouraged from using such subject matter by many, he successfully used humor to draw attention to the seriousness of the current political situation.

Another Cleveland artist who studied at the Wiener Kunstgewerbeschüle was Russell Barnett Aitken. Like Schreckengost, he produced stylized and humorous figurative sculptures, using imagery characteristic of the Cleveland school—

Viktor Schreckengost. *Apocalypse '42.* 1941. Red clay, engobe, with colored glazes, 16 x 20". Permanent collection, Renwick Gallery, Smithsonian Institution, Washington, D.C.

Russell Barnett Aitken. *Student Singers*. 1934. Earthenware, 12 x 12 x 5½". Everson Museum of Art, Syracuse, New York. Gift of the artist

mythological characters, black figures (he collected African sculpture), and animals—while adding his own unique stamp to the work. His *Student Singers* (1934) is a reminiscence of his student days in Vienna, when he was an honorary member of the dueling society Corps Hilaritas. In this sculpture, three duelists, dressed in the uniforms of the society, belt out a song over frothy mugs of beer, the repetitive diagonals of their legs and swords uniting the composition and generating a sense of movement. This piece has the lightheartedness, color, and plasticity typical of the works of the Cleveland school during this period.

Aitkin's *Futility of a Well-Ordered Life* (1935) is a tongue-in-cheek jab at artist-celebrity Salvador Dali. Aitken admired the work of Dali but was tired of the ongoing publicity surrounding the Surrealist's antics during a visit to New York. His response was to create what he described as "a bit of surrealism to end all surrealism."[7] The sculpture is a spoof of Dali's portrait of his wife in which she appears with lamb chops on her shoulders and, at her side, a bureau shape that was removed from her abdomen. Aitken's figure repeats the lamb-chop motif. She has clocks for breasts, and a section of her midriff has been removed and a vase placed in the resulting niche. A swag of mice drapes her abdomen, and football players on roller skates whiz across the base. The elongated figure is Viennese in style, with opaque glazes and applied decoration.

The figures of Thelma Frazier Winter are among the most "Viennese" of any produced by Americans in the 1930s. Although she never traveled to Vienna, her husband, Edward Winter, an enamelist from Cleveland, did study there, and she would have seen Austrian work in any number of exhibitions and galleries in the United States. Many of her figures, such as *The Sirens* (c. 1937) and *Marguerita and the Jewels* (1936–37), are much like those of Reni Schaschl, who studied at the Kunstgewerbeschüle and later worked at the Werkstätte and the Werkbund in Vienna. *The Sirens* is in the Austrian manner, formed as masks, with hair, fish, starfish, and a boat added as sculptural decoration. The modeling and the glazing are loose and summarily handled, calling attention to the tactility of the material and the process by which the work was created. *Marguerita and the Jewels* is another early piece that clearly illustrates the influence of the Austrian school on Winter's work. The figure is slim and elongated, with an opaque white glaze and details, such as the supporting *bocage,* added rather than modeled as part of the form; the almond-shaped eyes with high, arching brows, and the small, pinched mouth are typical of Viennese figures. Winter was aware that she and her colleagues were pioneers in the field of clay sculpture. Commenting on the work produced during this period, she said, "Much of the thinking has been experimental, a search to find out just what ceramic sculpture should be, an effort to make it grow up as a fine art."[8]

The Cleveland School was the first identifiable, cohesive group of ceramists to work in a particular style in the United States (aside from the art potteries, which were commercial ventures, and Native American potters). These young ceramists enthusiastically explored the medium, extended their knowledge and creative spirit to others through teaching and publications, and vigorously supported the Ceramic National Exhibitions as artists, jurors, and advisors. They were the nucleus around which the fledgling studio ceramics movement developed.

DIVERSITY IN AMERICAN CLAY SCULPTURE

Although the Cleveland artists formed a unified group, there was actually great diversity in American clay sculpture during this period. Alexander Archipenko worked in an abstract modernist idiom, while Elie Nadelman's small figurative works were conceived quite expressionistically. Isamu Noguchi, who had studied with Constantin Brancusi in Paris, created abstracted figures inspired by early Haniwa sculpture, using the traditional methods of the Japanese potter to produce sculpture that combined the Eastern and European modernist idioms. Bernard Frazier's large stoneware animals of the 1930s embody the spirit of the American prairie in much the same manner as a Regionalist painting.

Waylande Gregory is an important yet enigmatic figure in twentieth-century American ceramics. He defies categorization, for he never developed a consistent style, nor was his work consistently of the same quality. He was, however, invariably in the forefront of ceramic activity. His works range from lyrical portrait busts in the Renaissance style to sculptures for public works, from the energetic Art Deco figurines done for the Cowan Pottery Studio to animal sculptures reflecting his Kansas origins.

After leaving Cowan, Gregory taught briefly at the Cranbrook Academy of Art before establishing his own studio. To sustain himself financially, he designed limited-edition table settings, but his passion was large-scale figural clay sculpture. In 1939, Gregory created four monumental figures, representing the four elements, for *The Fountain of the Atom* at the New York World's Fair. They are surrounded by smaller "electrons"—eight childlike figures reminiscent of the putti that gambol about in Renaissance and Baroque paintings. Although many of Gregory's figures derive from more traditional sources, his approach to the medium was wholly modernist, and in his larger works he pushed clay to its limits, inventing unique methods of construction utilizing the clay itself for structural support.

THE CERAMIC NATIONAL EXHIBITIONS

The Ceramic National Exhibitions were initiated in 1932 with the opening of the "Robineau Memorial Exhibition" in Syracuse, New York. Anna Witherell Olmstead, the director of the Syracuse Museum of Fine Arts (now the Everson Museum of Art), mounted a juried exhibition open to ceramists working in New York State, in memory of Syracuse artist Adelaide Alsop Robineau. The exhibition was so successful that Olmstead was encouraged by Guy Cowan and other museum supporters to make it an annual event open to ceramic artists across the country.[9]

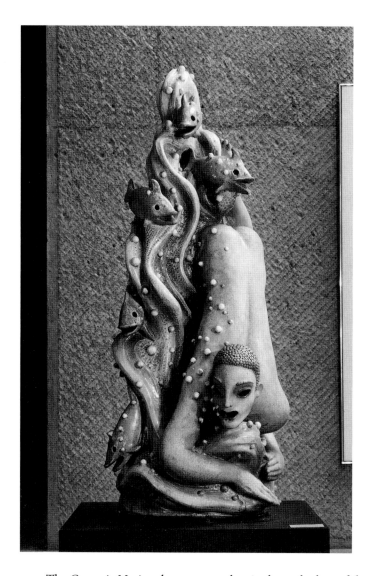

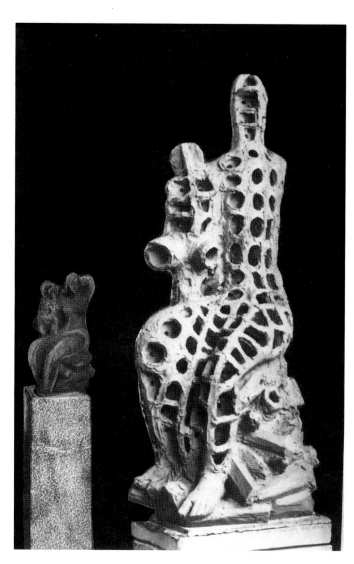

Waylande DeSantis Gregory. *"Water"* from *The Fountain of the Atom*. 1938. Stoneware, 6' x 39" x 35". Estate of Yolanda Gregory

Waylande DeSantis Gregory. Cellular inner structure of clay for *Mother and Child*. c. 1938. 6' x 34" x 32". As the clay hardened, additional clay was added until the figure was finished. This method used no support system other than the honeycombed clay structure itself.

The Ceramic Nationals were a catalyst in the early days of the modern ceramics movement in this country. In addition to providing a place for ceramists to show their work—few museums or galleries then exhibited ceramics—they provided a forum for the exchange of ideas and the discussion of the latest styles and techniques. In the days before color reproductions and media coverage were common, these exhibitions and discussion groups were vitally important in the dissemination of information.

Some of the most significant entries in the early Ceramic Nationals came from the pueblos of the Southwest. Maria Povera Martinez, of San Ildefonso Pueblo, sent three entries to the Second Ceramic National in 1933, and other Pueblo potters soon followed. There had been a revival in Native American potterymaking in the 1920s. Initially a re-creation of traditional forms and designs, it inevitably led to the introduction of new forms and more modern decorative motifs influenced by contemporary American and European design. Maria Martinez and her husband, Julian, abandoned their traditional polychrome wares and concentrated on the burnished blackwares for which they are now well known, adapting indigenous designs from objects found in ancient Pueblo ruins and combining them with modern motifs. These Native American wares were popular with collectors not only for their intrinsic values but also because their geometric motifs—zigzags, feather-and-wing designs, step motifs, and parallel lines—lent themselves to current Art Deco schemes.

This new interest in Native American pottery signaled another aspect of American ceramics to emerge in the period between the wars. The instability of the Depression years led to a rediscovery of America's cultural heritage—a con-

Waylande DeSantis Gregory. *Light Dispelling Darkness*. 1937. The fountain was created for the grounds of the Roosevelt Hospital in New Brunswick, New Jersey. It depicted in relief men whose technological inventions advanced civilization; these figures were surrounded by smaller sculptures representing War, Famine, Pestilence, Death, Greed, and Materialism. The original sculpture was destroyed by vandals.

scious effort to strengthen national unity through the collective embrace of that which is uniquely American. Regionalist painters Thomas Hart Benton, Grant Wood, and John Steuart Currey, and writers William Faulkner, Sinclair Lewis, and Thomas Wolfe, among others, portrayed what they saw as this country's heartland—its small towns and rural landscapes. Like the American Scene painters, a number of ceramists explored indigenous subject matter. Don Schreckengost and Hunt Diederich, using large plates rather than canvas as supports, painted cowboy scenes. Viktor Schreckengost and Edris Eckhardt portrayed Johnny Appleseed and Huckleberry Finn in clay. Folk pottery, especially that of the Appalachian highlands of Tennessee, inspired Edwin A. and Mary Goldsmith Scheier. They continued to produce vessels and functional wares in this idiom, even after they were transplanted to New England, where they taught at the University of New Hampshire at Durham.

In the 1920s, the growing pride of African-Americans in their heritage resulted in the Harlem Renaissance, an outpouring of new music, literature, and art. Sargent Johnson, who was active in the projects of the WPA, made figurative sculptures in wood and clay. Like many of the European abstractionists, he looked to non-Western art for inspiration, finding it in Africa, Asia, and Latin America. William E. Artis studied at the New York Art Students League, at Alfred University, and with Augusta Savage, an influential sculptor and teacher, in Harlem. Primarily a sculptor of figurative works in clay, Artis also handcrafted ceramic vessels in a modernist idiom. Both Johnson and Artis were recognized by having works accepted in the Ceramic National Exhibitions.

For some, like the ceramist Glen Lukens, the search for new forms of expression ended in the very earth of the country itself. Based in Los Angeles, Lukens explored the deserts and mountains of the West to find materials for his clay bodies and glazes. He ultimately developed a technique that exploited the characteristics of the clay and accented the viscosity of the glazes, allowing him to create free-form vessels with sensuous, tactile surfaces.

THE WORKS PROGRESS ADMINISTRATION FEDERAL ART PROJECTS

A positive outcome of the Depression was the number of public art projects sponsored by the various federally funded relief agencies established under the New Deal. One of the most successful of these projects was directed by Edris Eckhardt, a ceramist who had studied at the Cleveland School of Art and later worked at the Cowan Pottery Studio. Under the aegis of the Works Progress Administration (WPA), Eckhardt created a workshop environment in which artists in all media learned the basics of ceramic production, from moldmaking and finishing to glazing and painting. Eckhardt and her team designed and produced several series of small, meticulously crafted figurines, at first individually sculpted and then mold-formed, of characters drawn from American folklore, nursery rhymes, and literature, including Lewis Carroll's *Alice in Wonderland* and works by Charles Dickens, Rudyard Kipling, and others. Vases and bookends were produced as well. In each case, the size of the piece was dictated by the project kiln facilities.

Eckhardt also created larger sculptural works. *Earth* (1939), a sculpture in the Art Deco style but with Viennese overtones, was commissioned as part of the WPA Federal Art Project. For the WPA Ohio Art Program, Eckhardt, Henry Keto, Alexander Blazys, and others produced sculpted relief panels and decorative tiles depicting the history of Cleveland and other, more general subject matter for the exteriors of two housing developments, Valleyview and Woodhill Homes, in the Cleveland area.

The Art Deco style prevailed in many of the monumental clay sculptures produced under these federal programs. The massive neoclassical figures seemed most appropriate for government-sponsored projects, although many artists also worked independent of this style. Waylande Gregory's fountain group *Light Dispelling Darkness* (1937), commissioned for the grounds of Roosevelt Hospital in New Brunswick, New Jersey, took its inspiration from Thomas Edison, whose laboratory had been located in nearby Menlo Park. Gregory combined familiar Art Deco imagery—skyscrapers, lightning bolts, wavy lines of clouds, and allegorical figures—to represent Man's hopes for advancing civilization through the use of technology. Thousands of artists across the country participated in such government-sponsored production, and the ceramics projects were among the most successful.

BAUHAUS PRINCIPLES AND AMERICAN CERAMICS

The influence of the Bauhaus on American ceramics was less direct than that of Vienna, but no less strong. Its principal contribution, however, was a philosophy rather than a style, the theoretical basis for which was the unification of the arts and industry. Founder Walter Gropius emphasized the teaching of craftsmanship, which he believed should be put in the service of industry, and saw no essential difference between the artist and the craftsperson: "The artist is an exalted craftsman. . . . Proficiency in his craft is essential to every artist. Therein lies a source of creative imagination. . . . Let us create a new guild of craftsmen, without the class distinctions which raise an arrogant barrier between craftsman and artist."[10]

At the Bauhaus pottery studio, located 25 kilometers outside Weimar, in Dornburg, students learned the technical aspects of potterymaking from Max

Krehan, the Workshop Master, whose roots were in the Thuringian folk tradition;[11] and design from the historicist Gerhard Marcks, the Master of Form.[12] Most of the objects produced there were hand-thrown, and there was little initial interest in design for industry. In 1923, the studio was divided into separate workshops for technique and production, the latter focused on the creation of designs suitable for mass production. The forms produced in this workshop are in accordance with the dictums of simplicity and utility that are usually thought of in association with the Bauhaus, while the hand-thrown forms, in keeping with Gropius's philosophy of remaining true to the material at hand, exploit the expressive qualities of the clay.

The Bauhaus sought to unite art and industry in order to create objects that were both useful and beautiful. In this the school was not unique. What *was* exceptional was the speed with which its ideas were disseminated and accepted throughout both Europe and the United States.

Marguerite Wildenhain studied at the Bauhaus from 1919 to 1926, and when she arrived in the United States in 1940 she brought with her the Bauhaus tradition of functional pottery, both handcrafted and mass-produced. At first, she created designs for industry in the modernist style, but she later eschewed mass-production techniques in favor of a more expressive personal style, returning to the hand-thrown vessels that she had produced under Krehan. Her work exhibits a reverence for the nature of the clay and an unwavering dedication to functional pottery. Her concepts of ceramics and ceramics education—indeed, her whole way of life—were widely emulated by the students who attended her workshops at Pond Farm in Guerneville, California.

Perhaps the most obvious area of modernist influence, Bauhaus or otherwise, was in production pottery. The emphasis is placed on form and the avoidance of surface decoration in Frederick Hurten Rhead's Fiestaware (1936), produced by the Laughlin China Company; Eva Zeisel's Museum White (1943), made by Castleton China Company in 1946; and Russel Wright's American Modern (1937), produced by Steubenville Pottery beginning in 1939. The design decisions were in keeping with the tenets of the Bauhaus and other modernist schools: In each case, form was dictated by the object's function, and by the practical considerations of mass production. It was in these objects, particularly the elementary white forms favored by Zeisel, that the Bauhaus manifesto—"Art and technology, the new unity"[13]—was most fully realized.

OTHER EUROPEAN SOURCES OF MODERNIST INFLUENCE

The classicism of the modern style was never more clearly displayed than in the forms and glazes of the works produced by the Austrian ceramists Gertrud and Otto Natzler, who emigrated to the United States in 1939. Gertrud's thin-walled, elegantly formed vessels were the perfect complement to Otto's sensuous and inventive glazes. The malleability of the clay, the spin of the wheel, the vagaries of the kiln—all were vital to the realization of their work.

Majlis (Maija) Grotell, a Finnish émigré, brought another version of modernism to the American ceramics scene. Grotell taught at the Cranbrook Academy from 1938 to 1966, a period during which the name Cranbrook became synonymous with the best in ceramics education. She was important both as a teacher and as an artist. The vessels she produced during the 1930s and 1940s are simple but strong in form and often decorated with abstracted images of the urban industrial landscape—skyscrapers and factory smokestacks—similar to those in the paintings of Lyonel Feininger and Charles Demuth. Many of her stu-

Gertrud Natzler and Otto Natzler. *Bowl.* 1943. Earthenware; gray lavastone glaze with turquoise overflow, 3½ x 8½". Los Angeles County Museum of Art. Gift of Rose A. Sperry 1972 Revocable Trust

dents went on to become important teachers and/or ceramists in their own rights.

The English ceramist Sam Haile introduced the freedom of European expressionism to American ceramics. Working at Alfred University—then the bastion of conservatism in the field of American ceramics—Haile created freely thrown vessels decorated with amorphous linear figures influenced by Surrealism. His work was not in the "classic" Bauhaus tradition; rather, it spoke of other solutions to the problems of modern utilitarian design.

Modernism, then, appeared in American ceramics in many guises; in each, it proposed solutions to questions raised by young ceramists in the years following World War I. The limited editions produced at the Cowan Pottery Studio and the freedom granted to the young artists working there helped bridge the gap between the production pottery of the Arts and Crafts era and the emerging studio pottery movement. These young ceramists looked to Vienna for answers to their questions about what modern clay sculpture should be, and about the role of the medium in the creation of a work of art. Later, the Bauhaus influence united art with industry, bringing a more pragmatic approach to ceramics and reviving interest in the vessel form. The advent of modernist thinking and practices helped bring American ceramics out of the art pottery and into the studio, the factory, the marketplace, and the museum.

TEXTILES: SURFACE, STRUCTURE, AND SERIAL PRODUCTION

by Mary Schoeser

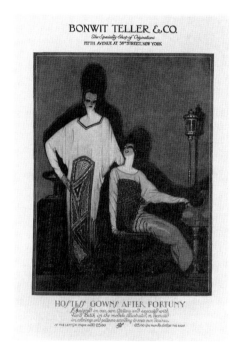

From *Arts and Decoration* (October 1922)

Manufacturing depression seems to have been handmade's opportunity, for never, even in "normal" times, has there been such marked steps forward in beauty and practicality. . . . The value of the handmade is first of all that it is handmade, next that if directed it sets the standard for manufacture.[1]

These remarks, made in 1921, identify the two most significant factors in the development of American handmade textiles in the years 1920–45. The first was the awareness that industrial production and hand production were to be inextricably linked; the second, and often contested, factor was the perception that handmade was better than machine-made. Exploring these issues is therefore essential to laying a foundation for the study of American textile arts of this period. Doing so relies on period commentaries that inevitably use the term "art" in place of "craft"—a choice that in itself was an important indicator of a mindset that allowed for both the elevated status of handmade objects and their use as prototypes for industry.

By 1920, "art" and "industry" had become paired, most notably in the work of the Wiener Werkstätte (founded 1903) and the Deutscher Werkbund in Berlin (1907). The latter was the first to have as a stated aim the reconciliation of craft, art, and industry, although by 1904, textiles and carpets were being manufactured from prototypes handmade by Werkstätte members Josef Hoffmann and Koloman Moser as well as by their students at the Vienna Kunstgewerbeschüle. Both the Werkbund and the Werkstätte were to influence American textile design. Of the two, the Vienna group held sway in the 1920s. The style was already well known in the United States through exhibitions; the much-feted but short-lived Werkstätte showroom in New York, opened by Joseph Urban in 1923; and the rugs and interiors of Wolfgang and Pola Hoffmann[2] and the textile designs of Urban and Werkstätte alumnus Valerie (Vally) Wieselthier.[3]

The Werkstätte represented both an idea and a style, but other Europeans were more influential in their exploration of technique, from the timeless handscreened and blockprinted fabrics of Fortuny, to the simple cloths woven of handspun and -dyed yarns at Gospels, the important English workshop founded in 1920 by Ethel Mairet. Batik on silk had been introduced into the United States by the Dutch shortly after 1902; the technique's application to different cloths was promoted in the 1920s by the atelier of Mme Pagnon in Paris. Also in France, Paul Rodier had become known for his technically inventive mixed-fiber fabrics; Bianchini-Férier for their intricate Jacquard handwoven silks; and Paul Poiret's Atelier Martine for its handpainted and -printed textiles. The Werkbund directly influenced Poiret, among others, but perhaps of equal importance in terms of the evolution of American textiles was the Werkbund's contribution to the founding of the Bauhaus. Bauhaus principles made the transatlantic crossing in the 1930s, arriving along with large numbers of European émigrés, including weavers Anni Albers and Marli Ehrmann. The immigration of European artists, designers, and craftspeople is another subtext critical to the development of American textiles. Far from having to till a lonely furrow, those who arrived after 1920 met with well-prepared ground.

In 1915 a group representing art and industry was assembled in New York by M.D.C. Crawford, research associate at the American Museum of Natural History; E. W. Fairchild, publisher of *Women's Wear;* and Albert Blum, partner in a Lyonnaise dye house and treasurer of the New Jersey silk firm United Piece Dye Works. Members of this working group included Richard F. Bach,[4] The Metropolitan Museum of Art; Harry Neyland, Swain Free School of Design; F. W. Purdy, Art Alliance of America; the artist Charles Prendergast; and representatives from the silk manufacturers Cheney Brothers, the silk printers H. R. Mallinson and Company, and the influential manufacturers/retailers B. Altman, Marshall Field, and Bonwit Teller.

Plate from *Women's Wear,* 1922; reproduced in *One World of Fashion* (4th edition, 1987)

Starting from the premise that the U.S. textile industry should make use of American collections of non-European objects as design sources, the group "published in *Women's Wear* and elsewhere information to the designers advising them of the great facilities before them. Next, a little booklet was prepared showing the technical details of mechanical patternmaking, and finally . . . a nation-wide contest in design [was] organized with the assistance of the art schools of America."[5] The juried Textile Design Competitions were held annually from 1916 to 1920. Among the entrants were many whose work is now widely recognized: Hazel Burnham Slaughter, Marion Dorn, Zoltan Hecht, Ilonka Karasz, Pieter Mijer, Winold Reiss, Ruth Reeves, Martha Ryther, and Marguerite Zorach. But there were many others: The 1920 competition attracted submissions from one thousand artists in thirty-four states and Canada.[6] A supplemental competition, named after Blum, was organized for finished fabrics, rather than designs on paper.

The initial impetus for the competitions, lectures, exhibitions, and articles that continued to be promoted by this group throughout the 1920s and 1930s was partly pure commercialism. As a result of World War I, the textile industry no longer had easy access to its European design sources. However, the Americans' desire for self-sufficiency had an idealistic element that was shared by many others, including George G. Booth, founder of the Cranbrook Academy of Art; and Albert Herter, founder of Herter Looms, who in the immediate postwar period discussed the "creation of truly American artistic expressions."[7] (Not surprisingly, Herter, a muralist and portrait painter who designed both tapestries and fabrics, was among the jurors and sponsors of the competitions.)

Artists searching for a new, distinctly American aesthetic had turned for inspiration to the arts of non-European cultures—just as their European counterparts had. Over the next twenty-five years, American artists created an independent style that took inspiration from textiles indigenous to the Americas, Africa, and the Pacific Rim, developing abstract idioms paralleling those of Europe. In the 1920s, printed patterns were derived from sources as diverse as Congo cloths, tapa cloths, and Cheyenne beadwork. Léon Bakst promoted the use of Native American designs in particular, creating Hopi Indian Motives for Mallinson's in 1927. Bakst's fabrics are believed to have spurred Winold Reiss's

Lorentz Kleiser. *Central Park*. c. 1926.
Tapestry

Tom Jones. "Machine Age," student design.
From *Design* (April 1934)

interest in similar motifs.[8] Reiss, an Austrian émigré perhaps better known for his later interiors, produced blockprinted textiles in addition to designing rugs.

Many American textiles attest to the influence of urban life. The heroic skyline of Manhattan was the subject of works by Lydia Bush-Brown, Slaughter, Reeves, and Zorach, as well as Clayton Knight, whose fabrics were machine-printed by Stehli Silks. Edgewater Tapestry Looms, founded by the Austrian émigré artist Lorentz Kleiser, explored both historical themes—for example, Kleiser's tapestry series based on the stories of Washington Irving—and contemporary ones such as a child playing in New York's Central Park.[9] Pride in American achievements, both past and present, was expressed in images ranging from covered wagons[10] to oil wells, the latter used by Brents Carlton as the inspiration for a batik of about 1927. The new relationship between industry and art was literally expressed in Marshall Fields's Speed Age collection of printed silks (1929). In 1934, University of Kansas students created a series of textile designs with "machine age motifs" representing electricity, light, power, movement, and traffic.[11] These textiles often incorporate pictorial elements associated with modern music and dance that are bold, brash, and rhythmic. Symbols of modern American urban life also appear as purely abstract pattern, exemplified by the Rhythmic series of handmade textiles by Henriette Reiss. These design trends paralleled developments in Europe, again suggesting that the vigor of the American campaign for self-sufficiency must be borne in mind if balanced conclusions are to be reached about the impact of European modernism on American textiles.

Finally, American life itself was an element of the new "primitivism"—the co-option of more primal forms in modern dance, music, and art—celebrated by the European avant-garde and fashionable society alike, evident even at the most trivial level. For example, in the vivid new colorings of Fair Isle handknits, called "jazz patterns," the pervasive influence of American taste was evident. It was also American taste that helped support avant-garde developments in European textiles. Until the Depression, Americans collectively represented the most powerful buying force. American patronage was particularly important for European haute couture, especially that of France, which fashioned its garments from handmade and hand-decorated cloths. This symbiotic relationship insured that European modernism would shape American tastes and be dependent upon them as well.

Such comparisons highlight the need to outline the relationship between Europe's own industry and craft, especially the meaning of U.S. textile manufacturers' traditional dependence upon French design. Great Britain was the first country to industrialize textile manufacture, but by 1920, Europe still had not. Thus the art-into-industry movement had a significance for Great Britain that it did not have on the continent.

In 1920, U.S. cotton production was more than double that of Great Britain, but the United States was not competitive in the production of wool or linen.[12] In addition, seventy percent of the Asian raw silk produced was sold to the United States, which processed more silk than any other country. Yet Lyons alone was exporting $11 million in handmade silks to the States, in the form of couture garments and lengths of cloth. In financial terms, French imports were dwarfed by the machine production of American silks—their value was nearly seventy times greater—and whatever the fiber, all the domestic markets, save those for luxury goods, were served by U.S. manufacturers. Nevertheless, the "best"—as defined by what the avant-garde and social elite purchased—was still European, which meant that many inexpensive, machine-made American textiles carried designs copied or purchased from Europe.

U.S. manufacturers were confident of the technical quality of their textiles.

In 1921, M. D. C. Crawford asserted on their behalf, "Silks made on a modern loom moving with incomprehensible speed can have the same charms as if made by the tedious technology of inserting each cross thread by hand. Silk printing on a modern roller printing machine can have the same quality of drawing and colour as silk decorated laboriously by hand from blocks of teak wood."[13] Nevertheless, the required aesthetic quality had to be rooted in art.

Artists had long provided imagery for textile manufacturers. Interest in American hand-decorated fabrics grew out of the desire, as Crawford put it, "to find designers rather than to secure designs."[14] And this is precisely what happened. Ryther went on to work on a free-lance basis for Belding Brothers, a leading American silk printing firm. By the end of the decade, Du Pont, the giant man-made fiber producer, was promoting its products through the use of designs by, among others, Ruth Reeves.

Until about 1928, hand-batiked fabrics dominated the Blum competitions and major exhibitions, and captured the interest of stores and journals. In that year, Bertram Hartman was singled out as "a most versatile talent . . . more generally known as a painter than as a decorator of fabrics or a designer of mosaics."[15] Hartman, Lydia Bush-Brown, Arthur Crisp, Dent Daniels, and Erika Lohmann had shown wall hangings in R. H. Macy's 1927 "Exposition of Art in Trade," which was given "the greatest credit for the rapid and general acceptance by the American producer and consumer of the modern note" within the previous year.[16]

Others who had previously worked in batik—Ilonka Karasz and Marguerite Zorach—were soon occupied elsewhere. By the late 1920s, the Hungarian-born Karasz was better known for her rugs, furniture, and designs for tapestry and embroidery, the latter worked by her sister Mariska.[17] Zorach, too, turned to embroidery. In 1935, her place as a leading exponent of "needlepainting" was confirmed with a retrospective at the Brummer Gallery, New York.[18] Reeves spent the years 1920–27 in Paris, where she studied with Fernand Léger, and became recognized for her hand-screenprinted textiles.[19]

Marguerite Zorach. *The Circus*. c. 1929. Wool on unbleached linen, 20½ x 22½". The Metropolitan Museum of Art, New York. Gift of Irwin Untermyer, 1964 (64.101.1404)

These artists had in common contact with Europe and training as painters. Zorach, a native of California, studied in Paris. Bush-Brown, whose parents were professional artists, studied at the Pratt Institute in Brooklyn, and her extensive travels included Syria.[20] Slaughter studied in Paris on a Cheney scholarship in 1922.[21] European modernism thus was observed first-hand or in the work of émigré designers in the United States.

For handmade textiles, the years 1920–28 were buoyant. They received widespread support from public and private patrons as well as from industry, particularly manufacturers of printed fashion fabrics. In the prosperous postwar years up to late 1921, industry was confident of its ability to use art to gain not only the remaining U.S. markets but the European ones as well.[22] In the next two years an oversupply of American textiles pushed prices down, but with the postwar building boom and the well-documented stir caused by the Paris Exposition Internationale des Arts Décoratifs et Industriels Modernes in 1925, the industry regained confidence and the subject of modern design received a wide airing. (It was in 1925, for example, that Stehli Silks introduced its Americana series of machine-printed, artist-designed silks.) All of these factors favored craftspeople who could provide art for industry. Their products, manufactured in limited quantities and less prone to devaluation, suited the desire for low-risk merchandising; and stores, galleries, museums, private patrons, and the expanding number of journals could use well-selected crafts to establish their commitment to modernism.

Until the Depression, the foremost concern among makers of textiles was surface imagery. Bush-Brown referred to her work as silk murals,[23] and although Zorach later made clear that she saw her embroideries as something quite separate from painting,[24] in general it was true that batik, embroidery, handprinting, and tapestry, while using different methods, shared an affinity with painting that enhanced the status of the objects. Their function was to carry images, a factor of particular importance in a period largely devoid of color reproductions; as one journal noted, "There is no doubt but that it is through fabrics that the art of today can most readily become known to the great public and influence its taste."[25]

As European modernism began to meld with influences from textiles indigenous to the Americas, the dominance of abstract images shifted the emphasis from surface imagery to the fibers and construction of the textile itself. Architecture replaced art as the muse for textiles. Tapestry floundered, withdrawing behind the edifice of the easel and relying even more heavily on the exact replication of artists' cartoons. In 1933, Edgewater Tapestry Looms closed.[26] That same year, Marie Cuttoli commissioned from Aubusson a series of tapestries designed by artists who, Jean Lurçat and Joan Miró excepted, condemned the technique to a period of lifelessness.[27] In 1939, Dorothy Wright Liebes included these tapestries in the textile section of the Golden Gate International Exposition in San Francisco. She granted that their impact was dependent upon "amazing cartoons by masters of art," but added as a cautionary note, "We should regard tapestry as a bona fide textile expression, not as a painting."[28]

In contrast, the techniques that readily were adapted to the new aesthetic were rugmaking, weaving, and hand-screenprinting, all of which were suited to the economic and ideological trends of 1930–45. Rugs were thrown into the spotlight of the "post-Paris" exhibitions held throughout the United States from 1926 to 1928. One of these, organized by Cuttoli and shown at the Arts Club of Chicago and at Lord & Taylor in New York, included Myrbor rugs handtufted in Algiers to designs by, among others, Léger, Lurçat, Louis Marcoussis, and Pablo Picasso. The artists were described as "well known and . . . the mainstay of such modern exhibitions of French art as have been shown in America."[29] Handtufted

French rugs could also be purchased at department stores such as B. Altman & Company. Their dominance of the U.S. market was such that one observer commented, "The plain carpet is the haven to which would-be modernists in America fly, if they cannot find a French rug that seems exactly to suit."[30]

If this was true in early 1928, it was not some few months later, when the designer and critic C. Adolph Glassgold observed, "There exists at present The New Age Group which employs the craftsmen of North Carolina to execute rugs designed by artists like Thomas Benton, George Biddle and Ilonka Karasz, and which expects to extend its operation to other decorative crafts."[31] Also known as New-Age Workers and the Blue Ridge Mountains Group, this collaborative project was organized by Zolton and Rosa Pringle Hecht. At the same time, hand-hooked rugs were being made to artists' designs by the New England Guild in Portland, Maine.

In 1929, the Metropolitan Museum featured American and European handmade rugs in their annual industrial design exhibition. A year later, The Newark Museum exhibited rugs by Donald Deskey, Lurçat, the influential Swedish studio of Marte Maas-Fjetterstrom, Poiret, Henry Varnum Poor, Reeves, Henriette Reiss, and Joseph Urban, as well as historical examples.[32] By 1931, *Creative Art* could record, ". . . of growing significance in the contemporary rug design in this country is the work of some of the small groups of craft workers, often directed by a designer who encourages originality or supplies patterns."[33] And in 1937, the Crawford Shops, New York, would produce rugs designed by Deskey, Poor, Walter Dorwin Teague, Sr., and Zorach for an exhibition at The Museum of Modern Art. The catalogue describes Poor as a painter and ceramist, Reeves as a designer, and Zorach, a painter.[34]

The superimposition of art—or design—onto rugmaking was in keeping with the current view of craft in the United States. Craft collectives were seen as the vehicle capable of carrying modernity to a wide market. As the reviewer of the Newark show said of the modern handmade rugs, ". . . when one talks of beauty and economy and mass production, it is [with] excitement."[35] No conflict was seen in the inclusion of handmade textiles in the many exhibitions that promoted industrial design in the 1930s and 1940s, partly because the trend toward serial production was in keeping with the nature of much modern European production.[36]

Exhibition of floor coverings at The Newark Museum, 1930. Wall-mounted rugs designed by Henry Varnum Poor; chair by Donald Deskey; flower stand and table by Eugene Schoen

Exhibition of floor coverings at The Newark Museum, 1930. Chenille rug on the floor designed by Joseph Urban; rug mounted on the wall at left from the studio of Paul Poiret, and at right, a rug designed by Henriette Reiss

But craftsmanship combined with a modern aesthetic survived, not only through the many projects set up by the Works Progress Administration and independent craft collectives and guilds between 1935 and 1942 but also in a form that more truly integrated design and production, epitomized by the handwoven rugs of Studio Loja Saarinen and the Cranbrook weaving department. Saarinen's rugs were created within set parameters. They were "always simple and impersonal in design as befits a floor covering in a contemporary house. More than this, they bespeak the contemporary spirit in their clean, logical patterns which impart a sense of great beauty and strength because of their definitely architectural quality."[37]

The history of Studio Loja Saarinen and the weaving workshop at the Cranbrook Academy of Art is well known.[38] So, too, is that of Black Mountain College, where Anni Albers taught weaving from 1934 to 1949.[39] László Moholy-Nagy's creation of the New Bauhaus in Chicago, and the subsequent founding of the Chicago School of Design, where Marli Ehrmann taught weaving from 1939 to 1947,[40] is also well documented. All were concerned with creating utilitarian fabrics suited to modern architecture and, as Marianne Strengell put it in 1942, with "texture, color and quality."[41] Cranbrook, where Strengell taught beginning in 1937, represented modern Swedish textile design (an extrapolation from peasant weaves); Black Mountain and the Chicago School, the design principles of the Bauhaus (the exploration of the ahistorical and nonpictorial). These institutions significantly contributed to the development of American textiles, both hand- and machine-made. However, the influence of their cloth weaving was not felt immediately, nor were their weavers, including Maja Andersson Wirde, who arrived at Cranbrook in 1929, among the first to stress materials and texture over pattern.

In 1924, Maria Kipp immigrated from Munich, where she had studied at the Kunstgewerbeschüle. She was reportedly the first woman to attend the textile school in Muenchberg, Bavaria, where the weaving course covered "all the processes involved from spinning yarn to finishing cloth and the absolute control and understanding of both the hand and the power loom."[42] Through her Los Angeles workshop Kipp built a reputation for innovative handwoven furnishing fabrics, which she custom-designed for decorators and architects.

When Kipp arrived in the United States, the most influential modern European weaves were undoubtedly the imports of Paul Rodier, who was famous for his subtle cotton and mixed-fiber fabrics. Woven and embroidered by an exten-

Maria Kipp at her loom, c. 1940s

sive network of cottage workers, they ranged from the semi-sheer to the densely textured, and reflected the influence on Rodier of French colonial cloths such as *sambots* (Cambodian *ikat* cloth).[43] By 1928, "Rodier fabrics" had become a generic term for modern weaves[44] (which may have prompted Dorothy Liebes to spend the following year in Rodier's Paris atelier).

Rodier made little use of silk in his highly textured cloths. This fiber—hand-painted, machine-printed, or woven on a mechanized Jacquard loom—had been the major vehicle for American textile innovation in the 1920s. Cost-cutting during the Depression and the introduction of improved yarns in cotton, wool, and the man-made fibers viscose and acetate had diverted attention away from silk and its associated quality, smoothness. This change was supported by modernist trends in architecture, interiors, and furniture design: "One of the chief style trends encouraged by the deornamentalized 'functionalism' now so popular in Europe mainly by reason of the economies it involves, has been a seeking for varieties of textures in fabrics."[45] By 1934, the impact of new yarns and hand-weaving was apparent. Innovative cotton fabrics and "marvelous and original new weaves,"[46] often in "woven in combinations of unusual materials—chenille, metal thread, horsehair, [and] cellophane,"[47] had appeared. It was also recognized that the "expensive handloomed things from abroad which have been so greatly admired the past few years have left their mark on machine design. . . . Design has become as much a matter of structure and materials as of pattern. . . . No longer is mass production necessarily a synonym for bad design."[48]

Contributing to this trend were a number of artists represented at the Metropolitan Museum's exhibition of contemporary industrial art in 1934. The selection was made with the intent of illustrating "all the elements of modern craftsmanship, but under the general proviso that quantity is the gauge" and with the understanding that "serial production implies and requires specialized organization, not only of process but also of design, for design itself must be construed as a model." Included were fabrics by Deskey, the architect Gilbert Rohde in collaboration with Grete Franke (of the Willich-Franke Studios), and Eliel Saarinen (Cranbrook Looms). In addition, there was "a collection of modern textiles effective chiefly because of their texture,"[49] including a velvet designed by Juanita Todd.

With the widespread adoption of European trends in architecture and the political changes occurring in Europe itself, the United States became the hotbed

Corner of a living room, with fabrics by Paul Rodier and furniture designed by Paul Frankl. As published in Frankl, *New Dimensions* (1928)

Example by Nellie Sargent Johnson of a simple free-weaving technique known as the "laid-in" method. From *The Weaver* (January 1937)

for modern textile design. Another contributing factor was the increased interest in North and Latin American textiles, especially weaves. This was reflected in Ruth Reeves's study trip to Guatemala in 1934 and the subsequent exhibitions of native fabrics and the designs they inspired; and in Hilarie Hiler's anthropological study of tribal customs, *From Nudity to Raiment* (1930), and his 1934 design for an Aubusson tapestry based on Native American figures. Beginning in 1930, *The Handicrafter* and its successor, *The Weaver,* ran articles on Mexican, Peruvian, Chilean, Guatemalan, Navaho, and other American weaves. Mary M. Atwater, founder of the Shuttle-Craft Guild, noted in 1936 that "many of the decorative forms we label 'modernistic' and 'new art' today are curiously akin to the patterns of primitive decoration. And this does not appear to be due to imitation, but to be the outgrowth of the fresh, new attitude towards art. . . ."[50] Atwater also recommends Raoul d'Harcourt's 1934 publication on Peruvian textiles,[51] which were admired by many weavers. Both Albers and Nellie Sargent Johnson, a well-known weaver and writer who made a study trip to Peru in 1939, recognized the technical mastery of pre-Columbian weaves. Intrinsic parallels aside, the more general appreciation of textiles indigenous to the Americas also supported the more frequent choice of "coarser weaves with designs from native Indian blankets, upholstery which would be most effective in a sun-room where Navajo or other Indian floor coverings are used."[52]

In 1940, the Metropolitan Museum's fifteenth annual exhibition of industrial art included weaves by Saarinen and Strengell. The annual prompted an article in *The Weaver* that outlined the benefits of studying with Strengell, recommending the stimulation of "contact with one who occupies a high place in her field."[53] A more sculptural quality was now apparent in "the rough, nubby materials, often threaded with brilliant metal and . . . the spongy, loosely woven and ribbed fabrics in vigorous tones."[54] These are the weaves associated with Kipp and Liebes, both of whom were still working in California, the latter attaining celebrity status through her machine-produced designs for Good Fabrics. The wider influence of the Cranbrook, Black Mountain, and Chicago School of Design weaving departments was only just beginning to be felt.

In 1941, a debate between Albers and Atwater ran through the pages of *The Weaver.* Their views offer a window onto the dilemma that had been created by the need to "justify handcrafts in an industrial age."[55] Albers represented the designer-weaver, arguing that only speed differentiated hand- from machine-weaving. In her view, handweaving should be "conceived as a preparatory step to machine production" and so "take [a] responsible part in a new development."[56] Atwater, the older and at the time far more influential of the two artists, believed that the handmade object should have a unique appearance and essence. She stood for the "pleasure of creating—the artist's pleasure, the good craftsman's pleasure"; the "utility" of the artist's creation was "the greater comfort and seemliness of our lives" and "the value of this escape in hard and cruel times."[57] Associated as she was with instructional workshops, Atwater was stung by Albers's condemnation of "recipes . . . traditional formulas, which once proved successful." She responded: "'New exploring' is exciting, and is highly desirable if the explorer happens to be equipped with the technical knowledge and ability to take him somewhere, but the 'new exploring' of one not so equipped is no more than a clumsy fumbling, unlikely to produce anything of value."[58] Albers, in short, was an elitist, Atwater, an egalitarian.

The irony of their conflict is that Albers illustrated her article with work by Black Mountain students that looks remarkably like Bauhaus pieces of some fifteen years before. Ed Rossbach also observed at Cranbrook, where he was a student in the early 1940s, "a formula for producing 'contemporary weavings' that was not wholly unlike Mary Atwater's recipes."[59] Albers's article demonstrates an ignorance of American weaving that was to be found wherever geographical isolation combined with ideological commitment. At Cranbrook, for example, Strengell became head of the weaving department in 1942. She had been trained by Elsa Gullberg (who in the early 1930s was already handweaving prototypes for the Scandinavian industry). It was Strengell, rather than Albers or Ehrmann, who in 1945 installed a S1 powerloom selected by her teaching assistant and former student Robert D. Sailors, who had studied its use at the Rhode Island School of Design.[60] Sailors was familiar with Bauhaus architecture, but "was not aware of crafts anywhere" like those being produced at Cranbrook, and in his subsequent exploration of yarns exemplified Strengell's "idea, always, that you had to dig it

Rug designed by Marianne Strengell, 1938

119

Interior by George Farkas, with hand-screenprinted curtains by Dan Cooper, c. 1942. From *Interiors* (April 1945)

out of yourself."[61] Thus handweavers in whose work one could recognize the influence of European modernism demonstrated the diversity of modernist thinking, rather than adherence to one school of thought.

As was true for all textile crafts, the older U.S. colleges provided a reservoir of ideologies that supported the development of modernism in a way as yet not fully documented. Perhaps the best-known example is the Milwaukee State Teachers College. From 1935 to 1942 the college sponsored the WPA Milwaukee Handicraft Project, which was organized by staff member Elsa Ulbricht. Ulbricht, with Mary June Kellogg (Rice) as art director, implemented a program intended to "produce articles of superior quality and craftsmanship" to distribute to public institutions. "The word 'artistically,' was not used. . . . [This] was merely a program in the production of practical, useful things . . . [necessary to] fuller, richer living."[62] Ultimately, the project encompassed a range of objects, from dolls and furniture to block- and screenprints, hooked rugs, and textiles. For the latter, Ulbricht placed "emphasis not on the production of traditional patterns, but rather upon the fundamental technical possibilities and limitations of the loom and in the structure of fabrics through the use of a variety of yarns. . . . Waste materials from a carpet factory and ravelled burlap lent themselves very well to this idea."[63]

The American tradition of stencilling also contributed to the least understood development of this period—hand-screenprinting.[64] In both techniques, areas to remain uncolored are masked out. Like batik, they require little in the way of equipment, space, or financial investment, making them ideal for experimental work as well as for use in schools. Batik and screenprinting were in use in the 1920s, but the latter became more prevalent; it was faster than blockprinting and more suited to serial production than batik—factors of interest to textile companies as well as to individuals. Equally important was the ease with which highly textured ground cloths could be printed, as Reeves demonstrated when she used thirteen different cotton fabrics, including terry cloth and velvet, in a 1930 project for W. & J. Sloane.[65] By 1937, Reeves had collaborated with Robert McBraney (who handscreened her designs from a series of paintings of the Hudson River) and had played a pivotal role in the creation of the Federal Art Project's Index of American Design.

Although Reeves "[stood] out among American textile designers"[66] in the late 1930s, others were waiting in the wings. Estell and Erwine Laverne, a partnership "dedicated to merging the fine arts with applied design," created hand-screenprinted textiles through their firm, Laverne Originals.[67] The influence of modern architecture on textile design was represented by the work of Antonin Raymond, a Prague-born architect later associated with Frank Lloyd Wright. Raymond's screenprints illustrate the flexibility of the technique, with single-screen designs used alone or in overlapping patterns.

In 1943, the U.S. government asked "dealers and textile firms to give up copper printing rollers not in use last year."[68] The stock of patterns for machine printing was reduced just as wartime conditions were creating a ready market for American-made fabrics. Serial hand production of both printed and woven cloths flourished, and these were particularly heady days for hand-screenprinting. Not to be mechanized by manufacturers until after the war, screenprinting represented the most direct link among art, craft, and industry, and became the most visible expression, in textiles, of "that thing called 'American taste.' . . ."[69] In 1948, Angelo Testa articulated the philosophy that was expressed in his own work and that of Dan Cooper, Marion Dorn, Estelle and Erwine Laverne, Antonin Raymond, Ruth Reeves, and Ben Rose, among others: "Texture should be emphasized where the decorative function of the fabric is minimized, and color and form where the function is purely decorative."[70] These artists used hand-screenprinting to make marks uniquely suited to the process—marks that interact with the surface instead of merely being placed upon it. They explored a technique that was as untried in Europe as in the United States, and in so doing nurtured a new textile aesthetic through the years of World War II.

In a relationship with industry forged as much by U.S. economic and social trends as by European modernism, craft seemed at times to be in danger of becoming yoked to manufacturing during the interwar period. Yet in counterbalance was the very nature of European "mass production"; the determination of the craftspeople who explored their media on American soil and held that "the machine can do many things, but not the most important thing of all, that is, to think for us";[71] and the contradictory but equally inherent belief that we "are modern at heart and only too open to accept anything new; but [it] . . . must prove its practical and useful value and be rendered foolproof."[72] In the end, craft, in the development of prototypes by hand, and craftsmanship, in the creation of standards of excellence in the exploration of new fibers, weaves, and printing techniques, determined the parameters for the search for a modern idiom in textiles.

STRIKING THE MODERN NOTE IN METAL

by Jewel Stern

Marion Anderson Noyes. *Drawing for a Pewter Teapot with Mahogany Handles*. 1935. Pencil on paper, 10¼ x 13½". The Brooklyn Museum. Gift of Marion Anderson Noyes

American decorative arts underwent profound and swift stylistic changes in the period between the world wars. Arts and Crafts ideals prevailed until 1926, when French *art moderne* was introduced and enthusiastically adapted. The ferment in design subsided during the Depression, which brought the economy to a standstill in the early 1930s. When the recovery began in late 1933, the national mood was more sober, and designers turned to a lean, modern classicism, or streamlining, to express the Machine Age. Biomorphism emerged as an aesthetic later in the decade.

The acceleration of change from Arts and Crafts and historical-revival modes to one in harmony with the new, modern age was particularly hard on craftspeople working in metal. Most affected were those who specialized in silverware, objects deeply associated in the American consciousness with tradition and continuity. Compounding the stylistic dilemma was the Depression, which was devastating to craftspeople dependent upon the demand for nonessential luxury items. The struggle for economic survival was exacerbated by the emergence of a new competitor—high-styled manufactured wares in chromiumplated metals and aluminum. These were easy to care for, affordable, and aggressively advertised. Production-line silverplate in ultramodern designs was also marketed persuasively by manufacturers as an inexpensive alternative to silver. The machine, symbol of a new aesthetic and social order, was triumphant. In the 1930s, mass production and its corollary, mass consumption, made the special commission more rare, and the toll on silversmiths was tremendous. Nevertheless, a younger generation would reinvigorate the craft and make its mark.

Prior to the landmark Exposition Internationale des Arts Décoratifs et Industriels Modernes, held in Paris in 1925, there had been limited exposure to progressive European design, and little interest in it, in the United States. Although The Newark Museum sponsored an exhibition of modern German applied art in 1922, and a branch of the Wiener Werkstätte, spearheaded by Austrian émigré architect Joseph Urban, opened the same year in New York, the American public generally remained aloof and isolated from early European modernism.[1] An exception was the successful entrance in 1922 of Danish silversmith Georg Jensen into the American market. From an outlet in New York City, the Jensen firm effectively promoted its blend of tradition and modernity, which found acceptance here in the 1920s.[2]

A European émigré design colony, centered in New York, did exist, however.

On the eve of World War I, a small but remarkably influential influx of Austrian and German architects and designers had occurred. Together with a handful of native professionals who had studied on the continent, they formed the nucleus of New York's progressive design community. Among them were German metalsmith Oscar Bach and Hungarian designer Ilonka Karasz, both of whom would create modern designs in metal in the late 1920s. The dire post–World War I economy in Europe propelled a second wave of emigrants that included silversmiths Peter Mueller-Munk of Germany, and Laurits Christian Eichner and Erik Magnussen of Denmark. New York's émigré design colony would play a major role in facilitating the rapid transition to modern design sparked by the 1925 Paris Exposition. Not surprisingly, in metalwork it was émigré silversmiths Mueller-Munk and Magnussen who became the modern superstars of the 1920s.

The tradition-bound state of American design had prevented the United States from participating in the exclusively modern Paris Exposition. The Exposition was visited by Americans nonetheless, and widely written about in American journals and newspapers. (Helen Appleton Read, the influential *Brooklyn Daily Eagle* art critic, heralded its importance in a series of four articles.[3]) Because of their previous detachment from progressive European design, many Americans were astonished. In New York, *art moderne* gained immediate credibility. Assisted by the talented émigré design colony, department stores (which emulated the promotional role of their French counterparts), museum exhibitions, and proselytizing journalists, *art moderne* was introduced throughout the United States in less than three years.

While most Arts and Crafts metalsmiths remained in the mold during the 1920s, two fiercely independent women born around 1880, Marie Zimmermann and Janet Payne Bowles, pursued personal visions. The shape, surface treatment, and ornamentation of ancient artifacts fascinated Zimmermann, a New Yorker who drew inspiration from the Egyptian, Far Eastern, and Greek galleries of The Metropolitan Museum of Art.[4] Reviews of her exhibitions at the Ehrich Gallery brought her national recognition in the early 1920s.[5] Zimmerman created architectural decoration and jewelry in addition to richly patinated tableware and accessories, and was technically proficient in iron, copper, bronze, gold, and silver. Small, richly embellished containers were her forte. In a stylized silver box of the 1920s that is reminiscent of the Biedermeier style, decorative elements in jade, enamel, and gilt were isolated and contrasted with smooth surfaces. Late in the decade, Zimmermann explored pure form in spun-copper and spun-silver bowls devoid of ornament.[6] Although the Depression and altered aesthetic values caused her production to taper off in the 1930s, a large selection of her jewelry and objects was shown in the 1936 Architectural League of New York's Annual Exhibition.[7]

Bowles was fascinated intellectually and culturally by the vanguard.[8] As a young woman, she studied psychology and philosophy with William James at Radcliffe College and later attended lectures in psychology given by John Dewey at Columbia University in New York,[9] where she opened a metalwork shop in 1907. A nonconformist in design and technique, Bowles created from instinct and emotion, aspiring to an expression of the eternal. Her forms evolved by working the metal spontaneously, in what she termed "creative flow."[10] The compositional teachings of Arthur Wesley Dow were an important influence, as were early Greek, Celtic, and Norse art. Several silver chalices, mature works of about 1925–31, forcefully demonstrate Bowles's use of expressionistic form and unconventional technique. Of one chalice W. Scott Braznell, the authority on Bowles, wrote: "[It] is an astonishing example of the daring sculptural elements Bowles brought to ritual vessels. Form is radically distorted to interact with space, light, and shadow. . . . Elements wrap, encircle, frame, penetrate, and enclose space. Hollows become important with negative space active in the overall arrangement. Allowing no rest for the eye, the play of light and shadow—moving in, out, and over changes of shape and texture—is constantly agitated and evanescent, but nonetheless it resolves formal harmonies of balance and proportion."[11] Bowles's subjective shaping of form and compositional freedom bears an uncanny affinity with post–World War II expressionist sculpture, and are a testament to her modernity.

In the 1920s, the workmanship of master jeweler Edward E. Oakes of Massachusetts and New Hampshire was unsurpassed. Oakes considered his masterpiece to be an extraordinary jewel casket he designed in 1928 and completed in 1929. Called "architectural in miniature" by a critic when it was first exhibited by the Society of Arts and Crafts, Boston, in 1929, the silver box was set in 14-karat green gold with 143 Siberian amethysts, 5 large South American amethysts, 86 pieces of onyx, and 78 Asian pearls, the stones specially cut for their placement in the design.[12] The Indian laurelwood base Oakes fashioned as a pedestal echoed the stepped details of the casket, and the ubiquitous setback motif of late-1920s American architecture and design. In this work Oakes brought the high standards of traditional craftsmanship to contemporary styling.

Other important Arts and Crafts metalsmiths from diverse geographical regions who, like Oakes, experimented with modernism were Rebecca Cauman of Boston and New York; William E. Brigham of Providence, Rhode Island; Porter George Blanchard of Burbank, California; John Pontus Petterson of Chicago; and William Waldo Dodge, Jr., of Asheville, North Carolina. Of Cauman's early life and training, little is known. She had bench space at the Society of Arts and Crafts, Boston, and exhibited silver and copperware in the Society's 1927 Triennial Exhibition.[13] After her inclusion in R. H. Macy's 1927 "Exposition of Art in Trade" in New York, Cauman, with her younger sister Josephine, opened a retail shop at 795 Madison Avenue, specializing in handcrafted tableware, decorative accessories, and jewelry, primarily of silver, pewter, and copper, often with enamelwork.[14] Cauman exploited the circle in one of her most modern works, a round pewter box on ball feet. Taut, incised radii segment the surface of the lid and underscore the geometry of the piece. Mounted vertically by small disks on

Edward E. Oakes. *Jeweled Casket.* 1929. Silver, green gold, amethyst, black onyx, pearls, 7½ x 6". Collection Oakes Family

the lid is the handle, a circle of colored glass framed in pewter. Cauman received considerable recognition in major exhibitions of the 1930s.

William Brigham was born in North Attleboro, Massachusetts, a jewelry manufacturing center in which his father worked. Brigham became an educator, teaching at the Cleveland School of Art and, from 1914 to 1927, the Rhode Island School of Design, his alma mater. His marriage to a prominent socialite relieved him of financial pressure, affording him the luxury of a studio at home, frequent European travel, and the means to acquire historical examples of decorative art.[15] Brigham's first love was the design and crafting of elaborate traditional jewelry.[16] A number of his silver holloware designs from the late 1920s, however, reveal his keen awareness of European avant-garde art movements. A pair of stepped candlesticks allude not only to New York skyscrapers but to de Stijl geometry as well.[17] By limiting his formal vocabulary and emphasizing line, proportion, and compositional balance, Brigham achieved spare, architectonic designs.

Like Cauman, Brigham, and Petterson, Blanchard was of the generation born in the 1880s. Trained by his father, silversmith George Porter Blanchard, he exhibited as a member of the Society of Arts and Crafts, Boston, and the Detroit Society of Arts and Crafts prior to moving from Massachusetts to Burbank, California, in 1923. Blanchard successfully marketed his wares through department stores in major cities. While wholesale business was his mainstay in the 1920s (at least twenty-five men were in his employ), he also operated a retail shop at the Burbank Studio.[18] Although Blanchard espoused Arts and Crafts principles, he did not disdain machine work. With the exception of noncircular pieces that were hand-raised, holloware was routinely spun on chucks designed by him. Handwork was reserved for chasing or a hammered finish; flatware was handwrought and later polished on a machine wheel.[19] With his emphasis on form over decoration, and the simplification of historical styles, Blanchard adapted easily to modernism. About 1928 he executed modern holloware in pewter by German émigré Kem Weber, one of the most progressive designers in California.[20] By 1930, he had introduced his own contemporary flatware patterns, including Lotus and Commonwealth. Commonwealth, displayed in the 1937 exhibition "Silver: An Exhibition of Contemporary American Design" at The Metropolitan Museum of Art (and soon after, in the 1937 Paris Exposition), was admired for its slim, rounded handles and simplicity—no trim, except for two incised lines at the join.[21] The enclave of wealthy, trend-setting patrons in Southern California provided Blanchard with special commissions. One, a striking, ultramodern three-piece coffee service—semicircular vessels on angular ebony bases, with round ebony handles—demonstrates Blanchard's strong propensity for form.

Understandably, the Swedish-born and Norwegian-trained silversmith John Pontus Petterson was influenced by modern Scandinavian rather than early American silver. In 1914, after working several years for Tiffany and Company in New York and Robert Jarvie in Chicago, Petterson opened a studio in which he executed holloware, trophies, flatware, and jewelry. His refinement in design and technique attracted a prominent clientele that included the Wrigley and Morton families.[22] In the early 1920s Petterson adhered to the Arts and Crafts aesthetic, but as the decade progressed, he sought alternatives in contemporary Scandinavian as well as French *art moderne* designs. His unpretentious jewelry projected a quiet elegance that was compatible with modern dress. Exemplar is a silver openwork pin with a moss-agate cameo in which he framed a stylized boss motif in a subtle, but stylish, octagonal shape. In the 1930s Petterson's work became more simplified. The sole decoration for the Neptune flatware pattern, which garnered a silver medal in the 1937 Paris Exposition, was a narrow panel of carved scallops.

During the interwar period, the Dodge Shop in Asheville, North Carolina,

Porter George Blanchard. *Flatware*. c. 1938. Silver; handforged. Collection Rebecca Blanchard Adler

John Pontus Petterson. *Pin*. 1920–29. Silver set with moss-agate cameo, 2¼ x 2¼". The Art Institute of Chicago. Americana Fund

William Waldo Dodge, Jr. *Coffee and Tea Service*. 1929. Silver, ebony; coffeepot: 7½ x 9¾ x 6"; teapot: 7 x 8⅞ x 5½". Collection Stephen Neal Dennis

Erik Magnussen. *Pair of Candlesticks*. c. 1928. Designed for Gorham Manufacturing Company. Silver, turquoise; height 13¾" each. Museum of Art, Rhode Island School of Design, Providence. The Gorham Collection. Gift of Textron, Inc.

appears to have been the only major producer of handwrought silver wares in the Southeast.[23] A practicing architect, Dodge learned silvercraft in the Arts and Crafts mode from an occupational therapist while recuperating from wounds sustained in France during World War I.[24] Tourists in the resort town of Asheville were a source of business, as were local country clubs that commissioned trophies, a Dodge specialty. Dodge's repertoire was broad, and included holloware, flatware, jewelry, and assorted novelties. Generally, he emphasized form and surface texture, but occasionally he imbued his creations with wit and charm.[25] A dolphin motif was employed by Dodge, a skilled carver, to enliven the ebony handles and finials and the tongs of a handsome five-piece coffee and tea set from 1929. Although traditional forms were the focus of the shop, Dodge's modern cocktail shaker, a dramatic vertical and angular version, was certainly up-to-date in 1930.[26]

All of these artists were Arts and Crafts practitioners who were open to modernism after it gained acceptance. The silversmiths who introduced modern design to the American public and were recognized early on in publications and exhibitions were Erik Magnussen and Peter Mueller-Munk. Shortly after the 1925 Paris Exposition closed, the Gorham Manufacturing Company brought Magnussen, an accomplished Danish silversmith, to Providence to design modern handwrought silver with an eye to developing a contemporary machine-made line.[27] Magnussen's conservative modernism was more compatible with American taste than the radical designs of French master Jean Puiforcat and other Europeans. Candlesticks from about 1928 with bases elevated on turquoise spheres demonstrate Magnussen's favorite strategies: restrained scrolling and beadwork, segmented volumes, and the addition of semiprecious stones. The segmenting of rounded, volumetric surfaces with radiating incised lines to emphasize the form was a Magnussen decorative device widely emulated by American silver manufacturers in the late 1920s. In his less formal work for Gorham, playful animal and marine subjects figured strongly, often as silhouetted supports for containers, or as finials, and may have inspired Dodge's coffee and tea set with dolphin motifs.

Out of character for Magnussen was the gilded and oxidized Cubic holloware of 1927. First exhibited in Gorham's Fifth Avenue show window, the coffee service, dubbed "Lights and Shadows of Manhattan," immediately became an object of controversy. The sharp facetting and the triangular planes of applied color proved too extreme for Gorham production (the design nonetheless provoked a profusion of watered-down, manufactured imitations). Magnussen's determination to create "something of America, and for America"[28] led to the design of Modern American, a production-line flatware and holloware pattern introduced by Gorham in 1928 that evolved more naturally from his formal work than had Cubic. Magnussen left Gorham the following year, and the Depression subsequently quashed the production of Modern American. Although his silver continued to be exhibited, Magnussen had had his day. After living and working in Los Angeles from 1932 to 1939, he returned to Denmark permanently.

The meteoric success of German émigré silversmith Peter Mueller-Munk reflected the feverish rush to be modern in the late 1920s. Mueller-Munk emigrated to America in 1926, working for Tiffany and Company and for German émigré metalsmith Oscar Bach before opening his own studio specializing in exclusive, modern silver.[29] By 1928, his work was illustrated and lauded in sophisticated journals and included in important modernist exhibitions in New York.[30] A solo exhibition in 1928 at the Detroit Society of Arts and Crafts led to a commission from the Detroit Institute of Arts funded by architect Albert Kahn. The result was a monumental pair of silver candelabra.[31] The applied strips resembling pilasters with faceted tips may have been influenced by Christian Fjerdingstad, a well-known Danish silver designer for Christofle in Paris who had used a similar decorative element when Mueller-Munk was a student in Berlin.

The influences on Mueller-Munk were diverse. He held his mentor Waldemar Raemisch in the highest esteem, and also admired modernists Georg Jensen, Dagobert Peche, and Jean Puiforcat.[32] He professed a profound respect for traditional metalwork yet accepted machinework if it did not imitate handwork.[33] He was not intimidated by Bauhaus functionalist theories, which he subscribed to in some works while selectively retaining applied and chased ornament in others. Although scenic and figurative chased decoration is characteristic of Mueller-Munk's work from the 1920s, he occasionally resorted to linear geometry. Surprisingly, a hairbrush, mirror, and comb from a dresser set dating from about 1931 have the identical chased geometric patterning he employed in the idiosyncratic 1931 silver tea service with ivory in The Metropolitan Museum, a design believed to have been unique.

Mueller-Munk survived the Depression by teaching and designing for industry. About 1933, he designed two series in silverplate for the Poole Silver Company's Silvermode line,[34] and his conviction grew that mass production was the wave of the future. In 1935, the year he began teaching industrial design at the Carnegie Institute of Technology, he designed for the Revere Copper and Brass Company a chromiumplated pitcher named for the new French ocean liner *Normandie*. Trained as a smith of the unique silver object, Mueller-Munk created in this sleek, mass-produced pitcher—his most celebrated design—a symbol of 1930s streamlining.

The early Depression years created a chasm between 1920s and 1930s design. In 1934, The Metropolitan Museum's "Contemporary American Industrial Art" exhibition sent a clear message that *art moderne,* the early, exuberant phase of modernism, was passé. The Depression had dampened the national mood, and austere European functionalism, advanced by The Museum of Modern Art in New York, was more in sync with the spirit of the time. Designers turned to powerful symbols of progress, transportation machines, and streamlining for inspiration.

The sphere, taken up by metalsmith Paul A. Lobel and architect Eliel Saarinen in two dramatic services commissioned especially for the 1934 Metropolitan Museum exhibition (both executed in silverplate by the International Silver Company), was seized upon by other metalsmiths. Among the spherical designs spawned was a teapot of 1935 by Marion Anderson Noyes. Harold Nock, head designer and talent scout for Towle Silver Company in Newburyport, Massachusetts, discovered Noyes's modern handwrought pewter at the University of Wisconsin and brought her to Towle as a consultant in 1935.[35] A year later, Noyes left Towle to produce hand-finished spun pewterware, which was sold until 1941 in her own Newburyport retail shop and in a few East Coast outlets. Noyes's production was small, and sales and distribution were "a very very hard struggle."[36] But the clean lines, fine proportions, and functional purity of her designs rank them among the best of the period to express the machine aesthetic.[37]

The upswing of the economy in 1933 ushered in a classical revival in architecture and design. In the forefront of the revival was silver manufacturer Rogers, Lunt & Bowlen, who trumpeted the revival in 1934 with a new pattern called Modern Classic. On its heels came Dorian, from the Watson Company; Classic Modern silverplate from Wallace Silversmiths; and more. The influence of this austere, or "stripped," neoclassicism is evident in a handwrought holloware series of the mid-1930s from The Kalo Shop, founded in Chicago by Clara Barck Welles. The footed bowl in the pattern has a fluted base and a notched rim, which allude to classical columns and moldings. Another application of modern classicism can be found in the reeded bases, handles, and finial of a three-piece hemispheric tea service of tinned copper by New York metalsmith Bernard W. Fischer, who was known for cutting-edge decorative accessories such as mirrors, waste baskets, lamps, and wall plaques in mixed metals.[38]

Tommi Parzinger, a German émigré of the 1930s who designed furniture and accessories for the Rena Rosenthal shop in New York before going out on his own in the late 1930s, independently produced exclusive silver holloware prior to World War II. Parzinger's silver designs were meticulously carried out by a fellow German émigré, silversmith Peter Reimes.[39] Parzinger drew inspiration from contemporary German silversmiths, especially Emil Lettré. His neoclassical bent was noted by critics, yet all of Parzinger's silver designs were imbued with the light-hearted charm and grace of modern Austrian decorative art, which he had studied in Vienna.[40] Although his penchant for decoration, especially incised and stylized floral motifs, was out of character with the prevailing aesthetic, the excellence of his silver was recognized almost immediately in major exhibitions.

During the vogue of *art moderne* in the 1920s, and of streamlining and modern classicism in the 1930s, the influence of Scandinavian silver design, especially that of Georg Jensen, was a constant. Peer Smed, William G. De Matteo, and Laurits Christian Eichner were outstanding metalsmiths who worked in this mode. Smed apprenticed to renowned Danish silversmith A. Michelsen before emigrating to the United States about 1904, but little is known of his work until the 1930s.[41] With the help of a few Scandinavian silversmiths Smed produced handwrought holloware, flatware, and jewelry in his Brooklyn studio. A staunch traditionalist, he repudiated machinework and permitted no division of labor; in his workshop, each piece was made entirely by one smith.[42] The holloware shapes often emulate the natural forms of gourds and melons, and the decoration, flowers, leaves, buds, wheat, corn, and cacti. Soft, curved, flared, and flowing lines are characteristic of his work. The metal subtly swells with organic life in a rare pair of triple-branched candelabra and a pair of candlesticks, both from 1934. Interestingly, in 1931 Smed collaborated with Frederick Stark, an in-house designer for the International Silver Company, on the flatware and holloware services of the new Waldorf Astoria Hotel. The peak of Smed's career came in 1937, when his contributions to the silver exhibitions at The Brooklyn Museum and The Metropolitan Museum were critically acclaimed.

Italian-born William G. De Matteo, and Laurits Christian Eichner, a Dane, were a generation younger than Smed. The work of De Matteo, who was trained in the United States, lacks the vegetal stamp of Smed and is closer in style to Jensen. In fact, he reinterpreted the stark 1920 Johan Rohde water pitcher for Jensen by adding a foot with a floral collar, the motif discreetly repeated beneath the top of the handle.[43] A silver gravy boat demonstrates how De Matteo emphasized shape and outline and contrasted plain sculptural volumes with lyrical, naturalistic accents.

While unemployed in 1934, the forty-year-old Eichner, an engineer and maker of scientific instruments, successfully turned his hand to his avocation: metalwork. Many of his designs were Scandinavian-influenced but more contemporary than those of Smed and De Matteo. Eichner demonstrated a flexibility in design ranging from Colonial revival in pewter to streamlining in copper and silver. He endowed a low, wide-rimmed copper bowl with the telescoping shape that was emblematic of modern design in the late 1920s; a version in silver appeared in "Silver: An Exhibition of Contemporary American Design" at The Metropolitan Museum in 1937.

Two distinctive pockets of creativity in metalwork blossomed and took hold in the 1930s: The Cranbrook Academy of Art formally opened in Bloomfield Hills, Michigan; and Grove Park, Pennsylvania, became the locus for innovation in handwrought aluminum.[44] In 1927, five years prior to the formal opening of the Cranbrook Academy, its founder, George G. Booth, invited English silversmith and jeweler Arthur Nevill Kirk to teach part-time at the Detroit Society of Arts and Crafts and to design and execute metalwork for Christ Church, Cranbrook.[45] From 1929 until 1933, Kirk directed the metals workshop at Cranbrook, and made impeccable objects in the English Arts and Crafts tradition. In addition to his own work, Kirk and his assistants executed the designs of Cranbrook's Finnish-born director, the celebrated architect Eliel Saarinen. A footed silver bowl of 1930 designed by Saarinen and wrought by Kirk is interesting because of

Peer Smed. *Candelabra and Candlesticks.* 1934. Silver; candelabra: 18⅜ x 11¼" each; candlesticks: height 16¼" each. The Art Institute of Chicago. Wesley M. Dixon, Jr., and Mr. and Mrs. Albert Pick, Jr., Funds

William De Matteo. *Gravy Boat.* c. 1935–40.
Silver

its relationship to the massive silver centerpiece bowl designed by Saarinen and produced by the International Silver Company for the Saarinen dining room in 1929. Though much smaller in size, the Cranbrook bowl, like the latter, has chased linear segmenting on the interior that subtly fans on the rim. The collaboration between Saarinen and Kirk, at times tense due to their conflicting philosophies, sparked a brief period of modernist experimentation on the part of Kirk, who remained deeply committed to the medieval precepts of the Arts and Crafts movement.

After financial difficulties caused the close of the metals workshop in 1933, Kirk left Cranbrook.[46] When the economic situation improved in 1938, the metals workshop was reopened under Italian-born Arieto (Harry) Bertoia, a promising young scholarship student who had emigrated in 1930 and settled in Detroit.[47] Bertoia, who was completely open to modernism, produced stunning streamlined coffee and tea services during his five-year tenure at Cranbrook. The juxtaposition of silver and Lucite, a material in vogue in the late 1930s but rarely used in combination with silver,[48] in Bertoia's sleek, elliptical service of about 1940 recalls Jean Puiforcat's silver-and-crystal service of 1925.[49] Rather than attaching the teapot handle directly to the body, Bertoia extended the horizontal planes at the base and lid to support a rectilinear column of Lucite—a device similar to the plinths in Puiforcat's 1925 service and to his spherical service with rosewood handles and knobs of 1928.[50] Bertoia exploited the coldness and polish of metal in this bold service, simultaneously exalting the Machine Age and the unique object.

The popularization of affordable new metals was a phenomenon of the 1930s. Aluminum, a versatile and economical material that is light, strong, and rustproof, could be stretched and rolled into almost any shape by hand, and was well suited for decorative accessories. Three producers of hand-forged and hammered aluminum wares—all working in Grove City, Pennsylvania—stand out: Wendell August, Arthur Palmer, and Arthur Armour. August, a blacksmith and the pioneer of handwrought aluminum tablewares and accessories, fabricated aluminum architectural decoration in the 1920s. When a job was completed, he presented customers with a small gift of aluminum repoussé, usually a bowl, vase, or candlesticks. After finishing the entrance gates for the headquarters of Alcoa, the Aluminum Company of America, in New Kensington, Pennsylvania, in 1929, the architect Henry Hornbostel asked August to make hammered aluminum gifts for company executives.[51] These came to the attention of Pittsburgh department store owner Edgar J. Kaufmann, Sr., and the production of decorative hammered aluminum began.[52] An unusual item for the Wendell August Forge was a desk set of the 1930s, a spare, constructivist design closer to the machine aesthetic than August's typical decorative work.[53]

Arthur Palmer, sales manager for Wendell August between 1933 and 1935, left the firm to establish his own business, the Palmer-Smith Company.[54] Palmer introduced incised decoration, which for a time was unique to Palmer-Smith, and created a sophisticated line of giftware. He preferred simple, bold shapes and strong outlines that emphasized form and surface. Decoration was kept to a minimum. A centerpiece and candelabra set demonstrate his penchant for stylizing one decorative motif and repeating it—in this instance, wheat.

Trained as an architect, Arthur Armour briefly designed patterns at Wendell August before striking out on his own in 1938.[55] Armour was a master of intricate detail, a highly skilled artisan who designed and executed all of his hand-cut dies.[56] Typical of Armour at his most modern is a serving tray from the 1930s that features the signs of the zodiac. In this design, negative space is balanced by a concentrated area of abstract decoration, a strategy Armour employed in his best work.[57]

Almost simultaneous with the advent of decorative handwrought aluminum wares in Grove City was the introduction, in 1931, of a line of modern, informal serving accessories of spun aluminum designed and produced by Russel Wright in New York and marketed throughout the country. After encountering difficulty with pewter and chromiumplated steel in the late 1920s, Wright switched to spun aluminum for ease of fabrication and for its similarity in color to pewter, which he preferred.[58] The immediate and continuing success throughout the 1930s of his spun-aluminum line was due to the new informality in home entertaining, on which Wright capitalized with a wide variety of smart, practical designs that were within the economic reach of the middle class during the Depression. One of his strongest designs is a cylindrical beverage pitcher that rises seamlessly to a flared spout; a wood dowel anchored to the body supports the handle, a large aluminum ring. Wright often accented his sleek metal shapes with details in wood, cork, cane, or rattan.

Only a handful of craftspeople produced significant architectural metalwork during this period. In this demanding field, almost all were born and trained in Europe.[59] Iron was the medium of Hungarian-born modernist Wilhelm Hunt Diederich, grandson of Boston painter William Morris Hunt and grandnephew of architect Richard Morris Hunt. The stylized, silhouetted animals in motion that enliven Diederich's functional wrought-iron objects resemble paper cutouts,

Palmer-Smith Company. *Centerpiece and Candelabra*. c. 1935–40. Hand-hammered aluminum. Courtesy Art Moderne, Tampa

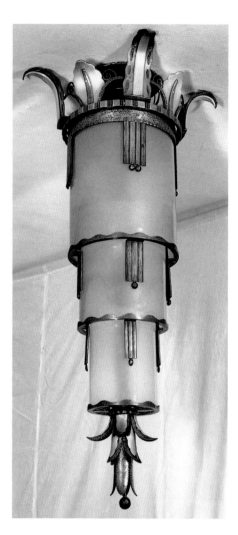

Paul Fehér. *Chandelier.* c. 1930. Designed for Rose Iron Works. Sandblasted glass cylinders, hot-rolled steel; forging, repoussé, height 39" overall. Rose Family Collection

an activity he enjoyed as a child.[60] A tripartite folding fire screen in a "fox and hounds" motif is a signature work from the 1920s, Diederich's most fertile period.

Winold Reiss, a painter, commercial graphic artist, teacher, and interior designer, arrived from Germany in 1914. He immediately became a force in New York's émigré design colony by cofounding the Society of Modern Art and its magazine, *Modern Art Collector.*[61] Interior decorative metalwork in a variety of metals figured in his restaurant commissions of the 1920s. For the Hotel Alamac in 1923, Reiss designed two thematic spaces, the rooftop Congo Room and a Medieval Grill. In a surviving panel from the latter depicting a harlequin, he combined brass, copper, aluminum, steel, and iron in repoussé for colorful contrasts.[62] The abstract composition reveals Cubist influences as well as Reiss's fascination with Native American motifs, particularly the rows of linked triangles and repetitive zigzag lines, a signature of his modern work and a characteristic of Blackfoot design, which he admired.[63]

Among the finest handwrought interior architectural metalwork and furnishings emulating the French *moderne* was that produced by the Rose Iron Works of Cleveland in a brief flowering at the end of the 1920s. A chance encounter brought Hungarian-born metalsmith Paul Fehér, an apprentice under Paul Kiss in Paris, to Cleveland as designer for Rose.[64] The fruits of the collaboration from 1928 to 1933 between Martin Rose, a Hungarian émigré, and Fehér are all the more remarkable because of their difference in age: Rose was twice as old as Fehér. The mixing of materials and finishes to achieve interesting contrasts in color and surface characterizes Rose-Fehér designs.[65] A variety of materials articulates the elements of an Art Deco desk set of 1929–31. Here, a satin-finished stainless-steel inkwell contrasts with a polished stainless-steel base and pen holders. The climax of the piece is a double-sided, carved aluminum dancing figure frozen in a bronze surround. Another work, a telescoping chandelier with frosted glass globes, features a forged Swedish-iron finish—highlighted, burnished, and lacquered—and cold-rolled aluminum overlays on a crown of leaves.[66]

The technical virtuosity of metalsmith Oscar Bruno Bach, a German émigré, has been compared to that of French master Edgar Brandt. Bach's early success was extraordinary. In 1904, at age twenty, he designed and executed all the metalwork for the Berlin City Hall.[67] Bach immigrated to the United States just prior to World War I, settling permanently in New York. By 1922, he was recognized in *Arts & Decoration* as the metalsmith most widely represented in the great homes of America.[68] His traditionally styled bronze, steel, and repoussé-silver doors for The Toledo Museum of Art were awarded the 1926 Architectural League of New York Medal of Honor in Design and Craftsmanship in Native Industrial Art.[69] Yet Bach kept pace with modernism. Before 1930, he designed and fabricated another pair of doors in steel with ornamental silverplated-bronze motifs as a tribute to heavy industry. The abstract uniformity of the geometrical bas-relief figures at once heroicizes and dehumanizes them—a fitting interpretation for the Machine Age.

The Bach shop also fabricated the designs of others. One of Bach's finest opportunities came in 1928, when he designed and made the wall clock for the Cranbrook School dining hall, and executed the entrance gate to the school designed by Eliel Saarinen.[70] In 1932, Bach produced four heroic mixed-metal-and-enamel plaques for Rockefeller Center that were designed by Hildreth Meiere.[71] Although architectural commissions diminished in the 1930s, he remained active until the outbreak of World War II.[72] During the war, the production of architectural metalwork ground to a halt; indeed, the moratorium on metals restricted the production of all kinds of nonessential wares, and many craftspeople closed their workshops for the duration of the war.

Margret Craver of Kansas led the first generation of twentieth-century American-born metalsmiths who trained after 1925, and she contributed significantly to the revitalization of the craft in the 1940s and, more importantly, in the 1950s. Two pieces by Craver that predate the war are noteworthy: a silver-and-enamel *bonbonnière* awarded first prize by the Philadelphia Art Alliance in a 1938 craft competition, and a silver-and-ebony teapot exhibited at the 1939–40 Golden Gate International Exposition in San Francisco. The teapot (c. 1936), her first fully realized work, was made while Craver was studying with Arthur Nevill Kirk.[73] Although the sleek design refers back to Art Deco styling, Craver's version has a powerful organic presence that prefigures post–World War II design. Of interest, too, is her interpretation of the extended columnar handle, a device associated with the work of Puiforcat in the 1920s and adapted by Bertoia.

In the 1930s, traditions associated with jewelry gave way in reaction to the profound cultural and socioeconomic changes in the United States. Artist-jewelers abandoned precious metals and stones for humbler materials and unorthodox decoration. New conceptions of form and space in jewelry design evolved, and new techniques developed. Among the pioneers were Alexander Calder, Harry Bertoia, Ruth Penington, Francisco Rebajes, and Margaret De Patta.

Beginning in 1931, Calder's creation of jewelry paralleled that of his wire sculptures and mobiles.[74] Calder made unconventional jewelry of silver, brass, or copper wire, which he cut, hammered flat, and twisted into tight spirals, sinuous curves, and abstract forms. As in his sculpture, he often portrayed creatures of the natural world—an insect or animal, a bird, fish, or flower—by joining elements with wires, which he twisted around each other. Occasionally, he added bits of colored glass and leather ribbon ties to pieces.[75] Repetitive motifs, especially spirals, proliferate in his necklaces, bracelets, and other ornaments.[76]

A strong stylistic connection to Calder can be discerned in the jewelry Harry Bertoia created at Cranbrook between 1938 and 1943.[77] Bertoia's jewelry, like Calder's, is primitive and whimsical, but the forms are more organic; there are also differences in the hammered finish of the metal and in the method used to join individual elements, which Bertoia accomplished by riveting or fusing. Bertoia was concerned chiefly with movement in space. Charged with energy, a riveted, multi-petaled silver pin from about 1938–40 appears to spring through space.

Ruth Penington of Seattle, the preeminent, trail-blazing metalsmith and jeweler in the Northwest, also drew on archaic and primitive art, including Northwest Coast Native American art, for inspiration.[78] Penington's identification with the Northwest was reinforced early on by the incorporation into her jewelry of natural found objects, such as the beach pebbles in a cross pendant of 1930. Penington had a firm grip on structure, and limited her vocabulary in the 1930s to simple geometric shapes and outlines; a forged and hinged silver bracelet of 1938 is an exemplar. Penington's major contributions to modern American jewelry would be made in her mature work after World War II.

Centered in New York were a number of modernist jewelers whose work was known through exhibitions mounted in the late 1930s and early 1940s. Gertrude Karlan, an artist who mingled in avant-garde circles, cleverly crafted a reversible silver necklace and earring set in a series of overlapping zigzag motifs. E. Byrne Livingston, an instructor in jewelry at the City College of New York and at Hunter College, set onyx and coral for color and enrichment in a silver ring and pin set of Machine Age styling. Francisco Rebajes and Leonore Doskow both embarked on production-line jewelry in the 1940s.[79]

Rebajes, an émigré from the Dominican Republic, realized the American dream. Penniless in New York during the late 1920s, the self-taught Rebajes began pounding and modeling tin cans into fanciful animal figures. With the proceeds

Alexander Calder. *Bracelet*. c. 1935–40. Gilded brass, height 5⅜". National Museum of American Art, Washington, D.C. Gift of Mr. and Mrs. Alexander Calder

from a large purchase at his Washington Square sidewalk display, he went into business in Greenwich Village in the early 1930s.[80] Rebajes had a sophisticated eye and was aware of early twentieth-century art movements. His sources of inspiration were diverse—nature, African sculpture, the machine, and the work of his contemporaries, especially Calder. In one bangle bracelet the copper was cut and thinly coiled to suggest eyes in the central motif—an abstract mask. Rebajes transformed metal into informal objects of charm, wit, and wearability. In less than ten years he had established himself and opened a store on Fifth Avenue to market his manufactured costume jewelry, primarily of copper.[81]

Margaret De Patta's rebellion against conventions in jewelry design began in 1929 when her direction shifted from painting as a career, for which she had been formally prepared, to metalwork.[82] With the establishment of a studio in San Francisco in 1935, her professional transition from painting to jewelry was complete. A year later, she began her association with the recently opened Amberg-Hirth Gallery in San Francisco, one of the earliest outlets on the West Coast for American craft objects.[83] The primitive overtones of De Patta's earliest experiments yielded to geometric clarity and machinelike precision by the late 1930s. The turning point in her creative growth came in 1940–41 with her study of Constructivist spatial theory and aesthetics under László Moholy-Nagy at the Chicago School of Design (now the Institute of Design). Structure, the placement of lines and planes within space, and the transparency of gemstones became a lifelong engagement. In a yellow-gold pin with topaz, citrines, and pearls of 1940, linear movement, the opposition of positive and negative space, and the "floating" of the stones with hidden wire circles anticipate De Patta's postwar development and the new direction in which she would lead jewelry.[84]

The period 1920 to 1940 presented formidable challenges to those whose métier was metal. Although the quantity of work and number of those engaged in the craft diminished because of the Depression, dwindling educational opportunities, and competition with manufactured wares, the quality of the work was outstanding. Metalsmiths survived mainly by teaching (Bertoia, Bowles, Eichner, Kirk, Livingston, Mueller-Munk, Penington) or by operating a shop (Armour, August, Bach, Blanchard, Cauman, Dodge, Eichner, Lobel, De Matteo, Noyes, Palmer, Parzinger, Petterson, Rebajes, Smed, Welles). In some instances, income was augmented by designing for industry (Lobel, Magnussen, Mueller-Munk, Noyes, Smed), in others, by gallery sales (Bertoia, Calder, De Patta, Diederich, Livingston, Mueller-Munk, Oakes, Zimmermann). All of these artists overcame the stylistic, economic, and social upheavals of the period, and in doing so, struck the modern note in metal.

CATALOGUE OF THE EXHIBITION

CERAMICS

GLEN LUKENS
Bowl. 1939
Earthenware, 4½ x 6¼ x 6¼"
Collection American Craft Museum, New
York. Gift of W. Osborn Webb, 1983.
Donated to the American Craft Museum
by the American Craft Council, 1990

MAJLIS (MAIJA) GROTELL

Flared Cylinder Vase. 1941

Glazed stoneware, 15 x 11½ x 11½"

Collection American Craft Museum, New

York. Museum Purchase, 1967. Donated

to the American Craft Museum by the

American Craft Council, 1990

KATARO SHIRAYAMADANI
Vase. 1930
Designed for Rookwood Pottery
Decorated by Lorinda Epply
Soft porcelain, 7¼ x 7 x 7"
Collection Stanley H. Shapiro

MONICA SILVIN
Jar with Geometric Design. 1941
Earthenware, 7½ x 6½ x 6½"
Collection Everson Museum of Art, Syracuse,
New York. Gift of the Pueblo Indian Arts and
Crafts Market

MARIA POVERA MARTINEZ AND
JULIAN MARTINEZ
Plate. c. 1939
Earthenware, 2 x 12¾ x 12¾"
Collection Everson Museum of Art, Syracuse,
New York. Gift of the Pueblo Indian Arts and
Crafts Market

CATHERINE VIGIL
Santa Clara Pueblo
Shallow Bowl. 1941
Earthenware, 3¼ x 14½ x 14½"
Collection Everson Museum of Art, Syracuse,
New York. Gift of the IBM Corporation

VIKTOR SCHRECKENGOST
Jazz Bowl. 1931
Designed for Cowan Pottery Studio
Earthenware, 11⅜ x 16⅛ x 16⅛"
Collection Cowan Pottery Museum at Rocky
River Public Library, Rocky River, Ohio

VIKTOR SCHRECKENGOST
The Seasons. 1931
Earthenware, 11⅛ x 8 x 8"
Collection The Cleveland Museum of Art.
Hinman B. Hurlbut Collection

WILHELM HUNT DIEDERICH
Russian Cossack Plate. February 1925
Ceramic, 3½ x 15 x 15"
Collection Dr. Tom Folk

HENRY VARNUM POOR
Plate. 1930
Glazed earthenware, 1½ x 11½ x 11½"
Collection American Craft Museum, New
York. Gift of the artist, 1967. Donated to the
American Craft Museum by the American
Craft Council, 1990

HENRY VARNUM POOR
Ten Nights in a Barroom. 1932
Ceramic, 15½ x 13 x 13"
Collection Dr. Tom Folk

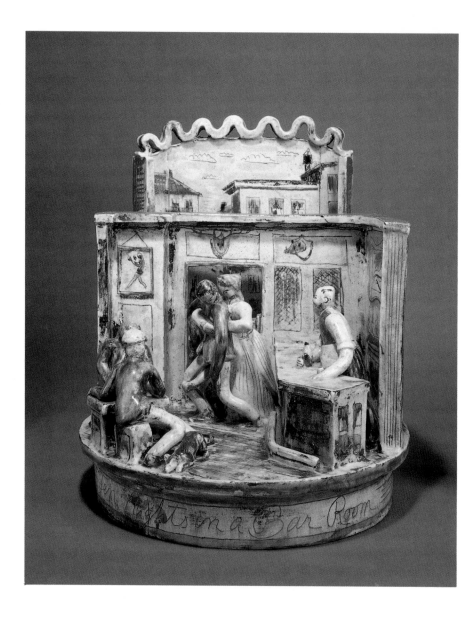

VIKTOR SCHRECKENGOST
The Dictator. 1939
Earthenware, 13 x 12½ x 10½"
Collection Everson Museum of Art,
Syracuse, New York. Gift of the artist

VALERIE (VALLY) WIESELTHIER
Europa and the Bull. 1938
Earthenware, 24 x 18 x 19"
Collection Christopher Kende

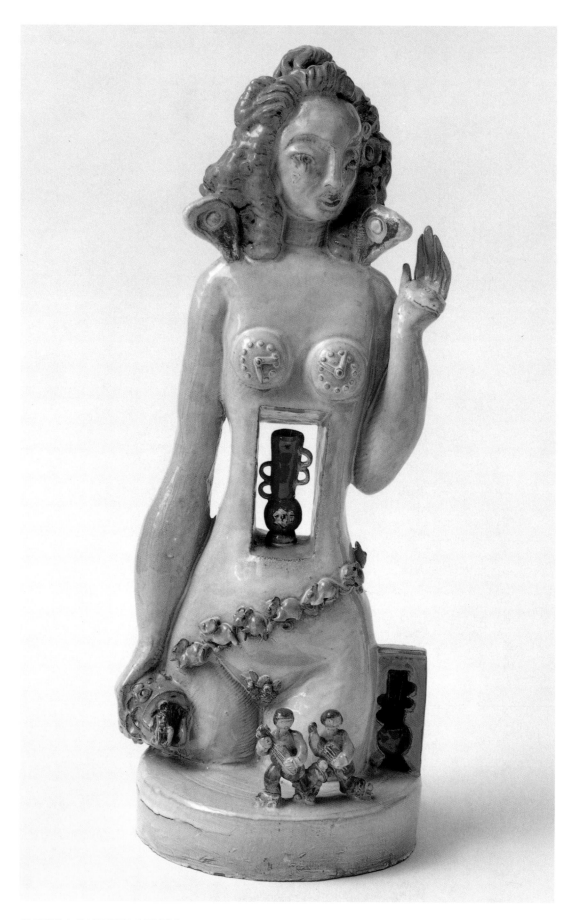

RUSSELL BARNETT AITKEN
Futility of a Well-Ordered Life. 1935
Earthenware, 18½ x 7 x 7"
Collection The Museum of Modern Art,
New York. Given anonymously

CARL WALTERS
Caterpillar. 1945
Earthenware, length of 16½"
Collection Detroit Institute of Arts.
Gift of Lillian Henkel Haass

THELMA FRAZIER WINTER
The Sirens. c. 1937
Earthenware, 18 x 15 x 4"
Collection Fred Silberman

EDRIS ECKHARDT
Earth. 1939
Earthenware, 13 x 8 x 6½"
Collection James L. Murphy
Photograph courtesy Everson Museum
of Art, Syracuse, New York

SARGENT CLAUDE JOHNSON
Negro Woman. 1933
Terracotta, 9¼ x 5 x 6"
Collection San Francisco Museum of Modern
Art, Albert M. Bender Collection. Bequest of
Albert M. Bender

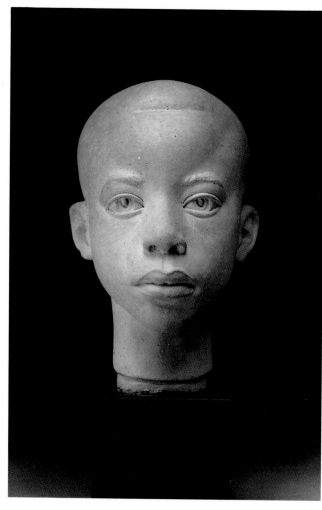

WILLIAM ELLSWORTH ARTIS
Michael. c. 1945
Terracotta, 10¼ x 6 x 8"
Collection North Carolina Museum of Art,
Raleigh. Purchased with funds from the
National Endowment for the Arts and
the North Carolina Art Society (Robert F.
Phifer Bequest)

WAYLANDE DESANTIS GREGORY

Head of a Woman. c. 1933

Porcelain, 24 x 9¾ x 12"

Collection Everson Museum of Art, Syracuse,

New York. Purchase

ISAMU NOGUCHI
Tsuneko-San (Head of a Young Girl). 1931
Ceramic, 9⅛ x 7 x 7½"
Collection Albright-Knox Art Gallery,
Buffalo, New York. Bequest of A. Conger
Goodyear, 1966

ALEXANDER BLAZYS

Moses. 1927

Designed for Cowan Pottery Studio

Earthenware, 19 x 6¼"

Collection The Cleveland Museum of Art. The

Harold T. Clark Educational Extension Fund

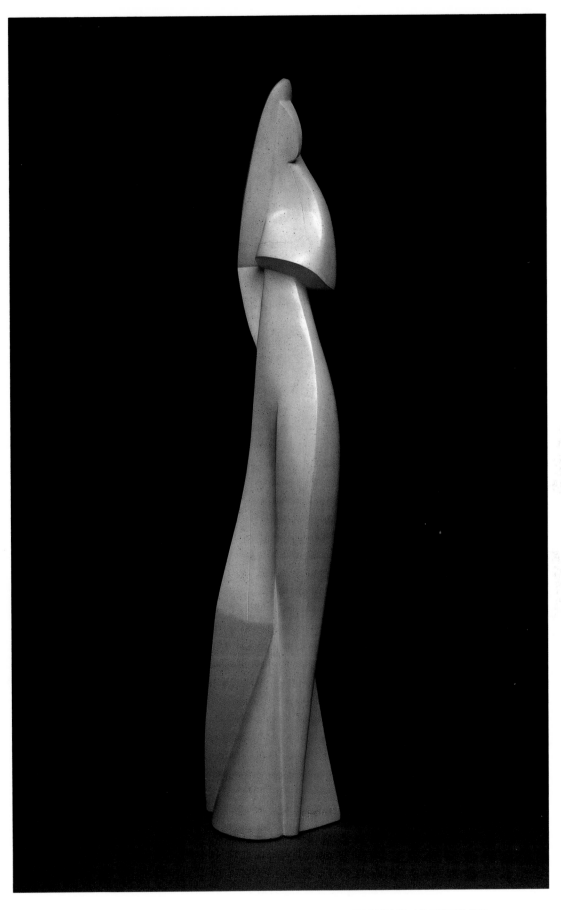

ALEXANDER ARCHIPENKO
The Bride. 1936
Terracotta, 34¼ x 6¹¹⁄₁₆ x 4¾"
Collection Seattle Art Museum. Eugene Fuller
Memorial Collection

EVA ALEXANDROVNA
POLANYI ZEISEL
Museum White Dinnerware. Designed c. 1943;
executed 1946
Designed for Castleton China Company
Glazed porcelain; coffeepot: 10½ x 7 x 5"
Collection Dr. Martin Eidelberg

FREDERICK HURTEN RHEAD
Fiestaware. 1936
Designed for Laughlin China Company
Earthenware; covered tureen: 5¾ x 9¾ x 8¼";
teapot: 6¼ x 9⅜ x 6⅛"; cup: 2¾ x 4⅞ x 3⁷⁄₁₆"
The Globus Collection

RUSSEL WRIGHT
American Modern Dinnerware.
Designed 1937; introduced 1939
Designed for Steubenville Pottery Company
Earthenware; pitcher: 10⅝ x 6⅞ x 8⅛";
teapot with lid: 4⅞ x 6¾ x 10"; covered
casserole: 3¼ x 12 x 9¼"
Collection William Straus

ROSEVILLE POTTERY COMPANY
Futura Vases. 1928
Earthenware; left to right: 7 x 5¼ x 5¼";
12 x 4½ x 4½"; 8 x 6⅜ x 6⅛"
Collection Everson Museum of Art,
Syracuse, New York. The Mary and Paul
Branwein Collection

EDWIN A. SCHEIER AND MARY
GOLDSMITH SCHEIER

Coffee Set. c. 1941

Stoneware; coffee pot: 8¼ x 9 x 9¼";
 sugar bowl: 3¼ x 3 x 3"; cup: 2¼ x 2½ x 3½"

Collection Everson Museum of Art,
Syracuse, New York. Purchase Prize given
by Richard B. Gump, Twelfth Ceramic
National Exhibition, 1948

MARGUERITE WILDENHAIN

Tea Set. c. 1946

Stoneware; teapot: 5 x 10 x 10"; sugar bowl:
2½ x 4¼ x 4¼"; creamer: 3 x 5½ x 5½"

Collection Everson Museum of Art,
Syracuse, New York. Purchase Prize given
by Richard B. Gump, Eleventh Ceramic
National Exhibition, 1946

GLASS

MAURICE HEATON
Bowl. c. 1930
Glass, 2⅞ x 16⅛ x 16⅛"
Collection The Metropolitan Museum of Art.
Gift of Theodore R. Gamble, Jr., in honor
of his mother, Mrs. Theodore Robert Gamble

WALTER DORWIN TEAGUE, SR.
Lens Bowl. c. 1934
Designed for Steuben Glass
Crystal, 2¼ x 11⅞ x 11⅞"
Collection William Straus

SAMUEL AYERS
Ship's Decanter. 1942
Glass, 10 x 8½ x 8½"
Collection Steuben Glass, New York

EDWIN W. FUERST (attributed)
Modern American Decanter and Glass. c. 1940
Designed for Libbey Glass Company
Crystal; decanter: height 11⅛";
cordial glass: height 2⅛"
Collection The Toledo Museum of Art.
Gift of Libbey Glass Company

EDWIN W. FUERST
Modern American Spiral Optic Bowl. 1940
Designed for Libbey Glass Company
Crystal; mold-blown and tooled, 8 x 9½ x 9½"
Collection The Toledo Museum of Art.
Gift of Libbey Glass Company

WALTER VON NESSEN
Stanhope Vase. 1938
Designed for Heisey Glass Company
Crystal, with Bakelite handles, 9½ x 8⅛ x 5⅛"
Collection William Straus

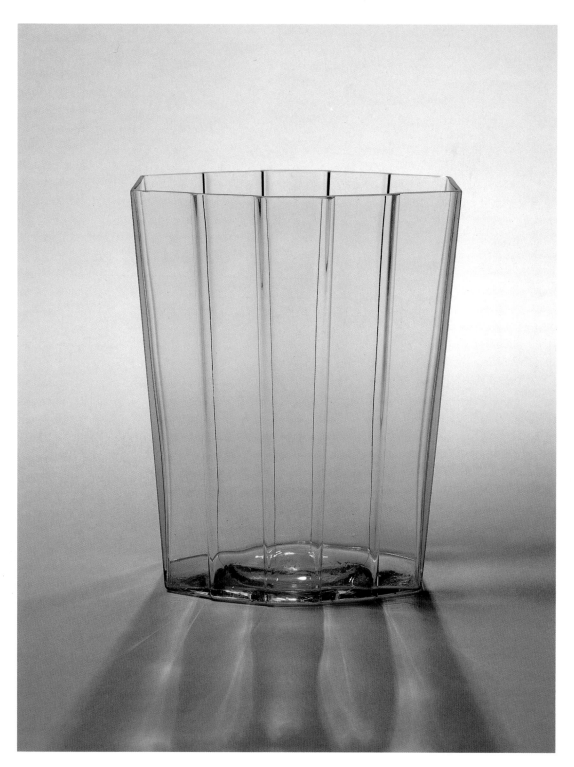

GEORGE SAKIER

Amber Stepped Vase. 1927–32
Designed for Fostoria Glass Company
Glass, 8¼ x 6¼ x 4⅝"
Collection William Straus

FREDERICK CARDER

Six Prong Green Jade Vase. c. 1930
Glass, 14⅞ x 7⅞ x 7⅞"
Collection Rockwell Museum, Corning,
New York

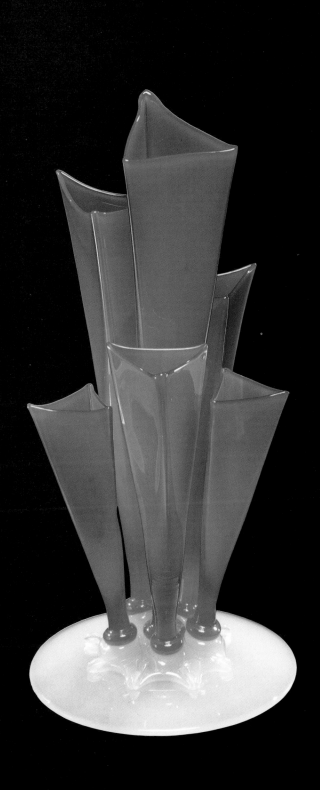

REUBEN HALEY
Ruba Rombic Vase. 1928–30
Designed for Consolidated Lamp &
Glass Company
Glass; molded, blown, and acid-etched,
16½ x 8⅛ x 8⅞"
Collection The Toledo Museum of Art.
Purchased with funds from the
Libbey Endowment. Gift of Edward
Drummond Libbey

REUBEN HALEY
*Ruba Rombic Whiskey Decanter, Tray,
and Glasses.* 1928–32
Designed for Consolidated Lamp &
Glass Company
Smoky topaz glass; mold-blown and pressed;
decanter: 9⅜ x 9¼ x 9¼"; tray: 11½ x 10⁷⁄₁₆ x 1";
glasses: 2¼ x 2 x 2" each
Collection The Corning Museum of Glass,
Corning, New York

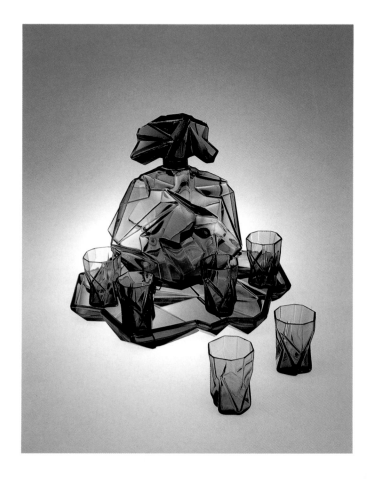

A. DOUGLAS NASH
Libbey-Nash Punch Bowl and Glasses. 1931–35
Designed for Libbey Glass Company
Glass; bowl: 7¾ x 13⅞ x 13⅞"; glasses:
3 x 2½ x 2½" each
Collection The Toledo Museum of Art.
Gift of Mrs. Carl R. Megowen in memory
of Carl R. Megowen

A. DOUGLAS NASH
Libbey-Nash Syncopation Cocktail Glass. 1933
Designed for Libbey Glass Company
Glass, 4 x 2¼ x 2¼"
Collection The Toledo Museum of Art.
Purchased with funds from the
Libbey Endowment. Gift of Edward
Drummond Libbey

SIDNEY BIEHLER WAUGH
Gazelle Bowl. 1935
Designed for Steuben Glass
Crystal; blown and cut, 7⅟₁₆ x 6⅛" x 6⅛"
Collection The Toledo Museum of Art.
Gift of William E. Levis

PAVEL TCHELITCHEW
Acrobats Vase. 1939
Designed for Steuben Glass, "Twenty-seven
Artists in Crystal" series
Crystal; blown and engraved, 13½ x 11³⁄₁₆ x 11³⁄₁₆"
Collection The Corning Museum
of Glass, Corning, New York. Gift of Harry W.
and Mary M. Anderson

PAUL MANSHIP
Woman and Centaur. 1939
Designed for Steuben Glass, "Twenty-seven
Artists in Crystal" series
Crystal; blown and engraved, 14½ x 24 x 24"
Collection The Corning Museum of Glass,
Corning, New York. Gift of Harry W. and
Mary M. Anderson

RUSSEL WRIGHT
Salad Serving Utensils. 1930–35
Glass, chrome; spoon: 1½ x 3¼ x 13⅛";
fork: 1¼ x 3½ x 13¼"
Collection William Straus

FREDERICK CARDER
Flatware. 1930s
Glass, silver; fork length: 7⅞";
spoon length: 7¼"
Collection The Corning Museum of Glass,
Corning, New York. Gift of the artist

LOUIS DIERRA (attributed)
Glass Chair. 1939
Designed for Pittsburgh Plate Glass Company
Glass, 29 x 22⅛ x 22½"
Collection The Brooklyn Museum
H. Randolph Lever Fund

FREDERICK CARDER
Paperweight Cologne Bottle. 1927–31
Cintra core surrounded by colored threadings,
controlled bubbles; cased in heavy crystal
with massive cutting, 8⅞ x 4 x 4"
Collection Rockwell Museum, Corning,
New York

FREDERICK VUILLEMENOT
DeVilbiss Atomizer and Powder Box. 1930
Enameled glass, platinum luster design;
atomizer: 5½ x 1½ x 1½"; box: 1½ x 3½ x 3½"
Collection Harvey K. Littleton

W. L. ORME
Pristine Table Architecture: Three-step
Candlesticks. 1938
Designed for Cambridge Glass Company
Crystal, 5⅜ x 5¼ x 1⅝" each
Collection William Straus

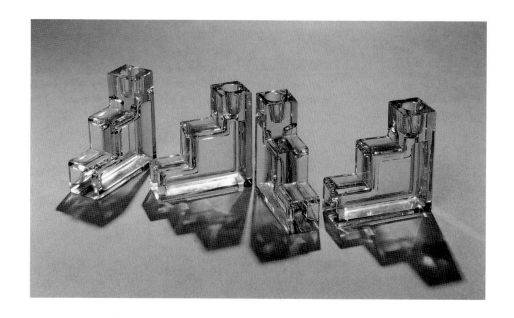

WAYLANDE DESANTIS GREGORY
Mermaid Bowl. c. 1940
Glass, 7⅛ x 12 x 12"
Collection New Jersey State Museum,
Trenton. Gift of the Friends of the New
Jersey State Museum, 1988 Forbes Benefit
and Museum Purchase

FRANCES HIGGINS
Slumped Glass Plate. 1992 (from 1942 mold)
Glass, 11¼ x 9 x 1½"
Collection Frances and Michael Higgins

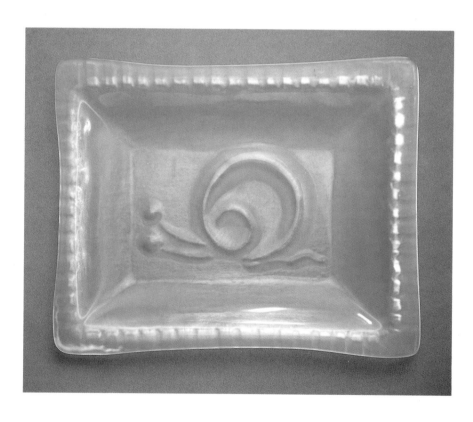

WAYLANDE DESANTIS GREGORY
The Airman. c. 1942
Ceramic, with crystal glaze, 12⅛ x 12¼ x 2"
Waylande Gregory Collection

METAL

WINOLD REISS
Harlequin Panel, Hotel Alamac, New York. 1923
Julius Ormos and Charles Bardosy, metalsmiths
Brass, copper, aluminum, steel, iron, 54½ x 47½ x ⅛"
Collection John P. Axelrod. Courtesy Museum
of Fine Arts, Boston

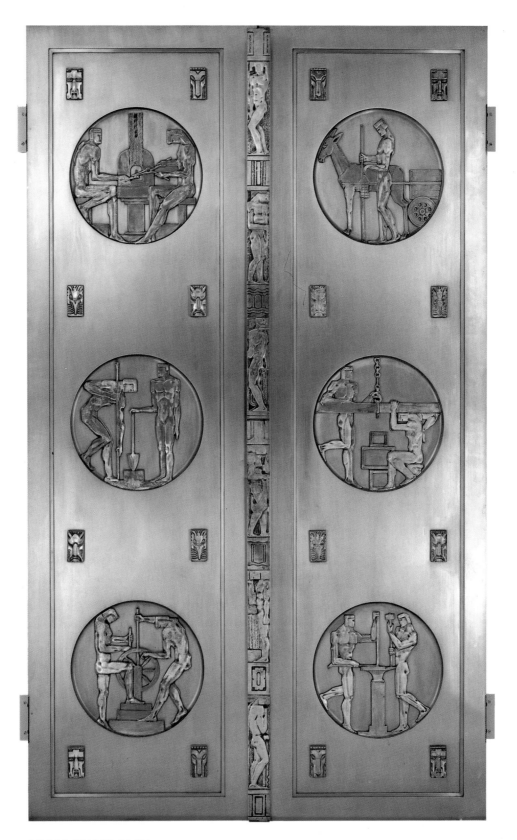

OSCAR BRUNO BACH

Pair of Art Deco Doors. c. 1925

Stainless steel over wood core, 8'5½" x 31¼" each

Collection Minneapolis Institute of Arts. The

Christina N. and Swan J. Turnblad Memorial Fund

MARGRET CRAVER

Teapot. c. 1936

Silver, gabon ebony, 5½ x 9¼ x 5"

Museum of Fine Arts, Boston. Gift in memory
of Joyce Goldberg with funds provided by
Mr. John P. Axelrod, Mr. and Mrs. Sidney
Stoneman, Mr. Charles Devens, Mr. and Mrs.
Peter S. Lynch, The Seminarians, Mr. James G.
Hinkle, Jr., The MFA Council and Friends

ARIETO (HARRY) BERTOIA

Tea Service. c. 1940

Silver, plastic; teapot: 5¼ x 7¼ x 4¼";
sugar bowl: 3¾ x 4¼ x 2¼"; creamer:
2⅝ x 4¼ x 2¼"

Collection Detroit Institute of Arts

ERIK MAGNUSSEN
Modern American Cocktail Shaker and Cups. 1928
Designed for Gorham Manufacturing Company
Silver; shaker: 12 x 6⅞ x 4"; cups: 5¼ x 3⁷⁄₁₆" each
Courtesy Denis Gallion and Daniel Morris,
Historical Design Collection, Inc., New York

WILLIAM WALDO DODGE, JR.
Cocktail Shaker, Tray, and Cups. 1929–31
Silver; shaker: height 18"; tray: 1⅛ x 15⅛ x 15⅛";
cups: 3¼ x 2¼ x 2¼" each
Collection William Waldo Dodge, III

JANET PAYNE BOWLES

Chalice. c. 1925–31

Silver, 10 x 5¼ x 5½"

Collection Indianapolis Museum of Art.

Gift of Jan and Mira Bowles in memory

of their mother, Janet Payne Bowles

BERNARD W. FISCHER
Tea Set. c. 1934
Tinned copper; teapot with cover: 6 x 8½ x 6¼";
creamer: 3 x 6½ x 5"; sugar bowl: 3 x 6½ x 5"
Collection Yale University Art Gallery,
New Haven, Connecticut. Gift of the Estate
of Bernard Fischer

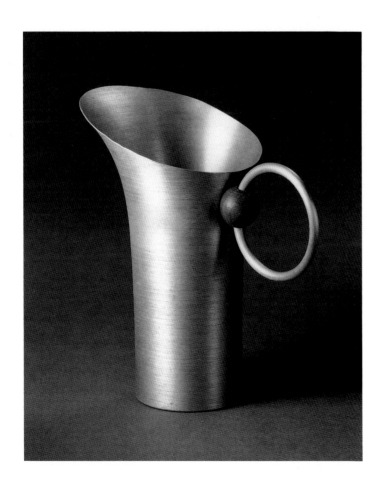

RUSSEL WRIGHT
Pitcher. c. 1935
Spun aluminum, wood, 10 x 10 x 6"
Collection William Straus

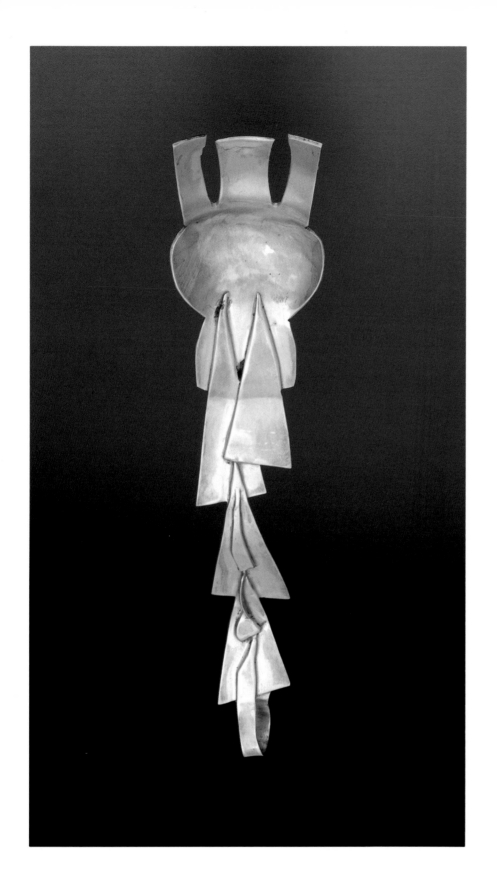

JANET PAYNE BOWLES
Fork. c. 1925–31
Silver, 9 x 1⅛ x ⅜"
Collection Indianapolis Museum of Art.
Gift of Jan and Mira Bowles in memory of
their mother, Janet Payne Bowles

JOHN PONTUS PETTERSON
Neptune Flatware Place Setting. c. 1937
Silver; dinner knife: 9¼ x ¾";
dinner fork: 7⅞ x 1"; teaspoon: 6⅛ x 1¼"
Collection John C. Petterson

LAURITS CHRISTIAN EICHNER
Shallow Bowl #40. c. 1935
Copper, 2 x 13¹³⁄₁₆ x 13¹³⁄₁₆"
Collection Mary Lou Wickham

ARTHUR NEVILL KIRK
Bowl. 1930
Designed by Gottlieb Eliel Saarinen
Silver, 4 x 8¾ x 8¾"
Collection Cranbrook Academy of Art
Museum, Bloomfield Hills, Michigan.
Gift of the Cranbrook Foundation

THE KALO SHOP
Compote. c. 1937
Silver, 2 x 8½ x 8½"
Courtesy Denis Gallion and Daniel Morris,
Historical Design Collection, Inc., New York

PETER MUELLER-MUNK

Candelabra. 1928

Silver, 17 x 19 x 10½" each

Collection Detroit Institute of Arts.

Gift of Mr. Albert Kahn

TOMMI PARZINGER
Candelabra. c. 1938–41
Peter Reimes, silversmith
Silver, 31¼ x 7¾ x 5½"
Courtesy Denis Gallion and Daniel Morris,
Historical Design Collection, Inc., New York

WILLIAM EDGAR BRIGHAM
Candleholders. c. 1930
Silver, 4½ x 3⅛₆ x 3½" each
Collection Museum of Art, Rhode Island
School of Design, Providence. Bequest of
William E. Brigham

REBECCA CAUMAN
Round Box with Finial. c. 1925
Pewter, glass, 4 x 5 x 5"
Collection Constance R. Caplan

MARIE ZIMMERMANN
Enameled Box. c. 1922
Silver, jade, enamel, gold, 7 x 4⅛ x 4⅛"
Courtesy Denis Gallion and Daniel Morris,
Historical Design Collection, Inc., New York

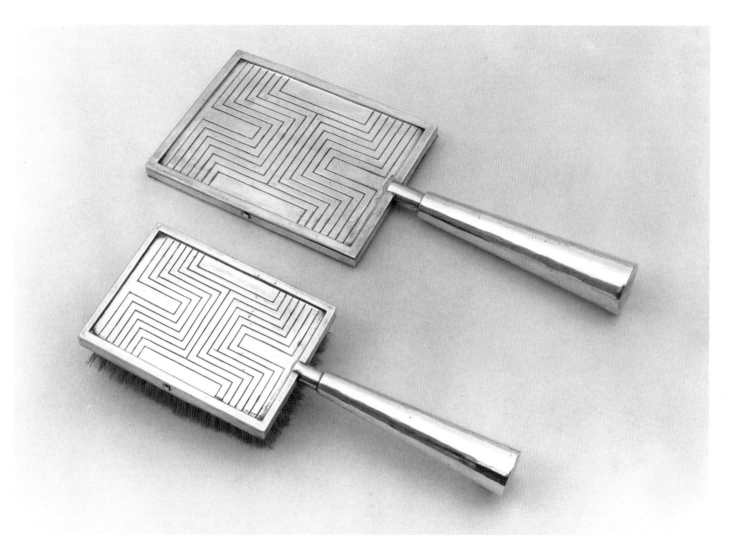

PETER MUELLER-MUNK
Hand Mirror and Brush. c. 1931
Silver; mirror: 12¼ x 4½ x 1¼"; brush:
9¾ x 3½ x ⅛"; comb (not photographed):
7½ x 1½ x ⅛"
Collection Constance R. Caplan

ARTHUR ARMOUR
Zodiac Tray. c. 1934–35
Hammered aluminum, 1 x 18 x 18"
Collection Dr. Thomas F. Armour

PAUL FEHÉR AND MARTIN ROSE
Art Deco Desk Set. 1929–31
Designed for Rose Iron Works, Cleveland
Hot- and cold-rolled steel, stainless steel,
bronze, brass, aluminum, black marble, with
cloisonné inserts, 12½ x 23 x 8"
Rose Family Collection, Cleveland

WENDELL AUGUST
Desk Set. c. 1930
Designed for Wendell August Forge Inc.
Hand-forged aluminum, glass, paper; letter
box: 1¼ x 10 x 13"; inkwell: 3¼ x 3⅛ x 3⅓";
blotter: 1½ x 6¾ x 2¾"
Mitchell Wolfson, Jr. Collection, The
Wolfsonian Foundation, Miami Beach and
Genoa, Italy

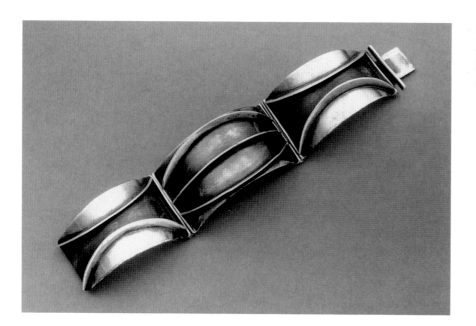

RUTH PENINGTON
Bracelet. 1938
Silver, 1¼ x 7"
Collection Ruth Penington

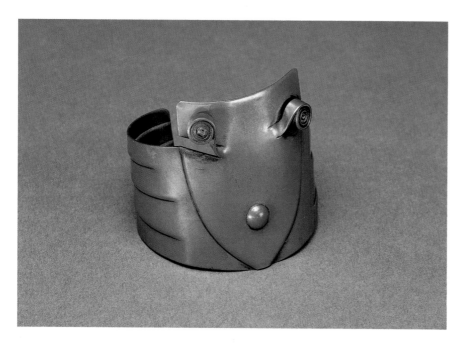

FRANCISCO REBAJES
Bracelet. c. 1945
Copper, 2 x 6⅛"
Collection Fern Simon

E. BYRNE LIVINGSTON
Ring and Pin Set. c. 1937
Silver, onyx, coral; pin: ⅞ x 2"; ring: diameter ⅞"
Collection The Metropolitan Museum of Art,
New York. Gift of E. Byrne Livingston

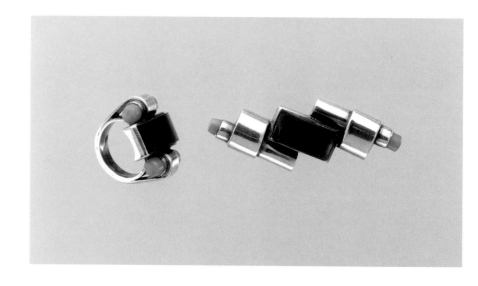

GERTRUDE KARLAN
Necklace and Earrings. c. 1937–41
Silver; necklace: 1⅛ x 15½ x ⅟₁₆"; earrings:
1⅞ x 1 x ⅟₁₆" each
Collection Mrs. Mildred Loew

MARGARET STRONG DE PATTA
Pin. 1940
Yellow gold, topaz, citrines, pearls, 1¼ x 3½"
Collection The Oakland Museum. Gift of
Mr. and Mrs. Hervey Parke Clark

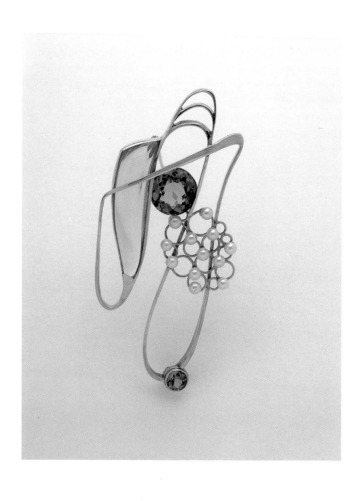

ARIETO (HARRY) BERTOIA
Pin. c. 1938–40
Hammered silver wire, 4¼ x 7"
Collection Patricia Shaw

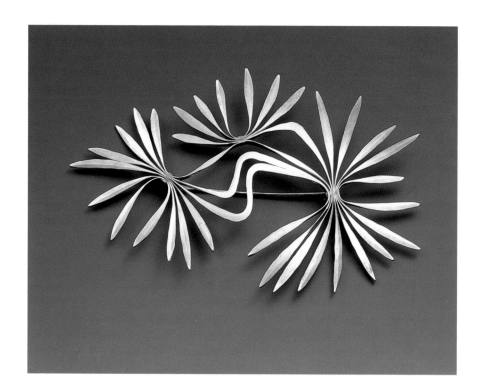

190

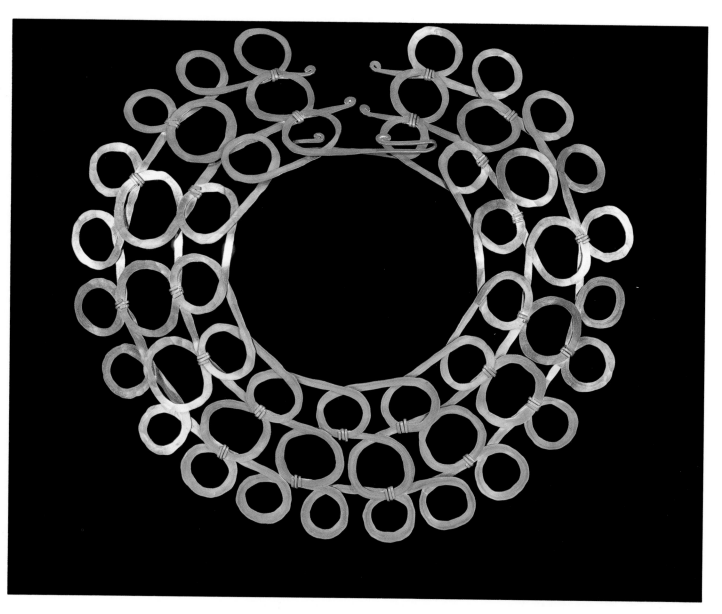

ALEXANDER CALDER
Necklace. c. 1940
Gilded brass, 12½ x 12½"
Collection National Museum of American Art,
Smithsonian Institution, Washington, D.C.
Gift of Mr. and Mrs. Alexander Calder

TEXTILES

H. R. MALLINSON AND COMPANY
Print Dress (detail). c. 1929
Silk
Collection The Museum at the Fashion
Institute of Technology, New York

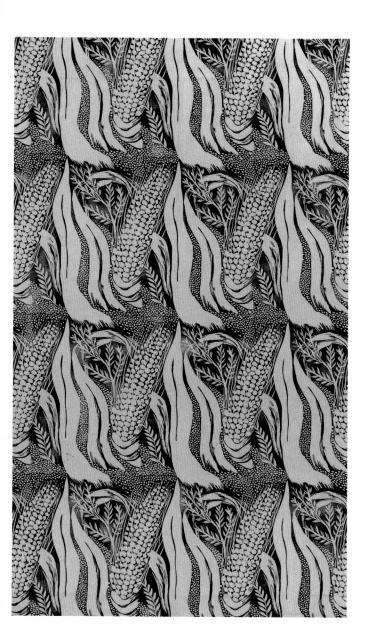

MILWAUKEE HANDICRAFT PROJECT
Block-printed Fabric. c. 1935–43
Designed by Barbara Warren
Muslin, 7' x 34½"
Collection Milwaukee Public Museum.
Gift of Elsa Ulbricht

HENRIETTE REISS
Rhythm Series. 1928
Cotton; screenprinted, 51⅛ x 50⅞"
Collection Goldstein Gallery, University
of Minnesota, St. Paul

BRENTS CARLTON
Batik Panel. 1927
Silk; wax-resist dyed, 50 x 38"
Collection John P. Axelrod

LYDIA BUSH-BROWN
New York Waterfront. c. 1928
Silk; wax-resist dyed, 35¼ x 48½"
Collection Cooper-Hewitt Museum, National
Museum of Design, Smithsonian Institution,
New York. Gift of Lydia Bush-Brown

ILONKA KARASZ
Rug. c. 1930
Cotton, wool, 8'11½" x 8'11"
Collection The Metropolitan Museum of Art,
New York. Purchase, Theodore R. Gamble, Jr.
Gift, in honor of his mother, Mrs. Theodore
Robert Gamble, 1983 (1983.228.2)

LORENZ KLEISER AND FREDERICK
AVINOFF
Jamaica Verdure Tapestry. c. 1927
Woven by Edgewater Tapestry Looms
Wool, 71 x 48½"
Collection Sharron Martin

MARGUERITE ZORACH
The Jungle. 1936
Commissioned by Crawford Shops
Wool, jute; handhooked, 42 x 60"
Collection The Museum of Modern Art,
New York. Gift of A. Conger Goodyear

Anonymous
Tulips. c. 1929–30
Produced by Schumacher
Cotton; airbrushed and stenciled,
6'6¼" x 45⅝"
Collection Goldstein Gallery,
University of Minnesota, St. Paul

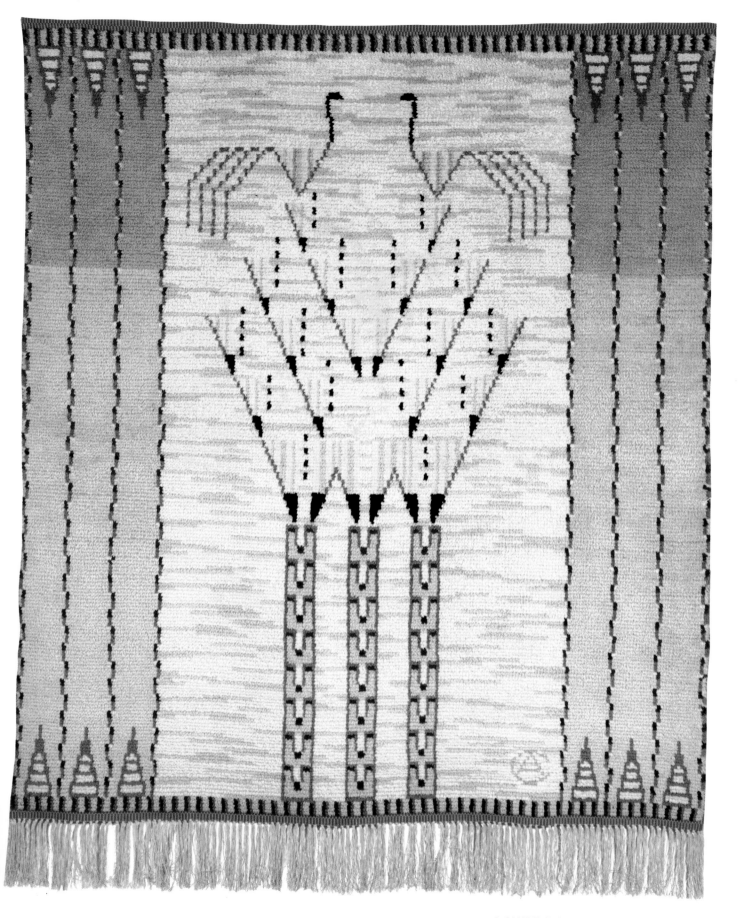

LOUISE (LOJA) SAARINEN
Tapestry #3 for Kingswood. 1928–29
Linen, wool, 66 x 50", including fringe
Collection Cranbrook Educational
Community, Bloomfield Hills, Michigan

MILWAUKEE HANDICRAFT PROJECT
WPA Hooked Rug. c. 1935–40
Wool, linen, 62½ x 47¼"
Collection Milwaukee Public Museum.
Gift of Mr. and Mrs. Quentin O'Sullivan

MARTHA RYTHER (attributed)
Grand Canyon Textile. 1927
Designed for H. R. Mallinson and Company
(Mallinson's Silks de Luxe)
Machine-printed silk, 16½ x 36"
Collection Goldstein Gallery, University
of Minnesota, St. Paul

NAVAJO
Shiprock Rug. c. 1920
Wool; handspun, 58" x 6'
Collection Tony Berlant

MARIANNE STRENGELL
Fringed Drapery Fabric. c. 1940s
Cotton, rayon, silver thread; handwoven,
10'8" x 41¼"
Collection Cranbrook Academy of Art
Museum, Bloomfield Hills, Michigan.
Gift of the artist

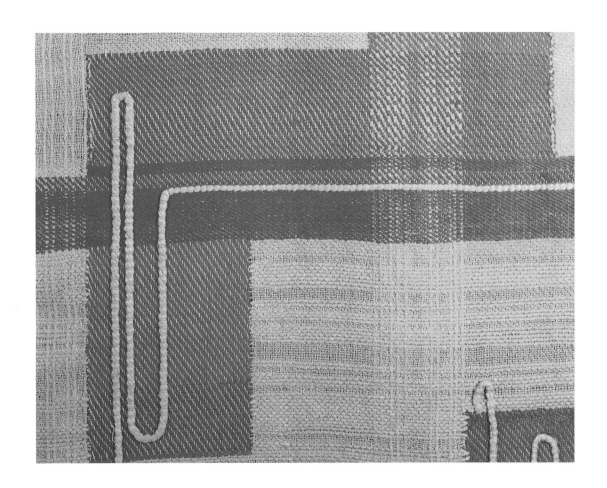

DOROTHY WRIGHT LIEBES
Wall Hanging (detail above). 1936
Cotton, silk, rayon; handwoven, 32 x 8'8"
Collection American Craft Museum, New York.
Gift of Dorothy Liebes Design, 1973.
Donated to the American Craft Museum
by the American Craft Council, 1990

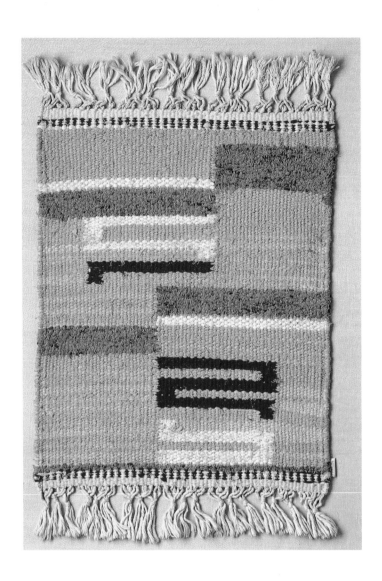

ROBERT DAVID SAILORS
Rug Sample #4. 1944
Cotton thread, cotton cloth, mosquito
netting, 17⅞ x 14¼"
Collection Cranbrook Academy of Art
Museum, Bloomfield Hills, Michigan.
Gift of the artist

ROBERT DAVID SAILORS
Rug Sample #32. 1944
Cotton, natural and dyed sisal, flannel,
11¼ x 14"
Collection Cranbrook Academy of Art
Museum, Bloomfield Hills, Michigan.
Gift of the artist

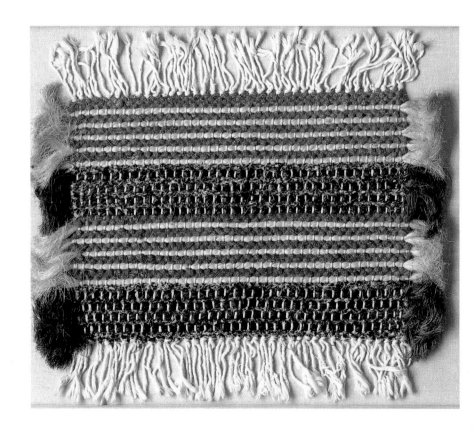

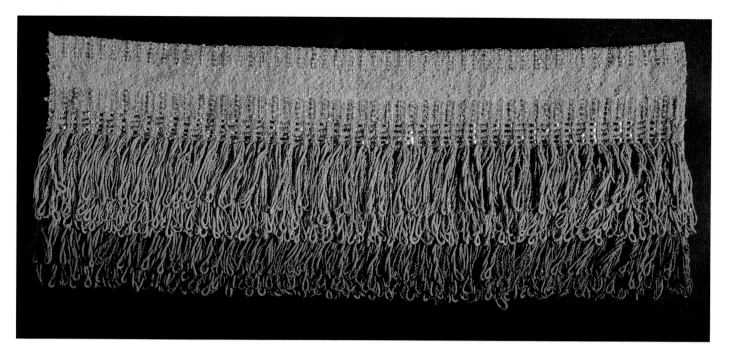

MARIA KIPP
Fabric. c. 1945
Cloth, 9½ x 25½"
Collection Doris Stein Research and
Design Center, Department of Costumes
and Textiles, Los Angeles County
Museum of Art. Gift of Harold Grieve

MARLI ERHMAN
Upholstery Fabric. 1941
Cotton; handwoven, 24⅝ x 24⅝"
Collection The Museum of Modern Art.
Gift of the designer

EVE PERI

Pillow Cover. 1942

Linen; embroidered and appliquéd,

17 x 17¼"

Collection American Craft Museum, New

York. Gift of Dr. Georgiana M. Peacher

MARION DORN
Headscarf. 1941–44
Silk, 36 x 34"
Collection Philadelphia Museum of Art.
Gift of Mrs. John Platt

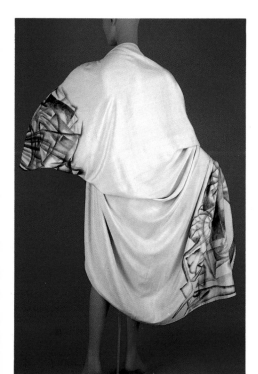

MADAME MARCELLE LABAUDT
Mantle. c. 1925
Silk; stenciled, 66½ x 62¼"
Collection The Oakland Museum

WOOD

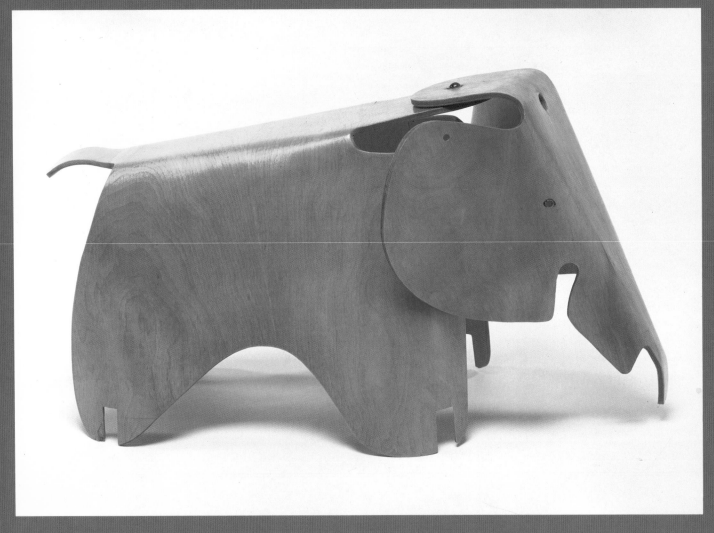

CHARLES O. EAMES AND RAY EAMES
Child's Elephant. 1945
Molded birch plywood, 16⅛ x 15¼ x 30⅛"
Collection Lucia Eames Demetrios, Eames
Office, Los Angeles

CHARLES O. EAMES
Tilt-back Lounge Chair with Metal Glides. c. 1944
Molded plywood, steel tubing,
29½ x 30⅛ x 30"
Collection The Museum of Modern Art, New York. Gift of the designer

BERTRAND GOLDBERG
Bentwood Settee. c. 1938–40
Mahogany plywood, 28 x 60 x 33"
Collection Bertrand Goldberg

209

JAMES L. PRESTINI
Lathe-turned Bowls. 1938–40
Left: beech, 5⅞ x 10⅝ x 10¼"; right: birch,
2¾ x 4¹⁵⁄₁₆ x 4⅞"
Collection American Craft Museum, New
York. Gift of Grace and Pauline Stafford
in memory of Cora E. Stafford, 1966.
Donated to the American Craft Museum by
the American Craft Council, 1990

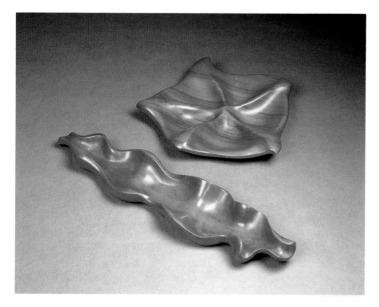

RUSSEL WRIGHT
Oceana Star-shaped Compartmented
Dish and Centerpiece Bowl. 1938
Wood; bowl: 1⅛ x 4⅝ x 19⅝";
dish: 1¼ x 13⅝ x 12½"
Collection William Straus

Anonymous
Hand Sculptures. c. 1940
Laminated wood; various sizes, ranging
from 2½ x 7½ x 3¾" to 2½ x 5½ x 5"
Collection Myron and Lois Kozman.
Courtesy Ubu Gallery, New York

RUSSEL WRIGHT
Oceana Wood Bowl. 1938
Gumwood, 4½ x 13¼"
Collection The Metropolitan Museum of Art,
New York. Gift of Russel Wright

FRANK LLOYD WRIGHT
Auldbras Plantation Chair (back view). c. 1939
Cypress plywood, 28 x 21 x 28"
Collection Mark A. McDonald

FRANK LLOYD WRIGHT
Auldbras Plantation Chair (front view). c. 1939

RUDOLPH MICHAEL SCHINDLER
Modular Chair. 1934
Plywood, 28 x 21½ x 33½"
Collection David Gebhard

FRANK LLOYD WRIGHT
Side Chair from the Imperial Hotel,
Tokyo. c. 1921
Wood, yellow-leatherette upholstery
(not original), 37¾ x 15½ x 17"
Collection Cooper-Hewitt Museum, National
Museum of Design, Smithsonian Institution,
New York. Given by Tetsuzo Inumaru

WHARTON ESHERICK
Dining Chair. 1928
Walnut, ebony, 36 x 14½ x 15"
Collection Mr. and Mrs. Peter Esherick

GOTTLIEB ELIEL SAARINEN
Dining Room Side Chair for Saarinen House. 1929–30
Fabricated by The Company of Master Craftsmen
Upholstery fabric by Loja Saarinen
Fir, horsehair, cotton, 37⅛ x 17 x 20"
Collection Cranbrook Academy of Art Museum, Bloomfield Hills, Michigan

WINOLD REISS
Red and Blue Armchair. c. 1920
Wood, 44 x 30½ x 27"
Collection Mr. and Mrs. W. Tjark Reiss

WHARTON ESHERICK
Side Chair. 1942–44
Designed for the Schutte-Koerting
Boardroom, 1938
Wood, 34¼ x 21 x 25¼"
Collection Philadelphia Museum of Art.
Gift of Schutte-Koerting Company

WHARTON ESHERICK
Sewing Cabinet (shown closed). 1933
Walnut burl, cherry, 30 x 27 x 19½"
Collection Helene Barbara Fisher Eldred

WHARTON ESHERICK
Sewing Cabinet (shown open). 1933

PAUL THEODORE FRANKL
Skyscraper Bookcase. 1926
Birch, lacquer, 84 x 39 x 14"
Collection High Museum of Art, Atlanta.
Purchase in honor of Darlene Schultz,
President of the Members' Guild,
1991–92, with funds from the Decorative
Arts Endowment

GOTTLIEB ELIEL SAARINEN
Cabinet for Saarinen House. 1929–30
Fabricated by Tor Berglund
African walnut, green hart, rosewood,
 and maple veneers, 60 x 38 x 18"
Collection Cranbrook Academy of Art
Museum, Bloomfield Hills, Michigan

EUGENE SCHOEN
Cabinet. c. 1930–32
Thuya burls, primavera, macassar ebony
door pulls, 36 x 48 x 21"
Courtesy Denis Gallion and Daniel Morris,
Historical Design Collection, Inc., New York

DONALD DESKEY
Sideboard. 1932
Mahogany, ebony, steel, 36 x 42 x 18"
Collection Radio City Music Hall Productions,
Rockefeller Center, New York

KARL EMANUEL MARTIN
(KEM) WEBER
Sideboard. c. 1930
Designed for the Grand Rapids Furniture
Company
Wood, 33⅓ x 72 x 19¾"
Collection The Metropolitan Museum of Art,
New York. Purchase, Theodore R. Gamble, Jr.
Gift, in honor of his mother, Mrs. Theodore
Robert Gamble, 1985 (1985.86.1)

PAUL THEODORE FRANKL
Bench. 1927
Lacquered and silvered wood, 24 x 34 x 15"
Collection Carol and Robert Goodman

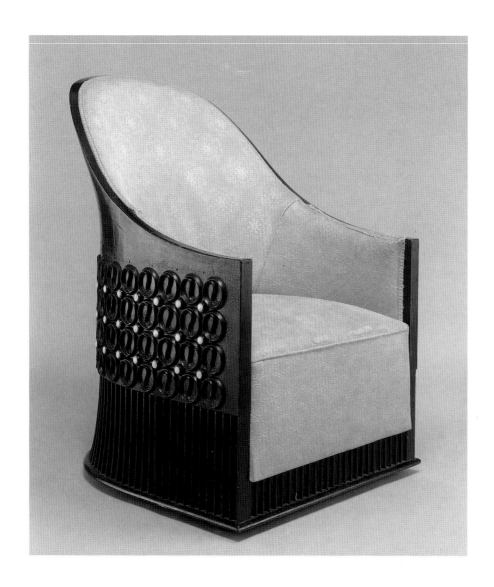

JOSEPH URBAN
Gondola Chair. c. 1922
Manufactured by Wiener Werkstäatte of
America, Inc.
Paint and silver leaf on wood, with mother
of pearl, 48 x 30"
Collection The Metropolitan Museum of Art,
New York. Purchase, Lita Annenberg Hazen
Charitable Trust Gift, 1985

TERRENCE HAROLD
ROBSJOHN-GIBBINGS
Low Table with Carved Rams' Heads. c. 1936
Wood, 24¾ x 19¼ x 19¼"
Collection Jorie Marshall Waterman

RESOURCE LIST

compiled by Tara Leigh Tappert

Artists and Advocates

Exhibitions

Periodicals and Books

Production Centers and Shops

Schools and University Programs

Societies and Associations

This resource list includes selected artists and advocates, exhibitions, publications, shops and manufacturing centers, educational institutions, and professional organizations that actively influenced the development of craft in the United States from 1920 to 1945. Its focus is the influence of European modernism upon American craft.

The material is organized in as useful a format for future study as possible, and is limited to what could be gathered from the most reliable sources. Categories are listed in alphabetical order, as are the listings within each category. Periodicals, institutions, and organizations, the names of which frequently change, are listed under the names in which they were founded; founders are identified where known. Active organizations are indicated by the word "present"; "n.d." is used where the closing date is uncertain.

T. T.

AALTO, HUGO ALVAR HENRIK

Born February 3, 1898, Kuortane, Finland;
died May 11, 1976, Helsinki, Finland
Architect, industrial designer

Aalto's contributions to modern design were manifold. In addition to residential and civic architecture, including major housing projects and city plans, he influenced furniture, lighting, and glass design. He established his own architecture practice in the small town of Jyäskylä after 1922, followed by Turku (1927–33), and Helsinki (1933–76). In 1924 he married Aino Marsio, an architect practicing in his office, and with her collaborated on design commissions for furniture and interiors. In the late 1920s he began designing the International Style buildings that catapulted him into world prominence in the 1930s. Aalto was a self-described humanist who emphasized organic forms and the use of natural materials. His experiments with tubular-metal furniture were at the forefront of avant-garde design in the 1920s. The molded-plywood furniture that he designed as "architectural accessories" for the Paimio sanatorium were conceived as part of the "biology" of the building. His earliest glassware dates from 1932, when he and his wife created geometric-patterned pressed-glass tableware for a competition. In 1935, they established the Artek design firm. The Museum of Modern Art in New York held an exhibition of Aalto's work in 1938, and from 1946 to 1948 he taught architecture at the Massachusetts Institute of Technology, in Cambridge.

AITKEN, RUSSELL BARNETT

Born January 20, 1906, Cleveland, Ohio
Ceramist, enamelist

Aitken was one of the youngest students to study in the ceramics program organized by R. Guy Cowan at the Cleveland School of Art in the 1920s. After graduating in 1931, he trained for two years in Berlin and in Vienna at the Kunstgewerbeschüle under architect-designer Josef Hoffmann and ceramist Michael Powolny. Upon his return to the United States, Aitken, with fellow ceramist Whitney Atchley, established the Pottery Workshop in Cleveland. In 1935 he opened a studio in New York, producing pottery and ceramic sculptures that consistently won prizes at the Cleveland Museum of Art's annual May Shows and at the Ceramic Nationals in Syracuse. In addition to the strong stylistic and iconographic influences of Vienna, Aitken's ceramics reflect his admiration for the work of the American sculptor Frederic Remington. Aitken worked with clay for only ten years, never returning to the medium after serving in the military during World War II.

ALBERS, ANNI (NÉE ANNELISE FLEISCHMANN; LATER, MRS. JOSEF ALBERS)

Born June 12, 1899, Berlin, Germany; died May 9, 1994, Orange, Connecticut
Weaver, textile designer, teacher

Albers was a leading textile artist and the wife of abstract painter Josef Albers. After graduating from the Dessau Bauhaus in 1930, she became an instructor in textiles at the school and acting director of its weaving workshop. After the Gestapo closed the Bauhaus in 1933, Albers met architect Philip Johnson in Berlin. Johnson, then a curator at The Museum of Modern Art in New York, arranged for the Alberses to emigrate to the United States. From 1934 to 1949 they taught at Black Mountain College, the progressive art school established by John Andrew Rice in Asheville, North Carolina. In 1949 Anni Albers became the first weaver to have a solo exhibition at The Museum of Modern Art. She embarked on a free-lance career after moving to New Haven, Connecticut, with her husband in the 1950s, and continued to weave and to publish books on weaving, including *On Designing* (1959) and *On Weaving* (1965). After the couple moved to Orange, Connecticut, in the early 1970s, Albers became a printmaker. In 1980 she was honored by the Women's Caucus for Art for outstanding achievement in the fields of weaving, design, and printmaking.

ALBERS, JOSEF

Born March 19, 1888, Bottrop, Westphalia, Germany; died March 24, 1976, Orange, Connecticut
Painter, teacher

Born into a family of craftsmen, Albers was initially trained as a teacher. He taught primary school in the Bottrop area while continuing his studies at the Berlin Kunstakademie (1913–15); the Essen Kunstgewerbeschüle (1916–19); with Franz von Stuck at the Munich Akademie (1919–20); and with Walter Gropius at the Weimar Bauhaus (1920–23). Albers began teaching at the Bauhaus in 1923, principally the preliminary course, but also wallpaper design, freehand lettering, and workshops in glass and furniture. He remained at the Bauhaus until it was forced to close in 1933, and shortly thereafter accepted a teaching position at Black Mountain College in Asheville, North Carolina. During his tenure Albers not only implemented an innovative, Bauhaus-based curriculum, but his active involvement in the art world helped identify the college as a center for experimental art. During the 1930s and 1940s Albers's fascination with geometric patterns and figure-ground relationships reinforced his interest in abstraction, optical illusion, and Gestalt theory. He became one of the leading proponents of abstract art in the United States, disseminating his ideas through numerous lectures and exhibitions. He remained at Black Mountain until 1949, when he was appointed chairman of the Graduate School of Design at Yale University in New Haven, Connecticut.

ANDRESON, LAURA

Born 1902, San Bernadino, California
Ceramist, teacher

Andreson received a B.A. from the University of California at Los Angeles (UCLA; 1932) and an M.A. in painting from Columbia University in New York (1936). While working toward her master's degree, she began teaching in the art department at UCLA during the summers, joining the faculty upon graduation and continuing to teach there until her retirement in 1970. From a student she had sent to train with ceramist F. Carlton Ball, Andreson learned Ball's technique for wheel-thrown pottery. She soon established a pioneering pottery course at UCLA, offering information that was not readily available to West Coast potters. Her early works were low-fired, gloss-glazed earthenwares, but the discovery in 1948 of stoneware clay deposits in Northern California, and an accidental reduction firing in her kiln, led Andreson to experiment with stoneware bodies and glazes. Andreson produced clean, simplified forms in the Scandinavian style, to which she added vibrant colors. Following her retirement from teaching, she participated in more than seventy invitational and one-woman exhibitions.

ARCHIPENKO, ALEXANDER

Born May 30, 1887, Kiev, Russia; died February 25, 1964, New York, New York
Sculptor, ceramist, teacher

Archipenko received his art training at the Kiev Art School (1902–05) and briefly at the École des Beaux-Arts, Paris, in 1908, before opening his own art school. He exhibited Cubist sculptures and reliefs with the Section d'Or beginning in 1910. In 1913 he was included in the New York Armory Show and had a one-man exhibition in the avant-garde Der Sturm Gallery in Berlin. In 1921 he moved to Berlin and opened an art school, but two years later moved to New York and founded schools in Manhattan and Woodstock. In 1929 he established Arko, a laboratory school for ceramics, in New York, and relocated and enlarged his Woodstock summer school. He reopened these schools in 1939, following moves to California and to Chicago, where he taught at the New Bauhaus from 1937 to 1938. Archipenko was an influential teacher, promoting a kind of animated painting that became known as "Archpentura." He frequently worked in polychrome terracotta, exploiting the material to emphasize its texture, modeling, and color. His ceramics were regularly exhibited in one-man shows, and occasionally at the Ceramic Nationals in Syracuse.

ARMOUR, ARTHUR
Born 1908, Conneaut Lake, Pennsylvania
Metalsmith, architect

Armour earned a degree in architecture from the Carnegie Institute of Technology (1931). He briefly designed patterns at the Wendell August Forge and was a practicing architect before opening his own metalwork shop in Grove City, Pennsylvania, in 1933. Armour was a competent designer-craftsman of hand-forged and -hammered aluminum wares; his success was such that his shop employed twenty people throughout the Depression. He continued to produce metalwork until his retirement in 1975.

ARTIS, WILLIAM ELLSWORTH
Born February 2, 1914, Washington, North Carolina; died April 3, 1977, Northport, New York
Ceramist, teacher

Artis worked as an artist-teacher from the earliest stages of his career. From 1933 to 1935 he taught pottery at the Harlem YMCA while studying at the Art Students League, and went on to earn a B.S. from Chadron State College in Nebraska as well as B.F.A. and M.F.A. degrees from Syracuse University. Artis worked as an artist for the Works Progress Administration in the late 1930s and served in the Army during World War II. In 1954, after teaching at the Pine Ridge Indian Reservation in South Dakota, he began a twelve-year association with Nebraska State Teachers College in Chadron. From 1966 until his retirement in 1975 he was a professor of art at Mankato State University in Minnesota. While he concentrated primarily on clay modeling, his later works include sculptural pottery. Artis was a recipient of the John Hope Prize for sculpture (1933 and 1935), a Rosenwald Fellowship (1947), and the Outstanding Afro-American Artist award (1970).

ATWATER, MARY (NÉE MEIGS)
Born February 28, 1878, Rock Island, Illinois; died 1956
Weaver, instructor

Atwater trained at The School of the Art Institute of Chicago and the Académie Julian and Académie Colorossi in Paris. After the death of her husband in 1922, she founded the Shuttle-Craft Guild, a popular business that she operated from her home. Through the *Shuttle-Craft Course of Instruction* (1923) and "Shuttle Craft Guild Bulletin"—a home-study weaving course—Atwater reached a national audience. A traditionalist who expanded on a variety of vernacular coverlet patterns, she compiled a "recipe" book of patterns, complete with threading and treadling instructions, that she published in 1928 as the *Shuttle-Craft Book of American Hand-weaving*. A sought-after and highly regarded teacher, Atwater directed workshops throughout the United States in the 1920s and 1930s.

AUGUST, WENDELL
Metalsmith, blacksmith

See Wendell August Forge: PRODUCTION CENTERS AND SHOPS—METAL

AYERS, SAMUEL
Glass artist

See Steuben Glass Works: PRODUCTION CENTERS AND SHOPS—GLASS

BACH, OSCAR BRUNO
Born December 13, 1884, Germany; died 1957
Metalsmith

Bach received his art training at the Royal Art Academy in Berlin. Upon emigrating to New York, he joined the Architectural League, winning a Medal of Honor in the League's 1926 exhibition for the traditionally styled bronze, steel, and repoussé-silver doors he designed for The Toledo Museum of Art. As a result, Bach received commissions for institutions such as Christ Church, Cranbrook; and Riverside Church and Temple Emanuel in New York. He also created four exterior plaques for New York's Rockefeller Center. Bach remained active until the outbreak of World War II.

BACH, RICHARD FRANZ
Born June 29, 1887, New York, New York; died February 16, 1968
Curator, writer

Bach was appointed associate curator for industrial art at The Metropolitan Museum of Art in 1918, and organized a number of the Metropolitan's American Industrial Art "annuals" beginning in 1921. In the late 1920s he became involved in the selection of the American Federation of Arts' International Exhibitions of Contemporary Industrial Arts, and was editor of the *Magazine of Art* from 1930 to 1932. He was an active member of various craft organizations, including the Architectural League, the Society of Designer-Craftsmen, and the American Institute of Architects in New York.

BAGGS, ARTHUR EUGENE
Born October 27, 1886, Alfred, New York; died 1947
Ceramist, teacher

When Baggs entered the newly established New York School of Clayworking and Ceramics at Alfred University in 1902, he was interested in studying drawing and design, but as a student of Charles Fergus Binns he developed an interest in ceramics. In 1904 Binns sent Baggs to Marblehead, Massachusetts, to assist Dr. Herbert J. Hall in the organization of a pottery department as part of the occupational therapy program at his sanatorium. In 1908 the pottery was reorganized as a commercial enterprise known as Marblehead Pottery, and soon had a weekly output of some two hundred matte-glazed pieces, the majority designed by Baggs. In New York from 1909 to 1915, Baggs taught elementary pottery, provided technical assistance for the Ethical Culture Schools, and studied at the Art Students League. He purchased Marblehead Pottery from Hall in 1915, and until it closed in 1936 spent his summers at the pottery, producing ceramics noted for their simple lines, matte finishes, and incised decoration. From 1925 to 1928 Baggs taught at the Cleveland School of Art and worked as a glaze chemist at the Cowan Pottery Studio. In 1927 he became head of the ceramics program at Ohio State University, where he taught until his death in 1947.

BALDWIN, BENJAMIN JAMES
Born March 29, 1913, Montgomery, Alabama
Architect, interior designer, textile designer

Baldwin majored in architecture as an undergraduate at Princeton University from 1931 to 1935. Following a year of study with painter Hans Hofmann in New York and Provincetown, Massachusetts, he entered the Graduate School of Architecture at Princeton, earning a master's degree in 1938. He attended the Cranbrook Academy of Art from 1938 to 1939, after which he worked briefly with the architectural firm of Saarinen and Saarinen. In 1940 Baldwin formed a partnership with Harry Weese in Kenilworth, Illinois, which was dissolved when Baldwin joined the Navy in 1942. After the war, Baldwin joined Skidmore, Owings and Merrill in Chicago, spending two years developing the interior design aspects of the firm's building projects. He practiced in partnership with William Machado from 1948 to 1956, and spent the remainder of his career as an independent designer of minimalist interiors. In addition to New York and Chicago, Baldwin practiced in Montgomery, Alabama; East Hampton, New York; and Sarasota, Florida.

BALL, F. CARLTON
Born April 2, 1911, Sutter Creek, California; died June 5, 1992, Tacoma, Washington
Ceramist, teacher

Ball studied at the University of Southern California (USC) from 1932 to 1935, when he began a peripatetic teaching career. He taught at the California College of Arts and Crafts (1935–38); Mills College, Oakland, California (1939–49); the University of Wisconsin, Madison (1950–51); Southern Illinois University, Carbondale (1951–56); USC (1956–68); and the University of Puget Sound, in Tacoma, Washington (1968 until his retirement). Ball is known for producing large pots with prominent surface texture, and for contributing significantly to the development of ceramics education. He wrote several books on the aesthetics and techniques of potting, including the highly regarded *Making Pottery Without a Wheel: Texture and Form in Clay* (1965), which he coauthored with Janice Lovoos.

BARR, ALFRED HAMILTON, JR.
Born January 28, 1902, Detroit, Michigan; died August 15, 1981, Salisbury, Connecticut
Museum director, curator

Barr attended Princeton University, earning a B.F.A. in art history (1922) and an M.A. in the same field (1923). He taught art history at Vassar College in Poughkeepsie, New York, in 1924 and also began work on a Ph.D. in art history at Harvard University. His growing passion for modern art found outlets in the organization of an exhibit of modern paintings at Harvard's Fogg Art Museum, and, at Wellesley College in 1926, in teaching the first contemporary art history course ever offered at an American university. By 1929, Barr's activities had come to the attention of a group of contemporary art collectors who were organizing a new museum. Following an interview with collector Abby Aldrich Rockefeller, Barr was appointed the first director of the nascent Museum of Modern Art in New York. Under Barr, the museum assumed a principal role in introducing the public to the art of its time, and the works the museum acquired formed the archetypal collection of modern visual art. Barr also established an architecture and design department that

featured craft objects, setting the standard in these fields for decades. While he was relieved of the directorship in 1944, he maintained an association with the museum until his retirement in 1967.

BATES, KENNETH FRANCIS
Born May 24, 1904, North Scituate, Massachusetts; died May 24, 1994, Euclid, Ohio
Enamelist, silversmith, teacher

Known as the dean of American enamelwork, Bates studied with the distinguished enameling instructor Laurin Martin at the Massachusetts College of Art in Boston. Bates first went abroad in 1928, the same year he began teaching design at the Cleveland School of Art. He returned to Europe in the summer of 1931, studying design at the École des Beaux-Arts Américaine, in Fontainebleau. He came under the influence of the geometric style advocated by the Union des Artistes Modernes, an approach evident in his metal- and enamelwork of the 1930s. Bates increasingly subordinated his metalwork to enameling, and by the 1950s was creating small-scale biomorphic forms that embodied his view of enamel as a precious medium. During the 1950s and 1960s he published several books and papers that remain standard texts for the field, including *Enameling, Principles and Practices* (1951), *Basic Design* (1960), and *The Enamelist* (1967).

BEL GEDDES, NORMAN
Born April 27, 1893, Adrian, Michigan; died May 8, 1958, New York, New York
Industrial designer

Known for popularizing the "streamline" style, Bel Geddes received formal arts training at the Cleveland School of Art, but as a designer he regarded himself as essentially self-taught. He first made theatrical stage sets for the Players Club and the Metropolitan and Chicago opera companies, designing scenery for ballets by Ruth St. Denis. Turning to industrial design in the early 1930s, Bel Geddes created the first streamlined ocean liner and ocean-going yacht, airplane interiors for Pan-American Airways, and the Futurama Building for the 1939–40 New York World's Fair. He also designed furniture, radios, and cabinets, and published the design treatises *Horizons* (1932) and *Magic Motorways* (1940).

BERTOIA, ARIETO (HARRY)
Born March 10, 1915, San Lorenzo, Udine, Italy; died November 6, 1978, Bally, Pennsylvania
Metalsmith, jeweler, furniture designer, teacher

Bertoia attended the Art School of the

Detroit Society of Arts and Crafts (1936–37) and the Cranbrook Academy of Art. He reopened the Cranbrook metals shop in 1938, teaching metalwork until 1943; from 1942 to 1943 he also taught graphic art at Cranbrook. After the metals shop was closed in 1943, Bertoia moved to California to work as a furniture designer with Charles and Ray Eames. Following World War II, he was employed by the Point Loma Naval Electronics Laboratory in California. By 1950, Bertoia had moved his family to Barto, Pennsylvania, and opened a studio in nearby Bally. There, he produced furniture designs for the New York firm Knoll Associates, Inc., and experimented with large freestanding metal sculptures, which were eventually incorporated into interior spaces he designed in collaboration with numerous architects.

BLANCHARD, PORTER GEORGE
Born February 28, 1886, Littleton, Massachusetts; died 1973, Los Angeles, California
Silversmith

Blanchard was trained by his father, the silversmith George Porter Blanchard, who had worked for Arthur J. Stone before opening his own shop in Gardner, Massachusetts. The junior Blanchard was a member of the Society of Arts and Crafts, Boston, and the Detroit Society of Arts and Crafts. Prior to 1923, when he moved to Burbank, California, Blanchard displayed his Colonial Revival silverwork in the two craft societies' exhibitions. In 1924 he helped found the Arts and Crafts Society of Southern California, and opened a business under his own name. The Blanchard shop employed several assistants and operated at various locations in the Los Angeles area, producing Colonial Revival tableware—including the Paul Revere, Colonial Antique, and Mayflower lines—as well as more progressive European-inspired designs. Blanchard's commitment to craft aesthetics is evident in the hand-hammered flatware and handspun holloware produced in his shop, which were sold in major department stores throughout the country.

BLAZYS, ALEXANDER
Born February 16, 1894, Lithuania, Russia; died 1963
Sculptor, ceramist

Blazys appeared on the Cleveland art scene in 1925. In the following year he joined the faculty of the Cleveland School of Art and won first prize for sculpture at the Museum of Art's May Show. Among his entries were two small bronzes of Russian dancers and a wood figure of Moses. Both figures appeared in the May Show of 1927 as ceramic sculptures produced by the Cowan

Pottery Studio, with which Blazys became associated. In a shift that added to the prestige of the firm while increasing its profits, Blazys centered the pottery's production on individually crafted decorative sculptures. While his active association with Cowan was short-lived, Blazys remained in Cleveland until 1938, and continued to teach at the School of Art.

BOGATAY, PAUL
Born July 5, 1905, Ada, Ohio; died 1972, Columbus, Ohio
Ceramist, teacher

During the mid-1920s Bogatay studied with R. Guy Cowan and, briefly, Arthur Eugene Baggs at the Cleveland School of Art. He continued his training under Baggs in the graduate arts program at Ohio State University, where Baggs was appointed a professor of ceramic arts in 1928. Bogatay joined the faculty as a ceramics instructor in the early 1930s, remaining until his retirement in 1971. He continued to explore the sculptural qualities of clay throughout his teaching career, producing work that secured two first prizes and a purchase prize at the Ceramic Nationals in Syracuse. He was the recipient of Tiffany and Rockefeller Foundation fellowships and served as an officer of the American Ceramic Society later in his career.

BOOTH, GEORGE G.
Born 1864, Toronto, Ontario, Canada; died April 11, 1949, Detroit, Michigan
Publisher, school founder, art patron

Booth assumed the presidency of The Evening News Association upon the death of his father-in-law, the publisher James E. Scripps, in 1906. An active patron of the arts, he became one of the leading proponents of the Arts and Crafts movement in America, crediting his interest in craftsmanship to his father and grandfather, who were metalworkers in the village of Cranbrook (Kent), England. Booth founded Cranbrook Press in 1900, and was instrumental in the establishment of the Detroit Society of Arts and Crafts in 1906. In 1915 he donated a substantial collection of contemporary crafts and sculpture to the Detroit Museum of Art (now the Detroit Institute of Art), and in the early 1920s he became involved with the architectural program at the University of Michigan. Booth's greatest contribution to American craft was the establishment of the Cranbrook Educational Community in Bloomfield Hills, Michigan, in 1925. In collaboration with Eliel Saarinen, who developed the site plan and formulated Cranbrook's holistic approach to arts education, Booth built a residential arts community where students worked closely with a distinguished faculty

of master craftsmen. The complex ultimately consisted of the Cranbrook Academy of Art; the Cranbrook Institute of Science; an elementary school, the Brookside School; two preparatory schools, Cranbrook School (for boys) and Kingswood School (for girls); and Christ Church. In 1929 Booth retired from The Evening News Association to devote himself full-time to Cranbrook.

BOUY, JULES
Born 1872, France; died June 28, 1937, New York, New York
Interior designer, furniture designer, metalsmith

Bouy served a metalworking apprenticeship with Edgar Brandt in France and directed an interior design firm in Belgium before emigrating to the United States around World War I. In New York he was associated with the Paris-based design firm L. Alavoine and Company from 1924 to 1927, and was the head of Ferrobrandt, Inc., a retail outlet for modern French design. During this period Bouy decorated the residences of several New York clients using modern and period-revival French furnishings. By 1928, he was president and director of his own firm, Bouy, Inc., which received interior design commissions from fashionable New Yorkers such as Lillie P. Bliss and Agnes Miles Carpenter.

BOWLES, JANET PAYNE (MRS. JOSEPH MOORE BOWLES)
Born June 29, 1882, Indianapolis, Indiana; died July 18, 1948, Indianapolis, Indiana
Metalsmith, silversmith, jeweler

Payne Bowles lived in Boston with her husband, Joseph Moore Bowles, editor of the journal Modern Art, from 1895 to 1902. She studied psychology and philosophy with William James at Radcliffe College, and learned the rudimentary techniques of metalsmithing in 1899 at a local shop. From 1902 until Payne Bowles and her husband separated in 1912, they lived in New York and in several experimental communities in the vicinity. By 1907, she had established her own studio, where she refined her metalworking skills and fulfilled commissions for jeweled ornaments, gold spoons and plates, and other metalware. In 1912 she won first prize at the competition of London and Paris Jewelers, and the following year, a prize from the International Goldsmiths. Returning to Indianapolis in 1914, she taught courses in metalsmithing, and continued to exhibit her metalwork and jewelry, garnering numerous international prizes. Payne Bowles's work was shown during the 1920s and 1930s in the annual exhibitions of the John Herron Art Institute in Indianapolis (now the Indi-

anapolis Museum of Art) and at the Art Center in New York. She continued to teach local students until her retirement in 1942.

BREUER, MARCEL LAJOS
Born May 22, 1902, Pécs, Hungary; died July 1, 1981, New York, New York
Architect, furniture designer

Breuer studied at the Akademie der Bildenden Künste in Vienna in 1920, but left shortly thereafter to enroll at the Weimar Bauhaus, where he studied furniture design. One of the first students to benefit from the school's integrated applied-arts program, he became a protégé of Bauhaus director Walter Gropius. He received a diploma in 1924, and the Bauhaus moved to new quarters in Dessau the following year. Gropius subsequently hired Breuer as master of the carpentry workshop, a position that he held until 1928. In the late 1920s Breuer designed a tubular-steel chair that was easy to manufacture. Light, resilient, and sleek, it became a hallmark of modernist design. In 1928 Breuer left the Bauhaus to establish his own architectural firm in Berlin. Most of the firm's work was interior design; it was not until 1932 that Breuer fulfilled an architectural commission, for the Harnischmacher House in Wiesbaden. He moved to England in 1935 and formed a partnership with F. R. S. Yorke, designing furniture for the Isokon company, and experimented with molded and cutout plywood furniture for Heal and Son. In 1937 he joined Gropius on the faculty of the Graduate School of Design at Harvard University. Breuer also practiced architecture in partnership with Gropius from 1937 to 1941 and continued to develop his cutout plywood furniture—through commissions for Bryn Mawr College (1938) and the Pennsylvania Pavilion at the 1939–40 New York World's Fair, and through competitions such as The Museum of Modern Art's "International Competition for Low-Cost Furniture Design" (1948) and "Designs for Modern Furniture" (1950). In 1949, after moving his office to New York, Breuer was asked by The Museum of Modern Art to design a house for installation in its sculpture garden, an event significantly enhanced his standing as an architect.

BRIGHAM, WILLIAM EDGAR
Born July 29, 1885, North Attleboro, Massachusetts; died 1962
Silversmith, teacher

After graduation from the Rhode Island School of Design (RISD) in 1910 and further study at Harvard University under Denman Ross, Brigham was appointed head of the design department at the

Cleveland School of Art. In 1914 he became director of the department of decorative design at RISD, a post he held until 1927. Financially independent, Brigham maintained a studio in his home, where he designed and crafted elaborate traditional jewelry. He exhibited his work at the Society of Arts and Crafts, Boston, in 1936, and at the Paris Exposition of 1937. During the 1940s his jewelry was sold in New York at America House, the retail shop established by the American Craftsmen's Cooperative Council in 1939.

BUFANO, BENIAMINO
Born October 14, 1898, San-Fele, Italy; died August 18, 1970, San Francisco, California
Sculptor, teacher

Bufano trained at the Beaux-Arts Institute of Design in Paris, and at the National Academy of Design and the Art Students League in New York, studying with such well-regarded sculptors as Paul Manship, James L. Fraser, and Herbert Adams. In the 1930s he taught sculpture at the California College of Arts and Crafts and executed numerous commissions for public sculpture in the Oakland area.

BUSH-BROWN, LYDIA (MRS. FRANCIS HEAD)
Born November 5, 1887, Florence, Italy; died 1984
Weaver, textile designer

Daughter of sculptor Henry Kirk Bush-Brown and portrait painter Margaret Lesley Bush-Brown, Lydia trained at Pratt Institute and studied batik techniques with Charles Pellew in Washington, D.C. She became a decorator, making her reputation in the 1920s and 1930s with exquisite "silk murals" inspired by her travels in the Middle East. Bush-Brown exhibited widely in this country and abroad, including the Paris Exposition of 1937, and published several articles on the potential uses of silk murals in interior decoration.

CALDER, ALEXANDER
Born July 22, 1898, Lawnton, Pennsylvania; died November 11, 1976, New York, New York
Sculptor, metalsmith, jeweler

Calder, the son of sculptor Alexander Stirling Calder, studied mechanical engineering at the Stevens Institute of Technology in Hoboken, New Jersey (1915–19), and later trained at the Art Students League (1923). He began working as an illustrator for the *National Police Gazette* in 1924, and would later create drawings for books such as *Fables of Aesop* (1931) and *Three Young*

Rats (1944). Calder went to Paris in 1926, and within a year began experimenting with animated toys and animals made of wire and wood. He later added metal disks and other colorfully painted abstract shapes to his wire sculptures, which were exhibited for the first time in Paris in 1931. Around 1932, Marcel Duchamp christened Calder's moveable constructions "mobiles"; the stationary pieces were given the name "stabiles" by Jean Arp. By 1934, Calder's work was being regularly exhibited at the Pierre Matisse Gallery in New York. His reputation was firmly established in 1937 with the completion of the monumental stabile *Whale* and his design for the *Mercury Fountain* in the Spanish Pavilion at the Paris Exposition. Calder also made whimsical wire and hammered-metal jewelry, exhibiting it for the first time at the Willard Gallery, New York, in 1941.

CARDER, FREDERICK
Born September 18, 1863, Brockmoor, Kingswinford, Staffordshire, England; died December 10, 1963, Corning, New York
Glass artist

In 1903 Carder was hired away from the prestigious English glassmaking firm of Stevens and Williams to establish the Steuben Glass Works in Corning, New York. The following year, he developed and began producing an art glass known as Aurene. Usually iridescent gold or brilliant blue, Aurene wares were highly competitive with Tiffany glass. In 1918 the Steuben factory was taken over by Corning Glass Works, and Carder remained as art director of the Steuben Division until 1932. His experiments with acid etching, casing, and deep, massive cutting during the 1920s resulted in the Cintra, Intarsia, and Cluthra lines, which rivaled the best French and Scandinavian glass. Carder was relieved of his duties as art director when Corning came under new administration in 1932, but was allowed to set up a private studio in the factory. He continued to experiment with non-production, lost-wax castings of double-walled Diatreta vases, cast-glass sculptures, *pâte de verre,* and molded architectural glass. He retired in 1959 to devote himself to painting.

CAUMAN, REBECCA
Born c. 1887, Ontario, Canada; died 1964
Metalsmith

Cauman was raised in Boston, where she earned bench space at the Society of Arts and Crafts in the 1920s. In 1927 her silver- and copperwork was included in the society's Triennial Exhibition, and in R. H. Macy's "Exposition of Art in Trade" in New York—an event that led Cauman and her younger sister Josephine to move there

and open a retail shop the following year. Located on Madison Avenue, the Cauman shop specialized in silver, pewter, and copper tableware, enamelwork, decorative accessories, and jewelry. In 1937 Cauman's silverwork was included in the Paris Exposition and in the exhibition "Contemporary Industrial and Handwrought Silver" at The Brooklyn Museum, and was illustrated in *Arts & Decoration* and *Interior Decorator*. In 1940 her work was shown in the Fifteenth American Industrial Art Exhibition at The Metropolitan Museum of Art. The Cauman shop remained open into the 1940s.

COOPER, DAN
No dates available
Textile designer, furniture designer

Cooper was a nationally known interior decorator and designer of woven and hand-screenprinted fabrics and furniture in a modern idiom. He established his own firm, Dan Cooper Inc., in New York, through which he designed interiors for public and private buildings throughout the country. Cooper was also a consultant for a number of Government-sponsored housing projects.

COWAN, R. GUY
Born August 1, 1884, East Liverpool, Ohio; died 1957
Ceramist, sculptor, teacher

Cowan studied with Charles Fergus Binns at the New York College of Clayworking and Ceramics at Alfred University, becoming one of the school's first graduates in 1907. Around 1912 Cowan set up a kiln behind the house of the Cleveland metalsmith Horace Potter. He incorporated the Cleveland Pottery and Tile Company the following year, and in 1917 won a first prize for pottery at the Art Institute of Chicago's Annual Exhibition of Applied Art. After World War I, Cowan moved the pottery to Rocky River, a suburb of Cleveland, and changed its name to Cowan Pottery Studio. In 1923 he joined the faculty of the ceramics department of the Cleveland School of Art and began to concentrate on molded, limited-edition ceramics, winning the Art Institute's Logan Medal for Beauty in Design in 1924. For several years Cowan worked alone, producing vessels and figurines in high-fired white porcelain but by 1927 he began to accept limited-edition design work from artists such as Alexander Blazys, Waylande DeSantis Gregory, Paul Manship, and Thelma Frazier (Winter). The quality and variety of Cowan's glazes were improved by Arthur Eugene Baggs, who briefly joined the studio in the mid-1920s. The Depression forced Cowan to close the pottery in 1931. Following a year as a research engineer with the Cleveland-based Ferro Enamel Company, he moved to Syracuse, New York, where he became the art director of the Onondaga Pottery Company and assumed a pivotal role in the organization of the Ceramic Nationals at the Syracuse Museum of Fine Arts.

CRAVER, MARGRET WITHERS
Born 1907, Pratt, Kansas; died 1991
Silversmith, metalsmith

Craver received her undergraduate degree from the University of Kansas, Lawrence (1929). During the 1930s she received private instruction in metalworking, studying with master craftsmen Wilson Weir of Tiffany's in New York; Arthur Nevill Kirk in Detroit; Leonard Heinrich, chief armor conservator at The Metropolitan Museum of Art in New York; Baron Erik Fleming, silversmith to the King, in Stockholm; and at the studio of Stone Associates in Gardner, Massachusetts. Craver also served as assistant director of the Wichita Art Association and as head of its craft program. In 1944 she met Gustav Niemeyer, president of Handy and Harman, a leading New York refiner of precious metals. For Handy and Harman Craver established the nonprofit Hospital Service Program, which worked directly with the Surgeon General of the U.S. Army and the chief occupational therapists in hospitals around the country. Craver trained the therapists in metalsmithing techniques and designed projects to help restore muscle strength and flexibility to the arms and hands of soldiers wounded during World War II. She continued to work for the firm after the war, renaming the division the Craft Service Department and turning her attention to the training of professional silversmiths. She organized five National Silversmithing Workshop Conferences between 1947 and 1953. Held at the Rhode Island School of Design and, later, at the Rochester Institute of Technology, the workshops were responsible for training the majority of metalsmiths working in the United States today. Craver resigned from Handy and Harman in 1953 and moved to Newburyport, Massachusetts, where she worked independently.

CRISP, ARTHUR
Born April 26, 1881, Hamilton, Ontario, Canada; no death date available
Industrial designer, teacher

Crisp studied at the Art Students League in the late nineteenth century, and became known primarily for his theater designs and for textiles commissioned for hotels, clubs, and schools on the East Coast and in Canada. He taught in New York at the Art Students League, the Cooper Union

Art School, and the National Academy of Design.

CULIN, STEWART
Born 1858; died 1929
Curator

One of the most important research collections of American textile and costume designs evolved under the auspices of Stewart Culin, curator at The Brooklyn Museum, in the early twentieth century. Special collections of books and other materials were set aside for practicing designers; by the 1920s, the design collection was used by artist-designers from throughout the country and abroad.

DANA, JOHN COTTON
Born August 19, 1856, Woodstock, Vermont; died July 21, 1929, New York, New York
Museum director, writer

Dana established The Newark Museum in 1909 in the Newark public library. Dana directed both the library and the museum, simultaneously creating the first library picture collection and mounting some of the earliest exhibitions of industrial art in the United States. The museum's modern German decorative art exhibit in 1912 was the first such show of contemporary design in America. It was followed by a series of exhibitions in the 1910s and 1920s that featured contemporary pottery, textiles, wallpaper designs, and metalwork. In 1926 Dana helped secure a separate building for the museum's collections. A prolific writer, he frequently contributed to magazines and newspapers and published several books, including *The New Museum* (1917) and *A Plan for a Useful Museum* (1920).

DE PATTA, MARGARET STRONG
(MRS. EUGENE BIELAWSKI)
Born March 18, 1903, Tacoma, Washington; died March 19, 1964, Oakland, California
Jeweler

De Patta studied painting at the Academy of Fine Arts in San Diego (1921–23), the San Francisco School of Fine Arts (1923–25), and the Art Students League (1926). In 1929 she established herself as a painter in San Francisco and began studying jewelry-making with Armenian émigré Armin Hairenian. By 1936, her jewelry, modeled on pre-Columbian and Near Eastern forms, was being sold through the Amberg-Hirth craft shop in San Francisco. Her work underwent a profound change in 1940, when she was introduced to Constructivism—the rigorous structuring of space by means of light, line, and color—by László

Moholy-Nagy during the summer session at Mills College in Oakland. In 1940–41 she studied with Moholy-Nagy at the Chicago School of Design (formerly the New Bauhaus) evolving an abstract formal vocabulary based on three-dimensional structure. She began to include obliquely angled planes, moving parts, pierced disks, and stainless-steel screening in her work, and to experiment with shadow as a compositional element. In 1941 she settled in the Bay Area with her new husband, Eugene Bielawski, and opened a jewelry studio. By 1946, the demand for De Patta's work was such that the couple established a limited-production shop. In addition to jewelry, she designed flatware, holloware, and ceramic vessels.

DESKEY, DONALD
Born November 23, 1894, Blue Earth, Minnesota; died 1989
Industrial designer, woodworker, teacher

Deskey studied architecture at the University of California, Berkeley, and painting at the Mark Hopkins Institute of Art (formerly the California School of Design), The School of the Art Institute of Chicago, and the Art Students League. In New York, he briefly worked in advertising before pursuing a career as a painter. In the early 1920s he made two trips to France, enrolling at the Académie de la Grande Chaumière in Paris, where he completed his art training. Before returning to the United States Deskey saw the influential Paris Exposition of 1925, traveled to the Bauhaus in Dessau, and found himself especially impressed by the work of the Dutch de Stijl group. In 1926 he began working as an interior designer in New York, creating high-fashion display windows for the Franklin Simon and Saks Fifth Avenue department stores that incorporated backdrops made of industrial materials. In 1927, in partnership with Phillip Vollmer, he established Deskey-Vollmer, Inc., which specialized in the design of screens, furniture, and lighting fixtures. Deskey also produced handpainted screens for the Paul Frankl Gallery, designed apartment interiors for Adam Gimbel and other prominent New Yorkers, and completed the interior design for Radio City Music Hall. He exhibited his work at the 1933–34 Century of Progress Exposition in Chicago, the 1937 Paris Exposition, and the 1939–40 New York World's Fair. In 1940 Deskey joined the faculty of New York University.

DIEDERICH, WILHELM HUNT
Born 1884, Hungary; died May 15, 1953
Ceramist, metalsmith

Grandson of Boston painter William Morris Hunt and grandnephew of architect

Richard Morris Hunt, Diederich was born in Hungary, where his father was a wealthy landowner and horse breeder. At twenty, Diederich studied sculpture at the Pennsylvania Academy of the Fine Arts in Philadelphia. He continued his art training in Paris and Rome, and had his first one-man show at the Paris Salon d'Automne of 1905. Primarily a metalsmith working in bronze, wrought iron, and sheet metal, Diederich specialized in undulating animal forms and figures for monuments and fountains. In the mid-1920s he also worked in ceramics, producing individual works as well as designing for industry. Diederich's monumental figures brought him numerous awards, including a Gold Medal from the Architectural League in 1927. His ceramic work, distinguished by superb draftsmanship and translucent glazing, was also included in the "International Exhibition of Ceramic Art" at The Metropolitan Museum of Art in 1928.

DIERRA, LOUIS
No dates available
Industrial designer

Louis Dierra worked in the structural glass department at Pittsburgh Plate Glass Company (PPG), where he was responsible for virtually all of the firm's special designs. The glass chair he created for PPG's representation at the 1939–40 New York World's Fair was manufactured at the company's Ford City, Pennsylvania, plant, where all industrial glass-bending took place. Dierra left the company during the 1940s.

DODGE, WILLIAM WALDO, JR.
Born February 6, 1895; died 1971
Silversmith

Dodge originally planned to follow in the footsteps of his father, a Washington, D.C., patent attorney, but shifted his focus from law to architecture after a year's study at Princeton University. He continued his studies at the Massachusetts Institute of Technology in Cambridge, earning a master's degree in architecture in 1916. Dodge learned silversmithing in an occupational therapy program while recovering from injuries sustained in World War I. By 1923, he was living in Asheville, North Carolina, where he established an architectural practice and opened a silver shop—an unusual vocational pairing that was noted in architectural journals. With the onset of World War II and the departure of his assistants for military service, as well as a lack of recognition for his work in contemporary exhibitions, Dodge closed his silver shop and devoted himself to architecture.

DORN, MARION (MRS. HENRY VARNUM POOR; later, MRS. EDWARD McKNIGHT KAUFFER)
Born 1899, San Francisco, California; died 1964, Tangier, Morocco
Textile designer, batik artist

Dorn was one of the leading textile and carpet designers in England and the United States in the 1930s and 1940s. After graduating from Stanford University in 1916, Dorn became a free-lance designer of resist-dyed fabrics, first in the United States and then in England, where she moved around 1924 with her future husband, the graphic designer Edward McKnight Kauffer. The couple began to design carpets, which were handmade by Wilton and first exhibited in London in 1929. Successive commissions for private residences and commercial interiors for hotels and ocean liners, including the *Queen Mary,* brought Dorn much publicity. By 1934, she was selling her carpets in her own shop in London. Dorn also supplied designs for woven and printed textiles to the leading manufacturers Donald Brothers, Edinburgh Weavers, Old Bleach Linen, and Warners. After Dorn returned to the United States in 1940, she continued to design fabrics, some of which were produced by Greeff.

EAMES, CHARLES O.
Born June 17, 1907, St. Louis, Missouri; died August 21, 1978, St. Louis, Missouri
EAMES, RAY (née KAISER)
Born December 15, 1913, Sacramento, California; died August 21, 1988
Furniture designers, woodworkers, architects

Charles Eames studied architecture at Washington University in St. Louis (1925–28). He established a partnership with Robert P. Walsh in 1934, supplementing residential architecture commissions with the design and production of furniture, rugs, and sculpture. In 1936 Eliel Saarinen offered Eames a fellowship at the Cranbrook Academy of Art. After studying there for a year, Eames accepted a position as instructor of design, remaining until June 1941. At Cranbrook, he met the painter and sculptor Ray Kaiser, a former student of Hans Hofmann, who had studied with him in New York and in Provincetown and Gloucester, Massachusetts. In collaboration with Kaiser and Eliel Saarinen's son Eero, Eames submitted furniture designs to The Museum of Modern Art's "Organic Design in Home Furnishings Competition" of 1940–41, winning the two first prizes. Kaiser and Eames married in June 1941 and moved to Los Angeles, where they founded their own design firm and began developing methods for molding plywood that were applicable to industrial design. The molded-plywood chairs

included in the Eameses joint exhibition at The Museum of Modern Art in 1946 attracted the attention of the Herman Miller Furniture Company, with whom the designers began a productive association. By the 1950s, the Eameses' innovative furniture was being produced by the thousands, making them two of the most influential furniture designers of the twentieth century.

ECKHARDT, EDRIS
Born January 28, 1912, Cleveland, Ohio
Ceramist, glass artist, teacher

Eckhardt studied at the Cleveland Institute of Art for five years, graduating in 1932. During her last year she was involved in a collaborative ceramics venture organized by the Cleveland School of Art, The Cleveland Museum of Art, and the Cowan Pottery Studio. The experience led her to become a ceramist, and after graduation she established a studio and involved herself in glaze chemistry. Participating in a pilot program for the Public Works of Art Project in 1933–34, Eckhardt conceived the idea of producing small-scale sculptural figures of popular nursery-rhyme characters for use in public library programs for children. When the Federal Art Project of the Works Progress Administration (WPA) began a program at the Cleveland School of Art in 1935, Eckhardt was appointed director of the department of ceramic sculpture and continued in the position until the program was discontinued in 1941. Under her leadership artists produced large-scale sculptures for public housing projects as well as bas-reliefs depicting scenes from American life and literature. One of Eckhardt's most interesting assignments during the WPA years was a ceramic statue of Huckleberry Finn commissioned by Eleanor Roosevelt in 1939. Eckhardt worked as a ceramist until the early 1950s, when she shifted her focus to glass, becoming one of the premier artists in that medium.

EHRMANN, MARLI (MRS. ELIEZER EHRMANN, née MARIE HELENE HEIMANN)
Born 1904, Berlin, Germany; died 1982, Santa Barbara, California
Weaver

Ehrmann was a student at the Weimar Bauhaus from 1923 to 1926, receiving a diploma in 1927. She continued her academic studies at the universities of Jena and Weimar and was qualified as a teacher in 1931. Dismissed from her teaching position in Holstein in 1933 because she was a Jew, she next found work at the Herzl School in Berlin, where she met her husband, Eliezer Ehrmann. In 1938 the couple emigrated to the United States. The following year, László Moholy-Nagy asked her to head the textile department at the Chicago School of Design. Ehrmann taught there until 1947, when the weaving program was discontinued by the school's new director Serge Chermayeff. Students regarded the closing of the textile department as a great loss and quickly reorganized themselves as an independent group called the "Marli-Weavers." Meeting once to promote the study of design and handweaving by organizing an exhibition of their work, the Marli-Weavers remained in existence from 1947 until 1991. Ehrmann was equally committed to teaching immigrant children and adults, offering weaving classes in the evening at Jane Addams's settlement school, Hull House. A talented designer-weaver as well as a gifted teacher, Ehrmann won first prize in the 1940–41 "Organic Design in Home Furnishings Competition" sponsored by The Museum of Modern Art in New York. She also worked as a free-lance designer and consultant to industry, creating prototypes for a number of textile firms. In 1956 she opened the Elm Shop in Oak Park, Illinois, an avant-garde source for modern design.

EICHNER, LAURITS CHRISTIAN
Born March 7, 1894, Stuer, Denmark; died 1967
Metalsmith

Trained as an engineer, Eichner later turned to metalsmithing, producing silver- and pewterwork that ranged from period reproductions to fine precision instruments. The quality of his work brought him a gold medal at the 1937 Paris Exposition. Eichner's clients included New York's Hayden Planetarium and the Franklin Institute in Philadelphia. During World War II he abandoned his craftwork to operate two small plants that made precision instruments for the U.S. Government, though he continued to teach at the Craft Students League in New York.

ESHERICK, WHARTON
Born July 15, 1887, Philadelphia, Pennsylvania; died May 6, 1970, Paoli, Pennsylvania
Furniture designer, sculptor

Esherick began his career as a painter, studying in Philadelphia at the School of Industrial Arts (1907) and the Pennsylvania Academy of the Fine Arts (1909). In 1916 he moved with his wife to rural Paoli, Pennsylvania, where he began creating the home and studio in which he would live and work for the next fifty-seven years. In 1919 he spent time at an experimental school for "organic learning" in Fairhope, Alabama, where he began carving wood

frames to complement his paintings and woodcuts. Returning to Paoli, he shifted his interests to wood carving and furniture-making, designing and fabricating chairs, sofas, tables, and cabinets whose forms were organically determined by the natural shapes of the wood itself. He created staircases, doors, hardware, and other furnishings for his home in Paoli, which is now the Wharton Esherick Museum. Esherick also conceived stage sets, created complete interiors for private clients, and illustrated books, including woodcuts for Walt Whitman's *Song of the Broadaxe* (1924).

FEHÉR, PAUL
Born August 18, 1898, Nagy-Kanizsa, Hungary; died 1992
Metalsmith, designer

Fehér trained at the Royal Art Academy, Budapest, and later exhibited his design work at the Salon des Artistes Decorateurs, the Salon d'Automne, and the Beau Salon des Artiste Decorateurs in France. After emigrating to the United States, he joined Rose Iron Works around 1928. Fehér frequently collaborated with the firm's founder, Martin Rose, and eventually became its head designer. Metalwork he produced for Rose was included in the Twelfth Annual Exhibition of Artists and Craftsmen at The Cleveland Museum of Art in 1931.

FISCHER, BERNARD W. (BEN)
Born 1900, Louisville, Kentucky; died August 1986
Metalsmith, teacher

Fischer studied painting and sculpture at the Albright Art School in Buffalo, New York, and at the National Academy of Design and the Grand Central School of Art in Manhattan. From 1923 to 1946 he taught arts and crafts in New York City public schools and designed glass and metal tablewares for the National Silver Deposit Company. In 1929 his work was included in The Newark Museum's "Modern American Design in Metal" exhibition and illustrated in the September issue of *House Beautiful,* in an article by Helen Sprackling titled "The Growing Use of Metal in Decorative Art." The following year, his metalwork was featured in interiors designed by Gilbert Rohde.

FRANKL, PAUL THEODORE
Born October 14, 1886, Vienna, Austria; died March 21, 1958
Industrial designer, writer

Frankl studied architecture and engineering in Vienna, Paris, Munich, and Berlin. Emigrating to the United States in 1914, he

applied his European training to theater design. While primarily a decorator, Frankl was listed as an architect in the Manhattan directory in 1916–17, and throughout his career he consistently relied on his architectural training in his industrial design work. In the mid-1920s he began designing modular furniture with setbacks like those of Art Deco skyscrapers, which he sold in his own New York gallery. Frankl's reputation rested on his innovative furniture designs and his staunch promotion of the modern movement in the United States. He contributed to the *Annual of American Design 1931* and was the author of the books *New Dimensions: The Decorative Arts of Today in Words and Pictures* (1928), *Form and Reform: A Practical Handbook of Modern Interiors* (1930), and *Space for Living: Creative Interior Decoration and Design* (1938).

FRAZIER, BERNARD (POCO)
Born 1906, near Athol, Kansas; died 1976
Sculptor, ceramist

Frazier attended Kansas Wesleyan University and graduated from the school of design at the University of Kansas, Lawrence (1929). He later apprenticed with sculptors Lorado Taft and Fred Torrey in Chicago and studied intermittently at the National Academy of Art, the Chicago School of Sculpture, The School of the Art Institute of Chicago, and the New Bauhaus. In 1938 Frazier was awarded an Andrew Carnegie Foundation grant to serve as sculptor-in-residence at the University of Kansas. At the end of the grant period he established the university's first formal department of sculpture. As a sculptor and ceramist, Frazier exploited the plasticity of his materials, massing and distorting elements of his forms to create an impression of brutal strength. This technique is evident in the series of ash-glazed ceramic horse sculptures he produced in the 1940s. Frazier gained an important local reputation and fulfilled numerous commissions throughout Kansas.

FUERST, EDWIN W.
Glass artist

See New England Glass Company: PRODUCTION CENTERS AND SHOPS—GLASS

GARDNER, PAUL V.
Glass artist

See Steuben Glass Works: PRODUCTION CENTERS AND SHOPS—GLASS

GATES, JOHN MONTIETH
Born June 25, 1905, Elyria, Ohio
Architect, glass designer

Educated at Harvard and Columbia universities, Gates was both an architect and a pragmatic businessman. Appointed vice president in charge of design at the Steuben Division of Corning Glass Works in 1932, he used aggressive new marketing techniques to expand the company's market during the Depression. Under Gates, the Steuben Division introduced art glass designed by Sidney Waugh, Samuel Ayers, and Edwin Fuerst. Gates also organized exhibits of Steuben glass for the major expositions of the period, including the 1937 Paris Exposition and the 1939–40 New York World's Fair. A practicing architect, he helped design Steuben's first shop, which opened in New York in 1934. In 1937, in association with Geoffrey and William Platt, Gates designed the Corning-Steuben Building—"The House of Glass"—at 718 Fifth Avenue in New York. Around 1937, Gates commissioned twenty-seven internationally known artists, including Paul Manship, Isamu Noguchi, and Pavel Tchelitchew, to create designs for a series of limited-edition glass engravings. An exhibition of the engravings, "Twenty-seven Artists in Crystal," was held at the Steuben gallery in the Corning-Steuben Building in 1940.

GILLIARD, JOSEPH W.
Born 1914, Taylors, South Carolina
Ceramist, metalsmith, teacher

Gilliard exerted a profound influence on generations of ceramics students during the four decades he taught at the Hampton Institute in Virginia. Innovative in both aspects of ceramics—form and glaze—he invented a special wheel on which vases and storage jars up to forty inches in height could be thrown. Gilliard's fascination with glazes and his experimentation with radical temperatures produced startlingly new effects, such as a gold-flecked glaze of unusual radiance. In the 1940s he cast organic forms which he then joined in abstract configurations. Equally competent as a metalsmith, Gilliard combined lathe-turned metal components with ceramic forms.

GIRARD, ALEXANDER HAYDEN
Born May 24, 1907, New York, New York; died 1993
Architect, industrial designer

A registered architect, Girard also designed interiors, furniture, graphics, industrial prototypes, and innovative museum installations. He was raised and educated in Florence, Italy, and trained as an architect at the Architectural Association in London, the Royal School of Architecture in Rome, and New York University. He opened his first architectural office, in Florence, in 1930, and in 1932 opened an office in New

York. Following his marriage to Susan Needham, Girard moved his office to Detroit in 1937, accepting commissions to design interiors for the Ford and Lincoln motor company buildings in 1943. In 1945 he was appointed color consultant by the General Motors Research Center, and in 1952 he became design director of the Herman Miller Furniture Company textile division. The following year, he moved his office yet again, to Santa Fe, New Mexico. Girard's principal commissions were the Ford Motor Company offices, Dearborn, Michigan (1946); the Irwin Miller residence, Columbus, Indiana (1955), designed in collaboration with Eero Saarinen; and the Herman Miller, Inc., Textiles and Objects Shop, New York (1961). As a textile designer Girard favored strong colors and clear compositions, with whimsical motifs frequently inspired by his extensive folk art collection. The collection is now housed in the Girard Wing of the Museum of International Folk Art in Santa Fe.

GOLDBERG, BERTRAND
Born 1913
Architect, furniture designer

Goldberg studied architecture at the Harvard University School of Architecture, the Dessau Bauhaus, and the Armour Institute of Technology, Chicago. In 1937 he opened his own architectural office in Chicago. Goldberg adhered to the Bauhaus tradition in which the architect also functioned as industrial designer, and created furniture constructed of plywood, steel, plastic, and other modern materials for many of his architectural commissions. In 1938 he designed a gracefully scrolled plywood chair and settee; crafted in Mexico, it was displayed at the New York World's Fair in 1939–40. As both an architect and an industrial designer Goldberg continued to experiment with shapes and materials, fulfilling such diverse commissions as the development of plastic freight cars for the railroad industry and the design of Chicago's Marina City, a unique residential-commercial-recreational complex whose interior spaces radiate from a central core, suggesting the petals of a flower.

GREGORY, MARY (MOLLY)
Born 1914
Woodworker, teacher

Educated at Bennington College in Vermont, Gregory began her teaching career at the Cambridge School in Weston, Massachusetts. In 1941 she became an apprentice woodworking instructor at Black Mountain College and was appointed to the faculty the following fall. Under Gregory's leadership the woodworking shop expanded to accommodate Black Mountain's construc-

tion program, which included the completion of the studio buildings and remodeling of the cottages. Her students produced furniture, easels, bulletin boards, and sculpture stands for the school's use, as well as wood plates and utensils and woven belts that were sold in a shop on the grounds. They also executed custom designs for faculty and visitors. Gregory's own furniture was constructivist and utilitarian. She designed a square modular unit in wood that could be used as a seat, a side table, grouped as a bench, or stacked for a sculpture stand. Gregory also produced the chairs that Josef Albers had designed for the school in the 1930s and which had been previously produced by woodworkers in Asheville. As a teacher, her emphasis was on good craftsmanship, traditional methods of joining such as dovetailing and wooden pegs, and inventive solutions to problems of functional design. In addition to teaching woodworking and running the shop, she kept the accounting books for the school's working farm. When the farmer managing the property left abruptly in 1943, Gregory took over the farm and operated it at a profit. She remained at Black Mountain until 1947.

GREGORY, WAYLANDE DESANTIS
Born June 13, 1905, Baxter Springs, Kansas; died August 18, 1971, Warren, New Jersey
Ceramist, sculptor, glass artist, teacher

Gregory was a sculptor and ceramist, working in bronze and clay. In the late 1920s he left the studio he shared in Chicago with Lorado Taft and joined the Cowan Pottery Studio, shifting his focus to ceramics. He produced some of the pottery's most significant work, including *Diana and Two Fawns,* which won first prize at the Cleveland Museum of Art's May Show of 1929. When Cowan went out of business in 1931, Gregory accepted a two-year artist's residency at the Cranbrook Academy of Art, where he experimented with glazes, mixing clay with minerals and oxides. Later in the 1930s, in his Metuchen, New Jersey, and New York studios, he developed a technique he termed "inner modeling," which allowed him to produce massive ceramic sculptures with the necessary internal supports. He used this method to complete the mammoth ceramic fountains *Light Dispelling Darkness* (1937) and the *Fountain of the Atoms* (1938). The latter, a 60-foot-wide sculpture with four central figures depicting Earth, Air, Fire, and Water and weighing more than a ton, welcomed visitors to the 1939–40 New York World's Fair. In 1940 Gregory moved his studio to Bound Brook, New Jersey, where he continued to produce large-scale ceramic pieces, as well as portraits and serially cast vessels and figurines. In the later years of his career he experimented with glass, wire, and sheet metal.

GROTELL, MAJLIS (MAIJA)
Born August 19, 1899, Helsinki, Finland; died December 6, 1973, Pontiac, Michigan
Ceramist, teacher

Grotell studied painting, design, and sculpture at the Central School of Arts and Crafts in Helsinki, graduating in either 1920 or 1921. She then pursued six years of postgraduate study in industrial ceramics and textiles. In 1927 Grotell emigrated to the United States, since artists' materials were limited in Finland. She settled in New York and commuted to Alfred University where she enrolled in pottery courses taught by Charles Fergus Binns. In 1928 Grotell began a ten-year association with the Henry Street Craft School, which was affiliated with Lillian Wald's Henry Street Settlement, a center for creative expression for the underprivileged. While teaching, she continued to practice her art, winning more than twenty-five major exhibition awards. In 1938 Eliel Saarinen hired Grotell to head the ceramics program at the Cranbrook Academy of Art, where she taught until her retirement in 1966. Grotell made Cranbrook a major center for ceramic art education, and while she insisted that her students learn the basics of wheel throwing, glazing, and firing, she also encouraged them to develop their own styles. Under her direction, ceramics became a profession rather than an avocation. Grotell's early work included simple ovoid or cylindrical forms with abstract-geometric Art Deco motifs. She developed a palette of applied colors—turquoises, reds, and burnt oranges—and, by using Albany slip under a clear Bristol glaze, created distinctive craterous glazes.

HAILE, THOMAS SAMUEL
Born 1909, England; died 1948, England
Ceramist

Haile studied painting and later trained at the Royal College of Art in London under the master artist-potter William Staite Murray. He emigrated to the United States in 1939, and was invited by Charles Harder to teach at Alfred University. At Alfred, and later at the University of Michigan, Ann Arbor, Haile left an indelible mark on American ceramics, bringing a new perspective to the medium in which the focus was on surrealistic surface decoration and the interplay of forms. Haile advocated a simpler approach to clay, with less emphasis on technical adroitness and more concern for the expressionist qualities of the medium. He won a prize for his pottery at the Tenth Ceramic National in 1941. He died in an automobile accident in England in 1948.

HALEY, REUBEN
Born February 5, 1872, Pittsburgh, Pennsylvania; died September 29, 1933, Beaver, Pennsylvania
Glass designer, metalsmith, sculptor

Haley specialized in decorative glasswork and produced a profusion of designs for several glass manufacturers and at least one pottery company over the course of his career. One of the few designers who first modeled his glassware in clay, Haley also worked as a sculptor and metalsmith. In 1911 he accepted the position of chief designer for U.S. Glass, a conglomerate with some thirteen manufacturers in the group. Over the fourteen years that Haley was with U.S. Glass he rose from chief designer to vice president. When the company was sold in 1925, Haley refused the presidency and left the firm. He reopened the Metal Products Company, which he had operated briefly around 1910, in space rented from Consolidated Lamp & Glass, producing a Mexican-style art glass and the Ruba Rombic line for Consolidated and other patterns for Morgantown Glass Works of West Virginia and the Indiana Glass Company in Dunkirk. Haley also designed a line of art pottery for the Muncie Pottery Company of Indiana.

HARDER, CHARLES MABRY
Born 1889, Birmingham, Alabama; died 1959
Teacher, ceramist

Harder graduated from The School of the Art Institute of Chicago (1925). In 1927 he became an instructor at the New York State School of Clayworking and Ceramics (now the College of Ceramics) at Alfred University, and was appointed assistant professor in 1931. While teaching, he trained under Charles Fergus Binns and earned a B.S. in ceramics in 1935. Following a year of postgraduate study in Chicago, Harder returned to Alfred as a professor of ceramic arts, reorganizing courses and curricula to conform to New York State requirements for industrial and professional design. He became the acting head of the department in 1938 and was appointed head in 1944. Harder was awarded a gold medal at the Paris Exposition of 1937 and the Charles Fergus Binns Medal of the American Ceramic Society in 1938. He was made a fellow of the American Ceramic Society, and was a member of the Ceramic Educational Council.

HATHAWAY, ISAAC SCOTT
Born April 4, 1874, Lexington, Kentucky; died 1967
Sculptor, ceramist, teacher

Hathaway was educated at Chandler College, Lexington, Kentucky; Pittsburg College, in Kansas; and the New England Conservatory of Music, Boston. He developed the ceramics program at Tuskegee Institute in 1937 and served as head of the ceramics department at Alabama State Teachers College in the 1940s. Hathaway was known for his portrait busts, the most famous of which are of Frederick Douglass, Paul Laurence Dunbar, and Booker T. Washington. He also designed memorial coins honoring Washington and George Washington Carver.

HEATON, MAURICE
Born April 2, 1900, Neuchâtel, Switzerland; died April 6, 1990, Rockland County, New York
Glass artist

Heaton was the son and grandson of English glass artists. His grandfather, Clement John Heaton, Sr., had his own London firm, Heaton, Butler & Bayne; his father established a thriving stained-glass business in the United States. A pioneer in studio glass, Maurice Heaton introduced modern alternatives to the revival styles dominant in American decorative arts of the 1920s and 1930s. From 1920 to 1921 he studied engineering at the Stevens Institute of Technology in Hoboken, New Jersey, enabling him to construct his own glass-making equipment, including kilns. In 1919 Heaton's father relocated his studio to Valley Cottage, New York, in rural Rockland County. Maurice joined him in 1923, fulfilling traditional stained-glass commissions until the Depression. In 1928 and 1929 some of his early experimental designs for glass tableware and lighting fixtures were exhibited at the American Designers' Gallery in New York. Heaton continued to design lamps and glass shades throughout his career, working for Lightolier throughout the 1930s and developing an association with interior designer Eugene Schoen, for whom he produced architectural glass panels decorated with abstract-geometric patterns or figural Cubist motifs. His most ambitious work, a glass mural titled *The Flight of Amelia Earhart Across the Atlantic,* was created in 1932 for the women's lounge of the Rockefeller Center theater. Heaton later took over his father's atelier, creating wall plaques, plates, and bowls using a technique of fusing enamel and glass that he developed. The studio remained active until Heaton's death in 1990.

HERTER, ALBERT
Born 1871, New York, New York; died February 15, 1950
Painter, textile designer

Herter studied painting with James Carroll Beckwith at the Art Students League and with Henri Laurens and Fernand Cormon in Paris. In 1910, only two years after his return from Europe, he was elected an associate of the National Academy of Design. An accomplished painter and a fiber designer with an impressive knowledge of textiles, Herter put his varied talents to good use when he established a tapestry atelier in New York about 1919. The atelier was extremely important for the development of modern textiles during the 1920s. Like William Morris, Herter was inspired by a desire to improve public taste, and through his atelier he attempted to produce material of sound aesthetic worth at reasonable prices.

HIGGINS, FRANCES (NÉE STEWART)
Born December 24, 1912, Haddock, Georgia
HIGGINS, MICHAEL
Born September 29, 1908, London, England
Glass artists

Frances Stewart received a B.S. degree from Georgia State College for Women (now Georgia College) in Milledgeville. She taught at the junior high school level in Atlanta from 1935 to 1943 and was an assistant professor at the University of Georgia, Athens, from 1944 to 1948. Stewart pursued art training with private teachers, in summer sessions at Columbia University Teachers' College and Ohio State University, and at the Institute of Design in Chicago, where she earned an M.F.A. and met and married Michael Higgins. Higgins attended Cambridge University, Eton College, and the London Central School of Arts and Crafts, and began working as a graphic artist in 1928. Emigrating to the United States in 1938, he was employed as a designing printer in New Orleans. He worked in Washington, D.C., as the Lend-Lease Liaison for India during World War II, and headed the department of visual design at the Institute of Design, Chicago, from 1946 to 1948. In 1948 the couple left their academic positions to produce and market fused enameled glass that incorporated iridescent, lustre, and "mother-of-pearl." Today, they are recognized as forerunners of the American studio glass movement.

HOFFMANN, WOLFGANG
Born 1900, Vienna, Austria; died 1969
HOFFMANN, POLA
Born 1902, Stryz, Poland
Interior designers

Wolfgang Hoffmann, the son of Josef Hoffmann, studied architecture and attended the Kunstgewerbeschüle in Vienna, and worked in his father's office for two years. Pola Hoffmann presumably met her husband while studying under his father at the Kunstgewerbeschüle. The Hoffmanns emigrated to the United States in 1925 and immediately became part of the vanguard design circles in New York. Establishing themselves as interior decorators known for urban apartments, the Hoffmanns also designed textiles, rugs, glassware, and metalwork. Their design commissions ranged from the interior of New York's Little Carnegie Playhouse to stylized asymmetrical ashtrays for the Early American Pewter Company, which were included in the American Federation of Art's "Decorative Metalwork and Cotton Textiles" exhibition in 1930–31. The Hoffmanns' marriage and design partnership dissolved in the 1930s.

HOLM, LILLIAN
Born October 20, 1896, Båstad, Sweden; died March 4, 1979, Båstad, Sweden
Textile designer, ceramist

Holm worked as a weaver at Märta Måås Fjetterström's Studio at Båstad, Sweden, in the 1920s, and may have arrived in the United States with fellow weaver Maja Andersson Wirde in 1929. In 1933 she was hired to teach weaving in the department of arts and crafts at the Kingswood School, Cranbrook, with which she maintained an association until her retirement in 1966. Holm was also an instructor of weaving at Studio Loja Saarinen (1934–37), an instructor of weaving and textiles in the Cranbrook Intermediate School (1937), and, beginning in 1941, an instructor of weaving at the Flint Institute of Arts. She returned to Sweden in 1966.

JOHNSON, SARGENT CLAUDE
Born October 7, 1887, Boston, Massachusetts; died October 10, 1967, San Francisco, California
Ceramist, sculptor

Johnson studied at the Boston School of Fine Arts, the A. W. Best School of Fine Arts in San Francisco, and the California College of Arts and Crafts under sculptors Beniamino Bufano and Ralph Stackpole. Of African-American, Cherokee, and Swedish descent, Johnson established his artistic reputation with award-winning work that was shown at the Harmon Foundation exhibitions in New York in the 1920s. In 1936 he was one of the first African-American artists hired for the West Coast Federal Art Project of the Works Progress Administration (WPA). As a senior sculptor and supervisor for the WPA Johnson completed an athletic frieze for George Washington High School in San Francisco and statues for the Sunnydale, California, Housing Project. Johnson worked in wood as well as terracotta and fired clay.

KAHN, ELY JACQUES
Born June 1, 1884, New York, New York; died September 5, 1972, New York, New York
Architect, industrial designer

Kahn was one of the most influential and prolific urban architects practicing in the United States during the 1920s; between 1925 and 1931 he designed more than thirty buildings in New York, including 2 Park Avenue (1927), 120 Wall Street (1930), and the Squibb Building (1930). In 1917 he formed a partnership with New York architect Jacob A. Buchman, with whom he practiced until 1929. He worked independently from 1930 to 1940, when he formed a new partnership with Albert Jacobs, an association that lasted until Kahn's death in 1972. Throughout his career, Kahn maintained a flexible attitude toward architecture, refusing to adopt any single, standardized design aesthetic. His aim was to serve the needs of his clients, not to be embraced as a theorist—a view he expressed in the books *Design in Art and Industry* (1936) and *A Building Goes Up* (1969). As the brother of Rena Rosenthal, Kahn also received interior design commissions. His work was included in the American Industrial Art annuals at The Metropolitan Museum of Art in 1929 and 1934; he selected the 1940 annual. In 1931 he was appointed director of the architecture department at the Beaux Arts Institute of Design in New York and in 1932–33 he headed the Industrial Arts Section of the Century of Progress Exposition in Chicago. He was a member of the New York Architectural League and served as president of the Municipal Art Society from 1942 to 1945.

KARASZ, ILONKA
Born July 13, 1896, Budapest, Hungary; died 1981
Weaver, textile designer, woodworker, silver designer

Trained at the Royal School of Arts and Crafts in Budapest, Karasz, with her sister Mariska, emigrated to New York in 1913. Shortly thereafter, she took a teaching position at the Modern Art School on Washington Square, one of the most progressive centers for art education during the 1910s. In addition to her teaching, she designed interiors and rugs, embroideries, and other textiles that were reinterpretations of either traditional European crafts or modern painting styles such as Fauvism and German Expressionism. She sold her work at the bookshop-gallery Sunwise Turn, which presented hand-dyed and embroidered textiles as serious art forms. Karasz also produced ceramics, silver, wallpaper, and furniture, as well as book illustrations and covers for *The New Yorker*. According to painter William Zorach, Karasz was one of the most talented and outstanding personalities in Greenwich Village during the 1920s.

KARLAN, GERTRUDE
Born 1901, New York, New York
Silversmith, jeweler, painter, teacher

Karlan was a designer and fabricator of jewelry who mingled in New York's bohemian circles in the 1920s. Her jewelry was first illustrated in "The Modern Note in Decorative Arts," an article by C. Adolph Glassgold published in the April 1928 issue of *The Arts*. During the 1930s Karlan taught piano and painting in New York at the progressive Walden School and provided instruction in handmade jewelry in classes at city settlement houses. She was included in The Museum of Modern Art's "Modern Handmade Jewelry" exhibition in 1946.

KIESLER, FREDERICK JOHN
Born September 22, 1892, Vienna, Austria; died 1966, New York, New York
Architect, industrial designer, furniture designer

Kiesler attended the Technische Hochschule in Vienna (1908–09) and studied painting and printmaking at the Akademie der Bildenden Künste (1910). He worked as a stage designer in Vienna and Berlin after World War I, and designed the utopian environment *City in Space* for the 1925 Paris Exposition. After emigrating to New York in 1926, Kiesler pursued a varied career as an architect, sculptor, and designer of stage sets, interiors, and furniture; a member of the Dutch de Stijl group, he later became involved with the Surrealists. Between 1928 and 1930 he created window displays for Saks Fifth Avenue, documenting his ideas regarding the American department store as a disseminator of modern European design in the book *Contemporary Art Applied to the Store and Its Display* (1930). His reputation was solidified in 1929 with the completion of the Film Guild Cinema in New York, the first theater in the United States designed specifically for film projection. Keisler began designing furniture in the late 1920s, showing a suspended office desk and tubular-steel furniture in the 1930 exhibition of the American Union of Decorative Artists and Craftsmen (AUDAC), an organization of which he was both a founder and director. As head of the Laboratory of Design Correlation at the Columbia University School of Architecture from 1937 to 1942, he patented several designs for multifunctional furniture, including a series of biomorphic cast-aluminum tables. In 1942 he designed the interiors and multi-use free-form modular furnishings for Peggy

Guggenheim's New York gallery, Art of This Century. Kiesler was director of scenic design at the Juilliard School of Music in New York from 1934 to 1957.

KIPP, MARIA
Born Germany; no dates available
Weaver, textile designer

Kipp trained in Munich at the Kunstgewerbeschüle and later became the first woman to attend the textile school in Muenchberg, Bavaria, where the weaving program covered all aspects of production, from spinning yarn to the operation of hand- and powerlooms. She later established a weaving workshop in Munich, where she specialized in dress fabrics. Following her emigration to Los Angeles in 1924, Kipp opened a studio in which she created innovative furnishing fabrics with modernistic motifs that were often custom-handwoven of rough and nubby materials; her clients were American decorators and architects. Kipp remained an influential representative of European modernism for some forty years.

KIRK, ARTHUR NEVILL
Born 1881, Lewes, Sussex, England; died 1958, Birmingham, Michigan
Silversmith, jeweler, enamelist

Kirk worked in his father's jewelry- and watch-repair shop before attending the Central School of Arts and Crafts in London. After graduating in 1920, he joined the faculty as an instructor in metalwork and miniature painting. In 1927 art patron George G. Booth invited Kirk to teach part-time at the art school of the Detroit Society of Arts and Crafts, and to design ecclesiastical plate for Christ Church, Cranbrook. In 1929 Kirk was appointed head of the Cranbrook silversmith workshop. With the help of two assistants he taught classes in jewelry and enameling while continuing to fulfill private commissions. He was one of a handful of American silversmiths with the knowledge and interest in making ecclesiastical objects. When working from Eero Saarinen's designs the results were modernist and exquisitely refined, but he usually worked in styles validated by the past, following historically acceptable working procedures. When the workshop was closed in 1933, a victim of Cranbrook's economic problems during the Depression, Kirk moved his studio to private quarters and began teaching at Wayne State University. He remained at the university until the effects of Parkinson's disease forced his retirement in 1947.

KLEISER, LORENTZ
Born May 26, 1871, Elgin, Illinois;

died 1963
Weaver, textile designer, interior decorator, painter

In 1892 Kleiser was apprenticed to a leading mural painter in Oslo and later trained in Munich. Upon his return to the United States in 1900, he became a designer and muralist for a New York decorator; his interest in handwoven tapestries dates from this period. By 1913, Kleiser had decided to pursue tapestry work as a profession, founding his own studio, Edgewater Tapestry Looms, Inc., and producing designs that earned him an international reputation. In New York Kleiser lectured on tapestry weaving at The Metropolitan Museum of Art and at New York University, and in 1935 a series of exhibitions of his tapestries circulated throughout the country. The following year the first exhibition of his paintings was held at the Ehrich-Newhouse Galleries, Inc., in New York.

KNIGHT, CLAYTON
Born March 30, 1891, Rochester, New York; no death date available
Textile designer, muralist, illustrator

Knight studied art with Robert Henri, George Bellows, and Giulia Von der Lancken. He established a career as a designer and illustrator, receiving commissions for a series of aviation murals for the Gorham Hotel in New York, and illustrations for the books *Pilot's Luck* (1928) and *Non-Stop Stowaway* (1929).

LABAUDT, MARCELLE (MADAME LUCIEN LABAUDT)
Born c. 1893, Bordeaux, France; died January 25, 1987, Sonoma, California
Textile designer

Apprenticed to a dress designer in Bordeaux at the age of twelve, Labaudt emigrated to San Francisco with a younger sister in 1916. Finding work as a dress designer and fabricator of hand-painted and -stenciled garments at the Labaudt School of Design during the 1920s, she soon became one of Lucien Labaudt's fashion models and eventually his wife. Known for his murals on the walls of Coit Tower and the Beach Chalet in Golden Gate Park, Lucien Labaudt was a war correspondent and illustrator for *Life* magazine during World War II, and was killed in a plane crash in 1943. In honor of her husband's enthusiasm and support for young artists, Madame Labaudt established the Lucien Labaudt Gallery in 1945 in her house at 1409 Gough St. in San Francisco. Over the next thirty-five years she sold work by nearly six hundred emerging artists. She also taught sewing and patternmaking at the gallery and dress design at the California School of Arts and Crafts in Oakland and served as secretary of the San Francisco Women Artists organization.

LESCAZE, WILLIAM EDMOND
Born March 27, 1896, Onez, Switzerland; died 1969, New York, New York
Architect

Lescaze received a master's degree in architecture in 1919 from the Eidgenössische Technische Hochschule in Zurich, where he trained under Karl Moser. After working in Arras and in the atelier of Henri Sauvage in Paris, he emigrated to Cleveland, and from 1919 to 1923 worked in the architectural offices of Hubbell and Benes, and Walter R. MacCormack. On his own and in partnership with George Howe from 1929 to 1933, Lescaze developed the prototypes for modernist architecture in the United States, from neoclassicism and Art Deco to the International Style. In 1932 Howe & Lescaze completed the Philadelphia Savings Fund Society Building, the first truly modern skyscraper. Lescaze reestablished his private practice in 1935, and during World War II experimented with new building materials and prefabrication systems. His postwar work, which evolved into a Miesian classicism, consisted primarily of large public, office, and apartment buildings.

LIEBES, DOROTHY WRIGHT (MRS. REHLMAN MORIN)
Born October 14, 1899, Santa Rosa, California; died September 20, 1972, New York, New York.
Weaver, textile designer, architect, arts administrator

Liebes received a B.S. from San Jose State Teachers College (1919), a B.A. in applied design from the University of California, Berkeley (1923), and an M.A. in art education from Columbia University (1928). After an internship at Rodier, the French textile firm, she opened a studio in San Francisco in 1930, becoming one of the first American weavers to adapt handweaving to mass production. Specializing in custom handwoven fabrics for architects and designers, Liebes was awarded two major architectural commissions for California public buildings in 1935. Two years later, she was selected to organize the Decorative Arts section of the 1939–40 Golden Gate International Exposition in San Francisco. Her success in that position brought Liebes numerous design commissions. In 1948 she moved her studio to New York, where she developed novelty yarns such as Lurex (a metallic yarn) and became equally well known for fabrics incorporating unusual and daring color combinations. She was a consultant to most of the major textile companies, including E. I. Dupont and De Nemours & Co.

LIVINGSTON, E. BYRNE
Born 1906
Silversmith, jeweler, teacher

Livingston was an instructor in jewelrymaking in New York during the 1930s, teaching at City College and Hunter College. In 1937 her modern jewelry designs were included in "Silver: An Exhibition of Contemporary American Design by Manufacturers, Designers and Craftsmen" at The Metropolitan Museum of Art and "Contemporary Industrial and Handwrought Silver" at The Brooklyn Museum. Livingston maintained a studio in New York and showed her silver at the Alma Reed Gallery in 1942.

LOBEL, PAUL A.
Born March 4, 1899, Romania; died 1983
Metalsmith, jeweler

Lobel was a design consultant for the International Silver Company and the Regal Art Glass Company. He also fulfilled commissions for the Hupmobile Company of Hartford, Connecticut, and the Barbizon Plaza and St. Moritz hotels in New York.

LOEWY, RAYMOND
Born November 5, 1893, Paris, France; died July 14, 1986, Monte Carlo
Industrial designer

One of the best known and most flamboyant industrial designers of the 1930s, Loewy was largely responsible for establishing the industrial design profession in the United States. Educated at the Université de Paris, he served in the French Army Corps of Engineers during World War I and was awarded the Croix de Guerre on four occasions. He received a degree in engineering from the École de Laneau in 1918, and the following year emigrated to New York, where he worked as a free-lance window designer for Saks Fifth Avenue and Bonwit Teller and created fashion illustrations for *Vogue, Vanity Fair,* and *Harper's Bazaar*. In 1929 Loewy established his own industrial design firm, making his reputation as a master of streamlining. His major commissions included a clean, sculptural exterior for the Gestetner mimeograph machine (1929), the Hupmobile (1932)—which won prizes in automobile competitions across the world—and two of his finest creations, the Coldspot refrigerator (1934), designed for Sears, Roebuck and Company, and the bullet-shaped S-1 locomotive (1937), commissioned by the Pennsylvania Railroad. By the time he became a U.S. citizen in 1938, Loewy was recognized as one of the foremost industrial designers in the country. He was also a master of corporate emblems and packaging. His redesign of the Lucky Strike cigarette package in 1942 brought him other commissions from Coca-Cola, Pepsodent, and the National Biscuit Company. By 1939, Loewy had offices in New York, Chicago, São Paulo, London, and South Bend, Indiana. With four partners he founded Raymond Loewy Associates in 1944 (the firm was incorporated as Raymond Loewy, William Snaith in 1961). The Raymond Loewy Corporation was formed in 1949 to handle specialized architectural commissions, and the independent Compagnie de l'Esthétique Industrielle (CEI) was established in Paris in 1953. This last firm stimulated industrial design in France.

LUKENS, GLEN
Born 1887, Cowgill, Missouri; died December 10, 1967
Ceramist, teacher

Lukens moved to Chicago to study ceramics at the Art Institute under Myrtle French. When the sewing machine he adapted to turn a potter's wheel came to the attention of the U.S. Surgeon General, Lukens was asked to manage a pottery program intended to help rehabilitate soldiers wounded in World War I. By 1924, he was teaching craft courses in California, and in 1936 he was appointed a professor of ceramics at the University of Southern California's School of Architecture, remaining on the faculty for the next three decades. Lukens was a gifted teacher who frequently reminded his students that "the new in art is incredibly old and the old is still vastly new." In his own work he combined oxides and desert stones to produce distinctively colored earthenware and used thick viscous glazes in strong yellows, turquoises, and greens that he developed from local raw materials. His *Yellow Bowl* won first prize for pottery at the 1936 Ceramic National, and he represented the West Coast at the Paris Exposition of 1937. Lukens was instrumental in organizing the first all-California Ceramic Art Exhibition in 1938, and his work was included in the 1939–40 New York World's Fair.

MAGNUSSEN, ERIK
Born May 14, 1884, Copenhagen, Denmark; died February 24, 1961, Denmark
Silversmith

Magnussen taught himself how to make jewelry and worked as a chaser for Danish silversmith Viggo Hansen (1902) and metalsmith Otto Rohloff in Berlin (1907–09). In 1909 he opened his own shop in Denmark, immersing himself in all aspects of the work, from preparing preliminary sketches to actually working with metals. In 1925 the Gorham Manufacturing Company brought Magnussen to the United States to develop a machine-made line of modern silver. The tea services and other works he designed for Gorham were less elaborate than his earlier European pieces and reflected the influences of Art Nouveau, Cubism, and modern urban architecture. After four years Magnussen left Gorham to work for August Dingeldein and Son. In 1932 he opened his own workshop in Chicago, and from 1932 to 1939 he worked in Los Angeles. He returned to Denmark in 1939.

MANSHIP, PAUL H.
Born 1885, St. Paul, Minnesota; died 1966
Sculptor, glass artist

Manship trained as a sculptor at the St. Paul Institute of Art, the Art Students League, and the Pennsylvania Academy of Fine Arts in Philadelphia. Using the cast-bronze technique and demonstrating a mastery of form and material, he fulfilled commissions for large sculptural groups and bronze figurines. Manship's mature work displays an elegant streamlining of form and clarity of design in the so-called style-conscious manner, incorporating the stylizations of Assyrian, Egyptian, Buddhist, Hindu, and archaic Greek art. His best-known sculpture, the gilded bronze *Prometheus* (1933) designed for the fountain in New York's Rockefeller Plaza, reflects these influences. In 1939 a commission from Corning Glass Works took Manship into glass design. John Monteith Gates, an architect and designer for Corning's Steuben Division, commissioned twenty-seven world-renowned artists, including Manship, to create working drawings for a series of limited-edition glass engravings. The engravings were exhibited in 1940, with Manship's design of a woman and centaur one of the more successful translations.

MARTINEZ, MARIA POVERA
Born 1887, San Ildefonso Pueblo, New Mexico; died July 20, 1980, San Ildefonso Pueblo, New Mexico
Ceramist
MARTINEZ, JULIAN
Born 1885, New Mexico; died 1943, New Mexico
Ceramist

Maria Povera Martinez was a self-taught ceramist who initially made polychrome pottery painted with red clays and a black pigment, called *guaco,* derived from wild spinach. She became known internationally as "the Potter of San Ildefonso" for her polished blackwares, which she began pro-

ducing in 1912. In 1919 her husband, ceramics painter Julian Martinez, developed a technique to produce a matte-black finish on polished blackware. The Martinezes instructed other potters of the San Ildefonso Pueblo in this technique, which evolved into a thriving cottage industry. Maria Martinez was invited to demonstrate her craft at the 1933–34 Century of Progress Exposition in Chicago and the 1939–40 Golden Gate International Exposition in San Francisco. Four Presidents feted her at the White House, and she was awarded two honorary doctorates; she was also chosen to lay the cornerstone of New York's Rockefeller Center. At the time of her death, her pottery was among the most sought-after examples of Native American art.

MIHALIK, JULIUS
Born 1874, Budapest, Hungary; died January 12, 1943, Cleveland, Ohio
Ceramist, teacher

Mihalik trained in Budapest at the E. Balli Art School. He taught in Budapest and in Vienna before joining the faculty of the Cleveland School of Art as an instructor in ceramics. In addition to his teaching, Mihalik contributed to the *American Magazine of Art* and to books on textiles.

MILLIKEN, WILLIAM MATHEWSON
Born September 28, 1889, Stamford, Connecticut; died March 14, 1978, Cleveland, Ohio
Museum director

Milliken was head of the Federal Art Project in Cleveland and director of The Cleveland Museum of Art during the 1930s and 1940s. His catholic tastes benefitted area artists and museum audiences alike. Not only was he a great supporter of the museum's annual May Shows, he also organized and circulated exhibitions of enamels, and found employment for Cleveland area artists with the various federal arts projects.

MOHOLY-NAGY, LÁSZLÓ
Born July 20, 1895, Borsod, Hungary; died November 24, 1946, Chicago, Illinois
Artist, teacher

As a teacher at the German Bauhaus, Moholy-Nagy promoted a vision of simple, functional design, and fostered the belief that "designing is not a profession but an attitude." In *Principles of Bauhaus Production* (1926) he wrote, "The Bauhaus workshops are essentially laboratories in which prototypes of products suitable for mass production and typical of our time are carefully developed and constantly

improved." By 1928, the German Government's increasing interference in the school's activities prompted Moholy-Nagy and several other instructors to resign. After living as a refugee in England in the early 1930s, he was invited by the Chicago Association of Arts and Industries to direct a school modeled on the Bauhaus. The New Bauhaus opened in Chicago in 1937 but closed after one year because of lack of funding. It reopened in 1939 as the Chicago School of Design and received academic accreditation as the Institute of Design in 1946. In addition to teaching and overseeing the administration of the school, with which he was associated until his death, Moholy-Nagy pursued an interest in photography and cinematography, publishing several books in these fields.

MUELLER-MUNK, PETER
Born June 25, 1904, Berlin, Germany; died March 13, 1967, Pittsburgh, Pennsylvania
Silversmith, industrial designer, teacher

Mueller-Munk received his art training at the Kunstgewerbeschüle, where he studied with noted German silversmith Waldemar Raemisch. Arriving in the United States shortly after the close of the Paris Exposition of 1925, Mueller-Munk designed for Tiffany and Company for three years before opening his own studio. Operating in New York and then in Chicago, he reinterpreted late eighteenth- and early nineteenth-century neoclassical styles in commissions for Revere Copper and Brass, Inc., and Elgin Watch, among other firms—work that was included in the major exhibitions of American silver in the late 1920s and 1930s. When the Depression severely diminished the U.S. market for custom-made silver, Mueller-Munk, along with Donald Dohner and Robert Lepper, founded the first American degree-granting program in industrial art, at the Carnegie Institute of Technology in Pittsburgh, in 1935. As an associate professor there until 1944, and later in lectures throughout the country, Mueller-Munk expounded on his belief in a broad-based liberal-arts education for industrial designers. In 1945 he established Peter Mueller-Munk Associates, a Pittsburgh-based firm that during its first decade was devoted almost exclusively to product design for a broad spectrum of U.S. industries. Its products included home appliances, cameras, and commercial machinery, for clients such as Westinghouse, U.S. Steel, Bell & Howell, and Waring Mixer Corporation.

NADELMAN, ELIE
Born October 6, 1885, Warsaw, Poland; died December 28, 1946
Sculptor, ceramist

As a sculptor living in Paris in the 1910s, Nadelman was a member of the avant-garde circle that included Gertrude and Leo Stein, Guillaume Apollinaire, Constantin Brancusi, and Pablo Picasso. With the assistance of Helena Rubinstein he moved to New York in 1915, and by 1920 was well established as a figurative sculptor. At the height of the Depression in the early 1930s, Nadelman lost his home and studio because he refused to exhibit or sell his work. He began experimenting with plaster and papier-mâché, and was introduced to clayworking by Mrs. Voorhess and Miss La Prince of Inwood Potteries, in Inwood Park, New York. Nadelman collected the toys of Central European folk artists, the baked-clay figures of Tanagra and Taranto, and preserved fragments of Tangerine and Myrrhine forms. His abiding interest in folk art gave him a respect for common materials, and from 1933 to 1935 he produced clay figures that he decorated simply with his own white, gray, yellow, and black glazes and fired in a home kiln. At his death, hundreds of small plaster and ceramic figures were found in his studio, a body of work that Nadelman believed achieved his sculptural intentions.

NASH, A. DOUGLAS
Born 1885; died 1940
Glass artist

Nash was the son of the English glassmaker Arthur J. Nash, with whom he worked at the Louis C. Tiffany factories at Corona, New York, until Tiffany retired from active participation in the firm in 1919. Nash purchased the assets of the Long Island factory and operated it as A. Douglas Nash Associates until 1920, when Louis C. Tiffany Furnaces, Inc., was formed. In 1928 Tiffany again withdrew its financial support, and Nash and his father formed A. Douglas Nash Corporation, a company that continued to make art glass in the Tiffany style, as well as tinted glass and lustred glass, and glassware embedded with air bubbles—a technique developed by Nash. When the firm ceased operation in 1931, Nash became a designer and technician for the Libbey Glass Company. Hired to help the company regain its position in the luxury glass field, Nash designed the Libbey-Nash line, an art-glass series with Tiffany influences that was far too expensive to succeed in a mass market. Nash left Libbey in 1935 and later worked for Pittsburgh Plate Glass Company as well as various other firms.

VON NESSEN, WALTER
Born 1889, Berlin, Germany; died 1943
Designer, woodworker, metalsmith

Von Nessen studied in Berlin with Bruno Paul, an important educator and furniture designer, and created furniture designs in Stockholm before emigrating to the United States in 1923. Shortly thereafter, he established his own company, Nessen Studio, Inc., in New York. The limited-edition objects produced by the studio were strongly influenced by the neoclassical style. Von Nessen also worked as an industrial designer for firms such as Chase Brass and Copper Company of Waterbury, Connecticut, for which he created a widely distributed coffee service in 1936.

NOGUCHI, ISAMU
Born November 17, 1904, Los Angeles, California; died December 30, 1988, New York, New York
Sculptor, ceramist, woodworker

Noguchi created sculpture as well as portraits, lamps, tables, stage sets, gardens, plazas, playgrounds, and interiors. His Japanese father was an internationally recognized poet and his American mother was a writer and teacher. In 1927 he won a Guggenheim Fellowship, and for the next two years he studied in Paris. Upon his arrival he met Alexander Calder and arranged to work for six months as a studio assistant to Constantin Brancusi, creating abstract sculptures in wood, stone, and sheet metal. In 1930 he spent eight months studying brush drawing with Ch'i Pai-shih in Beijing, and another seven months in 1931 examining haniwa figures, Bizen and Shigaraki ware, and Zen gardens and working with ceramist Uno Jinmatsu in Japan. When he returned to the United States Noguchi continued to produce sculpture in many styles and various media that ranged from the miniature to the monumental, the visionary to the utilitarian. His portrait sculpture led to one of his few mass-produced objects, an intercom called *Radio Nurse* that was manufactured in Bakelite by the Zenith Radio Company in 1937. In 1938 Noguchi executed the magnetite *Ford Fountain* for the 1939–40 New York World's Fair and the stainless-steel plaque *News* for the Associated Press Building in New York. There is now a museum dedicated to his work in Long Island City, New York.

NOYES, MARION ANDERSON
Born 1907, Wisconsin
Metalsmith

Noyes was influenced by the Scandinavian silver displayed at the 1933–34 Century of Progress Exposition in Chicago, as is evident in the handwrought pewter designs she created as a student at the University of Wisconsin, Madison. Following her graduation in 1933, she moved to Newburyport, Massachusetts, to become a consultant for the Towle Silver Company. Noyes left

Towle after one year, and in 1936 opened her own studio and retail shop in Newburyport. She closed the shop in 1941 and after World War II returned to Towle as a free-lance consultant.

OAKES, EDWARD EVERETT
Born March 5, 1891, Boston, Massachusetts; died 1961
Silversmith, jeweler

Oakes apprenticed in Boston with Frank Gardner Hale and Josephine Hartwell, becoming a master craftsman and working through the Boston Jewelers Guild of the Society of Arts and Crafts. Oakes made his own alloys and gained a reputation from his jewelry designs—clusters of leaves and flowers that were fabricated separately and then assembled. Today, Oakes's work is carried on by his son, Gilbert B. Oakes, in Sugar Hill, New Hampshire.

OLMSTED, ANNA WITHERELL
Born 1889, Syracuse, New York; died February 8, 1981
Museum director, art critic

Olmsted attended Syracuse University and began a career as an art critic for the *Syracuse Post Standard* in 1928. In 1930 she joined the staff of the Syracuse Museum of Fine Arts, assuming the director's position in 1932. Under her leadership the museum sponsored a memorial exhibition in honor of ceramist Adelaide Robineau. This ceramics show, held in 1932, was the first such national exhibition in the United States, and Olmsted developed it into a prestigious annual event that became known as the Ceramic National. In addition to her museum responsibilities, Olmsted continued as an art critic for the *Syracuse Post Standard* until 1944, and for the *Syracuse Herald-American* from 1945 until her retirement.

ORME, W. L.
Glass designer

See Cambridge Glass Company: PRODUCTION CENTERS AND SHOPS—GLASS

PARZINGER, TOMMI
Born 1903, Munich, Germany; died 1972
Silversmith, industrial designer

Parzinger studied art in Vienna, Munich, and Berlin and was well known as a designer of furniture, silver, enamels, and textiles before he emigrated to the United States in 1935. On his arrival in New York he associated himself with Rena Rosenthal's studio, and in 1940 he established Parzinger, Inc., a design house devoted to special orders and to custom-made furniture and accessories. Parzinger's work was included in the 1937 silver exhibitions at The Brooklyn Museum and The Metropolitan Museum of Art, in the Decorative Arts section of the 1939–40 Golden Gate International Exposition in San Francisco, and in the Metropolitan's "Contemporary American Industrial Art" exhibition in 1940. Between 1939 and 1942 his metalwork was illustrated in *Life, Arts & Decoration, The Connoisseur,* and *The Studio.* While Parzinger continued to design metalwork after World War II, he devoted himself primarily to the production of furniture and accessories until his retirement.

PENINGTON, RUTH
Born 1905, Colorado Springs, Colorado
Silversmith, metalsmith, jeweler

Penington entered the University of Washington in Seattle around 1923, beginning a forty-six-year association with the School of Art, first as a student and then as a faculty member. Many on the faculty, including painter Walter Isaac and printmaker-designer Helen Neilson Rhodes, had trained in Arthur Wesley Dow's pedagogical system of learning by doing, with which Penington was already familiar. In the mid-twenties Penington was attracted to the Art School's metal division, and advanced training outside the university further developed her metalworking skills. Her work was shown at the Seattle Art Museum in 1930 and in invitational exhibitions held at the Baltimore Museum of Art and the Cincinnati Art Museum in 1944. Also in 1944, she worked with designer Gilbert Rohde in New York, and in 1947, with the English silversmith William Bennett at a Rhode Island School of Design workshop arranged by Margret Craver. Penington's metalwork developed in two parallel directions: richly encrusted works of visual delicacy, and those marked with a monumental, architectonic feeling. Inspired by archaic and primitive art forms as well as the arts of Asia and Native American tribes of the Northwest Coast, her works incorporate spindle whorls, trade and tomb beads, amulets, feathers, unpolished beach pebbles, and agates. After teaching at the University of California, Berkeley, in the 1940s, Penington joined the faculty of the University of Alaska in Fairbanks. In 1955 she established the Fidalgo Summer School of the Applied Arts in La Conner, Washington.

PERI, EVE
Born 1896, Bangor, Maine; died March 14, 1966, Philadelphia, Pennsylvania
Embroiderer, painter

As a child Peri learned embroidery, appliqué, and quiltmaking from her New England mother and aunts, who were also skilled weavers. She moved to New York as a student and later established a studio in a Park Avenue brownstone, producing witty fabric forms called "Fabstracts" in the spirit of Jean Arp, Georges Braque, Joan Miró, and Pablo Picasso. Peri's approach to textile design was that of a painter. Some of her compositions are monochromatic and subtly varied in texture; others are bright, graphic abstractions; still others have the appearance of carvings in cloth. Peri had her first exhibition in 1937, at the Delphic Gallery in New York. Her work was subsequently used by interior decorators; her largest commission was a hanging for the San Francisco office of Container Corporation. Peri lived in Philadelphia in the 1950s and opened a shop in New Hope, Pennsylvania, where she sold her wall hangings, collages, and screens as well as her more conventional pillows and bed coverings.

PETTERSON, JOHN PONTUS
Born May 15, 1884, Göteborg, Sweden; died December 30, 1949
Silversmith, metalsmith

Petterson studied silversmithing at the Royal School of Arts and Crafts in Norway and served an apprenticeship with the renowned Norwegian silversmith David Anderson. In 1905 he emigrated to New York, where he worked for Tiffany & Company. He moved to Chicago in 1911 to work in the Jarvie Shop, and executed many of the splendid candlesticks and trophies that made the shop famous. In 1914 he opened his own business, the Petterson Studio. There, he and his assistants made hammered copperware and hand-wrought silver flatware, holloware, jewelry, and other special-order items. In 1937 Petterson won a silver medal at the Paris Exposition.

POOR, HENRY VARNUM
Born September 30, 1888, Chapman, Kansas; died December 8, 1970, New York, New York
Ceramist, painter, furniture designer

Poor studied economics and art at Stanford University. He later enrolled at the Slade School of Art in London and completed his art training at the Académie Julian in Paris. Returning to the United States in 1912, he taught at Stanford and at the Mark Hopkins Institute of Art in San Francisco (formerly the California School of Design). By 1923, Poor was living in New York and working in clay. Over the next ten years he established a national reputation with award-winning ceramics marked by bold cubistic patterning. His first ceramics exhibition took place at the Montross Gallery

in New York in 1923, and he received a Gold Medal for work exhibited at the Architectural League. Poor worked only sporadically as a ceramist after the mid-1930s. In 1946 he became the first president of the Skowhegan School of Painting and Sculpture in Maine, and in the early 1950s was an artist-in-residence at the American Academy in Rome, and a painting instructor at Columbia University, in New York. In 1954 he wrote *From Mud to Immortality,* in which he discussed the aesthetics of ceramics.

PRESTINI, JAMES L.
Born January 13, 1908, Waterford, Connecticut; died July 26, 1993, Berkeley, California
Woodworker, sculptor, teacher

Prestini trained as a machinist's apprentice and earned an undergraduate degree in mechanical engineering at Yale University (1930). While much of his career was spent as a research engineer specializing in construction materials, furniture, housing, and the relationship between research and design, his woodturning, begun in the early 1930s, brought him to the attention of curators and craft connoisseurs. Prestini used a lathe to make bowls and platters, creating extremely thin wood forms that were seen as the best possible expression of art through technology. He was influenced by social concerns and by Bauhaus utopian ideals, encountered as a student of László Moholy-Nagy at the Institute of Design in Chicago; Prestini was also an instructor at the institute from 1939 to 1946. His standing as a sculptor was confirmed in 1949 when he was part of the design team that won The Museum of Modern Art's "International Competition for Low-Cost Furniture" with a jointless chair made from durable wood pulp. After teaching at various schools and colleges in the 1930s and 1940s, Prestini joined the faculty of the University of California, Berkeley, in 1956, where he taught architecture until his retirement in 1975.

RAYMOND, ANTONIN
Born 1889, Prague, Czechoslovakia; died 1976
Architect, textile designer

Raymond earned a degree in architecture and engineering from the Higher Polytechnic Institute in Prague (1910). He moved to New York shortly thereafter to work in the office of architect Cass Gilbert. By 1916, he was employed by Frank Lloyd Wright, and the following year he designed the Théâtre du Vieux Colombier for Jacques Copeau in New York. During World War I Raymond served in Europe as an Army intelligence officer. In 1920 he went with Wright to Japan, remaining there to practice architecture from 1921 to 1938. He returned to the United States in 1939 and opened his own architecture, engineering, and design firm in New Hope, Pennsylvania, in partnership with his wife, designer Noemi Pernessin Raymond. In 1940 Raymond entered The Museum of Modern Art's "Organic Design in Home Furnishings Competition," winning first place in the Printed Fabrics category and honorable mention in the Furniture for a One-room Apartment category.

REBAJES, FRANCISCO (FRANK)
Born February 6, 1907, Puerto Plata, Dominican Republic; died 1990
Metalsmith, jeweler

Rebajes studied in the Dominican Republic and in Spain before emigrating to New York in the late 1920s. Penniless, he began modeling tin cans into animal figures, which he sold in sidewalk art shows around Washington Square. A large purchase in the early 1930s, purportedly by Mrs. Juliana Force, gave Rebajes the funds to establish his own business, Copper Craftsmen, Inc., in Greenwich Village. In 1937 his holloware and jewelry were given a full display case in The Brooklyn Museum's "Contemporary Industrial and Hand-wrought Silver" exhibition and were featured in "Silver: An Exhibition of Contemporary Design" at The Metropolitan Museum of Art. He won a bronze medal and a Diplôme d'Honneur at the 1937 Paris Exposition and displayed work in the Metals and Glass section of the Fifteenth American Industrial Art Exhibition at The Metropolitan Museum of Art in 1940. Rebajes had a shop on Fifth Avenue in the 1940s, where he sold copper costume jewelry of his own manufacture.

REEVES, RUTH
Born July 14, 1892, Redlands, California; died December 23, 1966, New York, New York
Textile designer, painter, woodworker, arts administrator

Reeves attended the Pratt Institute School of Art (1910–11), and received a scholarship to study at the Art Students League (1913), where she worked with Kenneth H. Miller. From 1920 to 1927 she lived and worked in France, studying under Fernand Léger at the Académie Moderne in Paris. Upon her return to the United States she produced handblocked textile designs in the Cubist-inspired idiom she had developed in Paris. Reeves's 1930 fabric design *Figures with Still Life* was a commission from W. & J. Sloane and was included in her 1932 one-woman exhibition at the Art Center in New York. From 1935 to 1936 Reeves served as the first national coordina-

tor of the Federal Art Project's Index of American Design. She then resumed work as a textile designer, developing motifs inspired by her study of vernacular design while in Guatemala on a Guggenheim Fellowship in 1934. Her works from this period include handpainted wall coverings for New York's Radio City Music Hall.

REISS, WINOLD
Born 1886, Karlsruhe, Germany; died August 29, 1953, New York, New York
Illustrator, interior designer, textile designer

Reiss emigrated to the United States in 1914, and while best known for his illustrations in *Survey Graphic* and Alain LeRoy Locke's *The New Negro* (1925), he was also a designer of interiors and textiles. His blockprinted fabrics and rug designs were shown in New York at the Art Alliance of America's Albert Blum Exhibitions of Hand Decorated Fabrics from 1916 to 1920. Reiss's interest in Native American motifs purportedly developed from an association with Léon Bakst, a design consultant to the textile manufacturer H. R. Mallinson and Company. Shortly after Bakst's pattern Hopi Indian Motives was produced by Mallinson in 1927, Reiss began visiting native tribes throughout the United States and Canada, portraying tribal members and also creating his own Native American–inspired designs.

REISS, HENRIETTE (MRS. WINOLD REISS)
Born May 5, 1889, Liverpool, England; died July 17, 1992
Textile designer

Reiss studied textile design in her native England and in Munich and Switzerland before emigrating to the United States with her husband, designer Winold Reiss, in 1914. By the 1920s, the couple was living in an artists' colony in New York that included Marion Dorn, Ruth Reeves, and Martha Ryther. In the latter part of the decade Reiss taught a number of promising students in addition to exhibiting her prints, handwoven textiles, and rugs. Rugs designed by Reiss and handhooked by the New England Guild of Portland, Maine, were included in a modern design exhibition at The Newark Museum in 1930. Other featured designers who worked in collaboration with the guild were Donald Deskey, Henry Varnum Poor, Ruth Reeves, and Joseph Urban.

RHEAD, FREDERICK HURTEN
Born 1880, Hanley, Staffordshire, England; died 1942, Newell, West Virginia
Ceramist

After working with the Roseville Pottery Company, and the Jervis Pottery in Oyster Bay, New York, Rhead moved to Southern California in 1913. He founded Camarata Pottery (later, Rhead Pottery) in Santa Barbara in 1914, specializing in decorative inlays and perfecting a Chinese black-mirror glaze. Rhead was director of research for the American Encaustic Tiling Company, of Zanesville, Ohio, from 1917 to 1927, when he became the head of the Laughlin China Company. For Laughlin Rhead designed Fiesta, one of the most enduring production lines introduced in the 1930s. The American Ceramic Society awarded Rhead the Charles Fergus Binns Medal in 1934.

RIEGGER, HAROLD EATON
Born 1913, Ithaca, New York
Ceramist, teacher

Riegger received a B.S. degree from the New York State College of Ceramics at Alfred University (1938) and an M.A. from Ohio State University, Columbus (1940). After graduation he relocated to Mill Valley near San Francisco and set up a workshop, where he experimented with *raku* and primitive firing techniques. Riegger taught ceramics at various art schools throughout the country, including the Haystack Mountain School of Crafts in Liberty, Maine; the California College of Arts and Crafts in Oakland; the California School of Fine Arts; the University of Oregon in Eugene; the Museum of Industrial Art in Philadelphia; and Ohio State. He is the author of several manuals on ceramics.

ROBSJOHN-GIBBINGS, TERRENCE HAROLD
Born 1905, London, England; died October 20, 1976, Athens, Greece
Interior designer, furniture designer, writer

Following an apprenticeship with a draftsman, Robsjohn-Gibbings studied at the University of Liverpool and the University of London, earning a B.S. in architecture. He was the head designer for Ashby Tab Ltd., art director for British International (motion) Pictures, and an antiques and home furnishings dealer under Charles Duveen at Charles of London before emigrating to the United States in 1930. In 1936 he established Robsjohn-Gibbings Ltd. in New York, attracting wealthy and socially prominent clients on both sides of the Atlantic. The rich, Robsjohn-Gibbings once said, are always with us, and we should learn to enjoy them. He gave panache to the homes of the social elite in a fiercely individual style, creating interiors for clients such as Elizabeth Arden and Neiman-Marcus. In 1946 he was commissioned to design furniture for the mass market by the Widdicomb Furniture Company of Grand Rapids, Michigan. The originality of the pieces he created for Widdicomb formed the basis for much of American furniture design in the postwar period, and represent Robsjohn-Gibbings's individual contribution to new standards for good design. He wrote two books satirizing American decorating habits, *Goodbye Mr. Chippendale* (1944) and *Homes of the Brave* (1954), and in 1964 he retired to Athens, Greece.

ROHDE, GILBERT
Born June 1, 1894, New York, New York; died June 16, 1944, New York, New York
Industrial designer

Rohde's innovative designs first received attention when he created the modular furniture for the "Design for Living House" at the 1933–34 Century of Progress Exposition in Chicago. From 1936 to 1938 he directed the Federal Art Project's Design Laboratory in New York, an industrial design school that followed the principles of the German Bauhaus. In his "Community Interests" installation at the 1939–40 New York World's Fair Rohde emphasized science and technology's impact on the community, with 1789 representing a period of "Man AND Community"—marked by self-sufficiency and little leisure time—and 1939 representing "Man IN the Community," enjoying better health, shorter working hours, increased educational opportunities, and a richer cultural life. Rohde illustrated this hopeful vision of the future through exhibits showing a colonial village green, inventions that changed the world, "Mrs. Modern" ordering dinner over the phone, and modern information systems. Rohde later worked as a consultant for General Electric, the Herman Miller Furniture Company, and Kroehler Manufacturing, among other firms.

ROOSEVELT, ELEANOR (MRS. FRANKLIN DELANO ROOSEVELT)
Born October 11, 1884, New York, New York; died November 7, 1962, New York, New York
Art patron, political advocate

Prior to her marriage to her cousin Franklin in 1905, Eleanor Roosevelt worked with the New York Consumer League, which sought to improve factory conditions and to outlaw child labor. During the early years of her marriage she devoted herself to her family and to her husband's political career. In 1920 she began working with the League of Women Voters in New York, an association that helped launch her as a powerful political advocate. Roosevelt's support of arts and crafts also had a political agenda. In 1925

she helped found Val-Kill Industries to provide employment for craftspeople. As First Lady she was an active participant in the design of the federally sponsored planned community of Arthurdale, West Virginia, in 1933.

RORIMER, LOUIS
Born 1872, Cleveland, Ohio; died 1939
Artist, teacher, businessman

Rorimer began his art training in Cleveland at the Manual Training School, and then studied abroad in the 1890s at the Kunstgewerbeschüle in Munich and at the École des Arts Décoratifs and the Académie Julian in Paris. As president of Rorimer Brooks Studios, he pursued a varied career as artist, teacher, and businessman, designing residences throughout the United States and interiors for the Statler Hotel chain. Many of his furnishings were based on French models. Rorimer was a member of the Hoover Commission that visited and reported on the 1925 Paris Exposition and was actively involved with the American Union of Decorative Artists and Craftsmen.

ROSE, BEN
No dates available
Textile designer

Rose had his own textile firm that manufactured hand-screenprinted fabrics in the 1940s. Using this technique he produced commercial fabrics employing a wide range of effects.

ROSE, MARTIN
Metalsmith

See Rose Iron Works: PRODUCTION CENTERS AND SHOPS—METALS

RYTHER, MARTHA
Textile designer

See H. R. Mallinson and Company: PRODUCTION CENTERS AND SHOPS—TEXTILES

SAARINEN, EERO
Born August 20, 1910 Kirkkonummi, Finland; died September 1, 1961, Ann Arbor, Michigan
Architect, designer

The son of Finnish architect Eliel Saarinen, Eero emigrated with his family to the United States in 1923. He studied sculpture at the Académie de la Grande Chaumière, Paris (1929), and received a B.F.A. from the Yale School of Architecture (1934). After traveling in Europe, the Mid-

dle East, and Africa, Saarinen worked with architect Karl Eklund in Helsinki from 1934 to 1936, later establishing an architectural practice with his father at Cranbrook, in Bloomfield Hills, Michigan. Saarinen taught architecture at the Cranbrook Academy of Art from 1939 to 1941, and during World War II worked for the Office of Strategic Services in Washington, D.C. From 1945 to 1947 he practiced in partnership with his father and Robert F. Swanson. Following Eliel Saarinen's death in 1950, he opened his own office, Eero Saarinen and Associates. Subsequent design projects included the General Motors Technical Center in Warren, Michigan; the Kresge Auditorium and Chapel at the Massachusetts Institute of Technology in Cambridge; Trans World Airlines Terminal, John F. Kennedy International Airport, New York; and the Jefferson Memorial Arch in St. Louis.

SAARINEN, GOTTLIEB ELIEL
Born 1873, Rautasalmi, Finland; died July 1, 1950, Bloomfield Hills, Michigan
Architect, teacher, woodworker

Saarinen studied painting and architecture in Helsinki from 1893 to 1897, entering a partnership with architects Herman Gesellius and Armas Lindgren in 1896. With offices in Helsinki and Kirkkonummi, the firm completed numerous projects before Saarinen left to establish his own practice in 1907. His entry in the competition for the design of the Chicago Tribune Tower in 1922 was awarded second prize and brought an invitation to visit Chicago. During his stay there Saarinen developed a visionary scheme for the city's lakefront, a project that proved his skill as an urban designer. In 1923 he began teaching architecture at the University of Michigan in Ann Arbor. One of his students was the son of Detroit newspaper publisher George Booth, who in 1924 commissioned Saarinen to draw up a site plan for Cranbrook, the arts and educational community Booth was committed to developing outside Detroit. The Cranbrook assignment launched a lifelong collaboration between the two men, allowing Saarinen the freedom to design buildings and develop educational programs encompassing all of the applied arts. Booth appointed Saarinen president of the Cranbrook Academy of Art in 1932. He relinquished the position in 1946 but continued to direct the architecture and urban design department until his death in 1950.

SAARINEN, LOUISE (LOJA) (NÉE GESELLIUS)
Born March 16, 1879, Helsinki, Finland; died April 21, 1968, Bloomfield Hills, Michigan
Textile designer, weaver

Saarinen trained as a sculptor, photographer, and model builder at the Konstforeningen Art School, Helsinki; the Taideteollinen Keskuskoulu (1898–99); the Suomen Taideyhdistyksen, Pirussuskoulu (1899–1902); and under Jean-Antoine Injalbert at the Académie Colorossi, Paris (1902–03). In 1903 she joined the Helsinki architectural firm Gesellius, Lindgren and Saarinen—in which her brother, Herman Gesellius, and Eliel Saarinen were partners—producing photographs, sculptures, and designs for the firm's interior commissions. Within a year she married Saarinen, and through him she met the major artists and designers of the day. Exposed to the textile arts as a student, she experimented with batik and weaving before emigrating to the United States with her family in 1923. Saarinen's textile skills played a key role in the development of the Cranbrook Educational Community, with which her husband became involved in 1925. With the idea that art should permeate the Cranbrook environment, founder George Booth asked her to design and weave textiles, carpets, and rugs for the community's buildings. In 1928 she established Studio Loja Saarinen, producing the furnishings for Saarinen House and designing textiles and carpets for the Kingswood School, Cranbrook. She was also director of the closely associated but quite separate weaving department that was founded under the aegis of the Cranbrook Academy of Art in 1929, a position she held until her retirement in 1942.

SAILORS, ROBERT DAVID
Born May 23, 1913, Grand Rapids, Michigan
Weaver, textile designer

After spending the summer of 1941 at the Cranbrook Academy of Art, Sailors was awarded a student fellowship for the following academic year, earning an M.F.A. in 1943. His accomplishments brought him a full fellowship for the 1943–44 academic year and an appointment to the Cranbrook faculty in June 1944. As assistant director and instructor in the weaving department, Sailors was sent to the Rhode Island School of Design to familiarize himself with the functions of a powerloom. A model S1 was installed at Cranbrook in January 1945, and instruction on the powerloom became Sailors's responsibility. Sailors stayed at Cranbrook until late 1947, when financial difficulties eliminated his position. He was next employed by the Celanese Corporation of America, but soon opened his own shop, Contemporary Textiles Weaving Company, in Bitely, Michigan. Advertising both handwoven and machine-loomed fabrics, Sailors employed twenty-three people and his work was represented in showrooms throughout the country. In 1962 he

moved his business to Grand Rapids, Michigan, and again, in 1974, to Cortez, Florida, changing the name to Robert D. Sailors Fabrics and producing handwoven textiles, shades, and rugs.

SAKIER, GEORGE
Born 1897, New York, New York;
died 1965
Industrial designer, glass artist

Sakier trained as an engineer at Columbia University and, after World War I, he also studied painting. As director of the Bureau of Design for the American Radiator and Standard Sanitation Company, he created the interiors for the firm's New York office building, which was designed by Raymond Hood in 1924. Sakier specialized in what he called "functional modern" bathroom accessories and fittings. Beginning in the late 1920s he also worked as a designer for the Fostoria Glass Company. Sakier's "classic modern" dinnerwares—including the popular and inexpensive Mayfair line—competed directly with those produced by Steuben Glass Works.

SAVAGE, AUGUSTA CHRISTINE (née FELLS; later, MRS. JOHN T. MOORE; later, MRS. JAMES SAVAGE; later, MRS. ROBERT L. POSTON)
Born February 29, 1892, Green Cove Springs, Florida; died March 26, 1962, New York, New York
Ceramist, arts administrator, teacher

The seventh of fourteen children born to an impoverished Methodist minister and his wife, Savage was producing clay figures by the time she was six and later taught clay modeling to fellow students at her secondary school. She originally planned to be a teacher and enrolled at the Tallahassee State Normal School (now Florida A & M University), but her desire for art training took her to New York in 1921. She attended the Cooper Union, which gave her financial support, and with the help of a librarian at the New York Public Library secured a commission for a bust of W. E. B. DuBois. Its success led to commissioned portraits of other black leaders, including Marcus Garvey. A scholarship awarded by the Julius Rosenwald Fund in 1930 allowed Savage to study at the Académie de la Grande Chaumière, Paris, under Félix Bueneteaux. On her return to New York in 1932 she established the Savage Studio of Arts and Crafts in Harlem, and by the mid-1930s was helping black artists obtain commissions from the Works Progress Administration. In 1939, at the request of the New York World's Fair Commission, Savage created her best-known work, the plaster sculpture *Lift Every Voice and Sing*. Inspired by James Weldon Johnson's

African-American anthem of the same title, it featured a young man kneeling in front of a choir grouped in a harplike configuration, a bar of musical notes in his hands. The most popular and most publicized statue by an African-American artist exhibited at the Fair, it brought Savage to national attention. Ironically, Savage could not secure the funds to cast or store the statue after the Fair closed. It was razed by the bulldozers demolishing the Fair's buildings—an event that went unnoticed in the press.

SCHEIER, EDWIN A.
Born November 11, 1910, Bronx, New York
SCHEIER, MARY (née GOLDSMITH)
Born May 9, 1910, Salem, Virginia
Ceramists

Mary Scheier studied in New York at the Grand Central School of Art, the Art Students League and the New York School of Fine and Applied Arts (1926–29), with a year of postgraduate study in Paris (1930). In 1935, the year she was appointed director of Big Stone Gap and Abingdon Art centers—the first federal art galleries established in Virginia—Edwin Scheier began two years of study at the New York School of Industrial Arts. In 1937 he became involved with the Federal Art Project in New York and was soon promoted to project field supervisor for Kentucky, North Carolina, and Virginia. The Scheiers met and married that year, and shortly thereafter resigned their administrative positions and began traveling with a puppet show throughout the South. In 1938 Edwin assumed the directorship of the Federal Art Project's Anderson County Federal Art Center in Norris, Tennessee, where both he and his wife taught puppet workshops and courses in metal-, wood-, and leatherworking, drawing, and painting. Through Hewitt Wilson they began making pottery at the Tennessee Valley Authority Ceramic Laboratory in Norris. In 1939 they discovered a superb red clay in Glade Spring, Virginia, and moved there to establish the commercial Hillcrock Pottery. At Hillcrock Mary made small figurative sculptures, vases, mugs, and pitchers. In 1940 the Scheiers won the second prize for pottery at the Ceramic National, the first of many their work would be awarded through 1958. In 1940 they were invited by the League of New Hampshire Arts and Crafts to teach at the University of New Hampshire in Durham, with Edwin as ceramics instructor and Mary an artist-in-residence. On a sabbatical in 1957–58 the Scheiers spent five months in Oaxaca, Mexico, where they became interested in the work of native weavers. They retired from the university in 1960, and from 1968 to 1978 lived in Oaxaca, where Edwin designed textiles and created wood sculptures, paintings, and prints. The couple returned to the United States in 1978 and currently live in Green Valley, Arizona. A retrospective of their work was organized in 1993 by the Currier Art Gallery in Manchester, New Hampshire.

SCHINDLER, RUDOLPH MICHAEL
Born 1887, Vienna, Austria; died 1953, Los Angeles, California
Architect

Educated in Vienna at the Imperial Technical Institute (1906–11) and the Academy of Arts under Otto Wagner (1909–13), Schindler graduated with degrees in both engineering and architecture. Emigrating to the United States in 1914, he worked as a draftsman for the Chicago firm of Ottenheimer, Stern, and Reichert, and in 1918 joined the office of Frank Lloyd Wright. Schindler remained in Wright's employ until 1921, when he opened his own practice in Hollywood and Los Angeles. One of his key buildings, the Schindler & Clyde Chase Duplex (1921–22), was the joint home of the Schindler and Richard Neutra families from 1925 to 1931. Schindler and Neutra often worked in collaboration, fulfilling joint commissions in differing but complementary styles. Most of Schindler's commissions were modest houses utilizing reinforced concrete, studwork, and plywood—an inexpensive construction method frequently used in Southern California. Though many of Schindler's buildings have not aged well and need conservation, they exhibit an imaginative use of three-dimensional space. Schindler created some 300 buildings during the course of his career.

SCHMITZ, CARL
Born 1900, France; died 1967
Sculptor, ceramist

Schmitz was educated in France and at the State School of Applied Arts and the State Academy of Fine Arts in Munich. In the 1920s he trained under Carl Paul Jennewein, Paul Manship, and Carl Milles at the Beaux-Arts Institute of Design in New York, where he established his own studio in 1930. He later taught at the National Academy of Design, and at Michigan State College in East Lansing. While Schmitz preferred to work in clay, he also produced work in other media. He frequently exhibited at the Ceramic Nationals in Syracuse, winning numerous awards.

SCHOEN, EUGENE
Born 1880, New York, New York; died 1957
Architect, industrial designer

After earning a degree in architecture from Columbia University in 1901, Schoen traveled on scholarship in Europe, where he met Otto Wagner and Josef Hoffmann. By 1905, he had established his own architectural practice in New York, adding an interior decoration service after seeing the 1925 Paris Exposition. He also operated a gallery that sold imported items as well as his own furniture and textile designs. Though occasionally inspired by contemporary French design, Schoen's furniture relies more on geometric arrangements of wood grain than applied ornament. In keeping with French traditions, each piece was individually made, unique in some of its details, and quite costly. His designs were executed at Schmieg, Hungate and Kotzian, Inc., and his clients included banks, theaters, and department stores throughout Manhattan and elsewhere. He also accepted numerous commissions for apartment interiors.

SCHRECKENGOST, DON
Born 1911, Sebring, Ohio
Ceramist, industrial designer, teacher

Born into a family of potters, Schreckengost had a long and varied career in both industrial and studio ceramics. He received his art training at the Cleveland School of Art and in Stockholm and Mexico, and in 1935 was appointed professor of industrial design at the New York State College of Ceramics at Alfred University. In 1945 he resigned to become design director of the Laughlin China Company. In 1960 he formed his own company, Design for Industry, whose clients included Hall China Company, Salem China Company, Summitville Tiles, and the Royal China Company. Schreckengost's nonproduction work includes scenes of the American West painted in a linear style on earthenware plates. He participated in the Ceramic Nationals from 1938 to 1946, and was included in the "Contemporary Ceramics of the Western Hemisphere" exhibition at the Syracuse Museum of Fine Arts in 1941. He is a recipient of the American Ceramic Society's Charles Fergus Binns Medal.

SCHRECKENGOST, VIKTOR
Born June 26, 1906, Sebring, Ohio
Ceramist, industrial designer, teacher

Schreckengost trained at the Cleveland School of Art (1924–29) and did postgraduate work at the Wiener Kunstgewerbeschüle, studying ceramics and sculpture under Michael Powolny (1929–30). Upon his return to Cleveland he joined the faculty at the School of Art and became a designer at the Cowan Pottery Studio. At Cowan he created a set of punch bowls on the theme of jazz for Eleanor Roosevelt, who commissioned the bowls for a party at the New York Governor's mansion in Albany. The design was so popular that the *Jazz Bowls* were later produced in a commercial edition. After the Cowan pottery closed in 1931, Schreckengost divided his time between the production of individual ceramic sculptures and designing for various U.S. ceramics companies. In 1933 he helped reorganize the American Limoges Ceramics Company in Sebring, Ohio, within a year expanding production with a fashionable *art moderne* dinnerware pattern that was sleek, unadorned, and sculptural. The style was soon imitated by other American potteries, with Schreckengost completing similar projects for the Sebring Pottery; Leigh Potters, Alliance, Ohio; and Salem China, in Ohio. After World War II he became chairman of the department of industrial design at the Cleveland Institute of Art (formerly the Cleveland School of Art) and served as art director and designer of the Murray Ohio Company, a Cleveland toy manufacturer. In the early 1950s Schreckengost developed a new style of carving vessels out of blocks of dry clay, and worked on numerous architectural commissions, including a series of terracottas for the Cleveland Zoo.

SHIRAYAMADANI, KATARO
Born 1865, Kanazawa, Japan; died 1948, Cincinnati, Ohio
Ceramics decorator and designer

While touring the United States as part of a group of Japanese artists and craftsmen in 1887, Shirayamadani was asked to join the decorating staff of the Rookwood Pottery. Except for a ten-year sojourn in Japan, he remained at Rookwood until his death in 1948. One of its finest artists, he is credited with developing the electrodeposit method of surfacing ceramics with metal, and with designing many of the standard Rookwood shapes. His work evolved from the refined linearity of the Arts and Crafts style to the rugged simplifications and geometries of his Art Deco–inspired ceramics of the 1930s.

SILVIN, MONICA
Active 1940s, Santo Domingo Pueblo, New Mexico
Ceramist

Silvin worked at the conservative pueblo of Santo Domingo, where traditional forms and decoration were carefully preserved. A bulbous earthenware jar with a high neck and flaring rim, with a black band and interlocking geometric designs painted over white slip, was shown at the Contemporary Ceramics of the Western Hemisphere exhibition at the Syracuse Museum of Fine Arts in 1941.

SINGER, SUSI (MRS. JOSEF SCHINNERL)
Born 1895, Vienna Austria; died 1956
Ceramist

Singer studied in Vienna at the Kunstgewerbeschüle under Michael Powolny before joining the Wiener Werkstätte in 1922. After her marriage to Josef Schinnerl in 1924, she moved to the rural Austrian village of Grünbach-am-Schneeberg, establishing Grünbacher Keramik and selling some of the pieces she produced through the Werkstätte. Singer soon demonstrated that she was one of Europe's leading ceramic artists, exhibiting pieces at the 1925 Paris Exposition and at world fairs in the 1930s, where her ceramics won numerous prizes. When her husband died in a mining accident in 1938, Singer, who was Jewish, approached the United States Consulate for permission to emigrate to America, persuading them that her ceramic work would allow her to be financially independent. The following year, Singer and her two-year-old son, Peter, arrived in California, eventually settling in Pasadena. An exhibition at the Amymay Gallery, held shortly after her arrival, and another at the Pasadena Art Institute in 1941 introduced her work in Southern California. In 1946 she received a Scripps College research grant from the Fine Arts Foundation, which allowed her to experiment with American slips and glazes. She created more than thirty ceramic figures under the grant, including *Saturn and Nymph, Adam and Eve, School Boy and Child,* and *Hat in Hand.*

STONOROV, OSCAR G.
Born 1905, Germany
Architect, woodworker

Trained at the École Polytechnique Fédérale in Zurich, Stonorov worked intermittently as a sculptor in Paris and Florence between 1925 and 1929. While working in the atelier of André Lurçat from 1927 to 1929, he cowrote a book on Le Corbusier with Willi Boesiger. In 1932, his own firm, Stonorov and Kastner, Associated Architects, won second prize in the international competition for the Palace of the Soviets. Stonorov emigrated to the United States later that year and began practicing architecture in Philadelphia. He completed commissions for housing projects in Philadelphia as well as Camden, New Jersey; New Britain, Connecticut; and Beaver County, Pennsylvania. In association with Willo von Moltke, Stonorov entered The Museum of Modern Art's "Organic Design in Home Furnishings Competition" of 1940–41, winning first place in the Furniture for a Bedroom category and honorable mention in the Seating for a Living Room category.

STRENGELL, MARIANNE (MRS. CHARLES DUSENBURY; LATER, MRS. OLAV HAMMARSTROM)
Born May 24, 1909, Helsinki, Finland
Weaver, textile designer

Strengell designed rugs and domestic fabrics in Helsinki from 1930 to 1936, and co-owned her own firm, Koti-Hemmet, from 1934 to 1936. In 1937, at Eliel Saarinen's invitation, Strengell joined the Cranbrook Academy of Art as the weaving instructor in the costume and textile department. There, she worked with Loja Saarinen teaching the design and creation of rugs, drapery fabrics, and dress materials. Following her belief that "good design is a way of life," Strengell encouraged students to incorporate an understanding of the client, raw materials, site conditions, the availability of labor and equipment, and cost into the development of their art. In 1942 she became head of Cranbrook's weaving and textile design department, a position she held until 1961. During this period Strengell designed fabrics for Knoll Associates, Cabin Crafts, Owens-Corning Fiberglas, Chatham Manufacturing, and Fieldcrest. Among her goals was the transfer of handweaving's design excellence to mass-produced textiles. She also designed ecclesiastical and residential interiors with her second husband, architect Olav Hammarstrom.

SWALLOW, WILLIAM
Born 1912, Pennsylvania
Ceramist

Swallow was educated in Philadelphia at the Pennsylvania Museum School of Art and the University of Pennsylvania. He taught at the Pennsylvania Museum School and at Muhlenberg College, in Allentown, Pennsylvania, and was director of art at South Whitehall Consolidated Schools in Allentown. Swallow's work displays Pennsylvania German and Amish motifs. The four tiles he submitted to the "Contemporary Ceramics of the Western Hemisphere" exhibition at the Syracuse Museum of Fine Arts in 1941 depict the tasks of everyday Amish life: a woman churning butter, women at market, men tending farm animals, and a man cutting wheat with a scythe. Swallow regularly participated in the Ceramic Nationals between 1940 and 1958, and his work was awarded several prizes.

SWANSON, J. ROBERT F.
Born June 14, 1900, Menominee, Michigan; died March 14, 1981, Birmingham, Michigan
Architect, designer

Swanson earned a B.A. in architecture

from the University of Michigan, Ann Arbor (1922). Following graduate study at the university under Finnish architect Eliel Saarinen, Swanson eloped with Saarinen's daughter, Eva Lisa (Pipsan), in 1926. He soon established his own architectural firm; his wife became the interior designer for the firm's projects. By the mid-1930s, the couple was designing furnishings for their contemporary interiors, developing a line of flexible furniture known as F.H.A.—Flexible Home Arrangements—that was introduced through the Johnson Furniture Company of Grand Rapids, Michigan. The Swansons also collaborated on printed fabrics for Goodall Fabrics, on metalwork for Cray of Boston, on lamps for the Mutual-Sunset Lamp Manufacturing Co. of New York, and on glassware for U.S. Glass of Tiffin, Ohio. In 1944 they formed a partnership with Pipsan's father and her brother, the architect-designer Eero Saarinen, completing architectural projects such as the Milwaukee Cultural Center, the Des Moines Art Center, and Drake University in Des Moines. In 1947 the Swansons established Swanson Associates, which accepted commissions from private institutions, schools, hospitals, banks, and churches. The firm was incorporated in 1954.

TCHELITCHEW, PAVEL
Born 1898, Moscow, Russia; died 1957, Frascati, Italy
Painter, glass designer

A neo-romantic painter, Tchelitchew made landscapes and figural scenes that consistently displayed exaggerated perspective and multiple hidden images. Trained at the Kiev Academy, he began his career as a stage designer in Berlin, working in a Cubist-Constructivist style. In 1923 he moved to Paris, where he became associated with Gertrude Stein and her circle. His first one-man show was held in London in 1928, and his first U.S. exhibition opened in New York at The Museum of Modern Art in 1930. Tchelitchew continued to work as a stage designer, creating the scenery and costumes for the Sergei Diaghilev ballets *Ode* and *L'Errante*, in Paris, and for various American productions after he emigrated to New York in 1934. In the late 1930s an unusual commission led Tchelitchew into glass design. John Montieth Gates, an architect and a designer for the Steuben Division of Corning Glass Works, commissioned twenty-seven world-renowned artists, including Tchelitchew, to create drawings that Steuben engravers could produce in limited editions. The engraved crystal pieces were exhibited at the Steuben building in New York in 1940.

TEAGUE, WALTER DORWIN, SR.
Born December 18, 1883, Decatur, Indiana; died December 5, 1960, Flemington, New Jersey
Industrial designer, glass artist

Teague is credited with establishing the industrial design profession in America in the first quarter of this century. After studying at the Art Students League, Teague began working in the art department of the New York advertising agency Calkins and Holden in 1908. While visiting Europe in 1926, he was introduced to the architecture of Le Corbusier, Walter Gropius, and Robert Mallett-Stevens. The following year, he accepted a commission to redesign the cameras and showroom of the Eastman Kodak Company, the success of which confirmed his reputation as an industrial designer. In 1932 Teague was contacted by Arthur Amory Houghton, Jr., president of Corning Glass Works, and offered a one-year contract to help reduce the company's diminishing profits, a result of the Depression. In addition to developing a modern line of colorless crystal tableware and decorative glass, Teague drew upon his advertising background to reorient the company's marketing approach, initiating an image-conscious promotional campaign that codified Steuben glass as a status symbol.

TESTA, ANGELO
Born August 15, 1921, Springfield, Massachusetts; died August 13, 1984, Springfield, Massachusetts
Weaver, textile designer

Between 1938 and 1945 Testa studied at the New York School of Fine and Applied Arts and the University of Chicago, and was the first graduate of the Institute of Design in Chicago (formerly the New Bauhaus). He studied with former Bauhaus instructor László Moholy-Nagy and with Bauhaus-trained weaver Marli Ehrmann, who, like himself, was intrigued by the structural components of weaving. Upon completion of his studies he established his own firm, Angelo Testa Designs, in Chicago. The Testa studio exploited the relationship of fabric to architectural interiors, and created the first mass-produced collection of fabrics with nonobjective imagery. Testa became both crusader and spokesman for the Bauhaus methodology. Its influence on his work was evident as early as 1942, in a textile with a printed free-form design of three overlapping shapes. Called Little Man, the design launched Testa professionally when it appeared in newspapers and magazines throughout the country. Testa was especially interested in making good design accessible to a mass market, and visible in public spaces as well as private institutions. Over the course of his career he designed woven and printed fabrics, furni-

ture, lamps, and graphics, and also worked as a muralist.

URBAN, JOSEPH
Born 1872, Vienna, Austria; died 1933
Architect, textile designer, woodworker, arts administrator

Urban was educated in Vienna, studying under Karl von Hasenauer at the Imperial Academy of Fine Arts (1890–93) and at the Polytechnicum. He traveled to the United States to design the Austrian Pavilion for the 1904 Louisiana Purchase Exposition in St. Louis, for which he won a gold medal. Urban settled permanently in New York in 1911, and fulfilled interior design commissions for the Metropolitan Opera and the Ziegfeld Follies. One of his most striking architectural commissions was that for the New School for Social Research, built 1929–30 on West Twelfth Street in Manhattan. From 1922 to 1924 Urban served as president of the Wiener Werkstätte's Fifth Avenue showroom.

VUILLEMENOT, FREDERIC ALEXANDRE
Born France; no dates available
Glass designer

Vuillemenot grew up in northeastern France near the textile center of Roubaix and attended schools where he could specialize in textile design and decoration. On a scholarship to the École des Arts Décoratifs in Paris, Vuillemenot concentrated on the application of industrial art to architecture. Emigrating to the United States in 1915, he was hired as a designer for the Libbey Glass Company in Toledo, and in 1924 he was appointed head designer of the atomizer division of the DeVilbiss Manufacturing Company, a perfumer. Under Vuillemenot's direction, DeVilbiss achieved an unprecedented level of excellence in product design; he was also responsible for the design of the company's advertising and packaging. In 1925, inspired by the recent Paris Exposition, which he attended in the company of the firm's owner, Tom DeVilbiss, Vuillemenot designed an eclectic array of atomizers, perfume lights, and other boudoir articles. The DeVilbiss catalogue he presented in 1928 contained atomizers and perfume droppers with chromeplating and sophisticated black glass. Among his most innovative designs were atomizers using component shapes that could be combined to create dramatic and imaginative multimedia sculptures. The Depression's impact on the purchase of luxury goods forced DeVilbiss to relegate Vuillemenot to a part-time free-lance position in 1932. When he was returned to full-time status in 1934, Vuillemenot was required to design spray-painting equipment in addi-

tion to working for the atomizer division. He left the company in 1948.

WALTERS, CARL
Born 1883, Fort Madison, Iowa; died 1955
Ceramist

Walters studied at the Minneapolis School of Art (1905–07) and under painter Robert Henri at the Chase School in New York (1908–11). He established himself as an artist in Portland, Oregon, continually exhibiting his work between 1913 and 1919 and gaining a reputation as one of the most promising young painters of the Northwest. In 1919 Walters returned to New York, where he shifted his focus to ceramics and spent nearly two years developing a popular Egyptian-blue glaze. In 1921 he opened his first workshop in Cornish, New Hampshire, and in the summer of 1922 he moved to Woodstock, New York, where he fired his earliest pieces of ceramic sculpture. In 1924 his work was exhibited in New York at the Whitney Studio Club and the Whitney Museum of American Art. Walters spent 1936–37 developing his work with the support of a Guggenheim Fellowship, producing painted pottery in a style similar to the whimsical folk-realist painting of the period. Though he seldom accepted students in his early years, he later established the ceramics department at the Norton School of Art in West Palm Beach, Florida. In 1955, shortly after his death, a memorial exhibition of his work was held at the Museum of Art in Ogunquit, Maine.

WARREN, BARBARA
Textile designer

See Milwaukee Handicraft Project: PRODUCTION CENTERS AND SHOPS—TEXTILES

WAUGH, SIDNEY BIEHLER
Born January 17, 1904, Amherst, Massachusetts; died 1963
Glass designer, architect, sculptor

Waugh attended Amherst College and the School of Architecture at the Massachusetts Institute of Technology, and spent four years studying under Emile Bourdelle at the École des Beaux-Arts in Paris. After winning the Prix de Rome, he studied sculpture for three years at the American Academy in Rome. On his return in 1932 Waugh settled into a studio on Bleecker Street in New York, where he concentrated on architectural sculpture, including the decoration of federal buildings in Washington, D.C. In 1936 Arthur Amory Houghton, Jr., and John Montieth Gates persuaded Waugh to participate in the reorganization of the Steuben Division of Corning Glass Works. Waugh was charged with developing a series of designs that would bring out the beauty of Steuben's new colorless crystal—sophisticated contemporary designs that could compete with those of Orrefors, Lobmeyr, and other well-established European manufacturers in an international market. His first use of glass as a sculptural medium was an illuminated crystal fountain with a slender column of concentric glass cylinders topped by a gazelle, created for Steuben's new glass shop on Fifth Avenue in New York. In 1939 Waugh designed the three-foot-high cast-crystal sculpture *Atlantica* for the Steuben booth at the New York World's Fair. Symbolizing the arrival of glassmaking in the New World, the sculpture, at 300 pounds, was one of the largest pieces of glass ever cast. During the 1940s and 1950s Waugh was responsible for the frequent selection of Steuben glass as the official United States presentation gift. His *Merry-Go-Round Bowl,* presented by President Truman to Princess Elizabeth and Prince Philip of England on the occasion of their marriage in 1947, was the first such state bestowal.

WEBB, AILEEN CLINTON HOADLEY (NÉE OSBORN; LATER, MRS. VANDERBILT WEBB)
Born June 25, 1892, Garrison-on-the-Hudson, New York; died August 15, 1979, Garrison-on-the-Hudson, New York
Philanthropist

Webb was born to a family of prominent philanthropists and scholars. Her father was president of The Metropolitan Museum of Art, and she grew up surrounded by his collection of French Impressionist paintings. Before her marriage to Vanderbilt Webb in 1912, she studied art in Italy. In the 1920s, after the birth of her children, she studied portrait painting under Cecilia Beaux, enameling under Kathe Berl, and ceramics under Maude Robinson. In the 1930s Webb began her life's work: elevating the status of the crafts in America. In 1930 she established a home-based relief project called Putnam County Products, which helped find markets for her neighbors' farm and dairy products, preserves, and handmade goods such as pottery, quilts, and other needlework. From this modest beginning Webb went on to found the American Craftsmen's Cooperative Council in 1939, which opened America House, a retail outlet for the marketing of American crafts, on West Fifty-third Street in New York, the following year. In 1941 the magazine *Craft Horizons* (now *American Craft*) began publication, with Webb as editor. Two years later, the American Craftsmen's Council received its charter as a nonprofit educational organization. Its founding chairman, Webb served until 1976. Under her leadership, the council

established, in 1944, the School for American Craftsmen, which later became a part of the Rochester Institute of Technology; and, in 1956, the Museum of Contemporary Craft (now the American Craft Museum).

WEBER, KARL EMANUEL MARTIN (KEM)
Born November 14, 1889, Berlin, Germany; died January 31, 1963, Santa Barbara, California
Industrial designer

One of the best-known industrial designers working on the West Coast in the 1920s and 1930s, Weber produced sleek, streamlined designs that epitomized the burgeoning "California style." Weber studied at the Unterichtanstalt des Kunstgewerbemuseums (School of the Decorative Arts Museum) in Berlin under Bruno Paul. From 1908 until his graduation in 1912, Weber assisted Paul with a variety of projects, including the German representation at the Brussels World's Fair in 1910. The worsening political situation in Germany prevented its completion, and left Weber, who had been sent to California to supervise its construction, stranded in the United States at the outbreak of World War I. After the war he moved to Santa Barbara, where he taught art and opened his own studio, designing architecture, interiors, and furniture. In 1921 he relocated to Los Angeles, serving as art director for Barker Brothers, a large decorating and furniture store, from 1922 to 1927. While employed there he created furniture, shop interiors, and packaging—displayed in the store's Modes and Manners shop—that suggested the witty, angular style of modern European decoration. Weber gained a national reputation in 1928 when his work was seen in New York at R. H. Macy's "International Exposition of Art in Industry." After resigning from Barker Brothers, he established his own industrial design studio in Hollywood. Architectural commissions included the Sommer and Kaufman shoe store in San Francisco, a design of 1929 that was closely allied with the International Style. Weber also designed hard-edged geometric silver objects for Porter Blanchard's Southern California shop and Friedman Silver in New York (1928–29); streamlined clocks for Lawson Time of Alhambra, California (1934); and plywood and tubular-steel furniture for Baker Brothers and the Lloyd Manufacturing Company of Menominee, Michigan (1934). During World War II Weber worked on a defense housing project and a system of prefabricated housing for the Douglas Fir Plywood Association of Tacoma, Washington. In 1945 he moved back to Santa Barbara and established a studio in his home.

WIESELTHIER, VALERIE (VALLY)
Born 1895, Austria; died September 1, 1945
Ceramist

Wieselthier trained at the Wiener Kunstgewerbeschüle under Michael Powolny (1914–20). Through her work at the Wiener Werkstätte under Dagobert Peche and Josef Hoffmann; the Binnini Werkstätte; and her own studio, Keramische Werkstätte Vally Wieselthier, Wieselthier established herself as one of Europe's leading ceramic artists in the 1920s. In 1928 her work was shown in New York at The Metropolitan Museum of Art's "International Exhibition of Ceramic Art." By the following year, Wieselthier was also in New York, where she began working for the Contemporary Group. She also became a designer for the Sebring Pottery in Ohio and taught at Tulane University in New Orleans, eventually opening her own workshop at 24 East Eighth Street in Manhattan. Her large ceramic sculptures, which fully exploit the expressive qualities of the medium, quickly established her as one of the most influential early figures in the development of ceramic sculpture in the United States. In addition to her work as a ceramist, Wieselthier also designed furniture, fabrics, wallpaper, glass, and jewelry.

WILDENHAIN, MARGUERITE (NÉE FRIEDLAENDER; LATER, MRS. FRANZ WILDENHAIN)
Born October 11, 1896, Lyon, France; died February 24, 1985, Guerneville, California
Ceramist, teacher

Wildenhain studied drawing and sculpture at the School of Fine and Applied Arts in Berlin, and designed porcelain for a factory in Thuringia. In 1919 she became an apprentice and a journeyman potter, working under Max Krehan and Gerhard Marcks at the Bauhaus Pottery Workshop until her certification as a pottery master in 1926. From 1926 to 1933 she headed the pottery department at the Municipal School of Arts and Crafts in Halle-Saale and designed ceramic models for the Royal Berlin Porcelain Manufactory. After the Nazis forced her dismissal in 1933, she and her new husband, Franz Wildenhain, moved to Putten in the Netherlands, establishing a pottery studio and creating designs for the Regout Porcelain Factory in Maastrict. In 1940 she emigrated to the United States, settling at Pond Farm in Guerneville, California; emigration restrictions prevented Franz from joining her until 1947. Wildenhain taught at the College of Arts and Crafts in Oakland from 1940 to 1942, and for a short time served as director of the pottery division of the Appalachian Institute of Arts and Crafts in Banner Elk, North Carolina. Returning to

Guerneville, she began working as an independent potter, and in 1949 helped establish the Pond Farm Community, where she was a teacher and potter-in-residence. The community was closed in 1953, but Wildenhain remained at Pond Farm until her death, managing a popular summer school that attracted students from as far away as China and India.

WINTER, THELMA (NÉE FRAZIER; LATER, MRS. EDWARD WINTER)
Born 1903; died 1977
Ceramist

Winter's work is perhaps the most Viennese of any produced in the United States during the 1930s and 1940s, displaying the gaiety, charm, and humor, as well as the same sculptural techniques, found in much of the Austrian work of the period. Though she did not study in Vienna, she was exposed to the style at the Cleveland School of Art, where she studied under ceramist Julius Mihalik, who had previously taught in Budapest as well as Vienna. Winter was also closely associated with the Vienna-trained Cleveland ceramists Viktor Schreckengost and Russell Barnett Aitken, and with the enamelist Edward Winter, whom she married in 1939. Following her graduation in 1929, she began working in cooperation with potter Richard O. Hummel at the Cowan Pottery Studio. A vase she created in collaboration with the pottery's founder, R. Guy Cowan, was awarded first prize for pottery at the Cleveland Museum of Art's May Show in 1930, and their 1931 Colonial Pattern tea set was a popular production piece. Winter also worked independently, creating a number of slip-cast production pieces under the pottery's auspices. When the pottery closed in 1931, she redirected her career, becoming a widely recognized ceramic sculptor, teacher, and writer. Deeply interested in ceramics education, she taught in the Cleveland public schools and at the Cleveland Institute of Art (formerly the School of Art). She was also a frequent contributor to *Design* magazine, an important sourcebook for art teachers. In 1939 Winter became the first woman to win a first prize for sculpture in the Ceramic Nationals.

WIRDE, MAJA ANDERSSON
Born November 14, 1873, Ramkvilla, Sweden; died February 11, 1952, Algutsboda, Småland, Sweden
Weaver

Educated in Stockholm, Wirde exhibited her work in New York in 1927 as part of The Metropolitan Museum of Art's "Swedish Contemporary Decorative Arts" show. In 1929 she was appointed instructor of weaving at the Cranbrook, teaching

courses at Studio Loja Saarinen, the Cranbrook Academy of Art, and the Kingswood School, Cranbrook. A carpet for the Kingswood School Study Hall Lobby, designed by Wirde and executed by Studio Loja Saarinen in 1931, fits neatly into the design vocabulary that Eliel Saarinen defined for the school. Filled with architectural motifs, it is stylistically similar to work Wirde had done in Sweden. Wirde left the school in June 1933 and spent the summer in Chicago on the staff of the Swedish pavilion at the Century of Progress Exposition. She then returned to Sweden and settled in Algutsboda, where she established a studio and formed a partnership with two other women. She executed ecclesiastical textiles and other commissions until her death in 1952.

WORMLEY, EDWARD J.
Born December 31, 1907, Oswego, Illinois
Furniture designer

Wormley trained at the School of the Art Institute of Chicago (1926–27) and was employed in the design studios of Marshall Field and at Berkey and Gay in Grand Rapids, Michigan, in the late 1920s. As chief designer and director of design at Dunbar Furniture, Inc., from 1931 to 1970, he became known for his prolific output and conservative adaptations of modern design. Wormley formed his eclectic approach from such diverse European designers as Le Corbusier and Émile-Jacques Ruhlmann. His perspective was that of an interior designer who did not believe any individual piece of furniture to be more important than the interior as a whole. During World War II Wormley headed the Furniture Unit of the Office of Price Administration in Washington, D.C. While he maintained his affiliation with Dunbar after the war, he also opened his own office in New York in 1945, accepting design commissions for residential and corporate interiors. He also designed lamps for Lightolier, furniture for Drexel, cabinets for RCA, carpets for Alexander Smith and Sons, and textiles for Schiffer Prints. In 1951 and 1952 his work was included in the "Good Design" exhibitions at The Museum of Modern Art in New York and The Merchandise Mart in Chicago. Wormley closed his New York office in 1967 but continued as a consultant to Dunbar until 1970, when he retired to Weston, Connecticut.

WRIGHT, FRANK LLOYD
Born June 8, 1867, Richland Center, Wisconsin; died April 9, 1959, Phoenix, Arizona
Architect

Wright's architectural and industrial design

theories profoundly influenced architects and craftspeople in Europe as well as the United States. According to Paul Frankl, in the 1920s, when there were few advocates of modern style in America, Wright played an important symbolic role as the originator of modern architecture and decoration. He designed the furniture for most of his important houses, emphasizing natural woods and functionality; he also designed metal grilles and lamps, and stained-glass windows with elaborate geometrical leading. While he advocated the use of machine-made furnishings, his reverence for wood and other natural materials, and his reliance upon forthright structures, made him an influential figure in the American craft movement. In the mid-1930s Wright displayed a renewed creativity, designing the S. C. Johnson Administration building in Racine, Wisconsin (1936); Fallingwater, for Edgar J. Kaufmann, Sr., in Mill Run, Pennsylvania (1936); and introducing the inexpensive Usonian houses, whose simple structure and furnishings could be completed in one operation, with most of the furniture built into the walls.

WRIGHT, RUSSEL
Born April 3, 1904, Lebanon, Ohio; died December 21, 1976, New York, New York
Industrial designer, ceramist, woodworker, glass artist

Wright attended the Art Academy of Cincinnati, studying under painter Frank Duveneck (1920); the Art Students League; and the Columbia University School of Architecture (1923). In 1924 he began working with Norman Bel Geddes as a stage designer. By 1927, Wright was casting nickelplated versions of papier-mâché stage props, which he sold through Rena Rosenthal's New York shop. Wright went on to design furniture, wallpaper, textiles, metalware, and tableware for firms such as the Wurlitzer Company, Chase Brass and Copper Company, Heywood-Wakefield Company, and Conant Ball Company. In 1935 he formed Russel Wright Associates in partnership with his wife, Mary, and designer Irving Richards. In 1937 the firm designed the sleek American Modern tableware line for Steubenville Pottery; produced in 1939, it was an artistic as well as a commercial success. Wright later added accessories to the pattern: stainless-steel flatware, produced by John Hull Cutlery (1951); glassware, manufactured by Morgantown Glass Guild (1951); and table linens, by Leacock (1946–48). In the 1940s Wright designed Highlight Dinnerware and Casual China for the Iroquois China Company, and several tableware lines in melamine; Meladur, a pattern created in 1945 for American Cyanamid, was one of the earliest attempts to bring plastic to the dining table. Wright's commissions, including the Easier Living collection for the Statton Furniture Company, complemented the casual American lifestyle, a design approach that he documented in *A Guide to Easier Living* (1951). During the 1950s and 1960s he designed metal folding chairs and tables for Samsonite (1950), school furniture for Shwayder Brothers (1955), small appliances, fabrics and vinyls, interiors, and packaging. Wright's appointment as a planning consultant to the National Park Service in 1967 marked the end of his design career.

ZEISEL, EVA ALEXANDROVNA POLANYI (NÉE STRIKER; LATER, MRS. ALEXANDER WEISSBERG; LATER, MRS. HANS ZEISEL)
Born November 11, 1906, Budapest, Hungary
Ceramist

One of this century's pioneer designers of ceramics for industry, Zeisel began her career in the fine arts, studying painting at the Royal Academy of Fine Arts in Budapest (1924). Attracted by the shapes and decoration of traditional Hungarian pottery, she apprenticed herself to one of the few remaining peasant potters. Within six months she became the first Hungarian woman to be admitted as a journeyman into the guild of potters and ovensetters. In 1928 Zeisel joined the German earthenware manufacturer Schramberger Majolika Fabrik, for which she designed tea sets, dinnerwares, lamp bases, inkwells, and ashtrays in simple geometric patterns that reflected the influence of the Bauhaus and the Deutscher Werkbund. She left Schramberger in 1929 to design for Carstens in Berlin, where she was involved in every stage of the production process, from design to manufacture and promotion. A short vacation to Russia in 1932 was extended when she began working for the Ukrainian Glass and China Industry, and then for Lomonosov, the former Imperial Porcelain Factory in Leningrad. She later moved to the huge Doulevo china factory in Moscow, founding an independent experimental design laboratory complete with artists, modelmakers, and moldmakers. Doulevo gave Zeisel the opportunity to pursue her objective of good design for mass production, and to inaugurate an apprentice system and improve the status and wages of factory workers. In 1935, at age twenty-nine, she earned the title of Artistic Leader (art director) of the China and Glass Industry of the Russian Republic. The following May, in a Stalinist purge, Zeisel was imprisoned by the State. Upon her release in 1937, she went to Vienna and, subsequently, England, and in 1938 she emigrated to the United States with her new husband, Hans Zeisel. By the end of the year, she was producing designs for Simon Slobodkin and the Keystone Watch

Company of New Jersey and for Henry A. Enrich & Company of New York. In 1939 she was asked to teach at Pratt Institute by Donald Dohner, head of the industrial design department. At Pratt, Zeisel introduced a more experiential approach to design, enabling her students to see their designs through to completion in the factory of the Bay Ridge Specialty Company in New Jersey, where she was a designer. Zeisel remained on the faculty for fifteen years, and from 1959 to 1960 she taught at the Rhode Island School of Design. She continued to work for various manufacturers, including Castleton China, and Red Wing Potteries of Minnesota, until the mid-1960s. In the early 1980s she accepted a commission for a series of fifteen ceramic pieces for the Zsolnay Factory in Pécs, Hungary.

ZIMMERMANN, MARIE
Born 1879, New York, New York; died 1972
Silversmith, jeweler

Zimmermann was a painter and sculptor, but it was in metalwork and jewelry that she achieved national recognition. By 1903, she had completed her studies at the Art Students League and exhibited at The Art Institute of Chicago. In 1915 and 1916 she began to show at the Ehrich Galleries in New York, and throughout the 1920s she received prestigious commissions for architectural metalwork in the East and Midwest. Zimmermann's metalwork was distinguished by highly skillful chemical treatments, gilding, and plating, which created a broad range of colors and textural effects, but she was also capable of an elegant simplification of forms.

ZORACH, MARGUERITE (NÉE THOMPSON; LATER, MRS. WILLIAM ZORACH)
Born September 25, 1887, Santa Rosa, California; died June 27, 1968, Brooklyn, New York
Embroiderer, weaver, painter, printmaker

Marguerite Thompson trained as a painter at the École de la Grande Chaumière in Paris, where in 1912 she married the American artist William Zorach. Her early paintings, which were included in the New York Armory Show of 1913–14—as were those of her husband—were influenced by the intense colors and strong brushwork of the Fauves. While the Zorachs' work was initially quite similar, it diverged around 1920, when William began devoting himself to sculpture. Marguerite continued to paint, and to produce etchings as well as embroideries that she called "needlepaintings," in styles ranging from Fauvism and Cubism to realism. She is considered a pioneer in the field of modern embroidery, and her back-

ground as a painter is visible in the sure draftsmanship of her textile designs. Her 1932 tapestry of the Rockefeller family, commissioned by Mrs. John D. Rockefeller, Jr., brought the artist considerable publicity.

EXHIBITIONS

THE AMERICAN FEDERATION OF ARTS (AFA)
"International Exhibition of Ceramic Art"
First International Exhibition of
Contemporary Industrial Arts
October 2–28, 1928
Washington, D.C.

This was the first of three international "one-material" industrial art exhibitions organized by the AFA. Directed by Charles R. Richards, with Helen Plumb and Metropolitan Museum of Art curator Richard Bach as associates, the series was intended "to bring to the American public and to American manufacturers, merchants and designers the best foreign achievements in a particular field of applied art side by side with our own creations in the hope that thus we may be able more readily to estimate our own position and to take advantage of whatever suggestions the contemporary work of other peoples may hold for us." Limited to contemporary Western European and American work, the shows emphasized new materials and techniques in individual media, with objects grouped by country of origin. The first exhibition, which opened at The Metropolitan Museum of Art and later traveled throughout the country, included functional, decorative, and architectural ceramics.

THE AMERICAN FEDERATION OF ARTS
"Decorative Metalwork and Cotton Textiles"
Third International Exhibition of
Contemporary Industrial Arts
October 15, 1930–April 5, 1931
Washington, D.C.

The last in a series of shows organized by the AFA under the direction of Charles R. Richards, the exhibition traveled to the Museum of Fine Arts, Boston; The Metropolitan Museum of Art; The Art Institute of Chicago; and The Cleveland Museum of Art. A vehicle for stimulating improved design in the objects produced by U.S. manufacturers, it presented the finest examples of contemporary textiles and metalwork by craftspeople from throughout Europe and the United States. The selection emphasized functional design and the suppression of ornament, with European work predominating. In his catalogue text Richards singled out a series of innovative blockprinted fabrics designed by Ruth Reeves for New York retailer W. and J. Sloane as a successful collaboration between artist and manufacturer. Blockprinted on cotton weaves ranging in texture from airplane cloth to toweling, they combined high styling with practicality.

ARCHITECTURAL LEAGUE OF NEW YORK
Annual Exhibitions
1880–present
New York, New York

The Architectural League was founded to represent the professions related to the art of architecture. Its membership includes painters, sculptors, designers, and designers as well as lay members representing the industrial sector. Throughout the 1920s and 1930s the league sponsored annual exhibitions of architectural drawings and photography, sculpture, murals, and interior furnishings, including furniture, lighting fixtures, ceramics, tilework, carpeting, wall coverings, and fabrics. Awards for excellence in architecture, painting, sculpture, landscape architecture, and design and workmanship in industrial art were presented to exhibiting artists. The last award was established in 1920 in recognition of the place occupied by the machine "in the production of beautiful things in quantity."

ART ALLIANCE OF AMERICA
Textile Design Competitions; Albert Blum
Exhibitions of Hand Decorated Fabrics
1916–20
New York, New York

Initiated by a working council that included curators M.D.C. Crawford and Richard Bach, *Women's Wear* publisher E. W. Fairchild, and textile industry representatives, the Textile Design Competitions were intended to promote design research and technical innovation in the textile industry. The competitions were organized under the auspices of the Arts Alliance of America, which also provided exhibition space, and with the assistance of U.S. art schools. With several hundred dollars in prize money donated by *Women's Wear*, the first competition attracted more than three hundred entries, of which 175 were included. Its success led to generous contributions from industry representatives for subsequent competitions juried by experts in the design field. The last exhibition, held in 1920, drew thirty-five hundred entries from one thousand artists representing thirty-four states and Canada, with prizes exceeding $2,300. Competing artists were allowed to keep their designs, and award-winners—including Zoltan Hecht, Ilonka Karasz, Hazel Burnham Slaughter, and Marguerite Zorach—often gained recognition in the industry. The Albert Blum Exhibition of Hand Decorated Fabrics was a supplemental competition for designers who preferred to work out their ideas in fabric rather than on paper.

BALTIMORE MUSEUM OF ART
"Contemporary American Crafts"

February 11–March 19, 1944
Baltimore, Maryland

This eclectic exhibition of handcrafted works was a compendium of American craft in the 1940s: utilitarian and decorative objects, in both traditional and highly experimental forms. Represented were Native American crafts of the Navajo, Zuni, Hopi, and Chitimacha tribes, as well as jewelry, rugs, blankets, basketry, pottery, and needlework loaned by the Indian Arts and Crafts Board in Washington, D.C.; folk art; and contemporary ceramics, textiles, glass, metalwork, and woodwork by artist-designers Laura Andreson, Paul Bogatay, Dan Cooper, Marli Ehrmann, Glen Lukens, Tommi Parzinger, and Ruth Penington, among others.

THE BROOKLYN MUSEUM
"Contemporary Industrial and
Handwrought Silver"
November 19, 1937–January 23, 1938
Brooklyn, New York

The focus of the exhibition was the interrelationship of machine production and handcraftsmanship, and the different technical processes involved in the manufacture of silver. Industrial silver was divided into three discrete sections: the work of firms producing traditional silver, those creating in more modern styles, and firms whose work was made predominately by hand or by machine. Works by individual silversmiths were displayed separately. The exhibition also included a gallery of modern electroplated silver, and contemporary works were shown in juxtaposition to conventional eighteenth-century designs. Rebecca Cauman, Arthur Nevill Kirk, Erik Magnussen, Tommi Parzinger, and Peer Smed were represented.

CENTURY OF PROGRESS EXPOSITION (CHICAGO WORLD'S FAIR)
"Design for Living House"
1933–34
Chicago, Illinois

The "Design for Living House" was one of several exhibits at the Exposition purporting to show how homes would be built and decorated in the near future. It was designed by architect John B. Moore, with interiors by Gilbert Rohde. Although the furniture—modular, mass-produced pieces designed by Rohde—was contemporary, the room settings were traditional.

THE CLEVELAND MUSEUM OF ART
Exhibition of Work by Artists and
Craftsmen of the Western Reserve ("The
May Show")
1919–present
Cleveland, Ohio

An enthusiastic commitment to the promotion of contemporary arts and crafts led the Cleveland Museum's first director, Frederic Allen Whiting, to establish the May Show, an annual exhibition devoted to the work of Cleveland-area artists. During the 1920s and 1930s this popular exhibition was an important showcase for students of the Cleveland School of Art and ceramists associated with the Cowan Pottery Studio.

EXPOSITION INTERNATIONALE DES ARTS DÉCORATIFS ET INDUSTRIELS MODERNES
1925
Paris

The Paris Exposition of 1925 represented a confluence of Austrian and French design, and marked the beginning of a design revolution in the United States. While French *moderne* objects dominated the central pavilion, the show also featured examples of functionalist architecture and design, most notably, Le Corbusier's Pavillon de l'Esprit Nouveau. Although American artists were not included, the show had a profound influence on American design and decoration. It was favorably reviewed by a U.S. trade commission organized by Secretary of Commerce Herbert Hoover, and widely discussed in American art and design journals. In 1926 Charles R. Richards, director of the American Association of Museums, organized an exhibition of over four hundred objects from the Paris Exposition for travel in the United States. Its purpose was "to bring about an understanding of this important modern movement in design in the hope that a parallel movement may be initiated in our own country." In the 1960s, design historians derived the term Art Deco from the Exposition's title to describe the American *moderne* style.

EXPOSITION INTERNATIONALE DES ARTS ET DES TECHNIQUES DANS LA VIE MODERNE
1937
Paris

As a forum for progressive industrial design, the 1937 Paris Exposition highlighted the best examples of *art moderne* styling from Europe and the United States. American craft was represented in an exhibition of silver organized by the American Federation of Arts for the Palais de l'Artisanat, and in a smaller show of metal objects chosen by the Society of Designer-Craftsmen for the American Pavilion. A Pavilion of Publicity, complete with neon lights spelling out the famous advertising slogans of the day, displayed promotional posters and photographs.

GOLDEN GATE INTERNATIONAL EXPOSITION
Palace of Fine and Decorative Arts
February 1939–September 1940
San Francisco, California

The Exposition was held on a 400-acre manmade island in San Francisco Bay, built by the city with a $3.8 million grant from the Works Progress Administration. The Decorative Arts section, organized by textile designer and arts administrator Dorothy Wright Liebes, included hand-crafted ceramics, metalwork, glass, textiles, and furniture. The Art in Action program featured demonstrations by artist-craftsmen in various media, including ceramists Maria Martinez and Glen Lukens.

R. H. MACY AND COMPANY
"An International Exposition of Art in Industry"
May 14–26, 1928
New York, New York

The R. H. Macy company sponsored two industrial art exhibitions in New York in the late 1920s: "Exposition of Art in Trade," in 1927, and "An International Exposition of Art in Industry." The latter show, installed by New York stage designer Lee Simonson, featured work by European and American artists and manufacturers, including Bruno Paul, Maurice Dufrêne, Josef Hoffmann, Vally Wieselthier, Edward Hald, Kem Weber, William Lescaze, Eugene Schoen, Ilonka Karasz, Peter Mueller-Munk, Walter von Nessen, Carl Walters, Henry Varnum Poor, Hunt Diederich, Frederick Carder, the International Silver Company, and the Cowan Pottery Studio. Richard Bach, associate curator for industrial art at The Metropolitan Museum of Art, wrote in 1928, "This exhibition closes a chapter in the history of contemporary art. The modern style . . . has come to stay."

THE METROPOLITAN MUSEUM OF ART
"The Architect and the Industrial Arts: An Exhibition of Contemporary American Design"
Eleventh American Industrial Art Exhibition
February 11–September 6, 1929
New York, New York

Held sporadically between 1917 and 1940, the American Industrial Art "annuals" were the first design exhibitions mounted by The Metropolitan Museum of Art. The series' basic premises were that good design would sell; that improved product design would insure the United States's ability to compete in international markets; and that better-informed manufacturers and industrial designers would come to

view their products as expressions of art in daily life. While the structure of the shows changed over the course of the series—the 1929 and 1934 exhibitions featured domestic and commercial room settings as opposed to individually displayed objects—they consistently represented "a cross section of the art industries," including furniture, textiles, ceramics, jewelry, drawings, costumes, lighting, and photography. Architect Eliel Saarinen was the principal designer of the 1929 exhibition, which was organized by curator Richard Bach. Architects rather than industrial designers participated, and all of the objects were of American conception and execution, designed specifically for the show. While one of the exhibition's goals was to present furnishings that could be mass-produced, in reality the rooms involved so much custom-finishing that few of the designs lent themselves to industrial production.

THE METROPOLITAN MUSEUM OF ART
"Twelfth Exhibition of Contemporary American Industrial Art"
October 12–November 22, 1931
New York, New York

This exhibition—a didactic installation of 524 objects from 240 lenders illustrating the current state of manufacturing—marked a return by curator Richard Bach to the more inclusive format of earlier annuals. In the catalogue's introduction Bach wrote at length about his view of contemporary design, discussing its determinants, terminology, and evolution: "The position of the Metropolitan Museum of Art with regard to contemporary industrial art is that of recorder and demonstrator, possibly also that of qualified observer. It assumes no authority, declines the power of arbitrator."

THE METROPOLITAN MUSEUM OF ART
"Contemporary American Industrial Art"
Thirteenth American Industrial Art Exhibition
November 5, 1934–January 6, 1935
New York, New York

For this exhibition Richard Bach installed a series of room settings similar to those he had designed for the industrial art annual in 1929. In contrast to that earlier exhibition, however, the objects in this show—stylishly modern yet practical furniture and housewares designed for mass production—reflected the economic realities of the Depression. Donald Deskey, William Lescaze, Raymond Loewy, and Russel Wright were among the young designers represented.

THE METROPOLITAN MUSEUM
OF ART
"Silver: An Exhibition of Contemporary
American Design by Manufacturers,
Designers and Craftsmen"
Fourteenth American Industrial Art
Exhibition
April 11–May 23, 1937
New York, New York

This was the first of several exhibitions
devoted to handmade and industrially manufactured objects in a single medium.
Organized by Richard Bach, it included
more than three hundred decorative
objects drawn from sixty-four collections.
Forty of the pieces were exhibited in the
United States Pavilion at the Paris Exposition later that year.

THE METROPOLITAN MUSEUM
OF ART
"Contemporary American Industrial Art"
Fifteenth American Industrial Art
Exhibition
April 29–September 15, 1940
New York, New York

By 1940, a pronounced reaction had set in
against the machine aesthetic—both modernism and the *moderne*—evident in the
shift toward biomorphic forms, texture, and
the use of natural materials in interior and
architectural design. For this exhibition,
twelve architects and ten designers created
thirteen domestic room settings under the
general direction of architect Ely Jacques
Kahn. While the designer-architects Eugene
Schoen and Ralph Walker had participated
in the conceptually similar 1929 exhibition,
a younger generation now dominated,
including architects Wallace Harrison, Louis
Skidmore, and Edward Durell Stone, and
industrial designers Donald Deskey, Gilbert
Rohde, and Russel Wright.

THE MUSEUM OF MODERN ART
"Machine Art"
March 5–April 29, 1934
New York, New York

Architect and Museum of Modern Art
curator Philip Johnson organized this seminal exhibition devoted to the machine
and the machine aesthetic. The show was
divided into six categories: Industrial
Units, Household and Office Equipment,
Kitchenware, Home Furnishings and
Accessories, Scientific Instruments, and
Laboratory Glass and Porcelain. Johnson's
goal in assembling this exhibition was to
emphasize both the usefulness and the
beauty of the objects displayed.

THE MUSEUM OF MODERN ART
"Modern Architecture: An International

Exhibition"
February 10–March 23, 1932
New York, New York

Organized by Henry-Russell Hitchcock and
Philip Johnson, the exhibition consisted of
models, building plans, and photographs
(including aerial views) of projects by the
most influential architects and planners
then working in America and abroad,
including Walter Gropius, Otto Haesler,
Le Corbusier, William Lescaze, J. J. P. Oud,
and Frank Lloyd Wright. Two models, one
by Wright, the other by Haesler, dominated
the exhibition. Similar in their flowing open
plans, reliance on mass-produced materials,
and lack of applied ornamentation, the
designs nonetheless polarized the critics,
and reflected the sociopolitical reality of the
early 1930s. Whereas Haesler's sprawling
low-income community development in
Kassel, Germany, was regarded as a "fine
piece of economical planning, social
thinking, and harmonious organization,"
Wright's spacious and beautifully composed
House on a Mesa was deemed wasteful and
elitist. Museum of Modern Art director
Alfred H. Barr, Jr., noted in the catalogue of
the exhibition that, "just as the modern
architect has had to adjust himself to modern problems of design and structure, so the
modern public, in order to appreciate his
achievements, must make parallel adjust-
ments to what seems new and strange."

THE MUSEUM OF MODERN ART
"New Rugs by American Artists"
June 30–August 9, 1942
New York, New York

The exhibition featured rugs designed by
contemporary artists at the invitation of
The Museum of Modern Art and executed
by the textile manufacturer V'soske. Participating artists included Stuart Davis,
Arshile Gorky, Edward McKnight Kauffer,
and Marguerite Zorach, among others.

THE MUSEUM OF MODERN ART
"Organic Design in Home Furnishings
Competition"
1940–41
New York, New York

In October 1940 the Modern's department
of industrial design inaugurated an inter-
American competition for the design of
furniture, fabrics, and lamps, with the purpose of engaging promising designers in
the creation of a better living environment.
The competition was sponsored by twelve
U.S. companies—including Heywood-
Wakefield, Mutual-Sunset Lamp Manufacturing, and the Cyrus Clark Company in
New York—which offered manufacturing
contracts as prizes to the winners. There
were nine categories: Seating for a Living

Room, Other Furniture for a Living Room,
Furniture for a Dining Room, Furniture for
a Bedroom, Furniture for a One-room
Apartment, Furniture for Outdoor Living,
Moveable Lighting Equipment, Woven
Fabrics, and Printed Fabrics, with a separate division for Latin American designers.
Among the first-place winners were Benjamin Baldwin, Charles Eames and Eero
Saarinen, Marli Ehrmann, Antonin Raymond, and Marianne Strengell. Under the
supervision of the museum, contracts with
manufacturers were arranged for all of the
first-prize winners and for some of those
who received honorable mention. As a
result of the competition, Castleton China
proposed that the museum collaborate in
the development of a line of contemporary
tableware. While the project was under
consideration, Eliot F. Noyes, then director
of the museum's industrial design department, heard Eva Zeisel speak on design for
handwork and mass production at The
Metropolitan Museum of Art, and became
convinced that she should be the designer
of the Castleton line. Zeisel's translucent
porcelain dinnerware, called Museum
White, was the first contemporary pattern
mass-produced in the United States for
an upscale market. It was added to The
Museum of Modern Art's permanent
design collection and regularly featured in
its "Good Design" exhibitions of 1950–55
as a model for collaborations between
artists and manufacturers.

NEW YORK WORLD'S FAIR
"World of Tomorrow Exhibition"
"American Art Today"
1939–40
New York, New York

The "American Art Today" exhibition was
installed in twenty-three galleries in the
redwood Contemporary Art Building
designed by Frederick L. Ackerman,
Joshua D. Lowenfish, and John V. Van Pelt.
Art historian and Museum of Modern Art
curator Mildred Constantine served on the
organization committee for the exhibition,
which included contemporary American
paintings, sculpture, and prints. In 1940 a
Works Progress Administration Federal
Art Project community arts center was
recreated at the Fair. The exhibit show-
cased more than eight hundred works of
art by WPA artists and also featured handcraft demonstrations.

THE NEWARK MUSEUM
"Modern American Design in Metal"
March 19–April 18, 1929
Newark, New Jersey

The Newark Museum was one of the first
public institutions to stage exhibitions of
industrial art. This show of decorative met-

alwork featured a silver bowl designed and executed by Peter Mueller-Munk, a fire screen by Hunt Diederich, smoking stands by Gilbert Rohde, and lamps by Deskey-Vollmer, Inc. Deviating from its usual policy of acting as an intermediary between artists and manufacturers rather than as a collector of modern design, the museum acquired the Mueller-Munk bowl for its permanent collection.

PENNSYLVANIA MUSEUM OF ART; LATER, PHILADELPHIA MUSEUM OF ART
"Design for the Machine"
February 20–March 20, 1932
Philadelphia, Pennsylvania

"Design for the Machine" was one of the earliest exhibitions to give consideration to the machine "as a means of making beautiful things by methods natural to itself," advancing the pure, rational forms of the machine as a new design aesthetic. Curator Charles R. Richards wrote in the catalogue introduction: "the aesthetic problem facing the designer for the machine is twofold: first, to determine the limits beyond which the machine or process should not be required to function; second, to determine the artistic principles that should govern the design of repetitive production. Both of these considerations make for simplicity of form and the elimination of all but extremely reserved functional ornament." The exhibition was divided into twelve sections: Ceramics, Glassware, Enamels; Construction Materials; Furniture; Interiors; Leatherwork; Metalwork and Lighting Fixtures; Retail Stores; Rugs, Carpets, Linoleum; Silverware; Textiles; Wallpaper; and Miscellaneous—which included optics, precision instruments, and machine parts. Among the more than two hundred individual designers, craftspeople, and manufacturers represented were Fostoria Glass, Heywood-Wakefield, H. R. Mallinson, Bruno Paul, Paul Poiret, Ruth Reeves, Rodier, Rena Rosenthal, George Sakier, Vally Wieselthier, and AUDAC members Alexey Brodovitch (who designed the exhibition poster and catalogue), Donald Deskey, Ely Jacques Kahn, Ilonka Karasz, Paul Lobel, Walter von Nessen, Gilbert Rohde, Eugene Schoen, Kem Weber, and Russel Wright.

SYRACUSE MUSEUM OF FINE ARTS; LATER, EVERSON MUSEUM OF ART
National Robineau Memorial Ceramic Exhibitions; LATER, Ceramic National Exhibitions; LATER, Ceramic Nationals
1932–1970s
Syracuse, New York

The Ceramic Nationals were the most important annual exhibitions in the United States devoted exclusively to ceramics. They were inaugurated in 1932 by Syracuse Museum of Fine Arts director Anna Witherell Olmsted as a memorial to ceramist Adelaide Robineau. The first exhibition was restricted to artists from New York State, and no funds were available for a catalogue or proper installation. The following year, the show was declared "open to potters of the United States," drawing work by seventy-two ceramists from eleven states; a total of 199 pieces was listed in a simple catalogue. Under Olmsted's direction, and through the corporate fundraising efforts of R. Guy Cowan, the annuals continued to expand throughout the 1930s. In 1937, with financial support provided by the Rockefeller Foundation, 133 pieces were selected from the five previous annuals for the first exhibition of American ceramics to be sent abroad. After traveling to Helsinki, Göteborg, Copenhagen, and the Hanley Museum in Stoke-on-Trent, England, the show was installed at the Whitney Museum of American Art in New York, where it was enthusiastically received by the public and the press.

VIRGINIA MUSEUM OF FINE ARTS
"An Exhibition of Silver: French, British, American Modern"
November 19–December 30, 1940
Richmond, Virginia

While much of the exhibition was devoted to collections of seventeenth- and eighteenth-century French, English, and Colonial American silver installed in individual galleries, curator Edward Morris Davis III included a selection of modern American silver to illustrate a continuity of good design. Davis noted that, just as the historical pieces were "indicative of the spirit of their time," the modern masterpieces were "indicative of the spirit of today."

WORCESTER ART MUSEUM
"An Exhibition of Contemporary New England Handicrafts"
October 10–December 12, 1943
Worcester, Massachusetts

Defining "handicrafts" as "those things which people make with their hands, either for their own use or for others"—including products made with tools and machinery, as long as the handmade aesthetic was maintained—the exhibition included rugs, quilts, woven commercial fabrics, pottery, wood objects, baskets, model ships, and pewter produced between 1938 and 1943.

PERIODICALS AND BOOKS

AMERICAN ART ANNUAL; LATER, AMERICAN ART DIRECTORY AND WHO'S WHO IN AMERICAN ART
1898–present
Publisher: The American Federation of Arts, Washington, D.C.

The American Art Annual published the annual reports of museums and national arts societies, biographical information on commercial and fine artists and art dealers, and a variety of art listings, including works of art sold at auction, art schools, magazines of art sold in the United States, and periodicals having art notes. This material was eventually divided into two publications, American Art Directory and Who's Who in American Art, which are now published by R. R. Bowker.

AMERICAN NEEDLEWORK: THE HISTORY OF DECORATIVE STITCHERY AND EMBROIDERY FROM THE LATE 16TH TO THE 20TH CENTURY
GEORGINA BROWN HARBESON
New York: Coward-McCann, 1938

This exhaustive survey presents a historical outline of decorative embroidery techniques, from quill-, lace-, and beadwork to appliqué, needlepoint, crewelwork, quilting, and cross-stitch. Harbeson selected examples from discrete periods that not only illustrate technique but also document American domestic life. While many of these traditional patterns derived from European and Asian sources, Harbeson observed that a uniquely American adaptation is consistently evident in the more simplified designs. The book includes chapters on contemporary needlework illustrated with the work of Marguerite Zorach and others.

THE AMERICAN SILK JOURNAL; LATER, THE AMERICAN SILK AND RAYON JOURNAL
January 1882–March 1938
Publisher: Clifford & Lawton, Inc., New York, New York

Issued in affiliation with the Silk Association of America, The American Silk Journal was the voice of the silk and rayon industries. It was absorbed by Rayon Textile Monthly in 1938.

ARCHITECTURAL RECORD
July 1891–present
Publisher: F. W. Dodge Corporation, New York, New York

The journal of record for architecture in

the United States, *Architectural Record* has also served as a sourcebook for examples of European and non-Western architecture. It absorbed the journal *American Architect* in 1938 and *Western Architect and Engineer* in 1962. It continues to be published in New York by McGraw-Hill.

ART AND INDUSTRY
January 1936–December 1958
Publisher: Studio Ltd., London and New York

Superseding *Commercial Art* (vols. 4–11) and *Commercial Art and Industry* (vols. 12–20), *Art and Industry* was neither a technical journal nor a supply catalogue, but rather a magazine that reported on the various facets of commercial and industrial design. It was absorbed by *Design for Industry* in 1959.

ART AND THE MACHINE:
AN ACCOUNT OF INDUSTRIAL DESIGN IN 20TH-CENTURY AMERICA
SHELDON CHENEY AND MARTHA CHANDLER CHENEY
New York: Whittlesey House, 1936

When *Art and the Machine* was written, no clear definition of "industrial design" existed. The Cheneys saw industrial design as a new form of art separate from that of the pre-industrial age, produced by separate forces in accordance with a new aesthetic. One of their intentions was to differentiate between the machine aesthetic and that of handcrafted decorative arts, highlighting the influences of the machine and abstract art on contemporary design. Their study was limited to the American scene as they believed the reliance on the machine and mechanized industry had no parallel in any other country. The book presents examples of products by U.S. manufacturers that reflect an acute awareness of industrial-design values.

ART IN INDUSTRY
CHARLES R. RICHARDS
New York: Macmillan, 1922

For this exhaustive survey of the industrial arts in the United States, Richards and his assistants investigated industries in fifty-five cities throughout the country, and compared the applied arts programs of institutions and organizations in the United States and Europe, including the Rhode Island School of Design, Pratt Institute, the California School of Arts and Crafts, the British Institute of Industrial Art, and the Wiener Werkstätte.

ARTS & DECORATION
November 1911–March 1942

Publishers: Adam Bunge (1910–18), New York, New York; Hewitt Publishing Co. (1919–42), New York, New York

A monthly journal devoted to art, architecture, and interior design and decoration, *Arts & Decoration* merged with *Art World* in 1918 and until 1919 was published as *Art World and Arts & Decoration*. The magazine incorporated *Spur* in 1940.

THE BOOK OF FURNITURE AND DECORATION: PERIOD AND MODERN
JOSEPH ARONSON
New York: Crown Publishers, 1936

The book documents the evolution of furniture and interior decoration from the Gothic to the modern period, and highlights the symbiotic relationship between the architect and interior designer. It is divided into three sections: the stylistic development of decoration; types of decorative elements used, including woods, fabrics, wall and floor coverings, lighting, and windows; and the principles of decorating specific types of room. Aronson viewed the modern interior designer's subordination of individual pieces of furniture to the form of the room as a whole as being consistent with the suppression of ornament in contemporary architecture. Furniture designs by Donald Deskey, Eugene Schoen, and Russel Wright are illustrated.

CALIFORNIA ARTS AND ARCHITECTURE; LATER, ARTS & ARCHITECTURE
February 1929–January 1944; February 1944–present
Publishers: J. D. Entenza (1924–44), Los Angeles, California; Arts and Architecture (1944–present), Los Angeles, California

A monthly periodical concerned primarily with the documentation of West Coast architecture, it was formed by the merger of *Pacific Coast Architect* and *California Southland* in 1929. The title was changed to *Arts & Architecture* in 1944.

CRAFT HORIZONS; LATER, CRAFT HORIZONS WITH CRAFT WORLD; LATER, AMERICAN CRAFT
November 1941–present
Publisher: American Craft Council, New York, New York

The voice for craft and the decorative arts in the United States, *Craft Horizons* was published "as an educational service" of the American Handcraft Council and the Handcraft Cooperative League of America. Aileen Osborn Webb, founder of the Handcraft Cooperative League, was the magazine's first editor.

CREATIVE ART
October 1927–May 1933
Publisher: Albert and Charles Boni, New York, New York

Creative Art was first issued as an edition of *The Studio*. A monthly publication, it was absorbed by the *American Magazine of Art* in 1934.

DECORATION: PAST, PRESENT AND FUTURE
SARAH M. LOCKWOOD
New York: Doubleday, Doran & Co., 1934

Lockwood approached home decoration from a historical perspective, believing that an enhanced understanding of period styles would result in more cohesively designed modern interiors. The book includes a series of chapters devoted to the decorative motifs and symbols of various cultures and historical periods, including the influences of ancient Egypt, Greece, and Rome; a discussion of Renaissance fashions; and a survey of American styles from the Colonial period to the modern era. Lockwood defined the modern home as not relying on any single definable tradition.

DECORATIVE ARTS: OFFICIAL CATALOG, DEPARTMENT OF FINE ARTS, DIVISION OF DECORATIVE ARTS
GOLDEN GATE INTERNATIONAL EXPOSITION, DEPARTMENT OF FINE ARTS
San Francisco: San Francisco Bay Exposition Co., 1939

Organized by arts administrator Dorothy Wright Liebes, the Decorative Arts section of the Golden Gate International Exposition was a four-part presentation of contemporary European and American craft. The exhibition opened with a historical survey of the decorative arts in thirty miniature rooms designed by Thorne, followed by fifteen full-size rooms created by noted architects, decorators, and designers. A third section, called Art in Action, was composed of workshops in which craftspeople demonstrated the techniques of various media. A series of small international galleries featuring glass, silver, ceramics, textiles, rugs, lace, metal, enamel, jewelry, and bookbinding surrounded the ateliers. Liebes appointed guest curators with expertise in various media to write short essays for the catalogue and to select the objects for display. Most of the pieces were created especially for the exhibition, and all of the work was for sale.

FORM AND RE-FORM: A PRACTICAL HANDBOOK OF MODERN INTERIORS
PAUL T. FRANKL
New York: Harper, 1930

In *Form and Re-form* Frankl examined the development of a distinctive American style in the 1920s and defined "the inner necessity upon which this art-revolution [was] based." Frankl believed that contemporary expression in the decorative arts was the logical and necessary outcome of a new, progressive spirit, manifest in every phase of American life, expressed in "skyscrapers, motor-cars, airplanes, in new ocean liners, in department stores, and great industrial plants." His point regarding the dynamics of artistic creation in a "machine age" is underscored with illustrations of buildings and decorative objects by leading architects, designers, and craftspeople.

GOOD FURNITURE MAGAZINE; LATER,
GOOD FURNITURE AND DECORATION
August 1925–September 1931
Publishers: Dean-Hicks Co. (1925–29), Grand Rapids, Michigan; National Building Publications (1929–31), New York, New York

A monthly periodical devoted to the presentation of good furniture and fashionable interior decoration, it merged with *Interior Architecture & Decoration* in 1931.

GOOD-BYE MR. CHIPPENDALE
TERRENCE HAROLD ROBSJOHN-GIBBINGS
New York: Alfred A. Knopf, 1944

Written in an amusing and whimsical style, the book takes aim at the use of European antiques and reproductions for American home decoration. Robsjohn-Gibbings observed that the proliferation of housing projects in the mid-1940s brought a crisis to the home furnishings industry, which lagged behind in the production of furniture suitable for these stripped-down, modern homes. Systematically debunking the period furniture factories of Grand Rapids, Michigan, and conservative tastemakers such as Elsie de Wolfe, he admonished his readers to furnish their homes with simple, comfortable furniture in keeping with the more informal American lifestyle.

*THE INTERNATIONAL STYLE:
ARCHITECTURE SINCE 1922*
HENRY-RUSSELL HITCHCOCK, JR., AND
PHILIP JOHNSON
1932. Reprinted as *The International Style.*
New York: W. W. Norton, 1966

Written while the authors were organizing "Modern Architecture: International Exhibition" for The Museum of Modern Art in 1931, the book documents the inception and distinguishing aesthetic principles of the International Style: an emphasis on volume and proportion, as opposed to mass

and symmetry; and a reliance on technical perfection, fine proportions, and the intrinsic values of materials rather than applied ornament. The work of European architects Walter Gropius, Le Corbusier, Ludwig Mies van der Rohe, and J. P. P. Oud is contrasted with that of the Americans Raymond Hood, George Howe, William Lescaze, Richard Neutra, and Frank Lloyd Wright.

*THE LOGIC OF MODERN
ARCHITECTURE: EXTERIORS AND
INTERIORS OF MODERN AMERICAN
BUILDINGS*
RANDOLPH WILLIAM SEXTON
New York: Architectural Book Publishing Company, 1929

Sexton believed it was the responsibility of contemporary architects to design buildings that logically met the complex demands of modern American life. While acknowledging the prevalence of regional influences in contemporary private residences, he identified the skyscraper as a distinctively American architectural form that was particularly responsive to the needs of a modern society. The book includes sections on modern architectural details such as ceramic tiles, grillwork, and lighting fixtures, and a chapter on furnishings for modern interiors.

*MODERN ARCHITECTURE:
ROMANTICISM AND REINTEGRATION*
HENRY-RUSSELL HITCHCOCK, JR.
New York: Payson & Clarke Ltd., 1929

The book traces the historical antecedents of modern architecture, beginning with a survey of the Age of Romanticism, continuing the chronology through the stylistic transitions of the late 1800s, and culminating with the work of the "new pioneers" of the early twentieth century. Hitchcock's approach was a radical departure from contemporary architectural discourse: Rather than insisting that modern architecture was something entirely new, he established the historical continuum out of which it developed.

*NEW DIMENSIONS: THE DECORATIVE
ARTS OF TODAY IN WORDS AND
PICTURES*
PAUL T. FRANKL
New York: Payson & Clarke Ltd., 1928

Frankl's definition of "What Is Modern" was based on a contemporary ideal of beauty in which simplicity predominated. Something of a manifesto on modern decoration, the book describes art as a mirror reflection of life, that in a complex age marked by "invention, machinery, industry,

science, and commerce," simplicity was sought in aesthetic expression: "Simple lines are modern. They are restful to the eye and dignified and tend to cover up the complexity of the machine age." Frankl identified continuity of line and sharp contrasts in light and shadow as characteristic of modern furnishings.

A POTTER'S BOOK
BERNARD HOWELL LEACH
London: Faber and Faber, 1940

In *A Potter's Book* Leach adapted his practical knowledge of traditional Japanese potterymaking to the needs of Western potters working singly or in small workshops. The book outlines the differences between *raku,* English slipware, stoneware, and porcelain; the qualities of different types of clays and pigments; and formulas for clay bodies, decoration, and glazes. Leach wrote the book "for students and teachers, for lovers of good pots and sound craftsmanship, and for those to whom the cultural meeting of East and West is the prelude to a human society." In it he formulated "a criterion by which good pots may be recognized in a manner similar to that by which a . . . classic standard encourages the appreciation of fine architecture, painting, writing, and music."

*STICKS AND STONES: A STUDY OF
AMERICAN ARCHITECTURE AND
CIVILIZATION*
LEWIS MUMFORD
New York: Boni and Liveright, 1924

In *Sticks and Stones* Mumford analyzed American architecture in terms of the development of Western civilization. Beginning with the Medieval period and ending with the Machine Age, the book appraises the historical, aesthetic, and sociological forces that impact on architecture and alter its forms from one age to another.

TECHNICS AND CIVILIZATION
LEWIS MUMFORD
New York: Harcourt, Brace, 1934

In an ambitious historical study that traces the sociocultural impact of the machine on Western civilization, Mumford occupied a middle ground between the "antimodern" sentiments of social reformers such as William Morris, Stuart Chase, and Allan Tate and the aggressive advocacy of efficient industrial production regardless of the cost to the individual. Mumford noted that humanity embraced the machine without fully comprehending it, and that to understand the machine—to assimilate the "objectivity, impersonality, neutrality, the lessons of the mechanical realm" was a first step toward the development of a more socially responsible civilization.

VERS UNE ARCHITECTURE
LE CORBUSIER (CHARLES-ÉDOUARD JEANNERET)
Paris: Éditions Crès, 1923. Published in English as *Towards a New Architecture*. Translated by Frederick Etchells. 1927. Reprint. New York: Praeger, 1970

Vers une Architecture had a profound influence on contemporary architectural discourse and brought Le Corbusier into the vanguard of international architecture. Translated into English in 1927, it was the first popular exposition in English of the "modern movement" in architecture. Le Corbusier saw contemporary architecture as a force in revolutionizing twentieth-century life. Positing the ocean liner, airplane, and automobile as icons of the modern era, he related their elements and structure to that of contemporary architecture. While noting that in this new age of streamlining architects could turn to classical architecture for inspiration, the demands of modern life required innovative solutions for housing, such as simple, mass-produced dwellings constructed in steel and concrete.

WOMEN'S WEAR DAILY
1927–present
Publisher: Fairchild News Service, New York, New York

A daily trade paper with a national circulation, *Women's Wear Daily* has covered the fashion industry for almost three-quarters of a century. It absorbed *Retail Executive* in 1941, and since 1976 has been published as *W.W.D.*

PRODUCTION CENTERS AND SHOPS

CERAMICS

CASTLETON CHINA, INC.
c. 1939–76
New Castle, Pennsylvania

Castleton China was a joint venture of the Shenango Pottery Company and Rosenthal China, formerly the U.S. distributor for the German manufactory Rosenthal Porzellan AG. The firm initially marketed Rosenthal dinnerware patterns decorated with transfer-prints of paintings by Marcel Vertès, Salvador Dali, and American regionalists Thomas Hart Benton and Paul Sample. In the early 1940s, Castleton, in collaboration with The Museum of Modern Art in New York, commissioned Eva Zeisel to design a modern dinnerware service. Known as Museum White, the translucent porcelain was introduced in 1946, and included in the Modern's "Useful Objects" exhibition of that year.

CLEVELAND POTTERY AND TILE COMPANY; LATER, COWAN POTTERY STUDIO, INC.
1913–31
Cleveland, Ohio; and Rocky River, Ohio
Founder: R. Guy Cowan

Ceramist R. Guy Cowan incorporated the Cleveland Pottery and Tile Company as a commercial enterprise, but it later became known as an art pottery specializing in high-fired porcelain and figurines. One of Cowan's earliest clients was the newly founded Cleveland Museum of Art, for whom he supplied unglazed red paving tiles for the inner garden court of the museum's new building. Cowan began pursuing his aesthetic interests as early as 1914, creating an inlaid terracotta sundial as well as two large vases with Persian designs. In 1917 twenty-two glazed vessels produced by the pottery were exhibited at The Art Institute of Chicago. In 1925, when Guy Cowan's *Female Figure and Bowl* won first prize for pottery at the Cleveland Museum of Art's annual May Show, the firm's aesthetic reputation was established nationally. Cowan moved the pottery to the Cleveland suburb of Rocky River, Ohio, in 1923, and four years later changed the firm's name to Cowan Pottery Studio, Inc. When Cowan began teaching in the ceramics department of the Cleveland School of Art, the studio provided employment for several students, including Paul Bogatay, Elizabeth Anderson (Mrs. Eliot Ness), Thelma Frazier (Winter), and Viktor Schreckengost. The studio also attracted other accomplished ceramists.

Arthur Eugene Baggs helped the pottery develop a new series of glazes with heavy *craqueleurs* or crystalline effects. Waylande DeSantis Gregory and Paul Manship produced award-winning vessels and sculpture designs, and Richard O. Hummel served as an advisor on matters of ceramic technology. Unable to survive the Depression, the pottery closed in December 1931.

ROOKWOOD POTTERY
1880–1967
Cincinnati, Ohio
Founder: Maria Longworth Nichols Storer

Rookwood was one of America's most successful art potteries, producing Cincinnati faience and employing many recognized potters and designers. Although the pottery is now known for its ceramics of the Arts and Crafts period, during the 1920s and 1930s its decorators—including Lorinda Epply, William Hentschel, Wilhelmine Rehm, and Jens Jacob Herring Krog Jensen—produced numerous innovative designs based on Asian, African, and ancient craft prototypes, as well as such modern painting styles as Cubism. Storer was the daughter of philanthropist Joseph Longworth, founder of the Art Academy of Cincinnati.

ROSEVILLE POTTERY COMPANY
1892–1954
Roseville, Ohio; Zanesville, Ohio
Founder: George F. Young

Roseville and its Zanesville competitor, the Weller Pottery Company, were among the few art potteries to survive the Depression. It produced Art Deco ceramics throughout the 1920s, including the well-known Futura line, and in the 1930s operated a tea room and showroom. Roseville developed a modern, oven-proof dinnerware pattern called Raymor in 1952, but it was unsuccessful—a failure the company blamed on the growing popularity of less expensive and more durable plastic products.

SIMS AND LAUGHLIN; LATER, HOMER LAUGHLIN AND COMPANY; LATER, LAUGHLIN CHINA COMPANY
1869–present
East Liverpool, Ohio; Newell, West Virginia

Incorporated under its present name in 1897, the Laughlin company operated four plants in East Liverpool, Ohio, and Newell, West Virginia, by 1905. The company is best known for its Fiesta, Harlequin, and Rhythm dinnerware patterns, which were produced under the design direction of Frederick Hurten Rhead (1927–42) and Don Schreckengost (1945–60).

STEUBENVILLE POTTERY COMPANY
1879–1959
Steubenville, Ohio

The Steubenville Pottery Company was formed in 1879 in association with English potter A. B. Beck, who produced ironstone and whitewares. In 1910 the firm was purchased by the Wintwringer family, which retained control until its closing. Steubenville's most famous pattern, Russel Wright's American Modern (1939), successfully retrieved the company from bankruptcy. The pottery closed in 1959, selling its building and pattern molds to Barium Chemicals, Inc., of Canonsburg, Pennsylvania. Barium marketed several of the original patterns under the Steubenville name.

GLASS

CAMBRIDGE GLASS COMPANY
1901–54
Cambridge, Ohio

Part of the National Glass Company consortium from 1901 to 1907, Cambridge produced high-end glassware in the 1920s and 1930s. W. L. Orme designed the Pristine Table Architecture series for Cambridge in 1938.

CONSOLIDATED LAMP & GLASS COMPANY; LATER, PHOENIX AND CONSOLIDATED
Active 1890s–1940s
Coraopolis, Pennsylvania

Originally a manufacturer of glass lighting fixtures, Consolidated Lamp & Glass entered the art glass market at the turn of the century with tableware designed by Nicholas Kopp. Under design consultant Reuben Haley in the 1920s, the company produced *art moderne* glassware in the style of French designer René Lalique, including the vases *Love Birds* and *Bird of Paradise*. In 1928 Haley diverged from conventional glass design in developing a line related to Cubist sculpture called Ruba Rombic. Consolidated's new glass lines were marketed in the 1920s by advertising executive Howard G. Selden.

FOSTORIA GLASS SPECIALTY COMPANY
1887–present
Fostoria, Ohio; Moundsville, West Virginia

Fostoria was one of the largest makers of handmade glass in the United States in the early twentieth century. Its American line, introduced in 1915 and produced until the 1970s, was evenly faceted in a cubistic design intended to be ultramodern. In the 1930s Fostoria was one of several U.S. glass manufacturers that followed the lead of Scandinavian and Austrian companies such as Orrefors and J. and L. Lobmeyr, and the French glass designers René Lalique and Jean Luce, producing colorless, engraved tablewares for the modern dining room.

"THE HOUSE OF GLASS"
Corning-Steuben Building
New York, New York

The first Steuben shop opened at 748 Fifth Avenue in February 1934. Designed by John Monteith Gates in consultation with MacMillen, Inc., the architectural firm of Charles A. Platt, it was evocative of a fine arts gallery, with quiet tones of white and gray chosen to complement the "brilliant color and lustre of the glass" displayed. An illuminated crystal fountain sculpture by Sidney Waugh dominated the décor, and there was a permanent display of architectural glass panels, in production at Steuben since the late 1920s. In 1937 the shop occupied the ground floor and mezzanine of the new six-story Corning Glass Works building at 718 Fifth Avenue and Fifty-seventh Street. Designed by Geoffrey and William Platt in association with Gates, "The House of Glass," as it came to be known, featured walls of Corning Pyrex glass blocks—their first use as a building material in New York. The shop's interior walls were papered with a thin layer of kapa shells, and a circular staircase, with posts of air-twist cane glass, rose to the mezzanine.

INDIANA GLASS COMPANY
Active 1910s–1970s
Dunkirk, Indiana

The Indiana company was one of the major producers of Depression glass—inexpensive lines of glassware commonly produced in clear pinks, greens, blues, and browns, as well as colorless glass. Patterns were typically made in complete dinner services with matching serving pieces; sold at five-and-dimes and department stores, they were affordable to buyers with limited incomes. Today, Depression glass provides a guide to popular taste in the 1920s and 1930s. Designer Reuben Haley was a consultant to the firm during this period.

NEW ENGLAND GLASS COMPANY; LATER, LIBBEY GLASS COMPANY; LATER OWENS-ILLINOIS GLASS COMPANY; LATER, A DIVISION OF OWENS-CORNING
1888–present
Toledo, Ohio
Founder: William L. Libbey

The New England Glass Company was the leading U.S. manufacturer of commercial glass products, including bottles and lightbulbs, in the early part of the century, and produced elaborate cut crystal until it lost its popular appeal in the mid–1920s. In the early 1930s, in an effort to recapture its position as the leading U.S. manufacturer of fine glassware, the Libbey Glass Company commissioned A. Douglas Nash to design a new series of leaded glassware. Introduced in 1933, the Libbey-Nash line proved too expensive to succeed in a mass market, despite aggressive promotion. The firm became a division of the Owens-Illinois Glass Company, which in 1936 hired Edwin W. Fuerst to design its Modern American line. Produced for private customers beginning in 1939 and released publicly in 1940, the simple, heavy blown crystal was noted for its remarkable brilliance, a result of improvements in the mechanical mixing process. The line was discontinued in the early 1940s in favor of war production.

STEUBEN GLASS WORKS; LATER, STEUBEN DIVISION OF CORNING GLASS WORKS
1903–present
Corning, New York
Founders: Frederick Carder, Thomas G. Hawkes, Samuel Hawkes, Townsend Hawkes

In 1903 Carder, an English glassmaker, moved to Corning, New York, to work with Thomas G. Hawkes, president of T. G. Hawkes and Company, a factory noted for its cut and engraved glass. Hawkes provided the financial backing for Carder to establish his own glass factory to produce blanks which glass artisans then decorated. This was the beginning of Steuben. In 1904 Carder developed a gold metallic luster glass using a spray of chemical salts that dissolve in heat, leaving a soft, lustrous surface. The glass, which he patented as Aurene, was an immediate success, as was its counterpart, Blue Aurene. In 1918 Corning Glass Works purchased Steuben and adapted its facilities to emergency war use. After the war, the Steuben Division of Corning reverted to the manufacture of art glass. Carder was retired in 1932 when the Steuben Division was reorganized under the direction of business-man Arthur Amory Houghton, Jr., with the assistance of architect John Monteith Gates. Using aggressive new marketing techniques, the introduction of art glass designed by Samuel Ayers, Edwin W. Fuerst, and George Thompson, and regular displays in the major expositions of the period, Steuben became the most important glass manufacturer in the United States in the 1930s.

METALS

WENDELL AUGUST FORGE, INC.
1932–present
Grove City, Pennsylvania
Founder: Wendell August

August (c. 1885–1963) began experimenting with forged aluminum in the late 1920s, and specialized in the process when he opened the Wendell August Forge in 1932. After completing the entrance gates to the New Kensington, Pennsylvania, headquarters of the Aluminum Company of America (Alcoa) in 1929, August was commissioned by the architect Henry Hornbostel to make hammered aluminum gifts for the company's executives. These favors soon came to the attention of Pittsburgh department store owner Edgar J. Kaufmann, Sr., who commissioned a line of decorative hammered-aluminum wares from the Wendell August Forge. Though he understood the mechanics of fabricating handwrought aluminum, August did not design or cut his own dies, instead directing the work of artisans in his employ.

EDWARD F. CALDWELL & CO.
c. 1900–35
New York, New York

The Caldwell company manufactured fine-quality metal reproductions that ranged from handcrafted period-revival desk sets to metalwork for the interiors of the Waldorf-Astoria Hotel in New York.

AUGUST DINGELDEIN AND SON
Active 1920s–1930s
New York, New York

Dingeldein and Son had a retail outlet in New York and factories throughout Germany, including Hanau. Silversmith Erik Magnussen worked for the company from 1929 to 1932.

DODGE SILVER SHOP
1924–41
Asheville, North Carolina
Founder: William Waldo Dodge, Jr.

The only major source of handwrought silver wares in the Southeast during this period, the Dodge shop produced largely traditional holloware, flatware, jewelry, and novelties such as trophies. The firm also accepted commissions for copperwork, stained glass, and woodwork.

FERROBRANDT, INC.
c. 1924–28
New York, New York

Ferrobrandt was an American retail outlet for *moderne* design, headed by French designer Jules Bouy. The firm not only produced Bouy's own designs but also sold the work of French metalsmith Edgar Brandt.

GORHAM MANUFACTURING COMPANY
1831–present
Providence, Rhode Island
Founder: Jabez Gorham

An important presence in American silver since the nineteenth century, Gorham manufactures complete lines of silver tableware, silver bowls and serving platters, and crystal. During the 1930s the firm was identified with the ideal of the independent craftsperson through advertisements featuring an elderly silversmith. Gorham is now a part of Dansk International Designs Ltd.

INTERNATIONAL SILVER COMPANY
1898–n.d.
Meriden, Connecticut

The International Silver Company was formed by the merger of seventeen silver-plate manufacturers, including Holmes and Edwards; Simpson, Hall, Miller & Company; Meriden Britannia; Meriden Silver Plate; and Wilcox Silver Plate. In the late 1920s the firm introduced several modern silver patterns, including a sterling-silver knife designed by architect Eliel Saarinen—represented in The Metropolitan Museum of Art's Eleventh American Industrial Art Exhibition in 1929—and Silhouette, a streamlined flatware pattern advertised as the latest in Parisian fashion. Intent on attracting both conservative and progressive customers, the firm also introduced New Sophistication, a neoclassical pattern that was produced in a smaller scale better suited to contemporary apartment life. In 1930 the firm's sterling division hired New York interior decorator Elsie de Wolfe, an arbiter of good taste, who lent her name to *Correct Table Silver*, a guide designed to encourage the careful acquisition of silver during the Depression. During the early 1940s the company devoted its significant manufacturing capability to war production, fulfilling more than eighteen hundred contracts for surgical instruments and military hardware.

THE KALO SHOP
1900–70
Chicago, Illinois
Founder: Clara Barck Welles (Mrs. George Welles)

The Kalo Shop was Chicago's largest producer of handwrought silverware, serving

generations of customers. Begun as a women's cooperative that produced handwoven textiles and leather goods, the workshop was producing ultrasimplified neoclassical silver holloware by the early 1930s.

NESSEN STUDIO, INC.
c. 1925–n.d.
New York, New York
Founder: Walter von Nessen

The Nessen studio supplied architects and interior designers with innovative lighting fixtures and metal furnishings. Eliel Saarinen used Nessen's lamps in the interiors of the Cranbrook Academy of Art.

ROSE IRON WORKS; LATER, ROSE METAL INDUSTRIES
1904–present
Cleveland, Ohio
Founder: Martin Rose

From 1928 to 1933 Rose (1870–1955) collaborated with fellow Hungarian-born metalsmith Paul Fehér, creating handwrought interior architectural metalwork in the French *moderne* style. Using a variety of materials and finishes, Rose and Fehér created metal objects marked by unusual contrasts of color and surface texture. Many of their unique samples are in the collection of the Rose family, which continues to operate a business in Cleveland under the name Rose Metal Industries.

TEXTILES

CHENEY BROTHERS
1838–1955
Manchester, Connecticut; Hartford, Connecticut
Founders: Ralph Cheney, Ward Cheney, Rush Cheney, Frank Cheney

Cheney Brothers was the leading U.S. manufacturer of decorative silks. In the 1920s the company introduced the idea of using fabrics in seasonal coordinated colors to modernize the look of traditional furniture. Cheney also imported French Art Deco fabrics, which were supplied directly to its customers from its Paris studio. After members of the firm saw the work of French metalsmith Edgar Brandt at the 1925 Paris Exposition, Cheney commissioned the designer to produce a wrought-iron entranceway and window decorations for its New York offices. In 1929 the company produced a series of fabrics for automobile interiors based on Brandt's work.

EDGEWATER TAPESTRY LOOMS, INC.
c. 1913–33; c. 1934–n.d.

Edgewater, New Jersey; California
Founder: Lorentz Kleiser

Kleiser's studio produced tapestries inspired by American history and literature, such as the series fashioned after the stories of Washington Irving, and also explored themes of modern-day life through such wall hangings as *Child Playing in Central Park*. Collaborative efforts between the studio and artists were also pursued. The studio produced several tapestries based on watercolors by Frederick Avinoff, director of the Natural History Museum of the Carnegie Institute. In the original tapestry Kleiser acknowledged the work on which it was based by combining his and Avinoff's initials. The New Jersey workshop closed in 1933 and reopened shortly thereafter in California. Edgewater tapestries were exhibited throughout the country in 1935.

HERTER LOOMS
c. 1919–n.d.
New York, New York
Founder: Albert Herter

Herter, an artist, established a tapestry atelier in New York in about 1919. Importing both his weavers and his looms from France, he sought to emulate the spirit and craftsmanship of Flemish tapestries produced during the reign of Charles V (1511–1556). An early commission from Detroit newspaper publisher George Booth, *The Great Crusade* (1920), is a symbolic representation of America rallying to save the cultural heritage of Europe after World War I. With its images of Joan of Arc, Charlemagne, and Philip the Good, the hanging resembles its medieval predecessors on first glance. But there are anachronistic images as well: at center, a youthful General Pershing seated on a horse; behind him, a phalanx of American soldiers; and in the far background, biplanes above a sea dotted with battleships.

LAVERNE ORIGINALS; LATER,
LAVERNE INTERNATIONAL
1934–65
New York, New York
Founders: Erwine Laverne, Estelle Lester Laverne

The Lavernes met and married in 1934, when both were students at the Art Students League. They established Laverne Originals as a showroom for wallpapers and giftware but soon began designing wallpapers, textiles, and furniture, specializing in these areas from 1935 to 1947. They produced textiles in three distinctly different styles: organic abstract designs and marble and wood-grain patterning; representational, often humorous motifs; and linear geometric patterning. All of the designs were hand-silkscreened on natural and synthetic materials. During the 1940s they also commissioned Alexander Calder, Ray Komai, Gyorgy Kepes, Alvin Lustig, and Oscar Niemeyer to design fabrics and wallpapers. While much of the Lavernes' furniture was strictly functional, they also produced some whimsical pieces in Lucite. In 1947 Laverne Originals received an award from the American Institute of Decorators for best printed fabric, and in 1948, the American Fabrics Award from The Metropolitan Museum of Art and a Good Design award from The Museum of Modern Art. Renamed Laverne International in 1948, the company thrived throughout the 1950s and early 1960s. A number of firms continue to carry their textile, wallpaper, and furniture designs.

H. R. MALLINSON AND COMPANY
Active 1910–1930s
Grand Canyon, Arizona

During the 1910s and 1920s Mallinson's developed abstract textile patterns based on African and Peruvian textiles and pottery, Native American sand paintings, and Southwestern basketry and pottery. Shortly after World War I the firm began exporting fabrics to London and Paris, where their designs contributed to the growing interest in abstract, geometric patterning. Mallinson design consultants Martha Ryther and Léon Bakst created the Hopi Indian Motives and Grand Canyon patterns in 1927.

SHUTTLE-CRAFT GUILD
1922–56
Seattle, Washington; Cambridge, Massachusetts; and Basin, Montana
Founder: Mary Meigs Atwater

The Shuttle-Craft Guild was a commercial concern through which Atwater marketed a popular home-study course in weaving, the "Shuttle-Craft Guild Bulletin." Atwater operated the guild from wherever she was living, and served as its president until her death in 1956.

STEHLI SILK CORPORATION
Active 1920s
New York, New York

Photographer Edward Steichen was one of several artists commissioned by the Stehli company to produce unconventional modern designs for its Americana print series (1925). Steichen's contribution—known as the "mothballs and sugar cubes" fabric—and the photographs on which it was based were included with other Stehli silks in R. H. Macy's 1927 "Exposition of Art in Trade" in New York. The firm's display was described as illustrating a "direct relationship between creative art and large-scale production."

STUDIO LOJA SAARINEN
1928–42
Bloomfield Hills, Michigan
Founder: Louise (Loja) Saarinen

Saarinen was approached by Cranbrook founder George Booth to design and produce rugs and textiles when the art and educational complex was in its infancy. They decided that the work could be done on-site, and in October 1928 Studio Loja Saarinen was established. Beginning with one loom (it would expand to include thirty) and a small staff of Swedish designers and weavers—including Maja Andersson Wirde and Lillian Holm—the Saarinen studio created handwoven fabrics, rugs, and window hangings by special commission. Its first task was producing furnishings for Saarinen House. The second assignment, creating carpets and textiles for Kingswood School, Cranbrook, to accommodate the opening of the school, was completed within a year by twelve weavers under Saarinen's supervision. Outside commissions included textiles and carpets for the Richard Hudnut Salon and the Yardley Shop in New York, and the Chrysler Showroom in Detroit.

WILLICH-FRANKE STUDIOS
Active 1930s
New York, New York

This fabric studio, in which textile designer Grete Franke was a principal partner, exhibited quality mass-produced fabrics created in collaboration with industrial designer Gilbert Rohde at The Metropolitan Museum of Art's Thirteenth American Industrial Art Exhibition in 1934. Work by the firm was also included in the Decorative Arts section of the Golden Gate International Exposition in San Francisco in 1939–40.

WOOD

DUNBAR FURNITURE, INC.; LATER,
DUNBAR FURNITURE
MANUFACTURING COMPANY; LATER,
DUNBAR FURNITURE CORPORATION
OF INDIANA
1919–present
Berne, Indiana
Founder: Aloysius Dunbar

The Dunbar company was originally a successful manufacturer of period rocking chairs. The company opened its first furniture showroom in 1927, and in 1931 appointed Edward J. Wormley director of design. Wormley designed all of the company's furniture for the next four decades, adding modern pieces to its lines of traditional English and Colonial Revival furniture. Wormley averaged one hundred new designs annually, spare, neoclassical, influenced by Swedish Modern. Under Federal contract during World War II, Dunbar manufactured wood tail sections for airplanes. By 1946, it resumed furniture production as the Dunbar Furniture Manufacturing Company. It was incorporated under its present name in 1950.

PAUL FRANKL GALLERY
c. 1922–n.d.
New York, New York
Founder: Paul T. Frankl

Frankl, an industrial designer noted for his "skyscraper" furniture, opened a gallery at 4 East Forty-eighth Street in New York around 1922. Frankl sold his own furniture through the gallery as well as handpainted screens by Donald Deskey and imported wallpapers and fabrics.

HEYWOOD-WAKEFIELD COMPANY
Active 1930s
Boston, Massachusetts

In the early 1930s the Boston-based Heywood-Wakefield Company commissioned industrial designer Gilbert Rohde to create a simple, inexpensive bentwood chair similar to those designed by Finnish architect Alvar Aalto. Some 250,000 copies of the Rohde chair were sold by the end of the decade. Russel Wright designed for Heywood in the early 1930s. The firm was a sponsor of The Museum of Modern Art's "Organic Design in Home Furnishings Competition" in 1940–41.

SCHMIEG, HUNGATE AND KOTZIAN, INC.; LATER, SCHMIEG AND KOTZIAN, INC.; LATER, S.K.J.S. CUSTOM FURNITURE, INC.
1908–present
New York, New York
Founders: Henry Kotzian, Karl Schmieg

Schmieg, Hungate and Kotzian was the premier U.S. cabinetmaking firm in the 1920s, producing custom furniture by important designers such as Donald Deskey and Eugene Schoen. Founded in England, the company relocated to New York in 1908, specializing in quality period furnishings and distinguishing itself through the use of exotic woods. In 1954 the firm was purchased by John Scalian and incorporated under the Schmieg and Kotzian name. It was sold to Nicola Leone and renamed S.K.J.S. Custom Furniture in 1978.

GENERAL

AMERICAN DESIGNERS' GALLERY
1928–29
New York, New York

A cooperative formed to promote, exhibit, and market the modern design work of its members, the American Designers' Gallery mounted some of the first non-museum shows of modern decorative and utilitarian objects by Donald Deskey, Maurice Heaton, Raymond Hood, Peter Mueller-Munk, Henry Varnum Poor, Ruth Reeves, and Joseph Urban, among others.

DESKEY-VOLLMER, INC.
1927–c. early 1930s
New York, New York
Founders: Donald Deskey, Phillip Vollmer

An interior design firm, Deskey-Vollmer specialized in Art Deco screens, lighting fixtures, and furniture.

MILWAUKEE HANDICRAFT PROJECT
1935–42
Milwaukee, Wisconsin

Initiated by the Works Progress Administration, the project was sponsored by the Milwaukee State Teachers College. Weaver and faculty member Elsa Ulbricht, with the assistance of her student Mary June Kellogg (Rice), implemented a program in which artisans created articles "of superior quality and craftsmanship" for distribution to public institutions, including dolls, furniture, hooked rugs, weavings, and block- and screenprinted fabrics. Using a variety of materials—including waste materials from a carpet factory and ravelled burlap—project weavers made fabrics that fully utilized the technical possibilities of the loom. Textile designers Nellie Sargent Johnson and Barbara Warren were members of the project.

NEW AGE GROUP; ALSO KNOWN AS NEW-AGE WORKERS AND BLUE RIDGE MOUNTAINS GROUP
c. 1928–n.d.
Founders: Zoltan Hecht, Rosa Pringle Hecht

The New Age Group was a short-lived collaborative arts project organized by painter Zoltan Hecht and his wife, Rosa Pringle Hecht, around 1928. The North Carolina artisans involved in the project produced rugs designed by artists such as Thomas Hart Benton, George Biddle, Pola Hoffmann, Ilonka Karasz, Henry Varnum Poor, among others. The Hechts later worked as textile designers and arts administrators for the Works Progress Administration.

W. AND J. SLOANE, THE COMPANY OF MASTER CRAFTSMEN
1843–present
New York, New York

The Company of Master Craftsmen was the deluxe furnituremaking division of the New York retail furniture store W. and J. Sloane. One of the major cabinet shops in New York, it produced extremely fine Duncan Phyfe reproductions in addition to more contemporary *art moderne* furniture. In 1929 the Master Craftsmen shop manufactured chairs designed by Eliel Saarinen, which were included in The Metropolitan Museum of Art exhibition "The Architect and the Industrial Arts" later that year. Shortly afterward, Saarinen commissioned the shop to produce the Art Deco dining room suite he designed for Saarinen House at Cranbrook.

STAR FURNITURE COMPANY; LATER, MICHIGAN STAR FURNITURE COMPANY; LATER, HERMAN MILLER FURNITURE COMPANY; LATER, HERMAN MILLER, INC.
1905–present
Zeeland, Michigan

Originally a manufacturer of ostentatious period-revival furniture, the company was purchased by Herman Miller and his son-in-law Dirk Jan De Pree in 1923. In the early 1930s, with the guidance of designer Gilbert Rohde, the Herman Miller Furniture Company became one of the chief manufacturers of modern furniture in the United States. Under Rohde, and his successor in 1944, George Nelson, the company executed such innovative designs as a biomorphic coffee table by Isamu Noguchi and plywood, fiberglass, and wire furniture by Charles and Ray Eames. In 1952 the firm expanded into fabrics and wall coverings, creating bright geometric patterns under the design direction of Alexander Girard. The company was incorporated under its present name in 1969.

SCHOOLS AND UNIVERSITY PROGRAMS

ALABAMA STATE TEACHERS COLLEGE; LATER, ALABAMA STATE UNIVERSITY, CERAMICS DEPARTMENT
1874–present
Montgomery, Alabama

The ceramics department at the Alabama State Teachers College was developed in the 1940s by Issac Scott Hathaway, a leading black ceramist known for his portrait busts of Frederick Douglass, Paul Laurence Dunbar, and Booker T. Washington.

ALFRED UNIVERSITY, NEW YORK SCHOOL OF CLAYWORKING AND CERAMICS; LATER, NEW YORK STATE COLLEGE OF CERAMICS AT ALFRED UNIVERSITY
1836–present
Alfred, New York

Alfred University was founded as a select school by Seventh Day Baptists; it was the first coeducational institution in New York State and the second in the nation. Today, the nonsectarian university is composed of the privately endowed College of Business, the College of Engineering and Professional Studies, the College of Liberal Arts and Sciences, and the New York State College of Ceramics (comprising the Schools of Ceramic Engineering and Sciences, and Art and Design). The College of Ceramics, originally called the New York School of Clayworking and Ceramics, was chartered in 1900 to train ceramists and to "conduct experiments for commercial purposes of clays and shales of New York State." Its director from 1900 to 1931 was the pioneering ceramics educator Charles Fergus Binns. In collaboration with the American Ceramic Society, the school reinvigorated the clay industries here and abroad, developing a coherent liberal arts curriculum in which two- and four-year programs in clay technology, clay testing, and graphic and decorative arts could be pursued.

ART STUDENTS LEAGUE
1875–present
New York, New York

The League was founded by a group of students who broke away from the National Academy of Design and began to hold art classes under the direction of Professor Lemuel Wilmarth. Its objectives were to maintain "a thorough course of study in painting, drawing, and modelling . . . and in anatomy, perspective, composition, and all that pertains to a complete system of education in Art, and also for the encouragement of a spirit of fraternity among art students." In 1889 the league joined with the Society of American Artists and the Architectural League to form the American Fine Arts Society. William E. Artis, Alexander Calder, Margaret De Patta, Erwine Laverne, Estelle Lester (Laverne), Mary Scheier, and Russel Wright were among the artists who trained at the Art Students League in the 1920s and 1930s.

BLACK MOUNTAIN COLLEGE
1933–56
Asheville, North Carolina
Founders: John Andrew Rice, Theodore Dreier

A progressive coeducational liberal arts college, Black Mountain was founded in 1933 by John Andrew Rice and other former members of the faculty of Rollins College in Winter Park, Florida. A cooperative, Black Mountain was owned and administered by the faculty, and offered a program of self-directed study in studio arts, intellectual disciplines, and community work. The structure made it a haven for the intellectually and spiritually curious, attracting a diverse constituency, including painters, writers, musicians, and dancers, as well as an unprecedented number of foreign refugees. Less than a month after the Dessau Bauhaus was closed in 1933, offers to teach at Black Mountain were extended to Josef and Anni Albers by Museum of Modern Art curator Philip Johnson on behalf of the college. The couple's traveling expenses and salaries were covered by the museum's trustees for the first year. Under the Alberses' leadership Black Mountain became a center for the dissemination of Bauhaus utopian idealism and a hub for experimental art in America. Josef Albers's method of teaching was one of discovery and invention, "a pedagogy of learning rather than a pedagogy of teaching." In his classes students were not taught "how to"; rather, they were given specific problems to solve. Anni Albers directed the weaving workshop, stressing a commitment to the social aim of designing for industry—an approach that evolved from her belief in the dominant role of mass production in meeting the needs of society.

CALIFORNIA SCHOOL OF DESIGN; LATER, MARK HOPKINS INSTITUTE OF ART; LATER, CALIFORNIA SCHOOL OF DESIGN OF THE SAN FRANCISCO INSTITUTE OF ART; LATER, CALIFORNIA SCHOOL OF FINE ARTS
1874–present
San Francisco, California
Founder: San Francisco Art Association

The School of Design was founded as a center for teaching the applied arts. In 1938 Alfred University–trained ceramist Harold Eaton Riegger joined the faculty and proselytized the Alfred ideas of the studio-potter. This approach not only emphasized the pleasure of making a shaped clay object but also gave students a working knowledge of all the technical aspects of clay and kiln firing.

CARNEGIE INSTITUTE OF TECHNOLOGY; LATER, CARNEGIE MELLON UNIVERSITY, INDUSTRIAL DESIGN PROGRAM
1900–present
Pittsburgh, Pennsylvania

In 1935 renowned silversmith and designer Peter Mueller-Munk, along with Donald Dohner and Robert Lepper, developed the first U.S. degree-granting program in industrial design at the Carnegie Institute of Technology.

CLEVELAND SCHOOL OF ART; LATER, CLEVELAND INSTITUTE OF ART
1882–present
Cleveland, Ohio

Since its founding the school's objectives have been the education of professional artists through a comprehensive liberal arts curriculum that includes philosophy, aesthetics, history, sociology, economics, anthropology, art history, and literature, together with an intensive five-year studio program. From the 1920s to the 1940s the school offered a well-regarded preparatory program in ceramics, taught by master ceramists such as Arthur Eugene Baggs, Alexander Blazys, R. Guy Cowan, and Viktor Schreckengost. The school changed its name to the Cleveland Institute of Art in 1949 and today awards baccalaureate degrees.

CRANBROOK ACADEMY OF ART
1932–present
Bloomfield Hills, Michigan
Founder: George G. Booth

The Cranbrook Academy of Art is part of a complex of small private schools founded by publisher and art collector Booth. The idea of establishing an artists' community was first suggested to him in 1919 by Detroit landscape architect William Tyler Miller. In 1925 Booth commissioned Finnish architect Eliel Saarinen to develop a site plan for the complex. Located on one hundred acres of Michigan farmland Booth purchased twenty miles north of Detroit, Cranbrook was conceived on the model of the American Academy in Rome, with resident artists pursuing their own work in on-campus studios. In exchange, they would supervise a few highly qualified apprentice "fellows" and create works of art for the community's buildings. Construction of the facilities and the development of a concrete educational philosophy for the academy proceeded slowly, and it was not until 1932 that the school was formally opened. With Saarinen as president, a faculty of distinguished European craftspeople, including Maija Grotell, Carl Milles, and Marianne Strengell, was assembled. Saarinen's approach to art education, which differed somewhat from Booth's master-apprentice concept, was also incorporated into the school's programs. Saarinen believed in the close relationship between art and life, and he conceived of Cranbrook as a place where students would learn the fundamental principles of art, enabling them to develop a mode of artistic expression reflective of modern existence.

HARVARD UNIVERSITY, GRADUATE SCHOOL OF DESIGN
1636–present
Cambridge, Massachusetts

Former Bauhaus director Walter Gropius became director of the Graduate School of Design in 1937. Under him, the school became the center for functionalist design and architecture in the United States in the late 1930s and 1940s. Gropius advocated a synthesis of art, technology, and social awareness, and stressed a practical approach to design based on the "peculiar conditions"—the functional requirements—of a building or object. Shortly after his appointment, Gropius asked architect-designer Marcel Breuer to join the faculty, and was instrumental in László Moholy-Nagy's appointment to head the proposed New Bauhaus in Chicago.

HOWARD UNIVERSITY
1867–present
Washington, D.C.

Originally conceived as a training school for African-American ministers and teachers, Howard University was ultimately chartered as a coeducational liberal arts college. It has since grown to become the largest historically black university in the United States, encompassing colleges of liberal arts, fine arts, pharmacy, and dentistry, and schools of engineering and architecture, medicine, law, religion, and social work. Joseph Gilliard, who succeeded Henry Letcher as ceramics instructor at Howard in the 1940s, influenced two generations of American ceramists.

NEW BAUHAUS; LATER, CHICAGO SCHOOL OF DESIGN; LATER,

INSTITUTE OF DESIGN, CHICAGO; LATER MERGED WITH ILLINOIS INSTITUTE OF TECHNOLOGY
1937–present
Chicago, Illinois
Founder: Chicago Association of Arts and Industries

In 1937 the Chicago Association of Arts and Industries asked László Moholy-Nagy to serve as head of an industrial arts school structured on the workshop model of the Dessau Bauhaus. Closed after one year because of lack of funding, the New Bauhaus reopened in 1939 as the Chicago School of Design, and received academic accreditation as the Institute of Design in 1944. Serge Chermayeff became director of the school upon Moholy-Nagy's death in 1946. It was incorporated into the Illinois Institute of Technology in 1949.

OHIO STATE UNIVERSITY, CERAMICS PROGRAM
1870–present
Columbus, Ohio

The Ohio State ceramics program, begun in 1927, was among the first in the country to include fine arts and history in a curriculum centered on ceramic engineering. Arthur Eugene Baggs headed the program from its inception until his death in 1947. During the 1930s, ceramics engineer Edgar Littlefield, designer Carlton Atherton, glaze expert Margaret Fetzer, and ceramic sculptor Paul Bogatay were on the program faculty. Today, the school offers B.F.A. and M.F.A. degrees in ceramics. Requirements for undergraduate degree candidates include classes in throwing, handbuilding, sculpting, plaster moldmaking, clay and glaze calculation, kiln building, and the history of ceramics. Advanced students study specific technical problems with a faculty member or visiting artists.

OTIS ART INSTITUTE; LATER, OTIS COLLEGE OF ART AND DESIGN
1918–present
Los Angeles, California
Founders: Harrison Gray Otis; County of Los Angeles

Otis, the founder and publisher of the *Los Angeles Times,* donated his MacArthur Park mansion to the County of Los Angeles in 1917, stipulating that it be used for a school of the visual arts. The Otis Art Institute was established by the County the following year, offering courses in design, pottery, textile decoration, wood carving, metalwork, and jewelry. It also served as the primary exhibition space for the City of Los Angeles. In 1976, as a result of state budget cuts, the Institute merged with the Parsons School of Design. It was restruc-

tured as an independent, private art school in 1979 and accredited as the Otis College of Art and Design in 1991.

POND FARM COMMUNITY
1949–53
Guerneville, California
Founders: Jane Herr, Gordon Herr

In 1939 California architect Gordon Herr traveled to Europe in search of participants for an artists' community that he and his wife, writer Jane Herr, hoped to establish. Ceramist Marguerite Wildenhain responded to Herr's offer, and arrived in Guerneville, California, in 1940. Over the next nine years, she and the Herrs remodeled an old barn into studio space. The Herrs completed Hexagon House, the community's signature building, and Wildenhain built her own house by hand. Pond Farm became a viable school and community in 1949, with a core faculty of Wildenhain, as potter-in-residence and teacher, and weaver Trude Guermonprez. Its educational program, like that of the Bauhaus, was built on the idea of the interrelatedness of craft, design, and architecture. Following the death of Jane Herr, the community's unifying force, Pond Farm closed in 1953.

PRATT INSTITUTE, SCHOOL OF ART AND DESIGN
1887–present
Brooklyn, New York
Founder: Charles Pratt

Realizing that rapidly industrializing society required a new approach to higher education, industrialist Charles Pratt founded a school combining a liberal arts curriculum and vocational training, including courses in mechanical drawing, wood carving, sewing, nursing, and typing. Pratt Institute was one of the first schools to recognize the need for advertising design as a specific academic discipline, and in 1935 the School of Art established a department of advertising design, the forerunner of its current communications design programs. A department of industrial design was added in 1936, making Pratt a pioneer in the development of this new field. The institute's interior design department was created in 1946, replacing the traditional interior decoration curriculum with more professional courses.

RHODE ISLAND SCHOOL OF DESIGN
1877–present
Providence, Rhode Island
Founder: Helen Metcalf

Considered the preeminent art school in America, the Rhode Island School of Design (RISD) was founded to provide theoretical and practical training for artists and to promote public art education. A strong liberal arts program provides courses in history, literature, and the social sciences as a means of complementing the art and design curriculum. Exhibitions of student and alumni work, mounted in the RISD Museum of Art, are an important part of the school's program. Silversmith William Brigham was on the faculty from 1914 to 1927, and in the early 1940s Cranbrook weaving instructor Robert Sailors studied the use of the powerloom at RISD.

SAVAGE STUDIO OF ARTS AND CRAFTS; LATER, HARLEM COMMUNITY ART CENTER
1932–n.d.
New York, New York
Founder: Augusta Savage

Savage opened an art school in a basement apartment on West 143rd Street in 1932. Shortly thereafter, a $1,500 grant from the Carnegie Foundation enabled her to provide tuition-free classes for young children. The studio program flourished, and in 1934 it became the Harlem Community Art Center, the largest program of its kind in the United States during the 1930s. Some fifteen hundred people of all ages participated in the Center's weaving, pottery, and quilting workshops.

THE SCHOOL FOR AMERICAN CRAFTSMEN AT DARTMOUTH COLLEGE; LATER AT ALFRED UNIVERSITY; LATER AT ROCHESTER INSTITUTE OF TECHNOLOGY
1944–present
Hanover, New Hampshire; Alfred, New York; Rochester, New York
Founder: American Craftsmen's Educational Council

The School for American Craftsmen grew out of the Rehabilitation Training Program sponsored by the American Craftsmen's Educational Council and a Dartmouth College student workshop. In 1946 the school became part of the Fine and Hand Arts Division of the Liberal Arts College at Alfred University, offering a two-year certificate program with the aim of lifting the "educational status of the Hand Arts from that of vocational training, on a par with radar or refrigerators, to training on the Liberal Arts level." It became affiliated with the Rochester Institute of Technology in 1950, after which the Educational Council had no further involvement in its operation.

SCHOOL OF THE ART INSTITUTE OF CHICAGO, DEPARTMENT OF DECORATIVE DESIGN
1886–present
Chicago, Illinois
Founder: Louis J. Miller

Miller, a well-known metalworker who executed designs for architect Louis Sullivan, founded and served as head of the decorative design department. The school soon expanded to include a department of applied design. Ceramists Charles Harder and Bernard Frazier, industrial designers Donald Deskey and Edward Wormley, and weaver Mary Atwater attended the school in the 1920s and 1930s.

SCHOOL OF THE CALIFORNIA GUILD OF ARTS AND CRAFTS; LATER, CALIFORNIA SCHOOL OF ARTS AND CRAFTS; LATER, CALIFORNIA COLLEGE OF ARTS AND CRAFTS
1907–present
Berkeley, California; Oakland, California
Founder: Frederick Henry Meyer

Founded in association with the California Guild of Arts and Crafts in 1907, the school integrated the study and practice of fine, applied, and industrial art, and trained teachers in these fields. Early courses included freehand and figure drawing, designing, wood carving, and clay and wax modeling. By 1908, the school was no longer affiliated with the Guild, and its name was changed to the California School of Arts and Crafts. Meyer negotiated the school's purchase of the Treadwell Estate in Oakland in 1922, and by 1924 the school was established there as the California College of Arts and Crafts. In the 1930s, West Coast sculptors Ralph Stackpole and Beniamino Bufano, and ceramist F. Carlton Ball were on the faculty. Today, the College awards undergraduate and graduate degrees in the fine and liberal arts as well as degrees in education.

STATE UNIVERSITY OF NEW YORK, FASHION INSTITUTE OF TECHNOLOGY
1944–present
New York, New York

The Fashion Institute of Technology is a coeducational school located in mid-Manhattan in the garment district, the center of the U.S. textile-apparel industry. A specialized college under the program of the State University of New York, F.I.T. is governed by a board of trustees, most of whom have made the fashion and textile industries their lives' work. The school is empowered to grant the associate degree in applied science as well as baccalaureate degrees in science and the fine arts.

SYRACUSE UNIVERSITY, COLLEGE OF FINE ARTS
1870–present
Syracuse, New York

The College of Fine Arts was founded in 1873, and first offered courses in art, architecture, and music. The college functions as an art school within the context of a liberal arts institution, and provides students with a selection of academic electives as well as professional studio courses in commercial art, printmaking, and metal crafts. The ceramics program—one of the first degree programs in ceramics in the United States—provides instruction in technique, glaze chemistry, and kiln construction.

TUSKEGEE NORMAL AND INDUSTRIAL INSTITUTE; LATER, TUSKEGEE UNIVERSITY
1881–present
Tuskegee, Alabama
Founder: Booker T. Washington

The school was founded as Alabama's first training school for African-American teachers and artisans. Known as Tuskegee Institute, it derived its curriculum from Washington's belief that only through the development of students' vocational skills would African Americans achieve civil and political rights as a result of economic gains. The institute employed a self-help program that allowed students to earn all or part of their expenses while pursuing courses in carpentry, masonry, tinsmithing, blacksmithing, mechanical drawing, architecture, farming, mechanics, and teacher education. Issac Hathaway established the school's influential ceramics department in 1937. The school became Tuskegee University in 1985 and now encompasses a college of arts and sciences and schools of agriculture and home economics, business, education, engineering and architecture, nursing and allied health, and veterinary medicine.

UNIVERSITY OF CALIFORNIA AT LOS ANGELES, ART DEPARTMENT
1881–present
Los Angeles, California

Laura Andreson developed an innovative ceramics course at the university in the late 1930s, providing instruction in glazing and throwing techniques not commonly known on the West Coast. From 1936 to 1970 she taught more than five thousand students.

UNIVERSITY OF SOUTHERN CALIFORNIA, SCHOOL OF ARCHITECTURE
1879–present
Los Angeles, California

In 1931 ceramist Glen Lukens established a ceramics program at the University of

Southern California under the auspices of the School of Architecture. The program intimately coordinated ceramics with architectural design. Appointed a professor of ceramics in 1936, Lukens taught at the university until the mid-1960s.

UNIVERSITY OF WASHINGTON, DESIGN DEPARTMENT OF THE SCHOOL OF FINE ART
1916–present
Seattle, Washington

During the interwar period, the School of Fine Art faculty included painter Walter Isaac, printmaker-designer Helen Neilson Rhodes, and metalsmith Ruth Penington, whose approach to arts education was informed by the work of Arthur Wesley Dow. The design department offered courses in pottery, metalwork, and needlework. Grace Denny, a noted textile designer, organized a program on the history of textiles that included technical instruction.

WAYNE UNIVERSITY; LATER, WAYNE STATE UNIVERSITY, ART DEPARTMENT
1868–present
Detroit, Michigan

During the 1930s and 1940s silversmith Arthur Nevill Kirk taught metalwork and weaver Nellie Sargent Johnson offered courses in textile design in the art department at Wayne University. These were the first courses in these fields offered by the university.

SOCIETIES AND ASSOCIATIONS

AMERICAN CERAMIC SOCIETY
1899–present
Columbus, Ohio
Founders: Edward Orton, Jr.; Theodore Randall

Orton and Randall founded the society in response to increased competition from European ceramics manufacturers in the late nineteenth century. Its purpose, then as now, is to support the ceramic arts and the development of ceramics technology in the United States. The society has evolved to include eleven technical divisions: Basic Science; Cements; Design; Electronics; Engineering Ceramics; Glass; Materials and Equipment; Nuclear; Refractory Ceramics; Structural Clay Products; and Whitewares. It has published a number of journals in the field, including *Ceramic Abstracts, Ceramic Bulletin, Journal of the American Ceramic Society, Advanced Ceramic Materials, Ceramic Proceedings,* and *Ceramic Source.* The Ross C. Purdy Museum of Ceramics, with a collection that includes sculptures, historical artifacts, and the latest product applications, is maintained in the society's Ohio headquarters.

AMERICAN HANDCRAFT COUNCIL AND HANDCRAFT COOPERATIVE LEAGUE OF AMERICA; MERGED TO FORM AMERICAN CRAFTSMEN'S COOPERATIVE COUNCIL, INC.; LATER INCORPORATED AMERICAN CRAFTSMEN'S EDUCATIONAL COUNCIL; LATER, AMERICAN CRAFTSMEN'S COUNCIL; LATER, AMERICAN CRAFTS COUNCIL; LATER, AMERICAN CRAFT COUNCIL
1939–present
New York, New York

The American Handcraft Council and the Handcraft Cooperative League of America—organizations with similar agendas but somewhat different focuses—were founded in 1939. The council underscored the study and development of contemporary craft, while the league, under founder Aileen Osborn Webb, sought to expand the market for the work of rural craftspeople; in 1940 the league opened America House in New York, a cooperative retail shop that continued to operate until 1971. In 1941 the council and the league merged to form the American Craftsmen's Cooperative Council, Inc., and began publishing *Craft Horizons* (now *American Craft*) "as an educational service" for its members. By 1943, an educational arm was added to the organization—the American Craftsmen's Edu-

cational Council, Inc., with the Board of Regents, on behalf of the Education Department of the State of New York, granting the group a charter to provide education in handcrafts and to stimulate public interest in, and appreciation of, the work of handcraftsmen. In 1949 the Educational Council inaugurated a new gallery at America House with an exhibition of embroidery, the first of many shows they would sponsor. In 1955 the Educational Council shortened its name to the American Craftsmen's Council (ACC) and amended its charter so that it could "own and operate a museum." The Museum of Contemporary Crafts (now the American Craft Museum) opened the following year. Now known as the American Craft Council, the organization continues to expand its educative mission, sponsoring exhibitions, competitions, workshops, and conferences, publishing books and catalogues, and awarding fellowships. The American Craft Museum became a separate, autonomous institution in 1990.

AMERICAN UNION OF DECORATIVE ARTISTS AND CRAFTSMEN (AUDAC)
1928–early 1930s
New York, New York

The American Union of Decorative Artists and Craftsmen (AUDAC) was formed "to give direction to contemporary design in America, particularly as it applies to industry." Based on European models—the Wiener Werkstätte, the German Werkbunds, and the French Société des Artistes Décorateurs—AUDAC was an association of designers, architects, artists, and craftspeople "engaged in giving our environment a new and appropriate appearance." Its activities included the publication of the illustrated *Annual of American Design 1931,* with essays by Paul Frankl, Norman Bel Geddes, Lewis Mumford, Frank Lloyd Wright, and others. The group also sponsored two major exhibitions of work by its members, at the Grand Central Art Galleries in New York, in 1930; and The Brooklyn Museum, in 1931. The more ambitious Brooklyn show was praised for presenting designs "suited to contemporary life in the United States, and not copied from European modes." AUDAC disbanded shortly after the exhibition closed, a victim of the deepening economic crisis of the 1930s.

DETROIT SOCIETY OF ARTS AND CRAFTS; LATER, CENTER FOR CREATIVE STUDIES, COLLEGE OF ART AND·DESIGN
1906–present
Detroit, Michigan
Founding President: George G. Booth

The Detroit Society of Arts and Crafts was founded to promote the ideals of the American Arts and Crafts movement—"[to] encourage good and beautiful work as applied to useful service." In 1911, with the financial support of Booth, the society established the Detroit School of Design. Economic pressures forced the closure of the school in 1918, but a second school was established in 1926; it continues today as the College of Art and Design of the Center for Creative Studies. Arthur Nevill Kirk taught metalwork at the school in 1927–28, and industrial designer Harry Bertoia trained there in 1936–37. The Detroit Society of Arts and Crafts maintained an active exhibitions program throughout the 1920s and 1930s. Silversmith Peter Mueller-Munk was given a solo exhibition in 1928, and in 1933 the Society mounted "Art in the Automobile Industry," the first exhibition to recognize the automobile as an art form.

SOCIETY OF ARTS AND CRAFTS, BOSTON
1897–present
Boston, Massachusetts
Founding President: Charles Eliot Norton

The Society of Arts and Crafts, Boston, was the foremost advocate of the Arts and Crafts aesthetic in America in the early twentieth century. Modeled on a medieval craft guild, it provided work space to, and exhibited the work of, its members, and parented specialized groups such as the Boston Jewelers Guild (founded 1920). The society sponsored a number of influential exhibitions, including a show of Danish arts and crafts in 1913 that introduced modern Scandinavian design in the United States. In the 1920s and 1930s it exhibited the work of metalsmiths Porter George Blanchard (before 1923), Rebecca Cauman (1927), Edward E. Oakes (1929), and William E. Brigham (1936), among others.

SOCIETY OF DESIGNER-CRAFTSMEN
1936–present
New York, New York

One of the first professional societies for contemporary crafts in America, the group organized an exhibition of metalwork for the Paris Exposition of 1937. Glass artist Maurice Heaton was a charter member and early president of the organization.

NOTES

KARDON
Craft in the Machine Age

1. Alistair Duncan, *American Art Deco* (New York: Harry N. Abrams, 1986), 21.

2. The Lord & Taylor exhibition was organized by Dorothy Shaver, Director of Fashion and Decoration, and contained furniture as well as some of the first works by Picasso and Georges Braque to be shown in this country. Virginia Hamill and Lee Simonson created fifteen rooms for R. H. Macy. *Art moderne* exhibitions at John Wanamaker's, Macy's, Lord & Taylor's, and B. Altman's preceded the founding, in 1929, of The Museum of Modern Art in New York. That same year, The Metropolitan Museum of Art mounted the exhibition "The Architect and the Industrial Arts," which included thirteen room settings; much of the furniture was handmade.

3. Jeffrey L. Meikle, *Twentieth Century Limited: Industrial Design in America, 1925–1939* (Philadelphia: Temple University Press, 1979), 24.

4. Ibid., 20.

5. Jeffrey L. Meikle, "American Design History: A Bibliography of Sources and Interpretation," *American Studies International* 23 (April 1985): 13.

6. Russel Wright, along with Charles and Ray Eames, Isamu Noguchi, and Frederick J. Kiesler, rejected the machine aesthetic, exploring organic forms and natural materials.

GREEN
Promise and Peril of High Technology

1. Lewis Mumford, *Technics and Civilization* (New York: Harcourt Brace, 1934), 363.

2. See, for example, Joseph Wood Krutch, *The Modern Temper* (New York: Harcourt Brace, 1929); Stuart Chase, *Mexico: A Study of Two Americas* (New York: Macmillan, 1931) and *Men and Machines* (New York: Macmillan, 1929); Robert Penn Warren, Allan Tate, et al., *I'll Take My Stand: The South and the Agrarian Tradition* (New York: Harper and Brothers, 1930). Chase wrote a series of articles for the *New Republic* titled "Men and Machines," the central theme of which was that technological innovation had produced a catastrophe, a cruel irony of displacement and "de-skilling" of workers by the very machines that had made the production of more goods possible; see "Skilled Work and No Work," *New Republic* 68 (March 20, 1929): 121; and "Leaning Towers," *New Republic* 68 (March 27, 1929): 171.

3. See Lewis Mumford, *Sticks and Stones: A Study of American Architecture and Civilization* (New York: Boni and Liveright, 1924) and *The Golden Day: A Study in American Literature and Culture* (New York: Boni and Liveright, 1926).

4. On Progressivism, see Gabriel Kolko, *The Triumph of Conservatism* (Chicago: Quadrangle Books, 1967); and Cecelia Tichi, *Shifting Gears: Technology, Literature, Culture in Modernist America* (Chapel Hill: University of North Carolina Press, 1987).

5. In reality, "laissez-faire" economics was a clever take on the application of individual liberties to economic relations with the government. While owners of large and small businesses were aghast at attempts to regulate working conditions, for example, they were delighted with government support in the form of land grants (particularly the railroads), unrestricted exploitation of mineral resources on government lands, and state and municipal police forces to control striking workers.

6. Lydia Sigourney, "Horticulture," *Godey's Lady's Book* 21 (October 1840): 179.

7. See Bevis Hillier, *Art Deco* (Minneapolis: Minneapolis Institute of Arts, 1971).

8. See Kathy J. Ogren, *The Jazz Revolution: Twenties America and the Meaning of Jazz* (New York: Oxford University Press, 1989); and Gunther Schuller, *Early Jazz: Its Roots and Musical Development* (New York: Oxford University Press, 1968). The Manhattan Casino could hold six thousand dancers. New York's Savoy opened its 200-foot-long dance floor in 1926.

9. See Jeffrey L. Meikle, *Twentieth Century Limited: Industrial Design in America, 1925–1939* (Philadelphia: Temple University Press, 1979).

10. See William J. Hennessey, *Russel Wright, American Designer* (Cambridge, Mass.: MIT Press, 1983).

11. *The Museum of Modern Art, New York: The History and the Collection* (New York: Harry N. Abrams in association with The Museum of Modern Art, 1984), 164–65.

12. Even popular romantic cinema of the era, especially the Busby Berkeley music extravaganzas, with their generally schmaltzy plots, were in some sense paeans to the Machine Age. In *Footlight Parade* (1933), Berkeley's choreography transformed women's bodies into parts of large machines, with arms and legs as gears and spokes.

13. Wilhelm Wagenfeld, quoted in *The Museum of Modern Art, New York,* 429.

14. See Roland Marchand, *Advertising the American Dream: Making Way for Modernity, 1920–1940* (Berkeley: University of California Press, 1985).

15. The exception to the "white is right" ideology in home furnishings in this era is to be found in the more expensive goods marketed for use in the bathroom. By the mid-1920s, several companies, including American Standard, Kohler, Crane, and Church, offered coordinated bathroom fixtures in pastel colors. It may have been a status totem of the self-appointed "smart set," who may have seen color as a rejection of the need to demonstrate cleanliness by means of whiteness. Towel makers introduced matched sets of colored bath towels by 1925.

16. For a cogent discussion of Popular Front politics in the United States, see Richard Pells, *Radical Visions and American Dreams: Culture and Social Thought in the Depression Years* (New York: Harper & Row, 1973), 294–99.

17. The first sit-down strikes occurred at the Goodyear Tire and Rubber plant in Akron, Ohio, in 1935. Workers intending to use this type of strike reported for work in the usual manner, and at a prearranged time simply quit working and refused to leave. By "sitting," the unions were able to keep replacement workers out. Management was reluctant to bring in the police or "goons" to throw out the strikers and thereby put at risk the usually expensive equipment found in most heavy industrial plants. Management and many average Americans denounced the strikers' abridgement of the company's property rights, but it was a brilliant tactic. In 1936, sit-downs were common in other rubbermakers' factories, and in 1937 almost five hundred thousand workers sat in the automobile, shipbuilding, baking, and steel industries. Between November 1935 and May 1937, more than nine hundred sit-down strikes took place.

18. See Robert Judson Clarke et al., *Design in America: The Cranbrook Vision, 1925–1950* (New York: Harry N. Abrams, 1983).

19. Neil Harris, "North by Midwest," in ibid., 15–20.

20. Meikle, *Twentieth Century Limited,* 160.

21. See Warren I. Susman et al., *Dawn of a New Day: The New York World's Fair, 1939–1940* (New York: New York University Press, 1980).

BLETTER
Myths of Modernism

1. See, for example, Peter Blake, *Form Follows Fiasco: Why Modern Architecture Hasn't Worked* (Boston: Little, Brown, 1977); Brent Brolin, *The Failure of Modern Architecture* (New York: Van Nostrand Reinhold, 1976); Charles Jencks, *The Language of Post-Modern Architecture* (New York: Rizzoli, 1977); and Tom Wolfe, *From Bauhaus to Our House* (New York: Farrar Straus Giroux, 1981).

2. See Henry-Russell Hitchcock, Philip Johnson, and Lewis Mumford, *Modern Architecture: International Exhibition* (New York: The Museum of Modern Art, 1932). See also Terence Riley, *The International Style: Exhibition 15 and The Museum of Modern Art* (New York: Rizzoli, 1992).

3. Henry-Russell Hitchcock and Philip Johnson, *The International Style: Architecture Since 1922* (New York: Norton, 1932); reprinted as *The International Style* (1966).

4. Walter Gropius, *Internationale Architektur,* Bauhausbücher 1 (Munich: Albert Langen, 1925); Adolf Behne, *Der moderne Zweckbau* (1926; reprint, Berlin, Frankfurt, and Vienna: Ullstein, 1964); Ludwig Hilberseimer, *Internationale neue Baukunst* (Stuttgart: J. Hoffmann, 1927). See also Walter Curt Behrendt, *Der Sieg des neuen Baustils* (The Victory of the New Building Styles; Stuttgart: Fr. Wedekind, 1927); and Bruno Taut, *Die neue Baukunst in Europa und Amerika* (Stuttgart: J. Hoffmann, 1929), published simultaneously in English as *Modern Architecture.*

5. For an extensive discussion of Bauhaus curricula, see Frank Whitford, *Bauhaus* (London: Thames and Hudson, 1984).

6. Quoted in ibid., 180.

7. See Gropius, *Internationale Architektur,* 5–6. The new "international architecture" was the subject of the exhibition *Bauhaus Ausstellung,* August 15–September 30, 1923.

8. Hilberseimer, *Internationale neue Baukunst,* 5. Author's translation.

9. See Alois Riegl, *Stilfragen* (Berlin, 1893).

10. Behne, *Der moderne Zweckbau,* 11. Author's translation.

11. Ibid., 44. Author's translation.

12. Le Corbusier, *Vers une Architecture* (1923); published in English as *Towards a New Architecture,* trans. Frederick Etchells (1927; reprint, New York: Praeger, 1970).

13. Henry-Russell Hitchcock, *Modern Architecture: Romanticism and Reintegration* (New York: Payson and Clarke, 1929).

14. See Siegfried Giedion, *Space, Time, and Architecture: The Growth of a New Tradition,* 4th ed. (Cambridge, Mass.: Harvard University Press, 1962); and Nikolaus Pevsner, *Pioneers of Modern Design: From William Morris to Walter Gropius* (Baltimore: Penguin, 1972), originally published as *Pioneers of the Modern Movement from William Morris to Walter Gropius* (1936).

15. Kenneth Frampton, "Modernization and Mediation: Frank Lloyd Wright and the Impact of Technology," in Terence Riley with Peter Reed, eds., *Frank Lloyd Wright, Architect* (New York: The Museum of Modern Art, 1994), 67–69. For Semper and his influence in Chicago, see Rosemarie Haag Bletter, "Gottfried Semper," in Adolf K. Placzek, ed., *Macmillan Encyclopedia of Architects,* vol. 4 (New York: Macmillan, 1982), 25–33.

16. Quoted in Cervin Robinson and Rosemarie Haag, *Skyscraper Style: Art Deco New York* (New York: Oxford University Press, 1975), 60.

17. Jeffrey L. Meikle, *Twentieth Century Limited: Industrial Design in America, 1925–1939* (Philadelphia: Temple University Press, 1979), 7 ff., 68 ff.

18. Rosemarie Haag Bletter, "The World of Tomorrow: The Future with a Past," in Lisa Phillips et al., *High Styles: Twentieth-Century American Design* (New York: Summit Books in association with the Whitney Museum of American Art, 1985), 113 ff.

19. Richard Guy Wilson, "Architecture in the Machine Age," in Wilson, Dianne H. Pilgrim, and Dickran Tashjian, *The Machine Age in America, 1918–1941* (New York: Harry N. Abrams in association with The Brooklyn Museum, 1986), 153.

20. Richard Guy Wilson, "Machine Aesthetics," in ibid., 57–58. Wilson is quite correct, however, in finding erotic overtones in both streamlined and biomorphic forms.

LUCIC
Seeing Through Surfaces

1. One notable example of a pioneering exhibition featuring the work of an American designer is *Kem Weber: The Moderne in Southern California, 1920–1941,* with a catalogue by David Gebhard and Harriette von Breton (Santa Barbara: Standard Print for The Art Galleries, University of California, 1969). For exhibitions of the 1980s, see Karen Davies, *At Home in Manhattan: Modern Decorative Arts, 1925 to the Depression* (New Haven: Yale University Art Gallery, 1983); Robert Judson Clarke et al., *Design in America: The Cranbook Vision, 1925–1950* (New York: Harry N. Abrams in association with the Detroit Institute of Arts and The Metropolitan Museum of Art, 1983); Lisa Phillips et al., *High Styles: Twentieth Century American Design* (New York: Summit Books in association with the Whitney Museum of American Art, 1985); Richard Guy Wilson, Dianne H. Pilgrim, and Dickran Tashjian, *The Machine Age in America, 1918–1941* (New York: Harry N. Abrams in association with The Brooklyn Museum, 1986). In addition, a traveling exhibition surveyed the career of Russel Wright; see William J. Hennessey, *Russel Wright, American Designer* (Cambridge, Mass.: MIT Press, 1983).

2. See Karen Lucic, "Educating the Manufacturer: Advocates for Style Change in the 1920s," in Lisa W. Baldauf, ed., *Merchandising Interior Design: Methods of Furniture Fabrication in America Between the World Wars* (New Haven, Conn.: Yale University, School of Architecture, 1991), 48–62.

3. Gebhard and von Breton, *Kem Weber,* 37–40.

4. Jeffrey L. Meikle, "A Problem of Style: Craft in the Machine Age?," a lecture given as part of the symposium "Craft in the Machine Age: 1920–1945: European and American Modernism," American Craft Museum, New York, March 20, 1992.

5. The term "Art Deco," however, was never used. This appellation was not invented until the 1960s, when the interest in the style was revived. "Art Deco" derives from the title of the 1925 Paris exhibition, Exposition Internationale des Arts Décoratifs et Industriels Modernes

6. To an audience familiar with Reyner Banham and Robert Venturi's writings, it is probably unnecessary to point out that Bauhaus material of this period embodied its own rhetorical inconsistencies. Brandt's early works, although intended as prototypes for mass production, remained handmade, one-of-a-kind objects, and she, too, employed luxury materials such as silver and ebony.

7. Jules David Prown, "Mind in Matter: An Introduction to Material Culture Theory and Method," *Winterthur Portfolio* 17 (Spring 1982): 1–2.

8. In actual practice, the field of material culture study embraces a variety of methodologies. My point of departure is the method outlined by Prown in "Mind in Matter," although because of space constraints, the analysis that follows is less thorough and systematic than the procedures Prown advocates. See also Jules David Prown, "Style as Evidence," *Winterthur Portfolio* 15 (Autumn 1980): 197–210; Ian M. G. Quimby, ed., *Material Culture and the Study of American Life* (New York: W. W. Norton, 1978); Thomas J. Schlereth, ed. *Material Culture Studies in America* (Nashville: American Association for State and Local History, 1982); and Steven Lubar and W. David Kingery, eds., *History from Things: Essays on Material Culture* (Washington, D.C.: Smithsonian Institution Press, 1993).

9. Interestingly, Eleanor Roosevelt bought several of these punch bowls for entertaining when her husband was governor of New York; this represents a fascinating congruence of the family's attraction to the imagery of alcoholic revelry and the fact that Roosevelt repealed Prohibition shortly after he became president. See

Cowan Pottery Museum (Rocky River, Ohio: Rocky River Public Library, 1978), 14.

10. Garth Clark, *A Century of Ceramics in the United States, 1878–1978: A Study of Its Development* (New York: E. P. Dutton in association with the Everson Museum of Art, 1979), 325–26.

11. Compare Schreckengost's idiom with the glossy, streamlined objects that came to dominate 1930s design. This mode seems to have evolved at least in part from a collusion between designers and manufacturers, who offered the public a mythical resolution to the ills of the Depression through designs that suggested effortless forward motion into a better future; see Jeffrey L. Meikle, *Twentieth Century Limited: Industrial Design in America, 1925–1939* (Philadelphia: Temple University Press, 1979).

12. See "Russel Wright," Russel Wright archive, George Arents Research Library, Syracuse University, Syracuse, New York.

13. Blanche Naylor, "American Design Progress," *Design* 33 (September 1931): 88.

14. Paul T. Frankl, *New Dimensions: The Decorative Arts of Today in Words and Pictures* (New York: Brewer & Warren, 1928); *Form and Re-form: A Practical Handbook of Modern Interiors* (New York: Harper, 1930).

15. Frankl, *New Dimensions,* 56–57.

16. Quoted in Martin Greif, *Depression Modern: The Thirties Style in America* (New York: Universe Books, 1975), 43.

17. Richard F. Bach, "Museum Service to the Art Industries," in *Industrial Arts Monograph,* no. 3 (New York: The Metropolitan Museum of Art, 1927), 1.

18. Frank Lloyd Wright's seminal 1901 address, "The Art and Craft of the Machine," heralded this concern for machine production. For a later, and extremely cogent, call for reform, see Lewis Mumford, "The Economics of Contemporary Decoration," *Creative Art* 4 (January 1929): xix–xxii.

19. From "The Cranbrook Development," an address given by Eliel Saarinen at the American Institute of Architects' Convention, San Antonio, Texas, April 1931; quoted in Robert Judson Clarke, "Cranbrook and the Search for Twentieth-Century Form," in Clarke et al., *Design in America,* 30.

20. Although Grotell encouraged her students in their efforts to design for industry, she was never personally interested in such ventures; see Martin Eidelberg, "Ceramics," in ibid., 230.

21. Christa C. Mayer Thurman, "Textiles," in

ibid., 187–88; Eidelberg, "Ceramics," in ibid., 221–23.

22. See R. Craig Miller, "Interior Design and Furniture," in ibid., 124–25.

MANHART
Charting a New Educational Vision

1. Michael E. Taylor, "Glass Education in the USA," *Neue Glas/New Glass,* no. 4 (October–December 1988): 290.

2. Paul Heyer, *Architects on Architecture: New Directions in America* (1966; 2nd rev. ed., New York: Walker and Company, 1978), 202.

3. Robert Judson Clarke et al., *Design in America: The Cranbrook Vision, 1925–1950* (New York: Harry N. Abrams in association with the Detroit Institute of Arts and The Metropolitan Museum of Art, 1983), 173.

4. Elaine Levin, "Pioneers of Contemporary American Ceramics: Maija Grotell & Herbert Sanders," *Ceramics Monthly* 24 (November 1976): 49.

5. Clarke et al., *Design in America,* 15.

6. Ibid., 211.

7. Ibid., 196.

8. Ibid., 203.

9. Ibid.

10. Ibid., 167.

11. Susan J. Montgomery, "The Sound and the Surface: The Metalwork and Jewelry of Harry Bertoia," *Metalsmith* 7 (Summer 1987): 22–29.

12. Clarke et al., *Design in America,* 122.

13. Paul S. Donhauser, *History of American Ceramics: The Studio Potter* (Dubuque, Iowa: Kendall-Hunt Publishing 1978), 95.

14. Levin, "Pioneers of Contemporary American Ceramics: Maija Grotell & Herbert Sanders," 50.

15. Ibid.

16. Clarke et al., *Design in America,* 225.

17. Ibid., 94.

18. Ibid., 91.

19. M. C. Richards, "Black Mountain College: A Golden Seed," *Craft Horizons* 37 (June 1977): 22.

20. Jeanne Patricia Moynihan, "The Influence of the Bauhaus on Art and Art Education in the United States," Ph.D. dissertation,

Northwestern University, Evanston, Illinois, 1980, 207.

21. Josef Albers, "A Note on the Arts in Education," *American Magazine of Art* 29 (April 1936): 233.

22. Mary Emma Harris, *The Arts at Black Mountain College* (Cambridge, Mass.: MIT Press, 1987), 17.

23. Ibid., 20.

24. Ibid., 24.

25. Ibid., 86.

26. Ibid.

27. Josef Albers, *Search Versus Re-search* (Hartford, Conn.: Trinity Press, 1969), 13.

28. Karen Davies, *At Home in Manhattan: Modern Decorative Arts, 1925 to the Depression* (New Haven, Conn.: Yale University Art Gallery, 1983), 104.

29. See Arthur J. Pulos, *American Design Ethic* (Cambridge, Mass.: MIT Press, 1983), 396.

30. Ibid., 399–400.

31. Karl Ann Marling, "New Deal Ceramics: The Cleveland Workshop," *Ceramics Monthly* 25 (June 1977): 25.

32. *American Studio Ceramics 1920–1950* (Minneapolis: University of Minnesota Art Museum, 1988), 83.

33. James Stubblebine and Martin Eidelberg, "Viktor Schreckengost and the Cleveland School," *Craft Horizons* 35 (June 1975): 53.

34. Roland Crawford, "Master Metalsmith: John Paul Miller," *Metalsmith* 4 (Fall 1984): 23.

35. The Savage Studio was renamed the Harlem Community Art Center in 1934.

36. Romare Bearden and Harry Henderson, *A History of African-American Artists: From 1792 to the Present* (New York: Pantheon Books, 1993), 173.

37. The awarding of the commission to Johnson outraged Bufano, who believed that his own design should have won, and their friendship ended; ibid., 220.

38. Pulos, *American Design Ethic,* 400.

39. Bearden and Henderson, *A History of African-American Artists,* 400.

40. Davies, *At Home in Manhattan,* 28.

41. JoAnn C. Ellert, "The Bauhaus and Black Mountain College," *Journal of General Education* 24 (October 1972): 144.

42. See Hans M. Wingler, *The Bauhaus* (Cambridge, Mass.: MIT Press, 1969).

43. See Cheryl Kent, *Designing the Future* (Chicago: Illinois Institute of Technology, 1993).

44. Ibid., 34.

45. László Moholy-Nagy, *Vision in Motion* (Chicago: Paul Theobald, 1947), 66. Renamed the Institute of Design in 1944, the school merged with the Illinois Institute of Technology in 1949.

46. Mark Foley, Foreword to *Structure and Ornament: American Modernist Jewelry 1940–1960* (New York: Fifty-50, 1984), 2–3.

47. Donhauser, *History of American Ceramics,* 66.

48. Charles Fergus Binns, *The Potter's Craft* (1910; reprint, Princeton, N.J.: D. Van Nostrand Company, 1967); Bernard Leach, *A Potter's Book* (London: Faber and Faber, 1940).

49. Melvin H. Bernstein, *Art and Design at Alfred: A Chronicle of a Ceramics College* (Philadephia: Art Alliance Press, 1986), 114.

50. Elaine Levin, "Pioneers of Contemporary American Ceramics: Charles Binns, Adelaide Robineau," *Ceramics Monthly* 23 (November 1975): 26.

51. This was the first four-year collegiate course in glass technology; see Bernstein, *Art and Design at Alfred,* 104.

52. Ibid.

53. Ibid., 116.

54. Ibid., 99.

55. Ibid., 98.

56. Ibid., 126.

57. "Necrology: Arthur Eugene Baggs," *Bulletin of the American Ceramics Society* 26 (March 1947): 105–06.

58. Baggs was fascinated by the self-glazing properties of Egyptian paste and their adaptation to industrial purposes. He experimented with commercially available alkaline materials, developing a formula that allowed the soluble salts to rise from the clay body to the surface when dry; upon firing, the salts melted, producing a glaze.

59. Donhauser, *History of American Ceramics,* 70.

60. Ibid.

61. Ibid., 72.

62. Lukens's interest in Egyptian paste was its intense color. His ambition to duplicate this "Egyptian blue" led Lukens to experiment with natural material he dug from the dry lakebeds of Death Valley, a terrain similar to that of Egypt. There he discovered a copper-imbedded clay and alkaline substances that produced the desired color when fired at low temperatures—a new discovery for the studio potter.

63. "Commentary by Martha Longenecker," in *Laura Andreson: A Retrospective in Clay* (San Diego: Mingei International Museum of World Folk Art, 1982), 85.

64. F. Carlton Ball and Janice Lovoos, *Making Pottery Without a Wheel: Texture and Form in Clay* (New York: Reinhold, 1965).

65. Marguerite Wildenhain, *Pottery: Form and Expression* (New York: Reinhold, 1962).

CARMEL
Against the Grain

1. See Lloyd Goodrich, *The Decade of the Armory Show: New Directions in American Art, 1910–1920* (New York: Whitney Museum of American Art, 1963).

2. C. Ford Peatross, "Winold Reiss: A Pioneer of Modern Design," in *Cincinnati Union Terminal and the Artistry of Winold Reiss* (Cincinnati: Cincinnati Historical Society, 1993), 38–39.

3. Ibid., 56. This same bold use of color had astonished the French when the Munich Werkstätten exhibited eighteen rooms of German design in Paris in 1910.

4. Long interested in decorative geometric compositions, Wright produced designs after a European trip in 1910 that suggest his familiarity with new forms of abstract art. Geometric designs in primary colors for the windows of the Coonley Playhouse (1912) and the Midway Gardens murals (1914) are reminiscent of the paintings of František Kupka and Robert Delaunay, whose use of similar motifs antedate Wright's compositions. In addition, Wright's abstract figurative sculptures at Midway Gardens indicate his knowledge of the Cubists, whose work he encountered either in Paris, in art journals, or at the Chicago venue of the touring Armory Show in 1913.

5. Frank Lloyd Wright, *An Autobiography* (New York: Longmans Green, 1932), 217.

6. The shop was closed within the year at considerable financial loss to Urban. For an extensive discussion, see Randolph Carter and Robert Reed Cole, *Joseph Urban: Architecture, Theatre, Opera, Film* (New York: Abbeville Press, 1992).

7. Robert Judson Clarke et al, *Design in*

America: The Cranbrook Vision, 1925–1950 (New York: Harry N. Abrams, 1983), 303, fn. 22. Originally conceived to have ebony inlay in the grooves, W. & J. Sloane seemingly changed the design to black painted decoration without Saarinen's permission when the ebony inlays proved too expensive or difficult to produce.

8. Ibid, 303, fn. 17. Tor Berglund was employed to set up a woodworking studio at Cranbrook in 1929, primarily to fabricate the furniture specified by Eliel Saarinen for Kingswood and Saarinen House. The woodworking studio was intended to eventually become self-sufficient by generating its own lines, and by providing classes to the public. This plan failed because of the Depression, as the public was unable to purchase the expensive products made at Cranbrook. Berglund left Cranbrook in 1932.

9. Source of information from caption on photograph forwarded to the American Craft Museum from Cranbrook, 1994.

10. For further discussion of how Schoen combined German and French influences, see Alastair Duncan, American Art Deco (New York: Harry N. Abrams, 1986), 47; and Derek Ostergard, "The Sincerest Form of Flattery: American Response to European Design," in Lisa W. Baldauf, ed., Merchandising Interior Design: Methods of Furniture Fabrication in America Between the World Wars (New Haven, Conn.: Yale University, School of Architecture, 1991), 17.

11. This form was shown in the "International Exposition of Art in Industry" at R. H. Macy's, New York, in 1928, and illustrated in The Arts 13 (June 1928): 376 and Good Furniture Magazine 31 (September 1928): 129. As noted by Duncan, American Art Deco, 46.

12. "Restricting his work to the demands of those who must have unique pieces, necessarily eliminates him as a commercial factor and places him among the specialists." Nellie C. Sanford, "An Architect Designer of Modern Furniture," Good Furniture Magazine 30 (March 1928): 117.

13. David A. Hanks with Jennifer Toher, Donald Deskey: Decorative Designs and Interiors (New York: E. P. Dutton, 1987), 193.

14. Ibid., 39. Skyscraper furniture relied on the variable positioning of recesses, shelves, and moldings for its character, which also made it impractical to produce in multiples. The Skyscraper line was fabricated in a number of different shops, which accounts for the great disparity in quality and construction from piece to piece.

15. Paul T. Frankl, Machine-Made Leisure (New York: Harper & Brothers, 1932), 70.

16. Paul T. Frankl, New Dimensions: The Decorative Arts of Today in Words and Pictures (New York: Payson and Clarke Ltd., 1928), 28.

17. Edward Weeks, "Trophy Rooms," House Beautiful (November 1929): 580.

18. Hanks and Toher, Donald Deskey, 103.

19. Ibid.

20. "Perspectives," Pencil Points (July 1944): 63.

21. Much of the furniture from Casa Encantada was branded "T. H. Robsjohn-Gibbings for Peterson Studios." This table and others are branded "Sans Epoque," the name of Robsjohn-Gibbings's New York firm and showroom.

22. David Gebhard, "The Moderne, 1920–1941," in David Gebhard and Harriette von Breton, Kem Weber: The Moderne in Southern California 1920–1941 (Santa Barbara: Standard Print for The Art Galleries, University of California, 1969), 27.

23. Don Wallance, Shaping America's Products (New York: Reinhold, 1956), 108–09.

24. Ibid., 111.

25. Nina Stritzler, "Design Moves On: The Ascendancy of American Design in The Decade of Recovery," in Baldauf, ed., Merchandising Interior Design, 70–71.

26. Wallance, Shaping America's Products, 112–13.

27. Christopher Wilk, Marcel Breuer: Furniture and Interiors (New York: The Museum of Modern Art, 1981), 128–59. Breuer, famous for his tubular-steel furniture, was drawn to the potential of the new plywood products. During two years of refuge in England (1935–37), he designed a group of molded and bent-plywood furniture for Isokon Furniture Company (a division of Venesta Plywood Company) and also furnished a series of houses with furniture made of free-form shapes cut from plywood sheets.

28. Ibid., 156–57. Most of the Frank House furniture was fabricated by Schmieg & Kotzian, New York cabinetmakers, or by Harry Meyers Co., also of New York.

29. Ibid., 157. Ultimately, Breuer abandoned this type of furniture due to its static, box-like quality—for no matter how imaginative the shape of the cutout sides, the chairs all shared a stiff, two-dimensional character.

30. Kathryn B. Hiesinger and George H. Marcus, Landmarks of Twentieth-Century Design (New York: Abbeville Press, 1993), 143.

31. Bertrand Goldberg in telephone interview with the author, July 26, 1994.

32. Ibid.

33. David A. Hanks, The Decorative Designs of Frank Lloyd Wright (New York: E. P. Dutton, 1979), 152, 154.

34. Carla Lind, The Wright Style (New York: Simon & Schuster, 1992), 139.

35. August Sarnitz, R. M. Schindler, Architect (New York: Rizzoli, 1988), 14.

36. Ibid., 25.

37. David Gebhard in telephone interview with the author, July 13, 1994.

38. John Neuhart, Marilyn Neuhart, and Ray Eames, Eames Design: The Work of the Office of Charles and Ray Eames (New York: Harry N. Abrams, 1989), 25.

39. Christopher Wilk, "Furnishing the Future: Bentwood and Metal Furniture 1925–1946," in Bentwood and Metal Furniture: 1850–1946 (New York: The American Federation of Arts, 1987), 163–65.

40. Neuhart, Neuhart, and Eames, Eames Design, 27.

41. Ibid.

42. Ibid., 33. Increasingly large and complex wartime military projects were brought to the Eameses to develop in molded plywood—including airplane stabilizers, pilots' seats, and the nose sections of giant cargo gliders. Although few of these projects went into production, the precision required and the access to restricted materials provided the Eameses and their team with invaluable experience in molding plywood.

43. Ibid., 35. A line of children's furniture was developed that could use the wartime tooling. A trial run of 5,000 chairs and stools was put into production in 1946, but the lack of marketing mechanisms for children's furniture curtailed further production. A group of nesting and stacking animals conceived as children's furniture or toys also seemed an amusing possibility for fabrication. Birch prototypes of an elephant and horses were made and shown at prestigious exhibitions in 1945 and 1946, but the animals never went into production.

44. Ibid. Each was to be a reductive statement in wood and hardware. Related molded tables, prototype lounge, and easy chairs were fabricated and various types of wire-rod or four-ply wood legs were attached. The 1946 promotional showings at the Barclay Hotel, the Architectural League preview, and The Museum of

Modern Art successfully launched the Eameses' furniture designs into an eager postwar market—but The Museum of Modern Art's Eames exhibition proved to be both the apogee and the dead-end of interest in innovative wood furniture for mass production. Soon all the molding and sculptural ambitions were transferred to the new fiberglass and plastic materials.

45. For further discussion, see Harold E. Dickson and Richard Porter, *Henry Varnum Poor 1887–1970: A Retrospective Exhibition* (University Park, Penn.: Museum of Art, Pennsylvania State University, 1983).

46. According to stepdaughter Annie Poor, this table was made about 1933–35 (interview with the author, August 1994).

47. *The Furniture and Sculpture of Wharton Esherick* (New York: Museum of Contemporary Craft, 1958).

48. Ibid.

49. Michael Stone, "Wharton Esherick, Work of the Hand, the Heart and the Head," *Fine Wood Working* (November–December 1979): 52. Esherick was physically involved with every work produced in his studio, and generally signed and dated each piece. On the other hand, he rejected impractical notions about handcraft, and made use of any machinery he found necessary. Finding joinery and finishing wearisome, he assigned this work to his shop assistants (all professional cabinetmakers) so that he could concentrate on the shaping of his material.

50. Isamu Noguchi, *A Sculptor's World* (New York: Harper & Row, 1968), 26.

51. Ibid.

52. George Nakashima, "A Feeling for Material," *California Art & Architecture* (November 1941): 30–31.

53. Derek Ostergard, *George Nakashima: Full Circle* (New York: American Craft Museum, 1989), 50.

54. According to Ostergard, the date of 1945–46 is based on a Brogen family photograph of 1946 in which this table can be seen; ibid., 116.

55. This dramatic change of direction was seen in their installation "La Maison du Jeune Homme" at the 1935 International Exposition, Brussels.

56. Ostergard, *George Nakashima,* 38–40.

57. The metal decorations and the first of the spun-aluminum accessories were retailed first at the Rena Rosenthal shop on Fifth Avenue.

58. This chair was also used at the time to furnish the Museum's Members and Board of Directors rooms. Though handmade, it was the only chair designed by an American to be included in the industrial design section of The Museum of Modern Art's Tenth Anniversary exhibition "Art in Our Time," on view during the time of the New York World's Fair in 1939.

59. "Eavesdropping on Russel Wright," *Craft Horizons* 2 (November 1943): 6.

60. Ann Kerr, *The Collector's Encyclopedia of Russel Wright Designs* (Paducah, Ky.: Collector Books, 1990), 70.

61. In 1937, on the recommendation of Gropius, The Association of Arts and Industries in Chicago offered the directorship of its newly formed design school to Moholy-Nagy. The school was to embody the principles and traditions of the first Bauhaus—an integration of art, craft, and technology. Moholy-Nagy transferred much of the playful and experimental Bauhaus program to the United States, and was instrumental in shaping a generation of American artists and industrial designers sensitive to matters of form and trained to understand the technical requirements of industry.

62. Rosamund Frost, "Form and Function = a U.S. Bauhaus," *Art News* 64 (August 1945): 23. The object was then studied in terms of its feasibility for mass production, especially the much neglected sense of touch. In turn the form was photographed, the camera revealing further aspects about the object in terms of light and shadow; and finally, the student prepared a meticulous rendering of the object.

63. David A. Hanks, biography of James Prestini, in Martin Eidelberg, ed., *Design 1935–1965: What Modern Was, Selections from the Liliane and David M. Stewart Collection*, (New York: Harry N. Abrams, 1991), 393.

64. Edgar Kaufmann, Jr., *Prestini's Art in Wood* (New York: The Pocahontas Press, 1950).

KINGSLEY
The Making of Modern Art Glass

1. I am grateful to William Warmus for this and other informative material provided in the early stages of preparing for the exhibition.

2. Robert Koch, *Louis C. Tiffany, Rebel in Glass* (New York: Crown Publishers, 1978), 153.

3. Laurelton Hall was destroyed by fire in 1957. The Foundation now restricts itself to giving grants to deserving younger artists.

4. Paul V. Gardner, *Frederick Carder: Portrait of a Glassmaker* (Corning, N.Y.: The Corning Museum of Glass; Rockwell Museum, 1985). Gardner was Carder's assistant for ten years.

5. Gardner quotes Carder as boasting that he "bought the materials, built the furnace, and retired 40 percent of the $50,000 indebtedness in the first year of operation" (ibid., 22).

6. Tiffany's legal challenge to Carder's approximation of his own golden Favrile glass collapsed when it was learned that its chemical make-up differed greatly from his own.

7. Carder's sources ranged from ancient Egyptian and Roman glass, through the Renaissance, to modern French, Scandinavian, English, and Italian glass. He even drew on eighteenth-century American lily-pad and threaded glass for his Colonial Revival glassware designs of the 1920s.

8. Casing is a process whereby two or more layers of glass are formed one inside the other. Often, though not in this case, the outer layer is cut away to reveal the color or colors beneath it.

9. Robert J. Charleston, *Masterpieces of Glass: A World History from The Corning Museum of Glass* (New York: Harry N. Abrams, 1980), 211.

10. Paul Hollister, "Frederick Carder and Sculpted Glass," in *Brilliance in Glass: The Lost Wax Sculpture of Frederick Carder* (Corning, N.Y.: Rockwell Museum, 1993), 5.

11. Apparently, the destruction was not extensive. Examples of each line were preserved, and later entered the Corning Museum of Glass in Corning, New York.

12. Gardner, *Frederick Carder,* 34.

13. Hollister, "Frederick Carder and Sculpted Glass," in *Brilliance in Glass,* 8.

14. Ibid, 6–8.

15. Paul Hollister, "USA Studio Glass Before 1962. Maurice Heaton, Frances and Michael Higgins, Edris Eckhardt: Four Pioneers and True Originals," *Neue Glas/New Glass* 4 (October 1985): 232–40. The well-known ceramist Edris Eckhardt, whose astonishingly inventive cast-glass sculptures, laminations, and fusions with materials such as gold and bronze lie outside of our period, also belongs in this group. She began researching her own colored glass formulas and melting the glass in her kitchen in 1952.

16. Karen Davies, "Maurice Heaton: American Pioneer in Studio Glass," *American Craft* 44 (August–September 1984): 52.

17. Hollister, "USA Studio Glass Before 1962": 232–34.

18. Eleanor Bittermann, "Heaton's Wizardry

with Glass," *Craft Horizons* 14 (May–June 1954): 10–14.

19. Ibid., 11.

20. Maurice Heaton, "Who Is the Craftsman?," *Art Education Today,* annual publication of Teachers College, Columbia University (1938): 1–7.

21. Joseph Kaye, "A Look at New York: Vanished Mural Adds a Poignant Mystery to Memory of the Missing Amelia Earhart," *The Kansas City Star,* July 2, 1961, sec. A: 13. Artist's file, American Craft Council Library, New York.

22. Crystal, "Jewels Imprisoned in Potter's Clay," *China and Glass* 65 (November 1945): 20.

23. The use of uranium was common in glass factories. Its studio use is what is remarkable. Gregory even built a cyclotron in 1932 at the University of California to try to split atoms, but only succeeded in chipping particles off the nucleus; ibid.: 10.

24. In 1990, when they were made fellows of the American Craft Council (ACC) at an awards dinner in Atlanta, the Higginses prepared a two-page joint résumé with a one-page handwritten narrative of their life together, which is the source for this information. It is on file in the ACC library.

25. Hollister, "USA Studio Glass Before 1962": 235.

26. Paul Perrot, "New Directions in Glassmaking," *Craft Horizons* 20 (November–December 1960): 24.

27. Ibid.

28. See Joan Falconer Byrd, "Harvey Littleton and Studio Glass," in *Harvey K. Littleton: A Retrospective Exhibition* (Atlanta: High Museum of Art, 1984), 5.

29. Littleton, in letter to Michael Higgins, May 11, 1959; quoted in Susanne K. Krantz, *Contemporary Glass* (New York: Harry N. Abrams, 1989), 46.

30. In 1945 the President of the British Board of Trade, Hugh Dalton, told a meeting of British glassmakers that, "Something like an industrial revolution has taken place in the United States in the last 15 years—a revolution of industrial design. It has made many of our exports old-fashioned and less acceptable." Dalton was talking about Steuben for the most part, but Libbey and some of the smaller glassworks were also part of this development. See "A Review of Varying Glass Techniques," *Craft Horizons* 4 (May 1945): 9.

31. Mary Jean Smith Madigan, *Steuben Glass: An American Tradition in Crystal* (New York: Harry N. Abrams, 1982), 70.

32. Walter Dorwin Teague, Sr., in memorandum to Arthur Amory Houghton, Jr., October 7, 1932; quoted in ibid.

33. Ibid., 73–75.

34. Ibid., 75.

35. Ibid., 76.

36. Ibid.

37. Ibid., 81.

38. Ibid., 91.

39. Ibid., 88–89.

40. Ibid., 84.

41. See John Webster Keefe, *Libbey Glass: A Tradition of 150 Years, 1818–1968* (Toledo: The Toledo Museum of Art, 1968).

42. Carl U. Fauster, *Libbey Glass Since 1818: Pictorial History & Collector's Guide* (Toledo: Len Beach Press, 1979), 97–99. As happened during World War I, production of lead crystal was halted by the government, which needed the lead for bullets and other purposes.

43. Hazel M. Weatherman, *Fostoria: Its First Fifty Years* (Springfield, Mo.: The Weathermans, 1972), 85.

44. Ibid., 223.

45. Jack D. Wilson, *Phoenix & Consolidated Art Glass, 1926–1980* (Marietta, Ohio: Antique Publications, 1989), 15.

46. Ibid., 40.

47. Christa C. Mayer Thurman, "Textiles," in Robert Judson Clarke et al., *Design in America: The Cranbrook Vision, 1925–1950* (New York: Harry N. Abrams in association with the Detroit Institute of Arts and The Metropolitan Museum of Art, 1983), 189.

48. Alastair Duncan, *Art Deco* (New York: Thames and Hudson, 1988), 69.

49. Ibid.

PERRY
Modernism and American Ceramics

1. Marlene S. Hamann, *The Ceramic Sculptures of Viktor Schreckengost,* Master's thesis, Syracuse University, Syracuse, New York, 1993, 21.

2. The Cleveland School was first recognized by James Stubblebine and Martin Eidelberg in "Viktor Schreckengost and the Cleveland School," *Craft Horizons* (June 1975), 52.

3. For a study of American clay sculpture during this period, particularly that of the Cleveland school, see Ross Anderson and Barbara Perry, *The Diversions of Keramos: American Clay Sculpture 1925–1950* (Syracuse: Everson Museum of Art, 1983).

4. The "International Exhibition of Ceramic Art," organized by the American Federation of Arts, traveled throughout the United States in 1928–29. It was shown at the Cleveland Museum of Art February 21–March 21, 1929.

5. Viktor Schreckengost, telephone conversation with the author, Summer 1983.

6. Vally Wieselthier, "Ceramics," *Design* 31 (November 1929): 101–02.

7. Quoted in *Time,* May 13, 1935: 34.

8. Quoted in Ernest W. Watson, "The Ceramic Sculpture of Thelma Frazier Winter," *American Artist* 16 (May 1958): 23.

9. That Olmstead undertook this monumental project in the midst of the Depression is an indication of the strength and determination of this remarkable woman. The exhibitions were a grand success and continue, with brief respites during the war and during the 1970s, to this day.

10. Quoted in Hans M. Wingler, *The Bauhaus* (Cambridge, Mass., and London: MIT Press, 1986), 31.

11. Frank Whitford, *Bauhaus* (London: Thames and Hudson, 1984), 73.

12. Wingler, *The Bauhaus,* 323–24.

13. Whitford, *Bauhaus,* 73.

14. Quoted in Paul Heyer, *Architects on Architecture: New Directions in America* (1966; reprint New York: Walker and Company, 1978), 202.

SCHOESER
Textiles

1. Norma K. Stahle, "Applied Arts Exhibition Cheers the Soul of Industry," *Arts & Decoration* 16 (November 1921): 33, 47.

2. "Art Moderne Rugs to the Fore: Hooked, Hand-Tufted and Machine Loomed," *Good Furniture Magazine* 31 (September 1928): 141–43. Wolfgang was the son of Josef Hoffmann.

3. See Werner J. Schweiger, *Wiener Werkstätte: Design in Vienna, 1903–1932* (New York: Abbeville Press, 1984); and Vally Wieselthier, "Modern Fabric Designing," *Design* 31 (January 1930): 145–47.

4. See *American Magazine of Art* 11 (1919–20) and 14 (1923) for articles by Bach, Associate Curator in Industrial Arts at The Metropolitan Museum of Art,

advocating the use of the museum's collection by designers; and R. Craig Miller, *Modern Design 1890–1900 in The Metropolitan Museum of Art* (New York: Harry N. Abrams in association with The Metropolitan Museum of Art, 1990), 8–32.

5. M. D. C. Crawford, *The Heritage of Cotton,* 2nd ed. (New York: Fairchild Publishing Company, 1948), 199.

6. M. D. C. Crawford, "Modern Silks: The First International Silk Exposition at the Grand Central Palace," *Arts & Decoration* 14 (February 1921): 279. For examples of designs by other entrants in the competition, see *Women's Wear* 13 (December 21, 1916): 1; and *Women's Wear* 18 (January 7, 1919): 202–03.

7. Christa C. Mayer Thurman, "Textiles," in Robert Judson Clarke et al., *Design in America: The Cranbrook Vision, 1925–1950* (New York: Harry N. Abrams in association with the Detroit Institute of Arts and The Metropolitan Museum of Art, 1983), 173.

8. Ethel Lewis, *The Romance of Textiles: The Story of Design in Weaving* (New York: Macmillan, 1937), 322.

9. Alice Maria Zrebiec, "American Tapestry Workshops," in Joan West, ed., *From American Looms* (Trenton: New Jersey State Museum, 1985), 13.

10. See *Decorative Metalwork and Cotton Textiles,* catalogue of the Third International Exhibition of Contemporary Industrial Arts (Portland, Me.: Southworth Press for the American Federation of Arts, 1930), n. 773, for an illustration of such a design by Dorothy Bird Trout, handprinted by the Lehman-Connor Company, New York.

11. Rosemary Ketcham, "Our Changing Point of View," *Design* 35 (April 1934): 16. See also "Printed Cottons with American Subjects," *The Bulletin of the Minneapolis Institute of Arts* 29 (February 17, 1940): 33–35.

12. For example, Gustav Stickley's "Craftsman Canvas" and other linen-and-jute fabrics were manufactured by Donald Brothers of Dundee, Scotland.

13. Crawford, "Modern Silks": 278.

14. M. D. C. Crawford, editorial, *Women's Wear* 18 (January 8, 1919): 1.

15. C. Adolph Glassgold, "The Modern Note in Decorative Arts," *The Arts* 13 (March–April 1928): 235. For comments on the influence of the Swedish contemporary decorative arts exhibition at The Metropolitan Museum of Art, New York, in January and February 1927, see 227.

16. Ibid., 227–28.

17. Glassgold, "The Modern Note in Decorative Arts": 232–33. For embroideries by Karasz, see Karen Davies, *At Home in Manhattan: Modern Decorative Arts, 1925 to the Depression* (New Haven, Conn.: Yale University Art Gallery, 1983), 42.

18. Nicola J. Shilliam, *Early Modern Textiles* (Boston: Museum of Fine Arts, 1993), 33. The term "needlepainting" was coined before 1938 by Georgina Brown Harbeson, herself an embroiderer and author; see Harbeson, *American Needlework: The History of Decorative Stitchery and Embroidery from the Late 16th to the 20th Century* (New York: Bonanza Books, 1938), 184.

19. Whitney Blausen, "Textiles Designed by Ruth Reeves," Master's thesis, State University of New York, Fashion Institute of Technology, New York, 1992. See "Mr. Crawford and Mr. Culin," 10–34; and "The Index of American Design," 79–92.

20. *Arts & Crafts in Detroit* (Detroit: Detroit Institute of Arts, 1976), 105.

21. *The American Silk Journal* 42 (December 1923): 65.

22. Herbert J. Spinder, *Exhibition of Industrial Art and Costumes* (New York: American Museum of Natural History, 1919), n.p. Spinder notes that "American goods are now selling in the discriminating markets of Paris and London."

23. "Modernistic Wall Hangings," *Good Furniture Magazine* 31 (August 1928): 108.

24. Marguerite Zorach, "Embroidery as Art," *Art in America* 44 (Fall 1946): 48; cited in Shilliam, *Early Modern Textiles,* 33. Zorach also states, "Yet were I not a painter my embroideries would never be what they are or have the stature they possess."

25. Marcel Valotaire, "New Textiles from France," *Creative Art* 3 (December 1928): 385.

26. Zrebiec, "American Tapestry Workshops," in West, ed., *From American Looms,* 13. Edgewater Tapestry Looms was later reconstituted in California, but it never regained its former prominence.

27. These were shown at the Bignou Gallery, New York, in 1936, as part of an international tour; see Martin Eidelberg, ed., *Design 1935–1965: What Modern Was. Selections from the Lillian and David M. Stewart Collection* (New York: Harry N. Abrams in association with the Musée des Arts Décoratifs de Montréal, 1991), 231.

28. Dorothy Wright Liebes, "Modern Textiles," in Liebes et al., *Decorative Arts,* official catalogue of the Golden Gate International Exposition (San Francisco: San Francisco Bay Exposition Company, 1939), 92.

29. "Art Moderne Rugs to the Fore: Hooked, Hand-Tufted and Machine-Loomed": 143. This, the following reference, and n. 34 courtesy of Sarah B. Sherrill, author of *Carpets and Rugs of Europe and America* (New York: Abbeville Press, forthcoming).

30. *Good Furniture Magazine* 30 (May 1928): 246.

31. Glassgold, "The Modern Note in Decorative Arts," *The Arts* 13 (1928): 235. In *Decorative Art 1929* (London: The Studio Yearbook, 1929), the same Biddle and Benton rugs are illustrated with the caption ". . . produced by CONTEMPORARY AMERICAN ARTISTS HAND-HOOKED RUGS, under the direction of Ralph H. Pearson . . . New York" (186–87). Henry Varnum Poor and Pola Hoffmann also designed rugs for the New Age Group.

32. *Good Furniture and Decoration* 35 (April 1930): 217–18.

33. "American Rugs for the Modern Age," *Creative Art* 6 (July 1931): 51, citing the recently formed Connecticut Handicraft Industry, founded by Mrs. Carleton H. Palmer and employing designs by the architect Theodore Muller.

34. *Rugs from the Crawford Shops Designed by American Artists* (New York: The Museum of Modern Art, 1937), n.p.

35. "American Rugs for the Modern Age": n. 34.

36. In rugmaking this impetus resulted in the introduction of the hand-guided but electrically powered tufting gun, used by V'Soske to make the rugs shown in the exhibition *"New Rugs by American Artists,"* The Museum of Modern Art, New York, June 30–August 9, 1942.

37. Florence Davies, "The Weavings of Loja Saarinen," *The Weaver* 2 (January 1937): 15.

38. See Thurman, "Textiles," in Clarke et al., *Design in America,* 173.

39. See *The Woven and Graphic Art of Anni Albers* (Washington, D.C.: Smithsonian Institution Press, 1985); Mary Emma Harris, *The Arts at Black Mountain College* (Cambridge, Mass.: MIT Press, 1987); and Mervin Lane, ed., *Black Mountain College* (Knoxville: University of Tennessee Press, 1990).

40. See Sigrid Wortmann Weltge, *The Bauhaus Weaving Workshop: Textile Art from the Bauhaus* (San Francisco: Chronicle Books, 1993). The Chicago School of Design was renamed the Institute of Design in 1944.

41. Marianne Strengell, "Texture, Color, and

Quality," *California Arts & Architecture* 59 (November 1942): 32–33.

42. *Creative Crafts* 2 (November–December 1961): 7.

43. Mary Schoeser and Kathleen Dejardin, *French Textiles from 1970 to the Present* (London: Lawrence King, 1991), 174–82.

44. See Paul T. Frankl, *New Dimensions: The Decorative Arts of Today in Words and Pictures* (New York: Payson and Clarke, Ltd., 1928), 78–79; "Historical and Modern Design for Fabric," *Good Furnishing* 30 (April 1928): 189; and "Mallinson-Rodier Alliance," *American Silk Journal* 43 (August 1924): 51.

45. *Fine Arts* (May 1932): 36.

46. Helen G. Thompson, "With Notebook and Pencil: A Forecast of Fall Decorating Trends," *Arts & Decoration* 34 (August 1933): 7.

47. Sarah M. Lockwood, *Decoration: Past, Present and Future* (New York: Doubleday, Doran & Co., 1934), 183.

48. "Custom-Made," *Creative Design* 1 (Winter 1934–35): 27. Many of the imported weaves referred to would have been from Great Britain, where handspinners such as Ethel Mairet had already influenced commercial spinners and weavers, including Edinburgh Weavers and Warner & Sons Ltd., both of which developed textural weaves in collaboration with Marion Dorn. See Mary Schoeser and Celia Rufey, *English and American Textiles from 1790 to the Present* (London: Thames and Hudson, 1989), 176–77 and *passim*.

49. All quotations in this paragraph, Ely Jacques Kahn, "Notes by the Chairman of the West Gallery Unit," *Bulletin of the Metropolitan Museum of Art* 29 (December 1934): 204–05.

50. Mary M. Atwater, "Some Ancient Peruvian Textiles," *The Weaver* 1 (March 1936): 26.

51. Raoul d'Harcourt, *Textiles of Ancient Peru and Their Techniques* (originally published as *Les Textiles anciens du Pérou et leurs techniques,* Paris, 1934), 4th ed., trans. Sadie Brown (Seattle: University of Washington Press, 1987).

52. Sara Sturgeon Small, "Choosing Your Spring Upholstery," *Arts & Decoration* 51 (April 1940): 40.

53. Mary Elizabeth Starr, "The Magic of Good Design," *The Weaver* 5 (July–August 1939): 3–5.

54. "Fabrics Woven with Imagination," *Arts & Decoration* 52 (August 1940): 38–39, illustrating, among others, weaves by Marianne Strengell, Haeckel Weaves, and Lili Berndt for Berndt & Schacht Handweaves.

55. Ed Rossbach, "Fiber in the Forties," *American Craft* 42 (October–November 1982): 17.

56. Anni Albers, "Handweaving Today," *The Weaver* 6 (January–February 1941): 3–7.

57. Mary M. Atwater, "It's Pretty—But Is It Art?," *The Weaver* 6 (July–August 1941): 13–14, 26.

58. Ibid.

59. Ed Rossbach, "Marianne Strengell," *The Weaver* 44 (April–May 1984): 11.

60. Thurman, "Textiles," in Clarke et al., *Design in America,* 197–203.

61. Marianne Strengell and Robert Sailors in conversation with the author, April 17, 1994, and April 24, 1994, respectively.

62. "The Milwaukee Project," *Design* 45 (January 1944): 7. The entire issue is devoted to this project.

63. "Weaving," *Design* 45 (January 1944): 7, 20. This and other information courtesy of Mrs. Elizabeth O'Sullivan.

64. For a contemporary description of the technique in an "industrial context," see A. H. Grimshaw and G. W. Searell, "Ornamentation by Means of Screen Printing," *The Melliand* 1 (January 1930): 1541–46.

65. Harry V. Anderson, "Ruth Reeves," *Design* 37 (March 1936): 25. Much of the publicity, including W. & J. Sloane's own, refers to all of Reeves's work as blockprints, a misnomer caused by the transitional term "screen block" (used in the article cited) and analogous to the continued use of "engraving" to refer to the process of putting the design on the screen.

66. Ethel Lewis, *The Romance of Textiles,* 322. Francis V. O'Conner, ed., *The New Deal Art Projects: An Anthology of Memoirs* (Washington, D.C.: Smithsonian Institution Press, 1972), also credits Dorothy Liebes with an involvement in the creation of the Index; see 257.

67. Eidelberg, ed., *Design 1935–1965,* 382.

68. "Fabrics from the New Spring Lines," *Interiors* 102 (February 1943): 45.

69. [Elinor Hillyer], "Backgrounds: A Study of the Determining Factors in Fall Decorating," *Arts & Decoration* 41 (August 1934): 29. Hillyer adds, "This is the first season I have heard it spoken of by a large number of people without an overtone of disrespect."

70. Angelo Testa, "Design vs. Monkey Business," *Interiors* 107 (February 1948): 82–84. Testa also attacks the "museum to consumer" design movement of the prewar years.

71. Maria Steinhoff, "The Creation of Smart Fabrics," *The Weaver* 1 (January 1936): 3.

72. Paul T. Frankl, *Space for Living: Creative Interior Decoration and Design* (New York: Doubleday, Doran, 1938), 22.

STERN
Striking the Modern Note in Metal

1. The Wiener Werkstätte arrived prematurely. It failed to find a sufficient market, and the showroom closed within two years.

2. For example, see "Art: Exhibitions of the Week. New Designs in Jensen Silver," *New York Times,* November 9, 1924, Sec. 8: 13. Illustrations of Jensen tableware proliferated in articles on silverware in 1920s periodicals.

3. Read was attached to the American Commission appointed by Secretary of Commerce Herbert Hoover to report on the Exposition. The first article in her series on the Exposition appeared in the *Brooklyn Daily Eagle* on August 16, 1925.

4. Gay Zimmermann, comp., "Metal Works by Marie Zimmermann," unpublished catalogue of an exhibition at the Colby College Museum of Art, Waterville, Maine, 1982. See also Joan Bamberger, " 'Nature in Her More Joyous Moods . . .' Metalsmith Marie Zimmermann," *American Craft* 53 (April–May 1993): 46–49.

5. Matlack Price, "Industrial Art and the Craftsman: Who Are Our Designers?," *Arts & Decoration* 16 (January 1922): 185–87; Mary Fanton Roberts, "Art," *Vogue* 59 (April 1922): 64, 78; Hanna Tachau, "On the Decorative Arts," *International Studio* 74 (January 1922): ccxxvii–ccxxviii; and Giles Edgeton, "An American Worker in the Crafts," *House & Garden* 41 (February 1922): 28–29, 78.

6. W. Scott Braznell, Marie Zimmermann entry in Wendy Kaplan, ed., *The Art That Is Life: The Arts & Crafts Movement in America, 1875–1920* (Boston: Museum of Fine Arts, 1987), 271.

7. See "Jewelry and Metal Art Objects," in *Index of Exhibits: 50th Annual Exhibition of Architectural League of New York Exhibition with American Institute of Decorators* (1936).

8. The definitive scholarship on Bowles was published in 1993 in conjunction with a retrospective exhibition mounted by the Indianapolis Museum of Art; see Barry Shifman, W. Scott Braznell, and Sharon S. Darling, *The Arts & Crafts Metalwork of Janet Payne Bowles* (Indianapolis: Indianapolis Museum of Art, 1993).

9. See Barry Shifman, "Janet Payne Bowles and the Arts & Crafts Movement in Indianapolis," in ibid., 12, 14.

10. Rena Tucker Kohlman, "Her Metalcraft Spiritual," *International Studio* 80 (October 1924): 54–55.

11. W. Scott Braznell, "The Metalcraft and Jewelry of Janet Payne Bowles," in *The Arts and Crafts Metalwork of Janet Payne Bowles,* 64.

12. The jewel casket was conceived as a communion piece to hold the wafers. A pair of candlesticks to make an ensemble with it was designed by Oakes and completed in 1952 by his son Gilbert B. Oakes. See G.H.C., "Silver and Precious Stones Make an Exquisite Jewel Casket," *Boston Evening Transcript,* October 16, 1929: 7; see also *Arts and Crafts in Detroit 1906–1976: The Movement, the Society, the School* (Detroit: The Detroit Institute of Arts, 1976), cat. no. 88.
   The Oakes Studio continues to this day in Franconia, New Hampshire, under the direction of Susan Oakes Peabody and Jon R. Peabody.

13. *Triennial Exhibition in Celebration of the Thirtieth Anniversary of the Society of Arts and Crafts, Boston* (Boston: Museum of Fine Arts, 1927), 6.

14. David Wolper, in telephone interview with the author, December 11, 1991.

15. "Little Museum of Rare Treasures Is Integral Part of Mr. and Mrs. William Brigham's Home," *Evening Bulletin, Providence,* February 14, 1935: W1; and "Mrs. Clara Brigham, 75, Dies; Art, Social and Club Leader," *Providence Journal,* October 21, 1954: n.p. (clipping, courtesy of Providence Public Library).

16. Garrett D. Byrnes, "Brigham Creates Individual Designs," *Evening Bulletin, Providence,* November 13, 1930: 4.

17. "The candlesticks originally had prickets and were altered by Brigham to have standard cylindrical candle sockets (which screw in) sometime before his 1963 bequest to the Museum" (Jayne E. Stokes, Assistant Curator of Decorative Arts, Museum of Art, Rhode Island School of Design, letter to the author, April 4, 1994). A pricket is the spike on which a candle is stuck.

18. Leslie Greene Bowman, "Arts and Crafts Silversmiths: Friedell and Blanchard in Southern California," in *Silver in the Golden State* (Oakland: Oakland Museum History Department, 1986), 52.

19. Ibid. for all descriptions of technique.

20. David Gebhard and Harriette von Breton, *Kem Weber: The Moderne in Southern California, 1920–1941* (Santa Barbara: Standard Print for The Art Galleries, University of California, 1969), 40, 64.

21. Helen Johnson Keyes, "Contemporary American Silver," *Christian Science Monitor,* May 1, 1937, sec. 5: 6.

22. Sharon S. Darling, *Chicago Metalsmiths* (Chicago: Chicago Historical Society, 1977), 91. See also the biographical questionnaire, John Pontus Petterson file, Chicago Historical Society.

23. Stephen N. Dennis, "Arts and Crafts Silver for the Historic House," *Historic Houses* 4 (February 1982): 6.

24. Stephen C. Worsley, "William Waldo Dodge, Jr., Silversmith," *Carolina Comments* 37 (September 1989): 148.

25. Dodge patented a distinctive hammered "waterfall" finish; ibid.: 152.

26. Surprisingly, Dodge was not recognized in contemporary exhibitions of the period, perhaps because he was not affiliated with an Arts and Crafts society, or other groups such as the Society of Designer-Craftsmen. He was an active member of the American Institute of Architects.

27. Charles H. Carpenter, Jr., *Gorham Silver, 1831–1981* (New York: Dodd, Mead & Co., 1982), 256–58.

28. Quoted in "Modern Silver Design: Erik Magnussen Leads a Trend Toward Plainer Patterns," *Good Furniture Magazine* 26 (June 1926): 291. See also "The Modern American," Gorham Company advertisement, *Jewelers' Circular* 96 (July 5, 1928): 2–3.

29. Peter Mueller-Munk résumé, c. 1934–35, and "Faculty Biography," Carnegie Institute of Technology, 1941. University Archives, Hunt Library, Carnegie Mellon University, Pittsburgh. See also Karen Davies, *At Home in Manhattan: Modern Decorative Arts, 1925 to the Depression* (New Haven, Conn.: Yale University Art Gallery, 1983), 33; and W. Scott Braznell, "The Advent of Modern American Silver," *Antiques* 125 (January 1984): 236–38.

30. Helen Appleton Read, "Twentieth-Century Decoration: The Modern Theme Finds a Distinctive Medium in American Silver," *Vogue* 72 (July 1, 1928): 58; Burton Stillman, "The Modern Spirit in Silver," *Spur* 42 (September 15, 1928): 98; and C. Adolph Glassgold, "The Modern Note in Decorative Arts," *The Arts* 13 (April 1928): 22. Mueller-Munk showed a group of silver holloware in R. H. Macy's "International Exposition of Art in Industry" in 1928.

31. A candelabra was illustrated in Peter Mueller-Munk, "Machine—Hand," *Studio* 98 (October 1929): 712. The pair was exhibited in the American Federation of Arts traveling exhibition of 1930–31, "Decorative Metalwork and Cotton Textiles."

32. Peter Mueller-Munk, "Handwrought Silver," *Charm* 9 (April 1928): 38–39, 81, 82.

33. Mueller-Munk, "Machine—Hand": 709–11.

34. "Original Design in Silver," *Arts & Decoration* 42 (April 1935): 28–29.

35. All biographical information from Marion Anderson Noyes, Key West, Florida, in telephone interview with the author, December 18, 1991.

36. Marion Anderson Noyes, letter to the author, [1991].

37. After World War II, Noyes was a freelance consultant to Towle Silversmiths. She gave a collection of her pewter, silver, and drawings to The Brooklyn Museum in 1991–92; other objects were given by the artist to the Historical Society of Old Newbury, Massachusetts.

38. See David L. Barquist, *American Tables and Looking Glasses* (New Haven, Conn.: Yale University Art Gallery, 1992), 351–53. The hemispheric form occurred frequently in silver services manufactured in the 1930s.

39. Parzinger's designs were fabricated in silverplate as well as sterling silver. Some pieces had enamelwork decoration attributed to William Stark; see *Contemporary American Industrial Art: 15th Exhibition* (New York: The Metropolitan Museum of Art, 1940), 13.

40. "Tradition in Contemporary Design," *Connoisseur* 104 (October 1939): 203–04.

41. "Modern Silver Achieved by Old World Technique," *The Jewelers' Circular–Keystone* 107 (February 1937): 77, 84–85.

42. See notes on Smed sterling flatware (1971.230.1–.114), departmental file cards, Twentieth Century American Art, The Metropolitan Museum of Art, New York.

43. De Matteo water pitcher in the collection of The Newark Museum (90.215).

44. Also of note was the metals program at Washington University in St. Louis, which nourished, among others, Maria Regnier, who matured after World War II.

45. See Robert Judson Clarke et al., *Design in America: The Cranbrook Vision, 1925–1950* (New York: Harry N. Abrams, 1983), 150–53.

46. Kirk taught at Wayne University and fulfilled commissions, many ecclesiastic, but his capacity was severely limited after 1939 by illness; ibid., 153, 270.

47. See Eidelberg, ed., *Design 1935–1965,* 363; and Clarke et al., *Design in America,* 268.

48. For more on the use of Lucite, see "A La Glassic," *Interior Decorator* 99 (April 1940): 26, 40; and Rosemarie Haag Bletter, "The World of Tomorrow: The Future with a Past," in Lisa Phillips et al.,

High Styles: Twentieth Century American Design (New York: Whitney Museum of American Art, 1985), 105–07. Plastics, especially colored Bakelite and Catalin, had been used by silver manufacturers for accents on sterling and silverplate holloware since 1927–28.

49. See Derek Ostergard, *Art Deco Masterpieces* (New York: Hugh Lauter Levin Associates, 1991), 32.

50. See Françoise de Bonneville, *Jean Puiforcat* (Paris: Éditions du Regard, 1986), 126.

51. Dannie A. Woodard and Billie J. Wood, *Hammered Aluminum Hand Wrought Collectibles* (Wolfe City, Tex.: Henington Publishing Company, 1983), 42; and A. D. LeMonte, "Business Built on Aluminum Art Work," *Youngstown Vindicator*, n.d.: n.p. (clipping, courtesy of Dr. Thomas Armour).

52. Soon afterward, Alcoa began manufacturing a line of aluminum accessories called Kensington. The Wendell August Forge is still in operation.

53. August understood the mechanics of designing and fabricating wrought aluminum, but he did not actually design or cut dies. He oversaw the work of forty craftsmen at the forge about 1940; see A. D. LaMonte, "Business Built on Aluminum Art Work," n.p.

54. Woodard and Wood, *Hammered Aluminum Hand Wrought Collectibles,* 151. Smith was the maiden name of Palmer's mother.

55. Arthur Armour, in telephone interview with the author, January 24, 1994. Armour received a Bachelor of Architecture degree from the Carnegie Institute of Technology in 1931.

56. When business was at its peak in the late 1930s, Armour retained as many as twenty in help; ibid. He continued to produce until his retirement in 1976.

57. Arthur Armour résumé, July 29, 1942. Courtesy of Dr. Thomas Armour.

58. William J. Hennessey, *Russel Wright, American Designer* (Cambridge, Mass., and London: MIT Press), 18, 21.

59. The unrivaled master of ironwork in the period was Samuel Yellin of Philadelphia, a European-trained Polish immigrant. The 1920s building boom brought large-scale architectural commissions to the Yellin Shop, which had sixty forges and two hundred employees at the height of the boom; see Jack Andrews, "Samuel Yellin, Metalworker," *Anvil's Ring* (Summer 1982): 2. Yellin never warmed to modernism, however; he reinterpreted and adapted historical styles until his death in 1940. Samuel Yellin Metalworkers continues to fabricate metal in Philadelphia under the guidance of Yellin's granddaughter, Clare Yellin.

60. F. Newlin Price, "Diederich's Adventure in Art," *International Studio* 81 (June 1925): 170. See also Davies, *At Home in Manhattan,* 37, 38; and Richard Armstrong, *Hunt Diederich* (New York: Whitney Museum of American Art, 1991).

61. C. Ford Peatross, "Winold Reiss: A Pioneer of Modern American Design," in Peatross, *Cincinnati Union Terminal and the Artistry of Winold Reiss* (Cincinnati: Cincinnati Historical Society, 1993): 38–41.

62. The panels were executed by Julius Ormos and Charles Bardosy. See Eugene Clute, "Today's Craftsmanship in Combining Metals," *Architecture* (October 1934): 203–04; quoted in Peatross, *Cincinnati Union Terminal and the Artistry of Winold Reiss,* 44.

63. Reiss became familiar with art native to the Americas while traveling in Montana, Colorado, New Mexico, and Mexico in 1920; see Peatross, *Cincinnati Union Terminal and the Artistry of Winold Reiss,* 46.

64. Melvin Rose, "Martin Rose, Master Art Smith," *Anvil's Ring* 19 (Summer 1991): 7.

65. A screen, the tour de force of the collaboration, traveled to Chicago, New York, and Boston during 1930 and 1931 in the American Federation of Arts exhibition "Decorative Metalwork and Cotton Textiles"; it is illustrated in Duncan, *American Art Deco,* 96.

66. Unique samples from this collaboration belong to the Rose family business, which continues to operate in Cleveland as Rose Metal Industries.

67. "Oscar Bach, Craftsman in Metal," *Interior Architecture and Decoration* 1 (May 1931): 100.

68. Perriton Maxwell, "Sonatas in Silver and Ballads in Bronze," *Arts & Decoration* 18 (November 1922): 27.

69. Jessie Martin Breese, "Bronze and Iron for Architecture and Decoration," *Country Life* 50 (May 1926): 110. The theme of the doors, depicted in the roundels, figuratively celebrated arts and crafts.

70. Clarke et al., *Design in America,* 156–57.

71. Eugene Clute, "The Story of Rockefeller Center: X. The Allied Arts," *Architectural Forum* 57 (October 1932): 355–58.

72. For Bach commissions of the late 1930s, see "Heed Well, Dictators!" *Art Digest* 13 (May 15, 1939): 8; and "Tin Can Cellini," *Time* 36 (August 19, 1940): 58.

73. Jeannine Falino, "MFA Boston Acquires Craver Silver Teapot," *Antiques and The Arts Weekly,* February 16, 1990: 50.

74. See *Calder,* introduction by H. Harvard Arnason and with comments by Alexander Calder (New York: Viking Press, 1971), 24. The first exhibitions devoted entirely to Calder's unconventional jewelry took place in Europe in 1938 and in New York in 1940.

75. "Modern Handmade Jewelry from an exhibition at the Museum of Modern Art," *Arts and Architecture* 63 (December 1946): 31–32.

76. Alexander Calder and Jean Davidson, *Calder: An Autobiography with Pictures* (New York: Pantheon Books, 1966), 178.

77. This connection was noted by contemporary reporters; ibid. See also "The Passing Show," *Art News* 43 (February 1, 1945): 25, a review of Bertoia's Nierendorf Gallery show.

78. LaMar Harrington, "The Making of a Modernist; Metalworker: Ruth Penington," *Archives of American Art Journal* 23 (1983): 18–21.

79. Two whose reputations as jewelers were made after World War II were Paul A. Lobel and Samuel Kramer. Lobel, a seasoned New York metalsmith, was beginning to work on a small scale; and Kramer, a Surrealist designer whose importance lay ahead, opened a retail shop in Greenwich Village in 1939 (see Eidelberg, ed., *Design 1935–1965,* 274–75, 380–81).

80. The art patron was reported to have been Mrs. Juliana Force; see Wallace B. Alig, "Man with a Hammer," *Americas* 5 (May 1954): 6, 44. See also *Rebajes 1907–1990,* brochure (Chicago: Arts 220 Gallery, 1991); and Matthew L. Burkholz and Linda Lichtenberg Kaplan, *Copper Art Jewelry: A Different Lustre* (West Chester, Penn.: Schiffer Publishing, 1992). Brochure courtesy of Fern Simon.

81. Alig, "Man with a Hammer": 6, 44.

82. *The Jewelry of Margaret De Patta: A Retrospective Exhibition* (Oakland, Calif.: The Oakland Museum, 1976), 24.

83. Ibid., 8, 12.

84. Ibid., 41.

SELECTED BIBLIOGRAPHY

This listing is confined to the most important or current surveys, the leading monographs, and the most useful writings of the period. It does not attempt to provide comprehensive information on individual artists or institutions.

Readers are referred to Robert Judson Clarke et al., *Design in America: The Cranbrook Vision, 1925–1950*; and Karen Davies, *At Home in Manhattan: Modern Decorative Arts, 1925 to the Depression*. Representative journals of the period are *The American Magazine of Art; Architectural Record; Art and Industry; Arts & Decoration; Craft Horizons; The Craftsman* (later *The Art World*); *The Handicrafter* (later *The Weaver*); *Industrial Design; Interior Architecture and Decoration; International Studio* (later *Connoisseur*); and *Pencil Points* (later *Progressive Architecture*).

Albers, Josef. *Search Versus Re-Search*. Hartford, Conn.: Trinity Press, 1969.

The American Federation of Arts. *Decorative Metalwork and Cotton Textiles*. Catalogue of the Third International Exhibition of Contemporary Industrial Arts. Portland, Me.: Southworth Press for The American Federation of Arts, 1930.

American Studio Ceramics, 1920–1950. Minneapolis: University of Minnesota Art Museum, 1988.

Anderson, Ross, and Barbara Perry. *The Diversions of Keramos: American Clay Sculpture 1925–1950*. Syracuse, N.Y.: Everson Museum of Art, 1983.

Applegate, Judith. *Art Deco*. New York: Wittenborn Art Books, 1970.

Arwas, Victor. *Art Deco*. New York: Harry N. Abrams, 1980.

Bach, Richard F. *Museum Service to the Art Industries*. Industrial Arts Monograph, no. 3. New York: The Metropolitan Museum of Art, 1927.

Baldauf, Lisa W., ed. *Merchandising Interior Design: Methods of Furniture Fabrication in America Between the World Wars*. New Haven, Conn.: Yale University School of Architecture, 1991.

Ball, Fred Carlton, and Janice Lovoos. *Making Pottery Without a Wheel: Texture and Form in Clay*. New York: Reinhold, 1965.

Banham, Reyner. *Theory and Design in the First Machine Age*. 1960. Reprint. Cambridge, Mass.: MIT Press, 1980.

Barquist, David L. *American Tables and Looking Glasses in the Mabel Brady Garvan and Other Collections at Yale University*. New Haven, Conn.: Yale University Art Gallery, 1992.

Battersby, Martin. *The Decorative Thirties*. New York: Collier Books, 1975.

Bauhaus Workshops: 1919–1933. Brochure. New York: Metropolis Magazine, 1994.

Bayer, Herbert, et al., eds. *Bauhaus 1919–1928*. New York: The Museum of Modern Art, 1938.

Bayley, Stephen, ed. *In Good Shape: Style in Industrial Products 1900 to 1960*. New York: D. Van Nostrand Reinhold, 1979.

Bearden, Romare, and Harry Henderson. *A History of African-American Artists: From 1792 to the Present*. New York: Pantheon Books, 1993.

Beeby, Thomas H., et al. *Samuel Yellin Metalwork at Yale*. New Haven, Conn.: Yale University School of Architecture, 1990.

Beer, Eileene Harrison. *Scandinavian Design: Objects of a Life Style*. New York: Farrar, Straus and Giroux, 1975.

Bel Geddes, Norman. *Magic Motorways*. New York: Random House, 1940.

Bernstein, Melvin H. *Art and Design at Alfred: A Chronicle of a Ceramics College*. Philadelphia: Art Alliance Press; London: Associated University Presses, 1986.

Bishop, Robert Charles. *Centuries and Styles of the American Chair*. New York: E. P. Dutton, 1972.

Bishop, Robert Charles, and Patricia Coblentz. *American Decorative Art: 360 Years of Creative Design*. New York: Harry N. Abrams, 1982.

Blausen, Whitney. "Textiles Designed by Ruth Reeves." Master's thesis, State University of New York, Fashion Institute of Technology, 1992.

Boilerhouse Project. *Art and Industry: A Century of Design in the Products We Use*. London: Conran Foundation, 1982.

Boydell, Christine. "Marion Dorn: A Study of the Working Methods of the Female Professional Textile Designer in the 1920s and 30s." Ph.D. diss., University of Huddersfield, 1992.

British Advisory Council for the International Exhibition of Modern Decorative and Industrial Arts. *Reports on the Present Position and Tendencies of the Industrial Arts as Indicated at the International Exhibition of Modern Decorative and Industrial*

Arts, Paris, 1925, with an introductory survey. [London]: Department of Overseas Trade, 1925.

Britton, Crystal, ed. Selected Essays: Art and Artists from the Harlem Renaissance to the 1980s. Atlanta: National Black Arts Festival, 1988.

The Brooklyn Museum. Contemporary Industrial and Handwrought Silver. Brooklyn: The Brooklyn Museum, 1937.

Burkholz, Matthew L., and Linda Lichtenberg Kaplan. Copper Art Jewelry: A Different Lustre. West Chester, Penn.: Schiffer Publishing, 1992.

Bush, Donald J. The Streamlined Decade. New York: Braziller, 1975.

Byrd, Joan Falconer. "Harvey Littleton and Studio Glass." In Harvey K. Littleton: A Retrospective Exhibition. Atlanta: High Museum of Art, 1984.

Calder, Alexander. Calder. New York: Viking Press, 1971.

Calder, Alexander, and Jean Davidson. Calder: An Autobiography with Pictures. New York: Pantheon Books, 1966.

Campbell, Mary Schmidt, et al. Harlem Renaissance: Art of Black America. New York: Harry N. Abrams in association with The Studio Museum in Harlem, 1987.

Caplan, Ralph. Connections: The Work of Charles and Ray Eames. Los Angeles: UCLA Art Council, 1976.

Carpenter, Charles H., Jr. Gorham Silver, 1831–1981. New York: Dodd, Mead & Co., 1982.

Carter, Randolph, and Robert Reed Cole. Joseph Urban: Architecture, Theatre, Opera, Film. New York: Abbeville Press, 1992.

Cartlidge, Barbara. Twentieth-Century Jewelry. New York: Harry N. Abrams, 1985.

Charleston, Robert J. Masterpieces of Glass: A World History from The Corning Museum of Glass. New York: Harry N. Abrams, 1980.

Chase, Judith Wragg. Afro-American Art and Craft. New York: D. Van Nostrand Reinhold, 1971.

Chase, Stuart. Men and Machines. New York: Macmillan, 1929.

Cheney, Sheldon, and Martha Chandler Cheney. Art and the Machine: An Account of Industrial Design in 20th-Century America. New York: Whittlesey House, 1936.

Christ-Janer, Albert. Eliel Saarinen: Finnish-American Architect and Educator. Chicago: University of Chicago Press, 1979.

Cincinnati Union Terminal and the Artistry of Winold Reiss. Cincinnati: Cincinnati Historical Society, 1993.

Clark, Garth. A Century of Ceramics in the United States, 1878–1978: A Study of Its Development. New York: E. P. Dutton in association with the Everson Museum of Art, 1979.

———. American Ceramics: 1876 to the Present. Rev. ed. New York: Abbeville Press, 1987.

Clarke, Robert Judson, et al. Design in America: The Cranbrook Vision, 1925–1950. New York: Harry N. Abrams in association with the Detroit Institute of Arts and The Metropolitan Museum of Art, 1983.

Clarkson, Leslie Linsley. Hooked Rugs: An American Folk Art. New York: Clarkson Potter, 1992.

Coatts, Margot. A Weaver's Life: Ethel Mairet 1892–1952. London: Crafts Council, 1983.

Crawford, M. D. C. The Heritage of Cotton: The Fibre of Two Worlds and Many Ages. New York: Fairchild Publishing Co., 1948.

Csikszentmihalyi, Mihaly, and Eugene Rochberg-Halton. The Meaning of Things: Domestic Symbols and the Self. New York: Cambridge University Press, 1981.

Cusker, Joseph P., et al. Dawn of a New Day: The New York World's Fair, 1939–40. New York: Queens Museum and New York University Press, 1980.

Darling, Sharon S. Chicago Metalsmiths. Chicago: Chicago Historical Society, 1977.

Davies, Karen. At Home in Manhattan: Modern Decorative Arts, 1925 to the Depression. New Haven, Conn.: Yale University Art Gallery, 1983.

Davis, Myra Tolmach. Sketches in Iron: Samuel Yellin, American Master of Wrought Iron, 1885–1940. Washington, D.C.: [George Washington University, Dimock Gallery], 1971.

Design History: Fad or Function? London: The Design Council, 1978.

Detroit Institute of Arts. Arts and Crafts in Detroit, 1906–1976: The Movement, The Society, The School. Detroit: Detroit Institute of Arts, 1976.

De Zurko, Edward Robert. Origins of Functionalist Theory. New York: Columbia University Press, 1957.

Dickson, Harold E., and Richard Porter. Henry Varnum Poor 1887–1970: A Retrospective Exhibition. University Park, Penn.: Museum of Art, Pennsylvania State University, 1983.

DiNoto, Andrea. Art Plastic: Machine Age Designs for Living. New York: Abbeville Press, 1984.

Donhauser, Paul S. History of American Ceramics: The Studio Potter. Dubuque, Iowa: Kendall/Hunt Publishing, 1978.

Drexler, Arthur. Charles Eames: Furniture from the Design Collection. New York: The Museum of Modern Art, 1973.

Drexler, Arthur, and Greta Daniel. Introduction to Twentieth Century Design. New York: The Museum of Modern Art, 1959.

Driskell, David C. Two Centuries of Black American Art. New York: Alfred A. Knopf for the Los Angeles County Museum of Art, 1976.

DuBois, J. Harry. Plastics History U. S. A. Boston: Cahners, 1972.

Duncan, Alastair. American Art Deco. New York: Harry N. Abrams, 1986.

———. Art Deco. New York: Thames and Hudson, 1988.

Eidelberg, Martin, ed. Design 1935–1955: What Modern Was. Selections from the Liliane and David M. Stewart Collection. New York: Harry N. Abrams in association with the Musée des Arts Décoratifs de Montréal, 1991.

———, ed. Eva Zeisel: Designer for Industry. Montreal: Château Dufresne, Musée des Arts Décoratifs de Montréal, 1984.

Fauster, Carl U. Libbey Glass Since 1818: Pictorial History & Collector's Guide. Toledo: Len Beach Press, 1979.

Ferebee, Ann. A History of Design from the Victorian Era to the Present. New York: D. Van Nostrand Reinhold, 1970.

Fitch, James Marston. Architecture and the Esthetics of Plenty. New York: Columbia University Press, 1961.

Fleming, Donald, and Bernard Bailyn, eds. The Intellectual Migration: Europe and America, 1930–1960. Cambridge, Mass.: Harvard University Press, 1969.

Foley, Mark. Foreword to Structure and

Ornament: American Modernist Jewelry 1940–1960. New York: Fifty-50, 1984.

Frankl, Paul T. Form and Re-form: A Practical Handbook of Modern Interiors. New York: Harper, 1930.

———. Machine-Made Leisure. New York: Harper & Brothers, 1932.

———. New Dimensions: The Decorative Arts of Today in Words and Pictures. New York: Payson & Clarke Ltd., 1928.

———. Space for Living: Creative Interior Decoration and Design. New York: Doubleday, Doran, 1938.

Frantz, Susanne K. Contemporary Glass: A World Survey from The Corning Museum of Glass. New York: Harry N. Abrams, 1989.

Frey, Gilbert. The Modern Chair: 1850 to Today. New York: Architectural Book Publishing Co., 1970.

Gardner, Paul V. Frederick Carder: Portrait of a Glassmaker. Corning, N.Y.: The Corning Museum of Glass; Rockwell Museum, 1985.

Gebhard, David, and Harriette von Breton. Kem Weber: The Moderne in Southern California, 1920–1941. Santa Barbara: Standard Print for The Art Galleries, University of California, Santa Barbara, 1969.

Giedion, Siegfried. Mechanization Takes Command: A Contribution to Anonymous History. 1948. Reprint. New York: W. W. Norton, 1969.

———. Space, Time, and Architecture: The Growth of a New Tradition. 4th ed. Cambridge, Mass.: Harvard University Press, 1962.

Golden Gate International Exposition, Department of Fine Arts. Decorative Arts: Official Catalog, Department of Fine Arts, Division of Decorative Arts. San Francisco: San Francisco Bay Exposition Co., 1939.

Goodrich, Lloyd. The Decade of the Armory Show: New Directions in American Art, 1910–1920. New York: Whitney Museum of American Art, 1963.

Greif, Martin. Depression Modern: The Thirties Style in America. New York: Universe Books, 1975.

Hanks, David A. The Decorative Designs of Frank Lloyd Wright. New York: E. P. Dutton, 1979.

———. Innovative Furniture in America from 1800 to the Present. New York: Horizon Press, 1981.

Hanks, David A., and Derek Ostergard. Gilbert Rohde. New York: Washburn Gallery, 1981.

Harbeson, Georgina Brown. American Needlework: The History of Decorative Stitchery and Embroidery from the Late 16th to the 20th Century. New York: Coward-McCann, 1938.

The Harmon Foundation. Negro Artists: An Illustrated Review of Their Achievements. New York: The Harmon Foundation, 1935.

———. Exhibit of Fine Arts by American Negro Artists. New York: The Harmon Foundation, 1930.

Harris, Mary Emma. The Arts at Black Mountain College. Cambridge, Mass.: MIT Press, 1987.

Hennessey, William J. Russel Wright, American Designer. Cambridge, Mass.: MIT Press, 1983.

Heskett, John. Industrial Design. New York: Oxford University Press, 1980.

Hiesinger, Kathryn B., and George H. Marcus. Landmarks of Twentieth-Century Design. New York: Abbeville Press, 1993.

Hiler, Hilaire. From Nudity to Raiment: An Introduction to the Study of Costume. New York: Educational Press, 1930.

Hillier, Bevis. Art Deco. Minneapolis: Minneapolis Institute of Arts, 1971.

———. Art Deco of the 20s and 30s. Rev. ed. New York: Schocken Books, 1985.

———. The Style of the Century, 1900–1980. New York: E. P. Dutton, 1983.

Hitchcock, Henry-Russell, and Philip Johnson. The International Style: Architecture Since 1922. New York: W. W. Norton, 1932. Reprinted as The International Style, 1966.

Hitchcock, Henry-Russell, Philip Johnson, and Lewis Mumford. Modern Architecture: International Exhibition. New York: The Museum of Modern Art, 1932.

Hoffmann, Herbert. Modern Interiors in Europe and America. London: Studio Limited, 1930.

Holland, Laurence B., ed. Who Designs America? The American Civilization Conference at Princeton. Garden City, N.Y.: Anchor, 1966.

Hollister, Paul. "Frederick Carder and Sculpted Glass." In Brilliance in Glass: The

Lost Wax Sculpture of Frederick Carter. Corning, N.Y.: Rockwell Museum, 1993.

Holme, Geoffrey. Industrial Design and the Future. London: The Studio, 1934.

Holmes, Oakley N., Jr. The Complete Annotated Resource Guide to Black American Art. Spring Valley, N.Y.: Macgowan Enterprises for Black Artists in America, 1978.

Huggins, Nathan Irvin. The Harlem Renaissance. New York: Oxford University Press, 1971.

———, ed. Voices from the Harlem Renaissance. New York: Oxford University Press, 1976.

Igoe, Lynn, comp. Artis, Bearden, and Burke: A Bibliography and Illustrations List. Durham: Museum of Art, North Carolina Central University, 1977.

Index of Exhibits: 50th Annual Exhibition of Architectural League of New York with American Institute of Decorators. New York: Architectural League of New York, 1936.

Johnson, Philip. Machine Art. New York: The Museum of Modern Art, 1934.

Kahle, Katharine Morrison. Modern French Decoration. New York: G. P. Putnam's Sons, 1930.

Kahn, Ely Jacques. Design in Art and Industry. New York: Scribner, 1936.

Kaplan, Wendy, et al. "The Art That Is Life": The Arts and Crafts Movement in America, 1875–1920. Boston: Museum of Fine Arts and Little, Brown and Company, 1987.

Kardon, Janet, ed. The Ideal Home 1900–1920: The History of Twentieth-Century American Craft. New York: Harry N. Abrams in association with the American Craft Museum, 1993.

Kaufmann, Edgar, Jr. Prize Designs for Modern Furniture from the International Competition for Low-Cost Furniture Design. New York: The Museum of Modern Art, 1950.

———. What Is Modern Design? Introductory Series to the Modern Arts, no. 3. New York: The Museum of Modern Art, 1950.

———. What Is Modern Interior Design? Introductory Series to the Modern Arts, no. 4. New York: The Museum of Modern Art, 1953.

Kaufmann, Edgar, Jr. (essay), and Barbara

Morgan (photographs). *Prestini's Art in Wood.* Lake Forest, Ill.: Pocahontas Press, 1950.

Kaufman, M. *The First Century of Plastics: Celluloid and Its Sequel.* London: The Plastics Institute, 1963.

Keefe, John Webster. *Libbey Glass: A Tradition of 150 Years, 1818–1968.* Toledo: The Toledo Museum of Art, 1968.

Kent, Cheryl. *Designing the Future.* Brochure. Chicago: Illinois Institute of Technology, 1993.

Kepes, Gyorgy, ed. *The Man-Made Object.* New York: Braziller, 1966.

Kerr, Ann. *The Collector's Encyclopedia of Russel Wright Designs.* Paducah, Ky.: Collector Books, 1990.

Kiesler, Frederick. *Contemporary Art Applied to the Store and Its Display.* New York: Brentano's, 1930.

Klein, Dan, et al. *In The Deco Style.* New York: Rizzoli, 1986.

Koch, Robert. *Louis C. Tiffany, Rebel in Glass.* New York: Crown Publishers, 1978.

Kouwenhoven, John A. *The Arts in Modern Civilization.* 1948. Reprint. New York: Octagon Books, 1975.

Krekel-Aalberse, Annelies. *Art Nouveau and Art Deco Silver.* London: Thames and Hudson; New York: Harry N. Abrams, 1989.

Krutch, Joseph Wood. *The Modern Temper: A Study and a Confession.* New York: Harcourt, Brace, 1929.

Le Corbusier (Charles-Édouard Jeanneret). *Vers une Architecture.* Paris: Éditions Crès, 1923. Published in English as *Towards a New Architecture.* Translated by Frederick Etchells. 1927. Reprint. New York: Praeger, 1970.

Leonard, R. L., and C. A. Glassgold, eds. *Annual of American Design 1931 by the American Union of Decorative Artists and Craftsmen.* New York: Ives Washburn, 1930.

Lesieutre, Alain. *The Spirit and Splendour of Art Deco.* New York: Paddington Press, 1974.

Levin, Elaine. *The History of American Ceramics, 1607 to the Present.* New York: Harry N. Abrams, 1988.

Lewis, Ethel. *The Romance of Textiles: The Story of Design in Weaving.* Macmillan Co., 1937.

Liebes, Dorothy Wright, et al. *Decorative Arts.* Official Catalog, Department of Fine Arts, Division of Decorative Arts. Golden Gate International Exposition. San Francisco: San Francisco Bay Exposition Co., 1939.

Lind, Carla. *The Wright Style.* New York: Simon & Schuster, 1992.

Locke, Alain LeRoy. *Contemporary Negro Art.* Baltimore: Baltimore Museum of Art, 1939.

Lockwood, Sarah M. *Decoration: Past, Present and Future.* Doubleday, Doran & Co., 1934.

Loewy, Raymond. *Never Leave Well Enough Alone.* New York: Simon and Schuster, 1951.

Longenecker, Martha. "Commentary." In *Laura Andreson: A Retrospective in Clay.* La Jolla, Calif.: Mingei International Museum of World Folk Art, 1982.

Lucic, Karen. *Charles Sheeler and the Cult of the Machine.* Cambridge, Mass.: Harvard University Press, 1991.

Lucie-Smith, Edward. *A History of Industrial Design.* New York: D. Van Nostrand Reinhold, 1983.

———. *The Story of Craft: The Craftsman's Role in Society.* Ithaca, N.Y.: Cornell University Press, 1981.

Lynes, Russell. *The Tastemakers.* New York: Harper, 1954.

McClinton, Katharine Morrison. *Art Deco: A Guide for Collectors.* New York: Clarkson N. Potter, 1972.

McFadden, David Revere, ed. *Scandinavian Modern Design, 1880–1980.* New York: Harry N. Abrams, 1982.

McKnight, Lola. "The Americana Prints: A Collection of Artist Designed Textiles." Master's thesis, State University of New York, Fashion Institute of Technology, 1993.

R. H. Macy & Company. *The Catalog of the Exposition of Art in Trade at Macy's, May 2 to May 7, 1927.* New York: R. H. Macy & Company, 1927.

———. *An International Exposition of Art in Industry from May 14 to May 26, 1928 at Macy's.* New York: R. H. Macy & Company, 1928.

Madigan, Mary Jean Smith. *Steuben Glass: An American Tradition in Crystal.* New York: Harry N. Abrams, 1982.

Mang, Karl. *History of Modern Furniture.* New York: Harry N. Abrams, 1979.

Marchand, Roland. *Advertising the American Dream: Making Way for Modernity, 1920–1940.* Berkeley: University of California Press, 1985.

Martin, Tony. *Literary Garveyism: Garvey, Black Arts and the Harlem Renaissance.* Dover, Mass.: Majority Press, 1983.

Meadmore, Clement. *The Modern Chair: Classics in Production.* New York: D. Van Nostrand Reinhold, 1975.

Meikle, Jeffrey L. *Twentieth Century Limited: Industrial Design in America, 1925–1939.* Philadelphia: Temple University Press, 1979.

Menten, Theodore. *Art Deco Style.* New York: Dover Publications, 1972.

The Metropolitan Museum of Art. *The Architect and the Industrial Arts: An Exhibition of Contemporary American Design.* New York: The Metropolitan Museum of Art, 1929.

———. *Contemporary American Industrial Art: 15th Exhibition.* New York: The Metropolitan Museum of Art, 1940.

———. *Contemporary American Industrial Art 1934: Thirteenth Exhibition.* New York: The Metropolitan Museum of Art, 1934.

Miller, R. Craig. *Modern Design in The Metropolitan Museum of Art, 1890–1990.* New York: Harry N. Abrams in association with The Metropolitan Museum of Art, 1990.

Moholy-Nagy, L[ászló]. *Vision in Motion.* Chicago: Paul Theobald, 1947.

Morse, Edgar W., ed. *Silver in the Golden State: Images and Essays Celebrating the History and Art of Silver in California.* Oakland, Calif.: The Oakland Museum History Department, 1986.

Moynihan, Jeanne Patricia. "The Influence of the Bauhaus on Art and Art Education in the United States." Ph.D. diss., Northwestern University, 1980.

Mumford, Lewis. *The Golden Day: A Study in American Literature and Culture.* New York: Boni and Liveright, 1926.

———. *Sticks and Stones: A Study of American Architecture and Civilization.* New York: Boni and Liveright, 1924.

———. *Technics and Civilization.* New York: Harcourt, Brace, 1934.

Museum of Fine Arts, Boston. *Collecting American Decorative Arts and Sculpture, 1971–1991*. Boston: Museum of Fine Arts, 1991.

The Museum of Modern Art. *Art in Our Time: An Exhibition to Celebrate the Tenth Anniversary of The Museum of Modern Art and the Opening of Its New Building, Held at the Time of the New York World's Fair*. New York: The Museum of Modern Art, 1939.

Neuhart, John, Marilyn Neuhart, and Ray Eames. *Eames Design: The Work of the Office of Charles and Ray Eames*. New York: Harry N. Abrams, 1989.

Noguchi, Isamu. *A Sculptor's World*. New York: Harper & Row, 1968.

Noyes, Eliot F. *Organic Design in Home Furnishings*. 1941. Reprint. New York: Arno Press, 1969.

The Oakland Museum. *The Jewelry of Margaret De Patta: A Retrospective Exhibition*. Oakland, Calif.: The Oakland Museum, 1976.

O'Connor, Francis V., ed. *The New Deal Art Projects: An Anthology of Memoirs*. Washington, D.C.: Smithsonian Institution Press, 1972.

Ogren, Kathy J. *The Jazz Revolution: Twenties America and the Meaning of Jazz*. New York: Oxford University Press, 1989.

Ostergard, Derek. *Art Deco Masterpieces*. New York: Hugh Lauter Levin Associates, 1991.

————. *George Nakashima: Full Circle*. New York: American Craft Museum, 1989.

Park, Edwin Avery. *New Backgrounds for a New Age*. New York: Harcourt, Brace, 1927.

Pells, Richard. *Radical Visions and American Dreams: Culture and Social Thought in the Depression Years*. New York: Harper & Row, 1973.

Pendergraft, Norman E. *Heralds of Life: Artis, Bearden, and Burke*. Durham: Museum of Art, North Carolina Central University, 1977.

Perry, Barbara, ed. *American Ceramics: The Collection of Everson Museum of Art*. New York: Rizzoli, 1989.

Pevsner, Nikolaus. *Pioneers of Modern Design: From William Morris to Walter Gropius*. Originally published as *Pioneers of the Modern Movement from William Morris to Walter Gropius*, 1936. Baltimore: Penguin, 1972.

Phillips, Lisa, et al. *High Styles: Twentieth Century American Design*. New York: Summit Books in association with the Whitney Museum of American Art, 1985.

Pile, John. *Dictionary of 20th-Century Design*. New York: Facts on File, 1990.

Pulos, Arthur J. *American Design Ethic: A History of Industrial Design to 1940*. Cambridge, Mass.: MIT Press, 1983.

Ransom, John Crowe, et al. *I'll Take My Stand: The South and the Agrarian Tradition*. New York: Harper & Brothers, Publishers, 1930.

Reynolds, Gary A., and Beryl S. Wright. *Against the Odds: African-American Artists and The Harmon Foundation*. Newark, N.J.: The Newark Museum, 1989.

Richards, Charles R. *Art in Industry*. New York: Macmillan, 1922.

Riley, Terence. *The International Style: Exhibition 15 and The Museum of Modern Art*. New York: Rizzoli, 1992.

Riley, Terence, with Peter Reed, eds. *Frank Lloyd Wright, Architect*. New York: The Museum of Modern Art, 1994.

Robinson, Cervin, and Rosemarie Haag. *Skyscraper Style: Art Deco New York*. New York: Oxford University Press, 1975.

Rochberg, Gene, comp. and ed. *Drawings by Wharton Esherick*. New York: D. Van Nostrand Reinhold, 1978.

Rocky River Public Library. *Cowan Pottery Museum*. Rocky River, Ohio: Rocky River Public Library, 1978.

Rosenthal, Rudolph, and Helena L. Ratzka. *The Story of Modern Applied Art*. New York: Harper, 1948.

Russell, Frank, ed. *A Century of Chair Design*. New York: Rizzoli, 1980.

Sarnitz, August. *R. M. Schindler, Architect*. New York: Rizzoli, 1988.

Schaefer, Herwin. "Design: An International Survey, 1851–1956." In *Modern Art: A Pictorial Anthology*. Edited by Charles McCurdy. New York: Macmillan, 1958.

Schmeckebier, Laurence. *Victor Schreckengost: Retrospective Exhibition*. Cleveland: Cleveland Institute of Art, 1976.

Schoeser, Mary. *Marianne Straub*. London: Design Council, 1984.

Schoeser, Mary, and Kathleen Dejardin. *French Textiles from 1760 to the Present*. London: Laurence King, 1991.

Schoeser, Mary, and Celia Rufey. *English and American Textiles from 1790 to the Present*. New York: Thames and Hudson, 1989.

Schomburg Center for Research in Black Culture. *Augusta Savage and the Art Schools of Harlem*. New York: Schomburg Center for Research in Black Culture; New York Public Library, 1988.

Schuller, Gunther. *Early Jazz: Its Roots and Musical Development*. The History of Jazz, vol. 1. New York: Oxford University Press, 1968.

Schweiger, Werner J. *Wiener Werkstätte: Design in Vienna, 1903–1932*. Translated by Alexander Lieven. New York: Abbeville Press, 1984.

Sherrill, Sarah B. *Carpets and Rugs of Europe and America*. New York: Abbeville Press, forthcoming.

Shifman, Barry, with contributions by W. Scott Braznell and Sharon S. Darling. *The Arts and Crafts Metalwork of Janet Payne Bowles*. Indianapolis: Indianapolis Museum of Art, 1993.

Shilliam, Nicola J. *Early Modern Textiles*. Boston: Museum of Fine Arts, 1993.

Sironen, Marta K. *A History of American Furniture*. East Stroudsburg, Pa.: Towse Publishing Co., 1936.

Sparke, Penny. *Consultant Design: The History and Practice of the Designer in Industry*. London: Pembridge Press, 1983.

Stone, Michael A. *Contemporary American Woodworkers*. Salt Lake City: Gibbs M. Smith, 1986.

Streichler, Jerry. "The Consultant Industrial Designer in American Industry from 1927 to 1960." Ph.D. diss., New York University, 1963.

The Studio Museum in Harlem. *New York/Chicago: WPA and the Black Artists*. New York: The Studio Museum in Harlem, 1978.

Teague, Walter Dorwin. *Design This Day: The Technique of Order in the Machine Age*. New York: Harcourt, Brace, 1940.

Tichi, Cecelia. *Shifting Gears: Technology, Literature, Culture in Modernist America*. Chapel Hill: University of North Carolina Press, 1987.

Van Doren, Harold. *Industrial Design: A Practical Guide*. New York: Braziller, 1968.

Venable, Charles L. *Silver in America, 1840–1940: A Century of Splendor*. Dallas: Dallas Museum of Art, 1994.

Vlach, John Michael. *The Afro-American Tradition in Decorative Arts*. 1978. Reprint. Athens: University of Georgia Press, 1980.

Vlack, Don. *Art Deco Architecture in New York, 1920–1940*. New York: Harper & Row, 1974.

Wallance, Don. *Shaping America's Products*. New York: Reinhold, 1956.

Walters, Thomas. *Art Deco*. London: Academy, 1973.

Weatherman, Hazel M. *Fostoria: Its First Fifty Years*. Springfield, Mo.: The Weathermans, 1972.

Weber, Eva. *Art Deco in America*. New York: Exeter Books, 1985.

Weltge, Sigrid [Wortmann]. *The Bauhaus Weaving Workshop: Source and Influence for American Textiles*. Philadelphia: Philadelphia College of Textiles and Science, 1987.

———. *Women's Work: Textile Art from the Bauhaus*. San Francisco: Chronicle Books, 1993.

West, Jean, ed. *From American Looms*. Trenton, N.J.: New Jersey State Museum, 1985.

Wharton Esherick Museum. *The Wharton Esherick Museum: Studio and Collection*. Paoli, Penn.: Wharton Esherick Museum, 1977.

Whitford, Frank. *Bauhaus*. London: Thames and Hudson, 1984.

Wildenhain, Marguerite. *Pottery: Form and Expression*. New York: American Craftsmen's Council, 1962.

Wilk, Christopher. *Marcel Breuer: Furniture and Interiors*. New York: The Museum of Modern Art, 1981.

———. "Furnishing the Future: Bentwood and Metal Furniture 1925–1946." In *Bentwood and Metal Furniture: 1850–1946*. New York: The American Federation of Arts, 1987.

Wilson, Jack D. *Phoenix & Consolidated Art Glass, 1926–1980*. Marietta, Ohio: Antique Publications, 1989.

Wilson, Richard Guy, Dianne H. Pilgrim, and Dickran Tashjian. *The Machine Age in America, 1918–1941*. New York: Harry N. Abrams in association with The Brooklyn Museum, 1986.

Wingler, Hans M. *The Bauhaus*. Translated by Wolfgang Jabs and Basil Gilbert. Cambridge, Mass., and London: MIT Press, 1986.

Withers, Josephine. "Margret Craver." In *Women's Caucus for Art: Honor Awards for Outstanding Achievement in the Visual Arts*. Philadelphia: Women's Caucus for Art, Moore College of Art, 1989.

Woodard, Dannie A., and Billie J. Wood. *Hammered Aluminum: Hand Wrought Collectibles*. Wolfe City, Tex.: Henington Publishing, 1983.

Woodward, Carla Mathes, and Franklin W. Robinson. *A Handbook of the Museum of Art, Rhode Island School of Design*. Providence: Rhode Island School of Design, 1985.

Worcester Art Museum. *An Exhibition of Contemporary New England Handicrafts*. Worcester, Mass.: Worcester Art Museum, 1943.

Wright, Frank Lloyd. *An Autobiography*. New York: Longmans Green, 1932.

CHECKLIST OF THE CATALOGUE

Note: Within each section checklist entries are in alphabetical order. For all dimensions, height precedes width precedes depth.

CERAMICS

Russell Barnett Aitken
Futility of a Well-ordered Life. 1935
Earthenware, 18½ x 7 x 7"
Collection The Museum of Modern Art, New York. Given anonymously

Alexander Archipenko
The Bride. 1936
Terracotta, 34¼ x 6 11/16 x 4¾"
Collection Seattle Art Museum. Eugene Fuller Memorial Collection

William Ellsworth Artis
Michael. c. 1945
Terracotta, 10¼ x 6 x 8"
Collection North Carolina Museum of Art, Raleigh. Purchased with funds from the National Endowment for the Arts and the North Carolina Art Society (Robert F. Phifer Bequest)

Alexander Blazys
Moses. 1927
Designed for Cowan Pottery Studio
Earthenware, 19 x 6¾"
Collection The Cleveland Museum of Art. The Harold T. Clark Educational Extension Fund

R. Guy Cowan
Scarf Dancer with Bowl. 1925
Designed for Cowan Pottery Studio
Porcelain; figure: height 6"; bowl: diameter 11"
Collection Cowan Pottery Museum at Rocky River Public Library, Rocky River, Ohio

Wilhelm Hunt Diederich
Russian Cossack Plate. February 1925
Ceramic, 3½ x 15 x 15"
Collection Dr. Tom Folk

Edris Eckhardt
Earth. 1939
Earthenware, 13 x 8 x 6½"
Collection James L. Murphy

Waylande DeSantis Gregory
Head of a Woman. c. 1933
Porcelain, 24 x 9¾ x 12"
Collection Everson Museum of Art, Syracuse, New York. Museum purchase

Waylande DeSantis Gregory
Nautch Dancer. 1930
Earthenware, 17⅜ x 8⅜ x 4¾"
Collection The Cleveland Museum of Art. Dudley P. Allen Fund

Majlis (Maija) Grotell
Flared Cylinder Vase. 1941
Glazed stoneware, 15 x 11½ x 11½"
Collection American Craft Museum, New York. Museum Purchase, 1967. Donated to the American Craft Museum by the American Craft Council, 1990

Sargent Claude Johnson
Negro Woman. 1933
Terracotta, 9¼ x 5 x 6"
Collection San Francisco Museum of Modern Art, Albert M. Bender Collection. Bequest of Albert M. Bender

Glen Lukens
Bowl. 1939
Earthenware, 4½ x 6¼ x 6¼"
Collection American Craft Museum, New York. Gift of W. Osborn Webb, 1983. Donated to the American Craft Museum by the American Craft Council, 1990

Maria Povera Martinez and Julian Martinez
Plate. c. 1939
Earthenware, 2 x 12¾ x 12¾"
Collection Everson Museum of Art, Syracuse, New York. Gift of the Pueblo Indian Arts and Crafts Market

Isamu Noguchi
Tsuneko-San (Head of a Young Girl). 1931
Ceramic, 9⅜ x 7 x 7½"
Collection Albright-Knox Art Gallery, Buffalo, New York. Bequest of A. Conger Goodyear, 1966

Henry Varnum Poor
Plate. 1930
Glazed earthenware, 1½ x 11½ x 11½"
Collection American Craft Museum, New York. Gift of the artist, 1967. Donated to the American Craft Museum by the American Craft Council, 1990

Henry Varnum Poor
Ten Nights in a Barroom. 1932
Ceramic, 15½ x 13 x 13"
Collection Dr. Tom Folk

Frederick Hurten Rhead
Fiestaware. 1936
Designed for Laughlin China Company
Earthenware; covered tureen: 5¾ x 9¾ x 8¼"; teapot: 6¾ x 9⅜ x 6⅛"; cup: 2¾ x 4⅝ x 3 7/16"
The Globus Collection

Roseville Pottery Company
Futura Vases. 1928
Earthenware; left to right: 7 x 5¼ x 5¼"; 12 x 4½ x 4½"; 8 x 6⅜ x 6⅜"
Collection Everson Museum of Art, Syracuse, New York. The Mary and Paul Branwein Collection

Edwin A. Scheier and Mary Goldsmith Scheier
Coffee Set. c. 1941
Stoneware; coffee pot: 8¼ x 9 x 9¼"; sugar bowl: 3¾ x 3 x 3"; cup: 2¼ x 2½ x 3½"
Collection Everson Museum of Art, Syracuse, New York. Purchase Prize given by Richard B. Gump, Twelfth Ceramic National Exhibition, 1948

Viktor Schreckengost
The Dictator. 1939
Earthenware, 13 x 12½ x 10½"
Collection Everson Museum of Art, Syracuse, New York. Gift of the artist

Viktor Schreckengost
Jazz Bowl. 1931
Designed for Cowan Pottery Studio
Earthenware, 11⅜ x 16⅜ x 16⅜"
Collection Cowan Pottery Museum at Rocky River Public Library, Rocky River, Ohio

Viktor Schreckengost
The Seasons. 1931
Earthenware, 11⅝ x 8 x 8"
Collection The Cleveland Museum of Art. Hinman B. Hurlbut Collection

Kataro Shirayamadani
Vase. 1930
Designed for Rookwood Pottery
Decorated by Lorinda Epply
Soft porcelain, 7¼ x 7 x 7"
Collection Stanley H. Shapiro

Monica Silvin
Jar with Geometric Design. 1941

Earthenware, 7½ x 6½ x 6½"
Collection Everson Museum of Art, Syracuse, New York. Gift of the Pueblo Indian Arts and Crafts Market

Catherine Vigil
Santa Clara Pueblo
Shallow Bowl. 1941
Earthenware, 3¼ x 14½ x 14½"
Collection Everson Museum of Art, Syracuse, New York. Gift of the IBM Corporation

Carl Walters
Caterpillar. 1945
Earthenware, length 16½"
Collection Detroit Institute of Arts. Gift of Lillian Henkel Haass

Valerie (Vally) Wieselthier
Europa and the Bull. 1938
Earthenware, 24 x 18 x 19"
Collection Christopher Kende

Marguerite Wildenhain
Tea Set. c. 1946
Stoneware; teapot: 5 x 10 x 10"; sugar bowl: 2½ x 4¼ x 4¼"; creamer: 3 x 5½ x 5½"
Collection Everson Museum of Art, Syracuse, New York. Purchase Prize given by Richard B. Gump, Eleventh Ceramic National Exhibition, 1946

Thelma Frazier Winter
The Sirens. c. 1937
Earthenware, 18 x 15 x 4"
Collection Fred Silberman

Russel Wright
American Modern Dinnerware.
Designed 1937; introduced 1939
Designed for Steubenville Pottery Company
Earthenware; pitcher: 10⅝ x 6⅝ x 8⅛"; teapot with lid: 4⅞ x 6¾ x 10"; covered casserole: 3¼ x 12 x 9¼"
Collection William Straus

Eva Alexandrovna Polanyi Zeisel
Museum White Dinnerware.
Designed c. 1943; executed 1946
Designed for Castleton China Company
Glazed porcelain; coffeepot: 10½ x 7 x 5"
Collection Dr. Martin Eidelberg

GLASS

Samuel Ayers
Ship's Decanter. 1942
Glass, 10 x 8½ x 8½"
Collection Steuben Glass, New York

Frederick Carder
Dancing Faun Panel. 1930s
Pâte de verre, 9 x 9¼"
Collection The Corning Museum of Glass, Corning, New York. Bequest of Gladys C. Wells

Frederick Carder
Elephant Bowl. c. 1940
Crystal; *cire perdue,* 7⅜ x 5¾ x 5¾"
Collection The Corning Museum of Glass, Corning, New York. Gift of Corning Glass Works

Frederick Carder
Flatware. 1930s
Glass, silver; fork length: 7⅝"; spoon length: 7¾"
Collection The Corning Museum of Glass, Corning, New York. Gift of the artist

Frederick Carder
Paperweight Cologne Bottle. 1927–31
Cintra core surrounded by colored threadings, controlled bubbles; cased in heavy crystal with massive cutting, 8⅞ x 4 x 4"
Collection Rockwell Museum, Corning, New York

Frederick Carder
Six Prong Green Jade Vase. c. 1930
Glass, 14⅞ x 7⅞ x 7⅜"
Collection Rockwell Museum, Corning, New York

Frederick Carder
Standing Glassblower. 1937
Cast crystal, $12\frac{11}{16}$ x $3\frac{5}{16}$ x 6"
Collection The Corning Museum of Glass, Corning, New York. Gift of Grace Fraas

Louis Dierra (attributed)
Glass Chair. 1939
Designed for Pittsburgh Plate Glass Company
Glass, 29 x 22⅜ x 22½"
Collection The Brooklyn Museum. H. Randolph Lever Fund

Edwin W. Fuerst
Modern American Spiral Optic Bowl. 1940
Designed for Libbey Glass Company
Crystal; mold-blown and tooled, 8 x 9½ x 9½"
Collection The Toledo Museum of Art. Gift of Libbey Glass Company

Edwin W. Fuerst (attributed)
Modern American Decanter and Glass. c. 1940
Designed for Libbey Glass Company
Crystal; decanter: height 11⅜"; cordial glass: height 2⅜"
Collection The Toledo Museum of Art. Gift of Libbey Glass Company

Paul V. Gardner
Empire State Building Architectural Panel. 1931
Crystal; intaglio, 10¼ x 13¼"
Collection The Corning Museum of Glass, Corning, New York. Gift of Corning Glass Works

Waylande DeSantis Gregory
The Airman. c. 1942
Ceramic, with crystal glaze, 12⅛ x 12¼ x 2"
Waylande Gregory Collection

Waylande DeSantis Gregory
Mermaid Bowl. c. 1940
Glass, 7⅛ x 12 x 12"
Collection New Jersey State Museum, Trenton. Gift of the Friends of the New Jersey State Museum, 1988 Forbes Benefit and Museum Purchase

Reuben Haley
Ruba Rombic Vase. 1928–30
Designed for Consolidated Lamp & Glass Company
Glass; molded, blown, and acid-etched, 16½ x 8⅞ x 8⅞"
Collection The Toledo Museum of Art. Purchased with funds from the Libbey Endowment, Gift of Edward Drummond Libbey

Reuben Haley
Ruba Rombic Whiskey Decanter, Tray, and Glasses. 1928–32
Designed for Consolidated Lamp & Glass Company
Smoky topaz glass; mold-blown and pressed. Decanter: 9⅜ x 9¼ x 9¼"; tray: 11½ x $10\frac{7}{16}$ x 1"; glasses: 2¾ x 2 x 2" each
Collection The Corning Museum of Glass, Corning, New York

Maurice Heaton
Bowl. c. 1930
Glass, 2⅞ x 16⅛ x 16⅛"
Collection The Metropolitan Museum of Art. Gift of Theodore R. Gamble, Jr., in honor of his mother, Mrs. Theodore Robert Gamble

Frances Higgins
Slumped Glass Plate. 1992 (from 1942 mold)

Glass, 11¼ x 9 x 1½"
Collection Frances and Michael Higgins

Paul H. Manship
Woman and Centaur. 1939
Designed for Steuben Glass, "Twenty-seven Artists in Crystal" series
Crystal; blown and engraved, 14½ x 24 x 24"
Collection The Corning Museum of Glass, Corning, New York. Gift of Harry W. and Mary M. Anderson

A. Douglas Nash
Libbey-Nash Syncopation Cocktail Glass. 1933
Designed for Libbey Glass Company
Glass, 4 x 2¾ x 2¾"
Collection The Toledo Museum of Art. Purchased with funds from the Libbey Endowment. Gift of Edward Drummond Libbey

A. Douglas Nash
Libbey-Nash Punch Bowl and Glasses. 1931–35
Designed for Libbey Glass Company
Glass; bowl: 7¾ x 13⅞ x 13⅞"; glasses: 3 x 2½ x 2½" each
Collection The Toledo Museum of Art. Gift of Mrs. Carl R. Megowen in memory of Carl R. Megowen

Walter von Nessen
Stanhope Vase. 1938
Designed for Heisey Glass Company
Crystal, with Bakelite handles, 9½ x 8⅛ x 5⅜"
Collection William Straus

W. L. Orme
Pristine Table Architecture: Three-step Candlesticks. 1938
Designed for Cambridge Glass Company
Crystal, 5⅜ x 5¼ x 1⅞" each
Collection William Straus

George Sakier
Amber Stepped Vase. 1927–32
Designed for Fostoria Glass Company
Glass, 8¼ x 6¾ x 4⅞"
Collection William Straus

Pavel Tchelitchew
Acrobats Vase. 1939
Designed for Steuben Glass, "Twenty-seven Artists in Crystal" series
Crystal; blown and engraved, 13½ x 11⁹⁄₁₆ x 11⁹⁄₁₆"
Collection The Corning Museum of Glass, Corning, New York. Gift of Harry W. and Mary M. Anderson

Walter Dorwin Teague, Sr.
Lens Bowl. c. 1934
Designed for Steuben Glass
Crystal, 2¼ x 11⅞ x 11⅞"
Collection William Straus

Frederick Vuillemenot
DeVilbiss Atomizer and Powder Box. 1930
Enameled glass, platinum luster design; atomizer: 5½ x 1½ x 1½"; box: 1½ x 3½ x 3½"
Collection Harvey K. Littleton

Sidney Biehler Waugh
Gazelle Bowl. 1935
Designed for Steuben Glass
Crystal; blown and cut, 7⁷⁄₁₆ x 6⅜" x 6⅜"
Collection The Toledo Museum of Art. Gift of William E. Levis

Russel Wright
Salad Serving Utensils. 1930–1935
Glass, chrome; spoon: 1½ x 3¼ x 13⅛"; fork: 1¾ x 3½ x 13¼"
Collection William Straus

METALS

Arthur Armour
Zodiac Tray. c. 1934–35
Hammered aluminum, 1 x 18 x 18"
Collection Dr. Thomas F. Armour

Wendell August
Desk Set. c. 1930
Designed for Wendell August Forge, Inc.
Hand-forged aluminum, glass, paper; letter box: 1¾ x 10 x 13"; inkwell: 3¼ x 3⅛ x 3⅓"; blotter: 1½ x 6¾ x 2¾"
Mitchell Wolfson, Jr., Collection, The Wolfsonian Foundation, Miami Beach and Genoa, Italy

Oscar Bruno Bach
Pair of Art Deco Doors. c. 1925
Stainless steel over wood core, 8'5½" x 31¼" each
Collection Minneapolis Institute of Arts. The Christina N. and Swan J. Turnblad Memorial Fund
(Not included in exhibition)

Arieto (Harry) Bertoia
Pin. c. 1938–40
Hammered silver wire, 4¼ x 7"
Collection Patricia Shaw

Arieto (Harry) Bertoia
Tea Service. c. 1940
Silver, plastic; teapot: 5¾ x 7¼ x 4¾"; sugar bowl: 3¾ x 4¼ x 2¾"; creamer: 2⅝ x 4¾ x 2¾"
Collection Detroit Institute of Arts

Porter George Blanchard
Coffee Set. c. 1938–40
Silver, ebony; coffee pot: 6½ x 8¼ x 3¾"; creamer: 4 x 4¾ x 2"; sugar bowl: 4¼ x 5⅛ x 2⅞"
Collection Mrs. William W. Hughes

Janet Payne Bowles
Chalice. c. 1925–31
Silver, 10 x 5¼ x 5½"
Collection Indianapolis Museum of Art. Gift of Jan and Mira Bowles in memory of their mother, Janet Payne Bowles

Janet Payne Bowles
Fork. c. 1925–31
Silver, 9 x 1⅝ x ⅝"
Collection Indianapolis Museum of Art. Gift of Jan and Mira Bowles in memory of their mother, Janet Payne Bowles

William Edgar Brigham
Candleholders. c. 1930
Silver, 4½ x 3¹⁄₁₆ x 3½" each
Collection Museum of Art, Rhode Island School of Design, Providence. Bequest of William E. Brigham

Alexander Calder
Necklace. c. 1940
Gilded brass, 12½ x 12½"
Collection National Museum of American Art, Smithsonian Institution, Washington, D.C. Gift of Mr. and Mrs. Alexander Calder

Rebecca Cauman
Round Box with Finial. c. 1926–29
Pewter, glass, 4 x 5 x 5"
Collection Constance R. Caplan

Margret Craver
Teapot. c. 1936
Silver, gabon ebony, 5½ x 9¼ x 5"
Museum of Fine Arts, Boston. Gift in Memory of Joyce Goldberg with funds provided by Mr. John P. Axelrod, Mr. and Mrs. Sidney Stoneman, Mr. Charles Devens, Mr. and Mrs. Peter S.

Lynch, The Seminarians, Mr. James G. Hinkle, Jr., The MFA Council and Friends

Margaret Strong De Patta
Pin. 1940
Yellow gold, topaz, citrines, pearls, 1¼ x 3½"
Collection The Oakland Museum. Gift of Mr. and Mrs. Hervey Parke Clark

Wilhelm Hunt Diederich
Fire Screen with Foxes and Hounds. c. 1925
Iron, 29 x 42"
Collection Alexander B. Slater

William Waldo Dodge, Jr.
Cocktail Shaker, Tray, and Cups. 1929–31
Silver; shaker: height 18"; tray: 1⅛ x 15⅛ x 15⅛"; cups: 3¼ x 2¾ x 2¾" each
Collection William Waldo Dodge, III

Laurits Christian Eichner
Shallow Bowl #40. c. 1935
Copper, 2 x 13 13/16 x 13 13/16"
Collection Mary Lou Wickham

Paul Fehér and Martin Rose
Art Deco Desk Set. 1929–31
Designed for Rose Iron Works
Hot- and cold-rolled steel, stainless steel, bronze, brass, aluminum, black marble, with cloisonné inserts, 12½ x 23 x 8"
Collection Rose Family, Cleveland

Bernard W. Fischer
Tea Set. c. 1934
Tinned copper; teapot with cover: 6 x 8½ x 6¾"; creamer: 3 x 6½ x 5"; sugar bowl: 3 x 6½ x 5"
Collection Yale University Art Gallery, New Haven, Connecticut. Gift of the Estate of Bernard Fischer

The Kalo Shop
Compote. c. 1937
Silver, 2 x 8½ x 8½"
Courtesy Denis Gallion and Daniel Morris, Historical Design Collection, Inc., New York

Gertrude Karlan
Necklace and Earrings. c. 1937–41
Silver; necklace: 1⅛ x 15½ x 1/16"; earrings: 1⅞ x 1 x 1/16" each
Collection Mrs. Mildred Loew

Arthur Nevill Kirk
Bowl. 1930
Designed by Eliel Saarinen
Silver, 4 x 8¾ x 8¾"
Collection Cranbrook Academy of Art Museum, Bloomfield Hills, Michigan. Gift of the Cranbrook Foundation

E. Byrne Livingston
Ring and Pin Set. c. 1937
Silver, onyx, coral; pin: ⅞ x 2"; ring: diameter ⅝"
Collection The Metropolitan Museum of Art, New York. Gift of E. Byrne Livingston

Erik Magnussen
Modern American Cocktail Shaker and Cups. 1928
Designed for Gorham Manufacturing Company
Silver; shaker: 12 x 6⅝ x 4"; cups: 5¼ x 3 7/16" each
Courtesy Denis Gallion and Daniel Morris, Historical Design Collection, Inc., New York

Peter Mueller-Munk
Candelabra. 1928
Silver, 17 x 19 x 10½" each
Collection Detroit Institute of Arts. Gift of Mr. Albert Kahn

Peter Mueller-Munk
Hand Mirror, Brush, and Comb. c. 1931
Silver; mirror: 12¼ x 4½ x 1¼"; brush: 9¾ x 3½ x ⅜"; comb: 7½ x 1½ x ⅜"
Collection Constance R. Caplan

Tommi Parzinger
Candelabra. c. 1940
Peter Reimes, silversmith
Silver, 31¾ x 7¾ x 5½"
Courtesy Denis Gallion and Daniel Morris, Historical Design Collection, Inc., New York

Ruth Penington
Bracelet. 1938
Silver, 1¼ x 7"
Collection Ruth Penington

John Pontus Petterson
Neptune Flatware Place Setting. c. 1937
Silver; dinner knife: 9¼ x ¾"; dinner fork: 7⅞ x 1"; teaspoon: 6⅛ x 1¼"
Collection John C. Petterson

Francisco (Frank) Rebajes
Bracelet. c. 1945
Copper, 2 x 6⅛"
Collection Fern Simon

Winold Reiss
Harlequin Panel, Hotel Alamac, New York. 1923
Julius Ormos and Charles Bardosy, metalsmiths
Brass, copper, aluminum, steel, iron, 54½ x 47½ x ⅜"
Collection John P. Axelrod. Courtesy Museum of Fine Arts, Boston

Russel Wright
Pitcher. c. 1935
Spun aluminum, wood, 10 x 10 x 6"
Collection William Straus

Marie Zimmermann
Enameled Box. c. 1922
Silver, jade, enamel, gold, 7 x 4⅙ x 4⅙"
Courtesy Denis Gallion and Daniel Morris, Historical Design Collection, Inc., New York

TEXTILES

Anonymous
Tires and Tire Treads (Speed Age Silk Print). 1929
Designed for Marshall Field and Company
Silk, 5⅛ x 4⅞"
Collection The Museum at the Fashion Institute of Technology, New York

Anonymous
Tulips. c. 1929–30
Produced by Schumacher
Cotton; airbrushed and stenciled, 6' 6¼" x 45⅝"
Collection Goldstein Gallery, University of Minnesota, St. Paul

Lydia Bush-Brown
New York Waterfront. c. 1928
Silk; wax-resist dyed, 35¾ x 48½"
Collection Cooper-Hewitt Museum, National Museum of Design, Smithsonian Institution, New York. Gift of Lydia Bush-Brown

Brents Carlton
Batik Panel. 1927
Silk; wax-resist dyed, 50 x 38"
Collection John P. Axelrod

Marion Dorn
Headscarf. 1941–44
Silk, 36 x 34"
Collection Philadelphia Museum of Art. Gift of Mrs. John Platt

Marli Erhman
Upholstery Fabric. 1941
Cotton; handwoven, 24⅝ x 24⅝"

Collection The Museum of Modern Art. Gift of the designer

Ilonka Karasz
Rug. c. 1930
Cotton, wool, 8'11½" x 8'11"
Collection the Metropolitan Museum of Art, New York. Purchase, Theodore R. Gamble, Jr. Gift, in honor of his mother, Mrs. Theodore Robert Gamble, 1983 (1983.228.2)
(Not included in exhibition)

Maria Kipp
Fabric. c. 1945
Cloth, 9½ x 25½"
Collection Doris Stein Research and Design Center, Department of Costumes and Textiles, Los Angeles County Museum of Art. Gift of Harold Grieve

Lorenz Kleiser and Frederick Avinoff
Jamaica Verdure Tapestry. c. 1927
Woven by Edgewater Tapestry Looms
Wool, 71 x 48½"
Collection Sharron Martin

Clayton Knight
Manhattan. 1925–26
Designed for Stehli Silk Corporation
Silk crepe, 6' 1" x 37¼"
Collection The Newark Museum. Gift of L. Bamberger & Co., 1926

Madame Marcelle Labaudt
Mantle. c. 1925
Silk; stenciled, 66½ x 62¼"
Collection The Oakland Museum

Dorothy Wright Liebes
Wall Hanging. 1936
Cotton, silk, rayon; handwoven, 32 x 8' 8"
Collection American Craft Museum, New York. Gift of Dorothy Liebes Design, 1973. Donated to the American Craft Museum by the American Craft Council, 1990

H. R. Mallinson and Company
Print Dress. c. 1929
Silk
Collection The Museum at the Fashion Institute of Technology, New York

Milwaukee Handicraft Project
Block-printed Fabric. c. 1935–43
Designed by Barbara Warren
Muslin, 7' x 34½"
Collection Milwaukee Public

Museum. Gift of Elsa Ulbricht

Milwaukee Handicraft Project
WPA Hooked Rug. c. 1935–40
Wool, linen, 62½ x 47¼"
Collection Milwaukee Public Museum. Gift of Mr. and Mrs. Quentin O'Sullivan

Navajo
Shiprock Rug. c. 1920
Wool; handspun, 58" x 6'
Collection Tony Berlant

Eve Peri
Pillow Cover. 1942
Linen; embroidered and appliquéd, 17 x 17¼"
Collection American Craft Museum, New York. Gift of Dr. Georgiana M. Peacher

Antonin Raymond
Strips, Trunks, Trees, Dots Fabric Panel. c. 1941
Cotton; handscreened, 7' 4" x 50"
Collection The Museum of Modern Art, New York. Gift of the designer

Ruth Reeves
Hudson River Series. c. 1933–34
Linen; screenprinted, 9' 2" x 33¼"
Collection Goldstein Gallery, University of Minnesota, St. Paul

Henriette Reiss
Rhythm Series. 1928
Cotton; screenprinted, 51⅛ x 50⅞"
Collection Goldstein Gallery, University of Minnesota, St. Paul

Martha Ryther (attributed)
Grand Canyon Textile. 1927
Designed for H. R. Mallinson and Company (Mallinson's Silks de Luxe)
Silk, 16½ x 36"
Collection Goldstein Gallery, University of Minnesota, St. Paul

Louise (Loja) Saarinen
Tapestry #3 for Kingswood. 1928–29
Linen, wool, 66 x 50" including fringe
Collection Cranbrook Educational Community, Bloomfield Hills, Michigan

Robert David Sailors
Rug Sample #2. 1944
Cotton thread, cotton rags, sisal, 13¾ x 8"
Collection Cranbrook Academy of Art Museum, Bloomfield Hills, Michigan. Gift of the artist

Robert David Sailors
Rug Sample #4. 1944
Cotton thread, cotton cloth, mosquito netting, 17⅜ x 14¼"
Collection Cranbrook Academy of Art Museum, Bloomfield Hills, Michigan. Gift of the artist

Robert David Sailors
Rug Sample #8. 1944
Cotton, Persian wool, wool floss, 9¾ x 9¼"
Collection Cranbrook Academy of Art Museum, Bloomfield Hills, Michigan. Gift of the artist

Robert David Sailors
Rug Sample #32. 1944
Cotton, natural and dyed sisal, flannel, 11¼ x 14"
Collection Cranbrook Academy of Art Museum, Bloomfield Hills, Michigan. Gift of the artist

Marianne Strengell
Fringed Drapery Fabric. c. 1940s
Cotton, rayon, silver thread; handwoven, 10' 8" x 41¼"
Collection Cranbrook Academy of Art Museum, Bloomfield Hills, Michigan. Gift of the artist

Marguerite Zorach
The Jungle. 1936
Commissioned by Crawford Shops
Wool, jute; handhooked, 42 x 60"
Collection The Museum of Modern Art, New York. Gift of A. Conger Goodyear

WOOD

Anonymous
Hand Sculptures. c. 1940
Laminated wood; various sizes, ranging from 2½ x 7½ x 3¾" to 2½ x 5½ x 5"
Collection Myron and Lois Kozman. Courtesy Ubu Gallery, New York

Donald Deskey
Sideboard. 1932
Mahogany, ebony, steel, 36 x 42 x 18"
Collection Radio City Music Hall Productions, Rockefeller Center, New York

Charles O. Eames
Tilt-back Lounge Chair with Metal Glides. c. 1944
Molded plywood, steel tubing, 29½ x 30⅛ x 30"
Collection The Museum of Mod-

ern Art, New York. Gift of the designer

Charles O. Eames and Ray Eames
Child's Elephant. 1945
Molded birch plywood, 16⅛ x 15¾ x 30⅜"
Collection Lucia Eames Demetrios, Eames Office, Los Angeles

Wharton Esherick
Dining Chair. 1928
Walnut, ebony, 36 x 14½ x 15"
Collection Mr. and Mrs. Peter Esherick

Wharton Esherick
Sewing Cabinet. 1933
Walnut burl, cherry, 30 x 27 x 19½"
Collection Helene Barbara Fisher Eldred

Wharton Esherick
Side Chair. 1942–44
Designed for the Schutte-Koerting Boardroom, 1938
Wood, 34¾ x 21 x 25¾"
Collection Philadelphia Museum of Art. Gift of Schutte-Koerting Company

Paul Theodore Frankl
Bench. 1927
Lacquered and silvered wood, 24 x 34 x 15"
Collection Carol and Robert Goodman

Paul Theodore Frankl
Skyscraper Bookcase. 1926
Birch, lacquer, 84 x 39 x 14"
Collection High Museum of Art, Atlanta. Purchase in honor of Darlene Schultz, President of the Members' Guild, 1991–92, with funds from the Decorative Arts Endowment

Bertrand Goldberg
Bentwood Settee. c. 1938–40
Mahogany plywood, 28 x 60 x 33"
Collection Bertrand Goldberg

James L. Prestini
Lathe-turned Bowls. 1938–40
Beech, 5⅞ x 10⅝ x 10¼"; birch, 2¾ x $4\frac{15}{16}$ x 4⅞"
Collection American Craft Museum, New York. Gift of Grace and Pauline Stafford in memory of Cora E. Stafford, 1966. Donated to the American Craft Museum by the American Craft Council, 1990

Winold Reiss
Red and Blue Armchair. c. 1920
Wood, 44 x 30½ x 27"
Collection Mr. and Mrs. W. Tjark Reiss

Terrence Harold Robsjohn-Gibbings
Low Table with Carved Rams' Heads. c. 1936
Wood, 24¾ x 19¼ x 19¼"
Collection Jorie Marshall Waterman

Gilbert Rohde
Dressing Vanity. 1939
Rosewood, burl redwood veneers, brass, brassplated steel, Plexiglas, vinyl-coated fabric, glass, ebonized plywood, 48 x 47 x 15"
Collection High Museum of Art, Atlanta. Purchase in honor of Hilda Cyphers, Associate Manager of the Members' Guild, 1979–94, with funds from the Decorative Arts Acquisition Trust

Gottlieb Eliel Saarinen
Cabinet for Saarinen House. 1929–30
Fabricated by Tor Berglund
African walnut, green hart, rosewood, and maple veneers, 60 x 38 x 18"
Collection Cranbrook Academy of Art Museum, Bloomfield Hills, Michigan

Gottlieb Eliel Saarinen
Dining Room Side Chair for Saarinen House. 1929–30
Fabricated by The Company of Master Craftsmen
Upholstery fabric by Loja Saarinen
Fir, horsehair, cotton, 37⅞ x 17 x 20"
Collection Cranbrook Academy of Art Museum, Bloomfield Hills, Michigan

Rudolph Michael Schindler
Modular Chair. 1934
Plywood, 28 x 21½ x 33½"
Collection David Gebhard

Eugene Schoen
Cabinet. c. 1930–32
Thuya burls, primavera, macassar ebony door pulls, 36 x 48 x 21"
Courtesy Denis Gallion and Daniel Morris, Historical Design Collection, Inc., New York

Joseph Urban
Gondola Chair. c. 1922
Manufactured by Wiener Werkstätte of America, Inc.
Paint and silver leaf on wood, with mother of pearl, 48 x 30"
Collection The Metropolitan Museum of Art, New York. Purchase, Lita Annenberg Hazen Charitable Trust Gift, 1985

Karl Emanuel Martin (Kem) Weber
Sideboard. c. 1930
Designed for the Grand Rapids Furniture Company
Wood, 33⅓ x 72 x 19¾"
Collection The Metropolitan Museum of Art, New York. Gift of Theodore R. Gamble, Jr., in honor of his mother, Mrs. Theodore Robert Gamble
(Not included in exhibition)

Frank Lloyd Wright
Auldbras Plantation Chair. c. 193
Cypress plywood, 28 x 21 x 28"
Collection Mark A. McDonald

Frank Lloyd Wright
Side Chair from the Imperial Hotel, Tokyo. c. 1921
Wood, yellow-leatherette upholstery (not original), 37¾ x 15½ x 17"
Collection Cooper-Hewitt Museum, National Museum of Design, Smithsonian Institution, New York. Given by Tetsuzo Inumaru

Russel Wright
Oceana Star-shaped Compartmented Dish and Centerpiece Bowl. 1938
Wood; bowl: 1⅞ x 4⅜ x 19⅝"; dish: 1¼ x 13⅝ x 12½"
Collection William Straus

Russel Wright
Oceana Wood Bowl. 1938
Gumwood, 4½ x 13¼"
Collection The Metropolitan Museum of Art, New York. Gift of Russel Wright

PHOTOGRAPH CREDITS

Howard Agriesti: 186 below; Albright-Knox Art Gallery: 149; American Craft Council, photo by Richard P. Goodbody, 27 below, 64 above; Arrow Shirt Company, photo by Richard P. Goodbody: 41; The Art Institute of Chicago: 125 below; Bauhaus Archiv, Berlin: 46; Bauhaus dessau archiv der Sammlung: 47 below; José A. Benitez: 124; E. Irving Blomstrann: 53 below; Del Bogart: 126 below, 183 below; Frank Borkowski: 168; The Brooklyn Museum: 122, 167; Will Brown: 137 above; Geoffrey Clements: 42; © The Cleveland Museum of Art: 16, 98, 140 above, 150; Cleveland Public Library: 67; Sheldan C. Collins: 83 below, 96 below, 97 above, 140 below, 145 below, 152 above and below, 157 above and below, 159 below, 160, 166 above, 169 below, 170 below, 171, 177 below, 179, 188 middle, 189, 197, 201, 210, 211 above, 222, 225; Cooper-Hewitt, National Design Museum, Smithsonian Institution/Art Resource: 78; The Corning Incorporated Department of Archives and Records Management, Corning, NY: 89, 94 below; The Corning Museum of Glass: 1, 5, 14, 15, 92, 95 below, 162 below, 164 below, 165, 166 below; Cowan Pottery Museum: 55; Dennis Cowley: 214; Cranbrook Academy of Art Museum: 30 below, 43 below, 61, 63, 216; Cranbrook Archives: 43 above, 119; Robert Damora, The Museum of Modern Art: 86; Lucia Eames Demetrios, Eames Office, Los Angeles © 1989: 82; © The Detroit Institute of Arts: 145 above, 174 below, 182; Mr. and Mrs Derrill G. Elmore and Ark Antiques: 130; The Equitable Life Assurance Society of the United States: 39 above; Estate of Yolanda Gregory: 105 right, 106; Fairchild Publications, a division of Capital Cities Media, Inc., a Capital City/ABC Inc., Company: 111; The Family of Lorentz Kleiser: 112 above; Claire Farkas: 120; Flint Institute of Arts: 60; Fondation Le Corbusier: 48; Paulette Frankl, photo by Richard P. Goodbody: 32, 77; Michael Fredericks: 217; Courtney Frisse: 64 below, 73, 83 above, 101 below, 103, 137 below, 138 above and below, 142 below, 146, 148, 154, 155 above and below; Richard P. Goodbody: 25 below, 59 below, 69, 75, 118 above; The Harvard University Art Museums: 65, 70; R. H. Hensleigh, Cranbrook Academy of Art Museum: 181 above, 202, 204 above and below, 220; John Herrmann: 131; Eva Heyd: 11, 13, 125 above, 135, 136, 141, 143, 153, 190 below, 199, 200 above, 203, 206, 207 below, 211 middle, 212; High Museum of Art: 12, 219; Historical Design Collection, Inc.: 57 above, 175 above, 181 below, 183 above, 184 below, 221; © 1994 Indianapolis Museum of Art: 176, 178; Isamu Noguchi Foundation, Inc.: 85; James Graham & Sons: 142 above; Jason McCoy, Inc.: 51 below, 81; Library of Congress: 38, 39 middle and below, 45, 96 above; Harvey K. Littleton: 169 above; Los Angeles County Museum of Art: 109, 117,